IRAQ
Sanctions and Wars

IRAQ
Sanctions and Wars

A.K. Pasha

STERLING PUBLISHERS PRIVATE LIMITED

> **Dedication**
>
> *This book is dedicated
> to the heroic people of Iraq*

STERLING PUBLISHERS PRIVATE LIMITED
A-59 Okhla Industrial Area, Phase-II,
New Delhi-110020.
Tel: 26386209, 26387070
Fax: 91-11-26383788 E-mail: ghai@nde.vsnl.net.in
www.sterlingpublishers.com

Iraq: Sanctions and Wars
© 2003, A.K. Pasha
ISBN 81 207 2561 1

All rights are reserved. No part of this publication may be reproduced, stored in a retrieval system or transmitted, in any form or by any means, mechanical, photocopying, recording or otherwise, without prior written permission of the original publisher.

PRINTED IN INDIA

Published by Sterling Publishers Pvt. Ltd., New Delhi-110020.
Lasertypeset at Vikas Compographics, New Delhi-110020.
Printed at Prolific Incorporated, New Delhi-110020.

Preface

The banks of the Tigris and the Euphrates rivers in present day Iraq have been the seat of several civilisations for over 7000 years; Hammurabi and Nebuchadnezzar were famous rulers who ruled this area. Subsequently, the Persians, Greeks, Romans, Arabs, Mongols, Ottomans and others dominated this area. Soon after the defeat of the Ottoman Empire in the First World War, Britain was granted mandate over Iraq. Although Iraq was a British creation, Iraqi Arab nationalists opposed British plans to impose Hashemite monarchy. Britain crushed the Iraqi opposition by using airplanes and the army and on July 11, 1921, King Faisal I was declared the King of Iraq. On October 3, 1932, Iraq was admitted to the League of Nations, thereby ending UK's mandate over Iraq. Iraq due to its virtually landlocked position has sought wider outlet to the Gulf and successive Iraqi rulers have staked their claims on Kuwaiti territory in order to be free from Iranian hegemony and mercy. The Iraqi Hashemite monarchy – due to its close identification with London in such schemes as the Baghdad Pact and its controversial stand during the 1956 Suez crisis and on Israel – had become discredited in the eyes of most Iraqis and was overthrown on July 14, 1958.

The new Iraqi ruler, Abdul Karim Qassem, soon after

Kuwait's independence from UK on June 19, 1961 declared Kuwait as an inseperable part of Iraq, thereby creating a major regional crisis which led to Baghdad's isolation as all the states supported Kuwait's independence. Qassem was overthrown in 1963 and the new ruler Abdul Salam Arif recognised Kuwait's independence on October 4, 1963, paving the way for Kuwait to become the 111th member of UN.

The emergence of a Baath Party government, under Hassan al Bakr and Saddam Hussein in July 1968, opened a new chapter in Iraq's history. Iraq's ties with Iran deteriorated in the wake of UK's decision to withdraw from the Gulf. Soon Iraq wanted Kuwait to cede Warbah and Bubiyan islands, which the Emir of Kuwait rejected. Iraq's treaty with USSR in April 1972 enabled the Baath leaders to nationalise all foreign oil companies in Iraq, which alarmed the UK/ US globally and Kuwait and Iran regionally. The growing assertiveness of the Iraqi regime led to amassing of troops on the Kuwaiti border in 1973 and 1976. The reasons why Kuwaiti rulers were so determined in rejecting Iraqi demands have been examined in the book. With the isolation of Egypt over the Camp David accords, Iraq emerged as the dominant Arab State. The Iranian revolution further pushed Iraq to primacy in Arab affairs. In August 1979, Saddam Hussein became President of Iraq and in September 1980 he invaded Iran to contain the so called export of Islamic revolution from Iran. Soon, in May 1981, the Arab Gulf states came under the GCC and began supporting Iraq in its war with Iran. Saddam Hussein fought his war with Iran for eight years, losing lakhs of Iraqis and billions of oil money and ruining the society Iraqis had built for centuries, especially since the oil boom. The GCC states gave Iraq substantial material help. The US also aided Iraq in order to contain Iran. For Saddam Hussein, the war brought Iraq none of the territorial gains or battlefield glories he was expecting. But he began to imagine that but for Iraq's 'victory' over Iran, most of the GCC states would have fallen to Iran. Apart from the large number of Iraqis killed and wounded, scarce resources had to be spent on maintaining a large military machine. The sharp fall in oil prices further aggravated his problems. All of this led him to mount pressure on the Kuwaiti rulers for financial aid and when that was not forthcoming he invaded Kuwait on August 2, 1990.

Just as there is a direct link between the Iranian Revolution and the eight year Iran-Iraq war – the 1990-91 Kuwaiti crisis would not have erupted but for the first Gulf war. Iraq emerged out of the war with a shattered economy and a huge foreign debt. Soon Saddam Hussein had to face UN sanctions for his blunder over Kuwait. The US-led attack on Iraq in 1991 further devastated the country. The civil war in the south by the Shias, and by the Kurds in the north and the subsequent no fly zones established by the US-UK over north and south of Iraq further curtailed Saddam's power. The UN sanctions and daily US-UK bombings and the UN inspectors working for Iraqi disarmament began to cripple and strangle Iraq. In 1991 it was believed that in view of the massive destruction inflicted on Iraq, Saddam Hussein would be overthrown by his own people particularly from within the army, Baath Party, Kurds and Shias. This optimism was misplaced, because he quickly regained control over the political system through his Baath Party which is a highly organised one with over one million supporters. He began to tighten his grip over Iraq although the UN sanctions had been gradually undermining his rule. The author believes that Saddam Hussein and his regime have survived due to his resourcefulness and his capacity for survival. Despite Iraqi cooperation with the UNSCOM in the disarmament of Iraq's weapons of mass destruction and IAEA to put an end to nuclear plans, the UN economic sanctions were retained primarily at the behest of the US and its allies (GCC) in order to reduce Iraq to an insignificant power. With great reluctance, Iraq accepted the oil for food UN plan which partly alleviated Iraqi suffering. From 1991 to 1998 Iraq was at war with US and its own people struggling to survive. The US called for Saddam Hussein's overthrow and began supporting Iraqi opposition backed by some GCC states. For the US it was clear that even though Saddam Hussein had been defeated on the battlefield, by no means was he defeated at home. More and more states began to normalise ties with Iraq. George Bush and his successor kept up US pressure on Saddam Hussein with the latter not changing his behaviour and defiantly rejecting the US and all his enemies. But continuing UN sanctions had reduced Iraq from a booming nation to a shadow of its former self. Since Saddam Hussein and his regime had survived for so long in the face of heavy odds, the US became determined to bring him down together with his regime. Unable to capture Osama bin Laden, George W Bush diverted his attention to Iraq and to overthrow Saddam Hussein with or without UN support. The UN Resolutions are being used as a pretext to control Iraq and its oil.

After September 11 and the outbreak of the second Intifada the US wants to redraw the map of the West Asian region in order to keep the beleaguered state of Israel as a predominant state and also to bring about changes in Iran, Syria, Jordan and Saudi Arabia. President Bush also wants to divert US public attention from the troubled American economy. The last chapter highlights US invasion of Iraq, which started on March 20, 2003. The US invaded Iraq without UN sanction, in clear violation of international law and against widespread public opposition throughout the world including in the US. The US did not want to give the UN arms inspectors more time as demanded by France, Russia, China, Germany and most of the UN members. The US occupied Baghdad on April 9, 2003 and since then, there have been daily demonstrations by the Iraqis demanding the withdrawal of US forces from Iraq. US inability to restore basic services in most of the cities has fuelled protests and Iraqi nationalism will ultimately prevail. There have been many violent incidents between US forces and Iraqi citizens and these are likely to intensify in future. To divert the attention, the US has been warning Iran and Syria against interfering in Iraq's internal affairs. Syria and Iran were supporting various Iraqi opposition forces before the collapse of Saddam Hussein. Such support included political and financial protection. Along with these two states, Saudi Arabia and Kuwait also have very important deep-rooted historical and social links with the Iraqi people, including family relations, which cannot be ignored by the US. These and many other crucial issues which have a direct bearing on major regional and global issues are presented in an impassioned and penetrating analysis. This book has both historical relevance and contemporary significance. It would be of interest to scholars, diplomats, journalists, opinion makers and other interested in the affairs of the Gulf region.

I take this opportunity to thank Mr. S K Ghai of Sterling Publishing House for bringing out this book for it is on his request that this book has been written.

April 30, 2003
New Delhi

A. K. Pasha
Director, Gulf Studies
School of International Studies
Jawaharlal Nehru University

CONTENTS

Preface — v

1. The Making of Modern Iraq — 1
2. War with Iran and Crisis with Kuwait — 18
3. War over Kuwait [1991] — 48
4. Shia and Kurdish Uprisings — 62
5. Sanctions, Bombings and Regime Change — 82
6. US Invasion of Iraq [2003] — 114

Select Bibliography — 147

Index — 153

1
The Making of Modern Iraq

The famous Sumerian civilisation flourished on the banks of the Tigris and Euphrates rivers four millenniums ago. This ancient place also contains such known historical places like Nineveh which was the capital of King Asurbanipal, Uruk, the scene of the Gilgamesh epic, and Hatra, the famous Parthian ruled city. Assur, the capital of the Assyrian Kingdom with its world famous Ishtar temple is also located in this area. The ancient civilisation of the Hittites, Assyrians, and many others also flourished in present day Iraq. Ur, near modern Nasiriyah, is believed to be the place where Prophet Abraham was born. Hammurabi and Nebuchadnezzar (604-538 BC) were great and famous rulers who ruled this area known in ancient period as Mesopotamia. Babylon was the capital of King Hammurabi – who codified the laws governing life of the citizens. Subsequently, the Persians, Greeks, Romans, Arabs, Mongols, Ottomans and others dominated this area. Soon after the Mongol invasion of the Abbasid empire and the destruction of its capital, Baghdad, in 1258 the Arabs had gone into a long deep slumber. The subsequent Ottoman domination further pushed the Arabs into insignificance. As the Ottoman grip over its possessions loosened, the Arab world became vulnerable to other influences. With the great changes in Europe like the Renaissance, the Reformation and a spate of geographical discoveries led by Columbus, Vasco da Gama and others, coupled with the Industrial Revolution, various European groups came to settle in different parts of the Arab world. The impact of modern science, new technology and other ideas stirred the otherwise virtually moribund Arab world. Some Arabs particularly the Syrian Christians, along with other ethnic groups, brought new ideas which slowly awakened the Arabs from Morocco to Iraq.

As the Ottoman grip became tenuous over its empire, European encroachments on its Arab possessions increased. The great turning point was Napoleon's invasion of Egypt in 1798, which also brought in its wake European culture, education and other aspects which initiated a massive process of modernisation in all fields. Interaction between various parts of the Arab world and Europe multiplied. Due to superior military, technological and economic capability, the Europeans carved out independent spheres of influence in various parts of the Arab world. Later the Europeans – especially the British and French – occupied and established their control and suppressed all opposition to their rule. This domination and brutal suppression of the Arabs produced a new breed of Arab nationalists who challenged European rule and domination and demanded independence. The struggle for freedom and full independence intensified in the second half of the nineteenth century. The Arab intellectuals who had their training in Europe returned with fresh ideas of liberty, equality, freedom and independence. They laid the intellectual foundations for the campaign to free their countries from the European yoke. Many Arabs rediscovered their rich contribution in various fields prior to the Mongol invasion which had, in fact, been the basis for the emergence of modern European states as major powers.

Slowly, a new consciousness grew among a great majority of the Arabs and, as they awakened to their strength, they began to concentrate on gaining full independence so that they could control and manage their own affairs. In order to finally rid themselves of Turkish control, some Arabs, in areas which were still under Ottoman rule, supported the British and French governments in the First World War after being promised full independence after the war. But the Arabs were unaware of the notorious duplicity of the Europeans. The contradictory pledges which Great Britain made to the Arabs and Jews, together with the governments of France and Russia, came to light only after the First World War with the publication of the Sykes-Picot Agreement by the new communist Soviet government. Soon after the war, the League of Nations mandate system lent legitimacy to European colonial domination and control of certain areas of the Arab world. Among the European powers Britain, France, Italy and Spain controlled vast areas of the Arab world.

The British took keen interest due to their commercial, maritime and strategic interests in present day Iraq as early as in seventeenth century, obviously through trade, as the Ottoman Sultan controlled this area. The British East India company established a factory at Basra in 1739, and a British Residency was permanently established in Baghdad in 1798. The period of 1834-1914 was characterised by a great expansion of British interest in Mesopotamia. In 1862 a British service between Iraq and India was instituted and telegraph lines were laid to connect Basra, Baghdad with Bombay, Constantinople and Tehran. By 1800 the British had a Resident at Basra and in 1802 a Consulate at Baghdad. The establishment of an agency of the East India Company at Basra gave the British an upper hand. This was reinforced by the deep personal interest of King William IV, which was largely responsible for obtaining a concession for British-owned vessels to use the Iraqi waterways for trade. Along with this breakthrough, the British influence in Iraq was increased when a telegraph line was established in mid-nineteenth century connecting the Gulf with the Mediterranean. At this time postal services were also established. The Ottoman Sultan's decision to grant Germany and Russia a concession to build a railway line upto Basra brought about additional British interest in Iraq. A railway line from Baghdad to Samarra was completed in 1914 and soon on November 7, 1914 Britain was at war with Turkey. Arab nationalist groups like Al Ahd from 1912 itself were very active in Iraq. Their main goal was to end the 'Turkish Yoke' and 'Ottomanism'.[1] During the war, despite setbacks, the British ultimately occupied Iraq from Basra to Mosul with the help of the Indian army. In April 1920, Britain, at the San Remo conference, received from the League of Nations a mandate for Iraq. Actually, in the case of Iraq, the terms of the mandate were never formally laid down by the League of Nations, but the relations between Iraq and Britain were defined in terms of an Anglo-Iraqi Treaty concluded on October 10, 1922 which was ratified in March 1924, in the face of strong opposition from the Iraqi Arab nationalists. Originally the treaty was to be for 20 years, but was modified by a protocol of April 30, 1923 in which it was agreed that the treaty should end upon Iraq's admission to the League of Nations. In 1925 the League of Nations recommended that the *vilayet* of Mosul be added to Iraq and this was done through the July 1926 treaty between Iraq,

Turkey and Britain. In 1930 a new treaty was signed between Britain and Iraq which established a close alliance for 25 years and gave Great Britain the right to use some of the Iraqi airbases. On October 3, 1932 Iraq was admitted to the League of Nations and the British mandate was terminated. Meanwhile in March 1921 Sharif Hussein's (of Mecca) son Amir Faisal bin Hussein agreed to rule as King of Iraq. His ceremonial accession took place on August 23, 1921. The British ruthlessly crushed the Iraqi Arab nationalist opposition (including use of air force) to the imposition of the Hashemite monarchy in Iraq. Thus, undoubtedly, Iraq is also a British creation like Kuwait.[2]

Whereas the Iraqi frontier with Najd was defined in the Treaty of Mohammara in May 1922 and a neutral zone of 7000 sq. km was established adjacent to the western tip of the Kuwait frontier; an agreement in May 1938, concerning the administration of this zone, was signed between the two states which more or less settled their boundaries, without however demarcating them. This was a relatively smooth event.

Equally smooth and swift was the agreement between Iraq and Kuwait. The Kuwaiti ruler, Sheikh Ahmad Al Sabah and the British High Commissioner for Iraq, Sir Percy Cox, on April 19, 1923 defined the Iraqi-Kuwait border. The Iraqi Prime Minister, Nuri es Saeed Pasha on July 21, 1932 confirmed the "existing frontiers" between Iraq and Kuwait to the British Resident in Kuwait — as defined in the Anglo-Ottoman Agreement of 1913, which included Warbah and Bubiyan as part of Kuwait. The frontier was described as :

> From the intersection of the Wadi el Audja with the Batin and thence northwards along the Batin to a point just south of the latitude of Safwan, thence eastwards passing south

of Safwan wells, Jebel Sanam and Umm Qasr leaving them to Iraq and so on to the junction of the Khor Zobeir with the Khor Abdulla. The islands of Warbah, Bubiyan, Maskan, Failakh, Auhah, Kubbas, Qaru and Umm el Maradim appertain to Kuwait.[3]

In an earlier exchange of letters on April 4 and 19, 1923 between the Sheikh of Kuwait and Sir Percy Cox the existing frontiers between Iraq and Kuwait had been clearly emphasised. The Kuwaiti ruler in a letter dated August 10, 1932 confirmed the boundaries as mentioned in Nuri Pasha's letter. In line with their deep interest in the establishment of Kuwait, the confirmation of the boundaries between Iraq and Kuwait was the zenith of the success of British diplomacy. Thus, Britain had finally established Kuwait as a legal entity which was recognised by Iraq. But there was a gap. The Iraqi-Kuwait boundaries had not been demarcated.

Meanwhile King Ghazi (second king of Iraq) became the first Iraqi ruler to lay claims to Kuwait. In fact he had raised the possibility of Iraq intervening in Kuwait and incorporating it just before his death on April 5, 1938 in a mysterious car accident which many suspected to be the work of Britain and their local Iraqi supporters. Kuwait, which raised the issue of border demarcation for the first time in 1951, found Iraq unenthusiastic on this issue and, when the Kuwaiti ruler pursued the issue, Baghdad expressed its desire to have Warbah in return for demarcation of their borders. Until then all had appeared smooth and satisfactory but, beneath this tranquility, a storm was building up which the British were fully aware and conscious of. Not surprisingly, the Kuwaiti ruler found the Iraqi demand unacceptable and opposed it. The Iraqis kept up their pressure on Kuwait when, in 1954 in the context of negotiations related to the supply of water from

Shatt al-Arab, Iraq increased her claims on Kuwaiti territory. This time it claimed about four kilometres of Khor al Sabiya coastline which is north of the island of Warbah and Bubiyan. Moreover, Nuri es Saeed Pasha invited Kuwait to join the British-sponsored Baghdad Pact in 1954 and, as *quid pro quo,* Kuwait was offered a definitive settlement of its undemarcated border with Iraq.

There was a specific and compelling reason for Iraq to advance the territorial claim and that was its virtual landlocked position which the British appeared to have deliberately enforced on Iraq. Since then, all Iraqi territorial claims could be linked to its desire to have a wider and more secure outlet to the Gulf rather than the Shatt al-Arab link which was virtually in the hands of Iran.

Successive Iraqi governments have staked their claims on Kuwaiti territory in order to be free from Iranian hegemony and mercy. The British realised the Iraqi predicament and they urged the Kuwaiti ruler to consider leasing Warbah island to Iraq in return for water from Shatt al-Arab. The ruler of Kuwait rejected the British proposal in 1956. Nuri es Saeed, in early 1958, called on Kuwait to join in a confederation between the two Hashemite monarchies of Jordan and Iraq "without effecting in anyway a change in its internal or external policy".[4] In return for Kuwait's adhesion, Iraq offered to demarcate the border and supply Kuwait with Shatt al-Arab water and to guarantee continuation of the existing degree of autonomy enjoyed by the Kuwaiti ruler.

The Iraqi Hashemite monarchy, which was created and sustained by the British, by its close identification with London in such schemes as the widely unpopular Baghdad Pact and its lukewarm support to Egypt in the 1956 Suez crisis and on Israel, had become discredited in the eyes of most Iraqi and

Arab people. When it was overthrown in a revolution on July 14, 1958 there was little surprise at the demise of King Faisal II, Crown Prince and Nuri es Saeed. Despite Iraq's territorial claim over parts of Kuwait, under the monarchy, relations between Iraq and Kuwait were more or less normal and at times cordial. The British due to their massive presence tried to keep things under control. When Iraq demanded Warbah in return for Kuwaiti demand for demarcation, they prevented things from getting out of hand and, in fact, outwardly tried to mediate to resolve the problem amicably. But, in the end, they had laid the basis for a future conflictual relationship as Iraq, due to its location, potential and other issues, was bound to demand wider access to Gulf waters which it felt was essential for its survival, stability and security.

The July 1958 revolution in Iraq, which led to the overthrow of the Hashemite monarchy, was as significant an event as the 1952 Egyptian revolution. The Iraqi revolution changed the very basic politics of the Gulf region. The Iraqi leader, General Abdul Karim Qassem, who established close ties with Soviet Union like Nasser of Egypt, not only withdrew Iraq from the hated Baghdad Pact on March 24, 1959 but also terminated the special agreement existing between Iraq and Britain. On March 31, 1959 the British evacuated from the Iraqi air bases. Soon Qassem called for the overthrow of monarchies in Iran and the Arab Gulf region. Like Nasser who decided to build the Aswan Dam, Qassem also wanted to build a port at Umm Qasr, barely a mile from Kuwait's side of the *de facto* border.[5] But his most controversial step was towards Kuwait which was granted independence by Britain on June 19,1961. The Kuwaiti ruler, Sheikh Abdullah al Salim al Sabah, applied for membership of the Arab League on June 22, 1961. But the Iraqi Prime Minister Qassem on

June 25, 1961 claimed Kuwait to be a part of the Basra province. He proceeded to designate the Kuwaiti ruler as *Qaimmaqam* of the Governor of Basra, like it was done during Ottoman Sultan's rule. This move came only six days after Kuwait signed a Treaty of Friendship and Mutual Consultation which terminated the British protectorate over Kuwait and the 1899 agreement which had given Britain the responsibility for the conduct of Kuwait's Foreign Policy. Qassem denounced the Anglo-Kuwaiti agreement as a "specially dangerous blow against the integration and independence" of Iraq and Kuwait and declared Kuwait as an inseparable part of Iraq.[6] On June 26, 1961 the Iraqi Foreign Ministry issued a formal statement enumerating the legal grounds for its claim over Kuwait. Among other things it also stated that Iraq succeeded to the rights of the Basra *vilayet* of the Ottoman empire. This led to a major crisis in the Arab world. Threatened with an Iraqi takeover, the Kuwaiti ruler applied for British military help under the June 19, 1961 agreement with UK. He also rejected all the Iraqi claims over Kuwait. The British on July 1, 1961 promptly responded by landing 6000 troops and "placed at the Rulers disposal"[7]. Interestingly the Sheikh of Kuwait also requested King Saud of Saudi Arabia to send troops whose contingents also immediately arrived. The Kuwaiti ruler also mobilized his own small force to safeguard the nascent independence of his oil-rich Emirate.

The British, already nervous due to a series of set backs since the 1952 Egyptian revolution, and particularly after their humiliation in the 1956 Suez crisis and the 1958 Iraqi revolution, promptly asked (on July 2, 1961) for the convening of a special session of the UN Security Council. Iraq also asked for a similar meeting of the Security Council complaining of the British threat to the "independence and security of Iraq". At the Council meeting, at which Kuwait was also called, Britain complained about the Iraqi threat to Kuwait's independence and moved a resolution condemning Iraq for its threat to Kuwait. The Soviet Union, which supported Iraq throughout the crisis, vetoed the resolution. The Soviet representative, Mr. Zorin, held Britain responsible for the crisis and defended Iraq saying that it had never sought to use force in the crisis. As expected he wanted the "provocative presence" of British troops to be withdrawn. The United Arab Republic (UAR) delegate, Mr. Loutfi, asserted that the Iraq-Kuwait dispute was an intra-Arab one and that it could be resolved through an Arab solution.[8]

It was Kuwait which took the initiative to solve the problem at the Arab level. On July 18, 1961 it sent a note to the Arab League expressing its desire to have the British troops replaced by an Arab force. Immediately the Arab League Secretary General, Khaleq Hassouna, visited Kuwait, Saudi Arabia and Iraq to defuse the situation and on July 20, 1961 the League reached the following decisions: it called for the withdrawal of British troops from Kuwait as quickly as possible; it urged Iraq to pledge that it would not resort to the use of force to annex Kuwait; it supported any Kuwaiti desire for union or merger with any Arab State. More significantly it welcomed Kuwait as a new member of the Arab League on July 21, 1961 and urged its members to support the request of Kuwait for UN membership. It also asked the Arab States to provide active help for guaranteeing the independence of Kuwait.[9]

On August 12, 1961 the Emir of Kuwait and the Arab League Secretary General reached an agreement about the nature and composition of the league force to be sent to Kuwait to replace the British troops as a guarantee of Kuwait's independence. Jordan, Saudi Arabia, UAR and Sudan contributed forces for the operation. These forces arrived in September 1961 and on October 10, 1961 the British troops were withdrawn. Due to the break up of UAR, its contingent was withdrawn in December 1961, and those of Jordan, Sudan and Saudi Arabia were also withdrawn before the end of the February 1963 *coup d'etat* when Abdul Karim Qassem was overthrown. The Soviet Union, which had vetoed resolutions in July and December 1961 in the UN Security Council, aiming at recognising the independence of Kuwait, relented after the changes in Baghdad and on May 14, 1963 Kuwait become the 111th member of the UN. This paved the way for the temporary resolution of the Iraq-Kuwait crisis. Thus, it was only with the overthrow of the Qassem regime that relations between Iraq and Kuwait improved.

The new Iraqi President, Abdul Salam Arif, realising the negative effects of isolation to which Iraq was subjected over its claims on Kuwait, recognised Kuwait's independence on October 4,1963 and said it wanted to clear "the sullied atmosphere created by the Qassem regime". The occasion was during a visit by a high-powered Kuwaiti delegation led by the Crown Prince and Prime Minister Sheikh Sabah al Salim al Sabah, the Interior Minister, the acting Foreign Minister and other officials. The delegation visited Iraq on an invitation from the Iraqi Prime Minister, Major General Ahmad Hassan al Bakr. At the meeting Iraq recognised the independence and complete sovereignty of Kuwait and its boundaries as specified in the letter of the Iraqi Prime Minister dated July 21, 1932 and which was accepted by the Kuwaiti Ruler in his letter dated August 10, 1932. Both agreed to immediately establish diplomatic relations at the level of ambassadors and pledged to work towards reinforcing the fraternal relations subsisting between the two states "inspired by their national duty, common interest and aspiration to a complete Arab unity".[10] They also agreed to work towards establishing cultural, commercial and economic cooperation and the exchange of technical information. Kuwait registered the agreed minutes as a Treaty with the UN. More significantly, Kuwait showed its readiness to review the 1961 agreement with Britain and made a grant of 30 million dinars to Iraq. Iraq, in return, agreed to provide sweet water to Kuwait from Shatt al-Arab. But this understanding did not lead to the resolution of their border demarcation problem. From 1964 until 1967 the Kuwait-Iraq joint committee met several times to discuss ways to demarcate the borders but, without success. Iraq is reported to have raised the question of the legality of the previous agreements and documents on the plea that these were signed at a time when Iraq was not really free. Iraq wanted a border adjustment in its favour as a *quid pro quo* to accept the previous agreements. Kuwait, as expected, rejected Iraqi interpretations and demands saying the duty of the joint committee was to implement the agreements and not to question their legality. In this stalemate, the border demarcation remained unsettled and the committee was winded up in 1967. Despite Iraqi reservations over Kuwait's territorial integrity, both cooperated in numerous fields including barter trade during the Arif brothers' rule. This phase was characterised by conflict and cooperation.

The emergence of a full-fledged Baathist party government in July 1968, in Iraq, opened a stormy chapter in Iraq-Kuwait relations. Initially, of course, relations appeared normal and in fact warm with Kuwait becoming the first state to accord state recognition to the new Baathist regime. Saddam Hussein, who become Vice-President under General Ahmad Hassan al

Bakr, made clear his desire to establish close ties with Kuwait. Moreover in 1969 both concluded several agreements extending to military and economic cooperation. This trend continued in 1971 when a new Customs agreement was concluded, allowing for the extension of the 1964 trade agreement, but providing for an increase in the volume of goods traded. Both denounced Iran's take over of the three Arab (UAE) islands in the Gulf. More significantly, following Britain's decision to withdraw from the Gulf, Kuwait and UK had concluded exchange of notes on May 13, 1968 terminating, from May 13, 1971, the defence agreement of 1961 which had been an irritant in the Kuwaiti-Iraq ties. Kuwait also supported the 1972 Iraqi nationalisation of the Iraqi Petroleum Company.[11]

But, beneath this facade of normal relations and cooperation in several fields trouble was brewing over the old issue of demarcation of their common border. A new element was added to their old problem. Iraq's ties with Iran deteriorated in the aftermath of the 1968 'Baath coup' and Britain's decision to withdraw from the Gulf. As the Shah of Iran intensified his pressure on Iraq, through support to Iraqi Kurds and other activities, the Baathist leaders requested Kuwait in April 1969 to allow it to station Iraqi forces near Bubiyan to safeguard Umm Qasr port from any Iranian mischief. Towards this end the Iraqi Defence Minister Hardan Takriti and the Interior Minister, Saleh Mahdi Ammash visited Kuwait to persuade the Emir of Kuwait to allow Iraqi forces to be deployed in a two sq. km area surrounding Umm Qasr. In return, Iraq told Kuwait that it could send its forces to Basra or any other place in Iraq. According to Iranian sources, Kuwait agreed to the stationing of Iraqi troops on its soil. This cannot be confirmed as neither Kuwait nor Iraq have acknowledged this move. Iraq is reported to have again urged Kuwait to cede Warbah and Bubiyan islands and Kuwait continued to reject Iraqi demands. Faced with persistent refusal, Iraq resorted to pressure tactics and massed troops in December 1971 on its border with Kuwait. Kuwait unsuccessfully tried to neutralise Iraqi hostility by making monetary payments and by making Kuwaiti investments in Iraqi industrial development projects. But Iraqi impatience was growing and it exploded in March 20, 1973 in an exchange of fire between the two states in which two Kuwaiti and one Iraqi soldiers died. Kuwait accused the Iraqis of erecting military installations inside Kuwaiti area of 'Al-Samita' in a protest note sent to Iraq on March 22, 1973. It also asked for the withdrawal of Iraqi troops from the Kuwaiti border. In a defiant mood, Iraq rejected the Kuwaiti contention and said that the two countries had not yet demarcated their boundaries. It eventually agreed to withdraw from the border post when PLO, Saudi Arabia, Syria and the Arab League intervened to defuse the crisis. Outwardly, Iraq had rejected Arab mediation in April 1973 arguing that it was purely a bilateral issue. It appears Iran and Saudi Arabia also played a significant role in coming to the rescue of Kuwait in the face of growing Iraqi assertiveness, mainly due to its expanding military capability, formalised and regularised by the April 1972 Friendship Treaty with Moscow which was received with concern by the two Gulf giants.

Meanwhile Iraq on April 28, 1973 suggested to Kuwait that the border demarcation talks should be resumed and that the "solution of the problem" should take into consideration not only the interests of the two countries, but also the larger interests of the Arab world. In a provocative reference Iraq called the previous border agreements correspondences as "indications".[12] Moreover, in another note on May 17, 1973 Iraq rejected previous border agreements saying they had not been ratified as required by Iraqi constitution. Around the same time the Iraqi foreign minister emphasised the importance of the two Kuwaiti islands of Warbah and Bubiyan to Iraq and asserted that, without them, it could not be a 'Gulf Power' and that it was prepared to give up "all of Kuwait" in return for the islands.[13] This clearly revealed that Iraq had not renounced its claim over Kuwait despite having recognised its sovereignty and territorial integrity in 1963. Sensing danger, on August 20-22, 1973 the Kuwaiti Crown Prince Sheikh Jaber al Ahmed al Sabah visited Baghdad to reach a settlement, but found the Iraqis again reiterating their demand for Warbah and Bubiyan islands. This time they wanted to be either ceded or leased to Iraq for defence purposes and would, in exchange, accept the existing borders. Sticking to its guns, Kuwait politely but firmly rejected the Iraqi proposal. In reaction, Iraq again moved its troops near the frontier in 1973, and repeated this in 1976 ostensibly over Kuwait's resumption of drilling at the oil-well at Jirjan in disputed territory and the border controversy continued till early 1977.

One crucial reason why Kuwaiti rulers were so determined in rejecting Iraqi demands over the two islands, was their desire not to antagonise the Shah of Iran who desired to be the policeman of the Gulf. These two islands would have surely strengthened the Iraqi position and desire to dominate the Gulf. The expected Iraqi challenge was sought to be nipped in the bud by the Kuwaiti rulers, whose tilt towards the Shah and the West was well known. Kuwait ultimately realised that leaving the two islands unused only attracted Iraqi demands. So they decided to have their presence.

Taking advantage of the confrontation in Kuwait between the *Al Sabahs* and the opposition over the dissolution of the National Assembly in September 1976, Iraq criticised Kuwait and revived the old claim it had renounced in 1963. Iraq even occupied a tiny area in northern Kuwait. The Kuwaiti rulers, in June-July 1977, again sent Interior and Defence Ministers to Iraq but the deadlock remained as before with Kuwait furiously denying reports that it had agreed to lease the two islands Iraq had been seeking for several years.[14]

With the isolation of Egypt over the Camp David agreements (on peace with Israel), Iraq, after the Baghdad Arab summits (1978-79), emerged as the dominant Arab state. The 1979 Iranian revolution further pushed Iraq to primacy in Arab affairs. In fact the Gulf region appeared ripe to respond positively to Iraqi goals. It had become well known that Saddam Hussein wished to spread Baath ideology in the Arab world especially the Gulf, under the Iraqi leadership. This Iraqi boldness emerged partly because of the perceived decline of Iranian power under the leadership of Ayatollah Khomeini.

NOTES AND REFERENCES

[1] Seton Lloyd, *Twin Rivers: A Brief History of Iraq* (London: OUP, 1961) p. 197; see also Abdul Qadir al Jasin, *The Political and Economic Development of Kuwait between the Two Wars, 1914-1939* (Cairo; 1973) (in Arabic) pp.145-88; Henry A.Foster, *The Making of Modern Iraq: A Product of World Forces* (Norman, University of Oklhahoma Press, 1935); *The Truth of the crisis between Kuwait and Iraq* (al-Kuwait al dairah, 1961) (In Arabic); For details see Rasheeduddin Ahmed Khan, *Political Developments in Iraq, 1914-1932* (Ph.D Thesis, University of Delhi, ISIS, 1959) pp.16.

[2] A.Shikara, "Faisal's ambitions of leadership in the Fertile Crescent", in Kelidar, ed., *The Integration of Modern Iraq*

(London: Croom Helm, 1979) pp 32-45; Thomas, Roy E, "Iraq and the Persian Gulf Region" *Current History*, Vol. 64, January 1973, pp.21-25 and 37-38.

3   See the text in A.H.H. Abidi and K.R. Singh ed., *The Gulf Crisis* (New Delhi, 1991) pp.260; and A.G. Noorani, *The Gulf War: Documents and Analysis* (New Delhi: Konark, 1991) pp.1-2; Hussein M. al Baharma, *The Arabian Gulf States; Their Legal and Political Status and their International Problems* (Beirut : 1975)

4   *Iraqi Regime's claims to Kuwaiti Territory - in Historical and Legal Perspectives* (New Delhi; Kuwait Embassy, n.d.) p. 4; For details see M.A. Saleem Khan, *The Monarchic Iraq: A Political Study* (Aligarh: Centre of West Asian Studies, 1977) p.71

5   M.S. Agwani, *Politics in the Gulf* (New Delhi: Vikas, 1978) p. 62

6   Zahra Freeth and Victor Winstone, *Kuwait: Prospect and Reality* (London: 1972) pp.123-4; Shwadran, Benjamin "The Kuwait Incident", *Middle Eastern Affairs*, vol. 13, January 1962 pp. 1-13 and February 1962, pp. 43-53.

7   Agwani, n. 5, p. 62

8   Abidi, n. 3, pp. 134-35; "Arab Reactions to Kuwait". *World Today* (London) vol. 17, August 1961, pp. 322-24

9   Iraqi Regime's claims to Kuwaiti Territory. n. 4, p. 4-5; see also A K Pasha, ed., *The Gulf in Turmoil: A Global Response* (New Delhi: Lancers Books, 1992)

10 Noorani, n. 3, p. 2-3.

11 Iraqi Regime's claims to Kuwaiti Territory, n. 4, p. 6; see also Adel Hussein, *Iraq: The Eternal Fire: 1972 Iraqi oil nationalization in perspective* (London : Third World Centre, 1981)

12 Ibid., p.7

13 Agwani, n. 5 p. 63; *Arab World Weekly* (Beirut), 24 March and 7 April 1973; De Candole, E.A.V., "Kuwait Today", JRCAS, vol.52, January, 1965, pp. 31-37; see also Sandra Mackey, *The Reckoning: Iraq and the Legacy of Saddam Hussein* (London: W W Norton, 2002).

14 Abidi, n. 3, p. 138.

2
War with Iran and Crisis with Kuwait

Just as the Iranian revolution alarmed the GCC states, they were also concerned with the export of the Iraqi revolution. They suspected the Iraqi intentions as outlined in Saddam Hussein's "Arab National Charter" of February 8, 1980. Undoubtedly, this charter was directed, at least in part, at the Saudi dominance of the lower Gulf states. Riyadh clearly resented Iraqi intrusions and attempts to spread its influence. Thus GCC states came to suspect both Iran and Iraq. Although the Iraqi threat (despite Saddam's recent moderation) in the long run was considerable, the Iranian threat was seen as more serious and immediate. It is against this backdrop that the Iran-Iraq war broke out in September, 1980. Although Iraq went out of its way to exploit GCC states' fears, the Arab pledge of support for Iraq before the war was not easily forthcoming. Initially, the GCC states, although concerned at the Iranian threat to export their Islamic revolution, gave only verbal support to Iraq. Even after the outbreak of the war, the Arab suspicion of Iraqi ideology and its export persisted, (besides not wanting to antagonise Iran). The full measure of

Iraqi irritation found expression in a passage of Saddam Hussein's speech on July 17, 1981 in which he complained not only of those Arab states "blatantly avowing total bias" in favour of Iran, but also of those who had failed to conform with the "minimum level of the pan-Arab bond" and had "outdone themselves in expressing neutrality".[1] In order to pre-empt any support from Gulf Arabs to Iraq, Tehran threatened to launch air strikes against any Gulf states that helped the Iraqi war efforts. Basically due to the revolution (and fears of the spread of the Gulf War) the GCC was formed in May 1981. The GCC leaders went out of their way to reassure Iran when they said, "We do not want the GCC to be misinterpreted as an alliance against Iran."[2]

As seen before, Iraqi threats to Kuwait had remained since 1961. Despite some improvement in ties, Kuwait remained deeply suspicious of Iraqi sincerity towards its independence and territorial integrity. Its stand on the Iran-Iraq ideological competition had been unique. Kuwaiti leaders had been working towards its own brand of a welfare state, neither sympathetic to Saudi Wahhabism nor to the Iranian brand. Apart from the Islamic revolution and the fear of its export to Kuwait, it had numerous reasons to be more than concerned about the Gulf war. Being a close neighbour to both combatants, Kuwait lay far more exposed and vulnerable. The substantial Shia population was another factor. All of these factors propelled Kuwait to maintain a neutral position in the initial stages of the war. Its neutral stance in the war underwent a significant change as the war dragged on with no clear-cut victory for Iraq in sight, and Kuwait incrementally shifted towards a pro-Iraqi position. Due to its crucial logistical role in channelling supplies to Iraq, (Iraq and Kuwait were reported to have signed an agreement on the use by the former of the

Kuwaiti port facilities at Shuweik) Kuwait was bombed several times by Iranian planes. Increasingly, Kuwait blamed Iran for prolonging the war.[3] Soon it became clear to Kuwait that Iran would not tolerate a situation whereby it functioned as an Iraqi 'extention'. Despite this agonising dilemma, Kuwait nevertheless continued to support Iraq. Interestingly, despite Iranian air attacks and mounting threat to its national security, Kuwait avoided any steps likely to lead to a deterioration in its relations with Iran. It made unofficial protest but otherwise relied on the GCC for support. It was opposed to the idea of seeking US support or even to its presence in the region. Relations with Iraq did not run smoothly either. Kuwait assisted Iraq by allowing Iraq-bound cargoes to transit via its ports and territory, and by granting an interest-free loan on a very large sum "for the reconstruction of installations destroyed in the war".[4] But it was adamant in refusing to lend any kind of direct wartime aid to Iraq, even refusing to admit wounded soldiers to its hospitals. The unresolved problem of the demarcation of the Kuwaiti-Iraqi border, coupled with the threats to internal security – which were an outgrowth of the wartime situation – also strained ties with Iraq. In early 1981, Iraq's Interior Minister visited Kuwait to propose that it should lease Iraq the offshore islands of Warbah and Bubiyan. President Saddam Hussein, in the summer of 1981, also expressed his desire to control the two islands for five years. Since Kuwait was opposed to the Iraqi proposal, as a reaction, it signed a contract in May 1981 to construct a bridge to connect the mainland with Bubiyan Island.[5] Despite Kuwait's attempt not to provoke Iran, its oil installations were bombed by the Iranian air force which prompted it to recall its ambassador to Tehran and lodge a complaint with the UN Security Council. At the same time,

Kuwait resisted Iraqi calls to break ties with Iran and struggled to maintain a conciliatory trend within the GCC towards Iran. With the Iraqis on the defensive since July 1982, in the face of several offensives launched by Iran, relations between Kuwait and Iran deteriorated steadily. On the other hand, to contain the Iranian offensive, Saddam Hussein brought about pressure on Kuwait to hand over Warbah and Bubiyan islands to it. Faced with the threat of Iran at its doorstep the Kuwaiti rulers agreed to place three of its islands under Iraqi control for security reasons. This agreement was signed in November 1984 by Kuwaiti Prime Minister, Sheikh Sabah during a visit to Iraq. Soon Iran accused Kuwait of giving logistics aid to Iraq by placing airfields, ports and transit routes at its disposal and objected to the hostile attitude of its media towards Iran. *Kayhan* wrote that so far "we have ground our teeth in silence", knowing that Kuwait acted only from fear of Iraq and Saudi Arabia; but now Kuwait should realise "tomorrow may be too late".[6] When the Iranians pressed their attack towards Iraq's Gulf coastline and the ports of al-Faw and Umm Qasr, the Kuwaiti island of Bubiyan became the object of unwelcome attention by both combatants. At the start of the offensive, Iran demanded that the Kuwaitis should not permit Iraqi forces to use Bubiyan in any attempt to push back the advancing Iranians. Otherwise, it warned, Iran might move in itself. Iraq has had its eye on this island and other areas on the Kuwaiti side of the border especially since the outbreak of the Gulf war. There had been several reported Iraqi incursions across the frontiers into Kuwait since the war began turning against Iraq in mid-1982. Kuwait took a serious view of these events. The Kuwaitis were clear that, notwithstanding their support for Iraq, they were not prepared to compromise their declared neutrality by allowing, even tacitly, their territory to be used by either of the warring states. The November 1984 agreement to allow Iraqi troops to use three islands for security reasons was reported to be a secret one. In fact, Kuwait had been opposed to the idea of allowing the GCC to become aligned with any one superpower and had rejected proposals to allow Western military forces to use Kuwaiti facilities. Kuwait had also refused to sign a bilateral security agreement with Riyadh. When Kuwait was rocked by a series of bombings in December 1983, Iraq emphasised that the bombings confirmed what it had been trying to explain to the Arab world, that Arab security was "an integral whole", and warned that any negligence to "purge your ranks (of them)... would inflict calamity on the Arabs" and necessitate the spilling of Arab blood to prevent Iran's swallowing the smaller Gulf states. In any case, Iraq was ready to continue to "stand as a barrier" and to participate in any collective security effort deemed desirable, including a Gulf intervention force. Speaking specifically of Kuwait, with which relations were now "excellent", Saddam Hussein declared a willingness to discuss the border demarcation and again mentioning an Iraqi desire to establish a military presence on the Kuwaiti islands of Bubiyan and Warbah.[7]

The blasts underlined Kuwait's essential vulnerability and the fact that it was the first in the firing-line should Iran seek vengeance against the GCC. Despite its anger with the Iranians, the Kuwaitis themselves redoubled their efforts to strike a more balanced position, attuned to current exigencies between the two warring parties. Despite intense war, Kuwait undertook another mediation effort, dispatching an envoy to Iran. One publication explained again Kuwait's basic position: during the four years of fighting "changes occurred in the Iraqi stance" but not in the Iranian one. "As we have refused

Iraq's war against Iran, despite the fact that its declared goals did not include changing the Iranian regime, we regret Tehran's offensive against Iraq and its declared aims of downing the Iraqi political regime".[8]

The response of the GCC to the Kuwaiti bombing was in essence a reiteration of its previous policy: some tough language towards the Iranian threat, followed by the return to a more moderate position. The GCC foreign ministers in June 1984 reiterated their calls for a peaceful end to the fighting. Concurrently, in order to "provide teeth" to their diplomacy, their military chiefs of staff met to plan responses in the event of further escalations. In the face of growing external threats and internal discontent, the Kuwaiti ruler dissolved the National Assembly in mid-1986, at the very time when Iran recaptured Mehran. The Iranian Majlis Speaker Rafsanjani linked the Kuwaiti move to Iraq's defeat and said, "To our belief, Kuwait's political crisis has nothing to do with the explosions at al-Ahmadi oil port but is linked with the (Gulf) war and the (Kuwaiti) people's growing opposition to support for Iraq."[9] Kuwait and Iran held diametrically opposite views on oil prices and oil production. Iranian hostility was also directed at Kuwait because of its oil policies which hurt Iran more than any other OPEC country. Iraq's intensified campaign of air strikes against Iranian economic and oil targets led to further Iranian reprisals against shipping on the Arab side of the Gulf. Iran stepped up attacks on vessels to and from Kuwait, identifying it as one of Iraq's key supporters. Kuwait went public and invited Soviet Union, China and US to reflag its oil tankers. This brought about massive naval presence in the Gulf of the US and other states. Kuwait became the target of vitriolic Iranian propaganda, and the government faced persistent requests from the US naval forces, for facilities in Kuwaiti territorial waters, which were politely but firmly turned down. Kuwait's determination to see its policy through despite Iranian intimidation is now widely praised. Kuwait's handling of the delicate issue showed considerable depth of experience in dealing with world powers. Said Tom Mc-Naugher of the *Brooking Institution*, "Kuwait is the most vulnerable country in the world. The fact that it survives suggests it has an acute sense of the balance of competing world forces".[10] Although Kuwait emerged from the crisis as an important regional, political and economic force retaining its political system intact, nevertheless, it had to pay a high price in terms of greater centralisation of domestic political power, deep alienation of Iran and some differences with other GCC states – some of which favoured a more conciliatory policy and some a tougher stance towards Iran. Perhaps, for Kuwait, circumstances had left no other viable alternative.

Soon after the Iran-Iraq ceasefire in August 1988, Kuwait, confident of Iraqi friendship, asked for the demarcation of its border. The Iraqis sent their Interior Minister Mr. Samir Abdur Razzaq to Kuwait and both agreed to constitute a joint committee to complete the task of demarcation. Again, Iraq raised the issue of Bubiyan island and was firm that unless this is transferred to Iraq, there would not be demarcation. As before, Kuwait turned down the Iraqi demand and the situation reverted to the stalemate. It must be stressed that the Al Sabah rulers were convinced that if they were to yield to Iraq on this issue, it would be seen as a grave provocation by Iran. [Later in October 1990 Iran told Kuwaiti exiled rulers (after Saddam Hussein had taken over Kuwait in August 1990) not to grant the island of Bubiyan to Iraq and that it would take appropriate measures (meaning they themselves would occupy it) if they actually did so as part of any settlement].

Convinced that, by providing financial and other support to Iraq during the Gulf war, they had earned its good will, Kuwait again tried to get its boundaries demarcated. But goodwill is an effervescent item in world politics and Kuwaitis learnt this soon. Kuwait's Crown Prince and Prime Minister Sheikh Saad Abdullah visited Baghdad in February 1989 because "the atmosphere in Baghdad could not be more conducive to resolving the border question finally". But the Kuwaiti delegation after reaching Baghdad "fell into the Iraqi trap" – a phrase coined by a prominent Kuwaiti political personality – even though this visit was billed as a "historic" trip whose "success" was assured in advance. As this personality puts it:

> Our policy has been simply to wait. We were in no hurry to delineate the border. We had and still have, plans for a border agreement that would institutionalize the *status quo*, without fear of provoking a confrontation with Baghdad. But what happened is that the Iraqi leadership lured us to Baghdad, and instead of approving the border, they informed us that it was necessary to redefine the border, to change the *status quo*. At no stage in the preliminary and preparatory discussions between us and Iraq had there been any mention of this.

The Kuwaiti personality adds bitterly.

They consider that our plans to populate the border area and build towns there are an act of 'confrontation' with Baghdad. This was the message in brief, though they tried to cool the temperature by offering us water from the Shatt al Arab. But such a water project has been discussed for 17 years. Talk of it started when Kuwait built its first water desalination plant. Did reopening this subject require a 'historic' visit such as this?"[11]

The Kuwaiti delegation, to their shock, discovered that Saddam Hussein intoxicated with the illusion of victory over Iran, made disparaging remarks on Kuwait's support to Iraq against Iran. Moreover he said "we expected that after the termination of the war the Emir of Kuwait would pay a visit to Iraq". Of course, the Kuwaitis quickly realised that there was no use expecting gratitude for the immense help given to Iraq. Rather, the Iraqis, by inviting other Arab countries "particularly Kuwait", to join the Arab Cooperation Council, which had given the Iraqis a stronger line of defence against Kuwaiti demands, were making it clear that Kuwaitis "still have dues to pay before they can expect a border agreement". *Al Azmina al Arabia* concluded that Kuwait's "hopes of drawing up a border agreement have been drowned in the waters of the Shatt al-Arab". Fed up with the protracted border problem, the Kuwaiti ruler, in a rare gesture, had gone to Baghdad in September 1989 to sort out the problem of demarcation, but "was sent packing in a manner that was barely polite".[12]

Saddam Hussein, by borrowing heavily from Kuwait, Saudi Arabia and others, had mortgaged Iraq's extensive oil resources far into the future to pay for a war that brought Iraq none of the territorial gains or battlefield glories that he had promised. However, he was convinced that, but for Iraq's "victory" over Iran, most of the Gulf Arab States would have fallen to Iran, the first being Kuwait. It is this assessment which propelled him to mount pressure on the Al Sabahs to be more generous in financial aid and, when this was not forthcoming, he invaded Kuwait on August 2, 1990.

Just as there is a direct link between the 1979 Iranian revolution and the eight-year Gulf war, the Kuwaiti crisis would not have erupted but for the Gulf war. Iraq emerged out of the Gulf war with a shattered economy and a huge foreign debt of nearly $100 billion (bulk of it to Saudi Arabia and Kuwait). Some 120,000 Iraqis had died in the war and about 300,000 were wounded, many of whom were left permanently disabled. Moreover a large part of the scarce resources were spent on maintaining a large military machine. The sharp fall in oil prices further aggravated Saddam Hussein's innumerable problems. But during and after the war, Iraq built up one of the finest and strongest military machines in the area.

Through his numerous speeches, statements and meetings, Saddam Hussein, during the Gulf war, had made it absolutely clear that the GCC states had not given adequate support to Iraq in its fight with Ayatollah Khomeini's regime, whose Islamic fundamentalism had threatened all of them seriously. Richard Murphy, former Assistant Secretary of State for Near Eastern and South Asian affairs under the Reagan administration, said:

> I was struck by the constant theme we heard from the Iraqis in 1988. They were clearly nettled and aggravated that the Arabs and, indeed, the world were not sufficiently grateful for Iraq's sacrifice in the war, that none of us appreciated what Iraq had done for all of us.[13]

Saddam Hussein, only eight days before he occupied Kuwait, in a meeting with the American ambassador to Baghdad, Ms Glaspie gave expression to his pent-up rage.

> Who else was there to protect the Gulf states against Iran? Who else would have fought a ground war to stop Iran? Would you have been able to lose 10,000 men in a single

battle one week, and then turn around and lose another 10,000 the next without concern that public opinion might force you to change your policy?[14]

Saddam Hussein who had promised his people peace, prosperity and democracy after the war found it difficult to fulfil his promise. His treasury was empty. Soldiers from some of the five demobilised divisions (some 300,000 soldiers) after reaching home complained about lack of jobs, shortages and other economic woes. Sensing danger, the regime allowed criticism and some open debate. Kuwaitis, who visited Iraq soon after the Gulf war, were surprised to see Iraqis "so openly voice their frustrations".[15] They concluded that Saddam's Baathist regime was in danger of imminent collapse. Elections were held in April 1989 for the Iraqi National Assembly and wages raised by 20 percent. By July 1989 things had come to crisis point. One Iraqi explained the regime's dilemma, "You Westerners don't see beneath the surface. People are fed up. The regime worries that one day there will be an explosion."[16] The dramatic changes in East European Communist regimes appear to have halted the liberalisation process inaugurated with much fanfare. In November 1988, Saddam Hussein told an Arab lawyer, "As you saw in Eastern Europe, democracy may not be the best thing. We have to be careful on how to proceed." The collapse of the Communist regime there had badly shaken Saddam Hussein and in an interview he told ABC's Diane Sawyer three times, "I am not Ceausescu".[17] He is reported to have repeated it to the US Ambassador April Glaspie shortly before his invasion of Kuwait. To sustain his "siege State Politics" and to stay and retain power in his "Republic of Fear", Saddam Hussein needed money, and very quickly, to keep his people contented and pacified.

Kuwait, Saudi Arabia and others do not seem to have realised the desperate financial position of Saddam Hussein. At the Arab Cooperation Council summit in Baghdad on February 19, 1990, Saddam Hussein for the first time revealed that he was in dire financial straits. He said that not only did it not matter whether the GCC states were willing to forgive his debts (all GCC states knew that Saddam Hussein would never repay the debt), he also needed more money. He told a closed session of the summit, "We cannot tolerate this type of economic warfare which is being waged against Iraq".[18] He wanted some $27 billion from Kuwait alone and the Al Sabahs flatly refused to bail him out. Saddam Hussein, in one more desperate move, sent Saddoun Hammadi, a high-ranking official to the GCC states for money. Wherever he went he pressed Saddam Hussein's request for a contribution of $ 10 billion in aid. To emphasise the seriousness, he seems to have produced a list of Kuwait assets to demonstrate that Kuwait had a sufficient sum of money to give to Iraq. The tightfisted Kuwaitis gave peanuts—only $ 500 million over three years.

Since the May 1990 Arab summit, Saddam Hussein, now virtually recognised as the leading Arab leader under attack from the US, made known his unhappiness over low oil prices and its negative impact on his country. Iraq accused, in early July 1990, Kuwait and UAE of exceeding their OPEC quota. In the first official criticism of these countries, Iraq's foreign minister Tariq Aziz assailed Kuwait and UAE in a letter to Arab League Secretary General Chadli Klibi on July 18, 1990. He raised a number of issues in the letter revolving around Kuwait-Iraq border, oil prices, OPEC ceiling, debts and Iraqi Pan-Arab role. This needs to be examined in some detail for a better understanding of the crisis.

Oil-prices and ceiling: Tariq Aziz accused Kuwait and UAE of "systematically, deliberately and continuously" harming Iraq's economy by exceeding OPEC oil quota and reducing its oil revenues to the tune of $89 billion between 1981-90. He said a drop of one dollar in price of a barrel of oil led to a drop of one billion dollars in Iraqi revenues annually. At a time when Iraq needed all the revenues to rebuild its war-ravaged economy, the fall in oil revenue was a terrible blow to Saddam Hussein, and his criticism of Kuwait on this score is partly justified because Kuwait had become one of the most avid practitioners of quota-busting and at one stage was almost boasting about its disregard for OPEC ceiling. The Kuwaiti oil minister stressed that a bigger market share, rather than high price should be OPEC's strategic aim. Moreover compared to Iraq, fall in oil prices did not severely affect Kuwait because it earned billions from its foreign investments. This made Kuwait less dependent on oil prices than Iraq and other OPEC members.

Apart from the above "premeditated abuses", Kuwait was also accused of stealing Iraqi oil since 1980 from the southern section of the Rumaylah oil field to the tune of $2.4 billion. Thus, Kuwait was accused of "theft tantamont to military aggression". Iraq says Kuwait was dumping this stolen oil on the world oil market. Since part of Kuwait's loans were on oil i.e., Kuwait sold oil on the account of Iraq (especially in the early years of the Gulf war when Iraq had problems in exporting directly); Baghdad links this oil to the stolen oil from the Iraqi Rumayleh oil field. Most of the technical and legal experts agree that since the Rumayleh oil field straddles the border, at the southern (lower) end Kuwait had been pumping oil to the clear disadvantage of Iraq.[19]

It must be noted that soon after the May Arab Summit, Kuwait was disturbed by Iraqi accusations of over-production. The Kuwaiti Emir as a concession to Iraq shifted his oil minister Sheikh Ali Khalifa al Sabah to the Ministry of Finance. Ali Khalifa had been a strong supporter of pumping more oil, irrespective of OPEC ceiling, to keep oil prices low. Moreover, before going public, Saddam Hussein at the end of June 1990 sent Saddoun Hammadi to GCC states to urge them to stick to OPEC quota so that oil prices would come to OPEC official price. Soon after on July 10, 1990 Gulf oil ministers met in Jeddah, Saudi Arabia, to study Iraqi complaints. Both Kuwait and UAE officially agreed to adhere to the OPEC quota.

This failed to pacify Iraq as Saddam Hussein needed immediate cash. The day Tariq Aziz sent the letter to the Arab League, an Arab summit meeting was taking place in Tunisia. Tariq Aziz again spoke bitterly about the Arab states, who had violated OPEC quota. Tariq Aziz told the Summit leaders, "we are sure some Arab countries are involved in a conspiracy against us. We want you to know our country will not kneel. Our women will not become prostitutes, our children will not be deprived of food."[20] To cap it all on July 17, 1990, Saddam Hussein renewed his attacks on Kuwait and UAE for over production even though they had agreed to abide by OPEC quota. For the first time sounding very belligerent, Saddam Hussein threatened millitary action if they failed to abide by the OPEC ceiling. He said "If words fail to afford us protection, then we will have no choice but to resort to effective action to put things right and ensure the restitution of our rights".[21]

The Kuwait ruler, shaken by the vehemence of Saddam Hussein's attacks and open military threat, convened a cabinet meeting on July 18, 1990. The minister of justice, Dhari-al

Othman said, "the Iraqi memorandum is just the beginning. God knows how far they will go".[22] His assessment was that Iraq had other intentions and that oil quota busting was merely a pretext. Badr al Yacoub, the minister of State for the National Assembly, and Abdul Rehman al Awadi, minister of State for Cabinet affairs, however, asserted that Saddam Hussein's basic motive was to get a substantial sum of money. The same day Kuwait sent a "troika of ministers" to GCC allies and other Arab friends to mobilise support.

In response to the Iraqi letter to the Arab League, Kuwait on July 19, 1990 sent a formal letter to the Arab League Secretary General expressing "astonishment and surprise" at Iraqi accusations. It mentioned that all the Iraqi allegations are "falsification of facts and the reverse of the truth". Moreover, Kuwait also sent a letter to the UN Secretary General on July 19, 1990 drawing his attention to the "unmistakable threatening" in the Iraqi note against Kuwait and said "it is regrettable". Iraq was simply furious at Kuwait's decision to approach the UN. *Al Jumhouriya* on July 23, 1990 launched an unprecedented personal attack on the Kuwaiti Foreign Minister Sabah al Ahmad and said his "malignant hand is behind all the harm inflicted on Iraq and he put himself as a tool to implement the American policy in Kuwait.... today he is the pivot of the conspiracy hatched by the Kuwait government against Iraq and the Arab nation". *Al Thawra* commented on the same day that "Sabah al Ahmed has been further exposed as a US agent when he abandoned the Arab choice and sent his message to international forums to take the issue out of the Arab League." Kuwait made a quick climbdown and denied it had any intention of making its dispute a global issue. They realised that this would infuriate the Iraqi's still more. Kuwait News Agency (KUNA), quoting an official reported, "Kuwait would like to assert here once again that when it submitted that memo, it never requested that it be distributed to member nations or that the UN Secretary General should act upon it. Kuwait is concerned that all issues that arise about relations between Arab brothers should be dealt with within the Arab League."[23]

The Pan-Arab and debt issue: Concerning Iraq's debt to GCC states there is no precise figure, but conservative estimates gave $100 billion, bulk of it to Saudi Arabia. Most of it was interest-free loans and Saudis commuted part of their loans to gifts, particularly those earmarked "for the reconstruction of Faw". Whereas Kuwait could only donate a mosque for Faw and firmly insisted on Iraq repaying the loan. For them the loans were not only a question of money, had they been gifts, even *ex post facto* Iranian taunts about Kuwaiti "co-belligerency" would have been difficult to deny. Kuwait repeatedly raised the debt issue as a bargaining chip whenever Iraq reiterated demands for territory or more money after the 1988 ceasefire.[24] The Kuwaitis had become used to Iraqi pressure and periodic demands – they would respond to such Iraqi tactics by discreetly inquiring about their debt to Kuwait. The Kuwaitis would also insist on demarcation of their borders in exchange for writing off the debt. For Saddam Hussein, such "insulting Kuwaiti intransigence" would be intolerable. Many Kuwaitis are now convinced that had the Al Sabah rulers given money to Saddam Hussein they could have prevented the Iraqi takeover. "When the lion is hungry," a US official said, "you don't tell it that there isn't going to be any dinner."[25]

When Kuwait rejected Iraq's request to cancel these debts, Baghdad reminded the tight-fisted Kuwaiti and other GCC rulers that Iraq was "obliged" to wage war (with Iran) not only to defend its sovereignty but also to "defend the eastern flank of the Arab homeland, especially the Arabian Gulf region". It must be pointed out that soon after the cease-fire in 1988, Saddam Hussein talked about Iraq's role in preventing the collapse of some of the GCC states in the face of Iranian onslaught, and spoke increasingly in a patronising tone. For Saddam Hussein, Iraq thus fought a Pan-Arab battle and defended Pan-Arab "sovereignty and dignity". But for this "rivers of blood of its youth", GCC states would have lost not only their wealth but also their dignity and sovereignty to others. Thus, Iraq claimed to have preserved oil revenues of these states. Iraq not only accused Kuwait and UAE of increasing oil production to the detriment of Iraq, but also said that the loans given to Iraq were not from their treasuries but from the increases in their oil revenues as a result of the drop in Iraqi oil exports over the war years. However, this claim is highly dubious and difficult to accept.[26]

But, there is some truth when Iraq claims to have protected Kuwait's territory, honour and wealth. When Iran achieved a breakthrough in Faw Peninsula and was close to Basra and had it succeeded in establishing its hegemony over southern Iraq, Kuwait's very existence, as an independent state, would have been gravely jeopardised. If this had become a reality, Saudi Arabia perhaps would have joined the Gulf war. Alternatively, it would have had to resign itself to having on its north-east doorstep a hostile Shia neighbour, flushed with military success, with Kuwait challenging the Gulf monarchies. Iran would have surely exploited the presence in eastern Saudi Arabia of a large, restive Shia population (in *Hasa*). In other words, had Iraq not pushed Iran away from Faw and Basra, and generally fought as energetically as it did, perhaps Kuwait would have become for Iran a springboard to destabilise the entire Gulf region.

When Saddam Hussein argued that what the Gulf states contributed during the Iran-Iraq war was 'protection money', most GCC leaders confirmed this to a large degree. Since their goal during the war was to stay out of war, Iraq was doing the job for them (in return for money). Moreover, since Pakistani troops had refused to fight for Riyadh, and since the latter's military capability was limited and that of Kuwait even weaker, both would have had to seek outside help (read US) to keep Iran at bay.

Even though Saddam Hussein's Pan-Arab ambitions were known as early as February 1980, when he outlined the "Arab National Charter" which was clearly directed, at least in part, at Saudi dominance of GCC states, the Gulf war and especially its successful conclusion in August 1988 provided Saddam Hussein an opportunity to reassert his Pan-Arab claims. Since then, and more particularly after the May 1990 Arab Summit, Saddam Hussein's Pan-Arab rhetoric increased. This was clearly reflected in Aziz's letter which said:

> *Iraq believes that the Arabs in all their countries are one nation. It also assumes that everyone should benefit from their wealth. If one is hurt or harmed, everyone will be affected.*[27]

This statement buried the so-called moderation which was ascribed to Saddam Hussein since 1979. The above statement was clearly aimed, not only at Kuwait, but Riyadh and other GCC members as well, who had provided not only money, but crucial support, by allowing their ports to be used for bringing in both civilian and military supplies, risking Iran's attacks. This was not only unjustified; Saddam Hussein was being ungrateful. The statement also "strikes unpleasant chords reminiscent of a time when Iraq tried to meddle in their internal affairs".

Finally, Tariq Aziz raised one additional point in his letter. He accused Kuwait of helping the US to achieve its goal i.e. lower oil prices. It was not difficult for Saddam Hussein to establish a link between Kuwait's oil policy and US designs in the area. Since the end of the Gulf War, when the US attacked him over Kurds being gassed, Saddam Hussein was aware of the US desire to contain and, if possible, to cut him to size. Now the sharp fall in oil prices gave him an opportunity to establish that Kuwait and UAE were implementing US strategy against Iraq. Tariq Aziz wrote that since Iraq began to call for regaining Arab rights in Palestine and to draw attention to the dangers of the US presence in the Gulf, Kuwait began to adopt an unjust policy, aimed at harming Iraq.

In a move designed to discredit pro-US, oil-rich Arab states and gain the support of non-oil Arab states, Saddam Hussein wanted an Arab fund for development to be established. This fund was to be financed by contribution of one dollar from the nearly 14 million barrels of oil sold by OAPEC linked to a price of $ 25. (The amount would have been around $5 billion per year). He also urged the setting up of a fund for *Intifada*. Saddam Hussein, fully aware of the cool attitude of GCC leaders towards pan-Arab ventures, floated these funds to discredit and expose them. Iraq continued to accuse Kuwait and UAE of implementing US inspired policies aimed at striking Pan-Arab security and interests, which Iraq claimed to have defended and was engaged in defending. More importantly, Iraq called the Kuwaiti Premier a traitor to the pan-Arab cause.

Concerning the border issue, Tariq Aziz accused Kuwait that it had set up military establishments, police posts, oil installation farms "as a plot to escalate the pace of the gradual systematic advance" towards Iraqi territory, and of "intentionally stalling border talks and contacts". These accusations should be seen in the light of their more than sixty year old border problem, whose demarcation had been stalled for various reasons.

The Jeddah Talks: The GCC leaders, in the face of this crisis and open Iraqi threats, were enraged at Saddam Hussein's behaviour. Kuwait, which at one time had actively campaigned for Iraqi membership in GCC, was rudely awakened as were the other GCC members, to whom it was a small consolation that Iraq had wisely been kept out. Descendants of wily Kuwaiti Emirs, had survived many crises and had succeeded in keeping many neighbouring predators at bay, first with British help and then with oil money. More recently, during the Gulf war, they were emboldened by the US decision to reflag their ships. They continued to have faith in their survival with shrewd maneouvrings. Not surprisingly, Kuwait on July 18, 1990 denounced the contents of the Iraqi memorandum. It said Kuwait "renounces the policy of violence, threats and blackmail" and reminded Iraq of its "material and moral" support during the Gulf war. It further said Iraq's allegations concerning the border were "a falsification of reality" and an "inversion of the truth as Iraq has a full history of violations, of Kuwaiti territory".

Some cabinet minister thought an Iraqi military strike was probable. Not leaving things to chance, the cabinet decided to cancel all military leaves and call an alert. The Americans by July 21,1990 learnt of Iraqi troop concentration on the Kuwaiti border but concluded that Saddam Hussein was merely sabre-rattling to raise oil prices and extort more money from the oil sheikhs. The next day Tariq Aziz again criticized Kuwait and UAE. The tone and vehemence surprised many.[28]

Egypt's President Hosni Mubarak was the first to sense danger and rushed to Baghdad to mediate the dispute. He got "assurances" from Saddam Hussein that Iraq would not resort to force in settling its disputes with Kuwait, as long as negotiations were under way. Saddam Hussein made the same assurance to Jordan's King Hussein and PLO's Yasser Arafat.[29]

Saudi Arabia's King Fahd, concerned at the mounting allegations and counter-allegations, intervened and talked to both Saddam Hussein and the Kuwaiti Emir especially of "the process of cooperation and solidarity between brothers". Arab mediation, was bringing some positive response from both sides, but US intervention aggravated and escalated the crisis. On July 24, the US deployed six combat vessels in the Gulf for joint maneouvers with the UAE. Moreover the Bush administration warned Iraq that "there is no place for coercion and intimidation in a civilized world." Even though America did not "have any defence treaties" with Kuwait and no special defence or security commitments, the US assured the Kuwaiti ruler that it was committed to supporting the individual and collective self-defence of its friends in the GCC.[30] At the same time, the US Senate on July 27, decided to cut off all food supplies and to prohibit the transfer of military equipment and technology to Iraq. The Senate vote meant denial to Iraq of $ 800 million in official US credits and required US representatives to vote against loans to Iraq by international financial institutions. This was done with a deliberate motive to unnerve Iraq's many foreign creditors and provoke a financial crisis.

On July 25, Saddam Hussein told the US Ambassador Ms April Glaspie that he badly needed money and that an invasion of Kuwait could not be ruled out unless Kuwait gave him the money he desperately needed. Glaspie innocently told Saddam Hussein, "We have no opinion on the Arab-Arab conflicts, like your border disagreement with Kuwait". She was confident that Saddam Hussein would not invade Kuwait. Perhaps he would seize a small amount of disputed land and, at the very worst, he would seize small Kuwaiti islands. As she later remarked to *New York Times,* "I didn't think – and nobody else did – that the Iraqis were going to take all of Kuwait."[31]

When told by the US Ambassador that her country had no opinion on Kuwaiti-Iraqi problems, Saddam Hussein finally made up his mind to invade Kuwait. On July 28 an Iraqi official is reported to have told an American retired official, "You will see by next week, we will be protecting the people of Kuwait." He also said *"the Americans are a paper tiger. They won't do anything."*[32]

Despite the aggressive signals from Iraq, Kuwait and Saudi Arabia appeared optimistic of a solution. This explains Kuwait's decision not to seek an emergency GCC summit on the issue. In fact, the Kuwaiti Minister of State for foreign affairs said it was "premature" to ask GCC leaders to hold an emergency summit in the light of Iraq's "complaint" against Kuwait. Moreover, the Kuwaiti foreign minister expressed the conviction that "what is between the brothers in Iraq and Kuwait is merely a summer cloud which will go away".[33] This clearly reveals the underestimation of the intensity of Iraqi anger and Kuwaiti confidence that it would tide over the crisis. The only small step which Kuwait took was to inform the UN Secretary General on the issue. Soon they were satisfied "over the positive and constructive stances" expressed by the GCC members. Interestingly, Kuwait did not challenge Iraqi accusation on its oil policy.

Meanwhile Egypt, Jordan, PLO, Saudi Arabia, realising the gravity of the problem intervened and arranged for a meeting between the two parties in Jeddah. It was also reported that Saddam Hussein had assured Egypt's Mubarak that Iraq had no intention of attacking Kuwait. But Iraq continued to mass troops on its border with Kuwait. Even though Kuwait agreed to hold talks with Iraq it rejected the latter's "methods of pressure and intimidation". The Jeddah talks originally scheduled for July 28 were finally held on July 31 but were doomed to fail because its outcome became known as early as 26th when Iraq reminded Kuwait that it should "know that whoever comes to meet us must be prepared to remove the harm and aggression which Iraq was subjected to, and respond to Iraq's *legitimate* rights". For Iraq the Jeddah meeting ought to be "decisive and fruitful", otherwise it would be a "preliminary, ceremonial meeting" which would be followed by a meeting in Baghdad where presumably Kuwait could be more easily pressurised and intimidated.[34]

Let us focus on what Iraq demanded from Kuwait as its "legitimate rights": 1) Promise by Kuwait to abide by OPEC oil ceiling; 2) Iraqi control over the entire Rumaylah oil field; 3) Kuwait to pay $2.4 billion as compensation for oil extracted from Rumaylah; 4) Gulf war debt to be cancelled; 5) compensation for loss in oil revenues due to Kuwaiti over-production and; 6) some territorial concessions on two islands, i.e. Warbah and Bubiyan.

In the face of mounting threats and clear warning signals from Iraq, Kuwait bought some time and partly agreed to Iraqi demands when the OPEC meeting at Geneva on July 27, 1990 agreed to raise oil prices to $21 a barrel. Kuwait and UAE agreed to abide by OPEC ceiling for production quotas. It was reported that Kuwait had tried but failed to cut a deal with Iraq, whereby its war loans would be cancelled, in return for a favourable solution of their border problem. This willingness to buy themselves out of the crisis came too late and, at any rate, they were unwilling to make any concessions having political and territorial implications. Whereas Kuwait first wanted technical experts to identify the exact areas of dispute and the leadership to take the final political decision, Iraq, saw this as a Kuwaiti ploy to delay and buy time (as it had accused them before) and looked for a political agreement first, with details to be sorted out later. Just before the Jeddah talks, Kuwait hoped that the meeting would be a step towards reaching a "final and just solution" to all pending problems and issues, while at the same time reiterating its "firm rejection of all forms of pressure, threats and use of force in settling the disputes between brothers".[35]

It is against this background that the Jeddah talks were held on July 31, 1990. Iraq was represented by the Revolutionary Command Council (RCC) Vice-Chairman Izzat Ibrahim and Dr. Saddoun Hammadi while Kuwait was represented by its Premier and Minister of State for foreign affairs. Kuwait's Crown Prince and Prime Minister, Sheikh Saad al Abdullah al Sabah, said he was "looking forward with an open heart" to the talks that, he hoped, would pave the way for the resolution of their problem. What exactly transpired at the talks is not known but Kuwaitis went for the talks in an intransigent mood. According to the Iraqi Ambassador to the US, the Kuwaitis had come to the meeting in bad faith, they had been unwilling to listen or to negotiate seriously. "They were arrogant," said Mohammed al Mashat. "The Kuwaitis were conducting themselves like small time grocery-store owners. The gap was irreconcilable so the meeting collapsed."[36] There is evidence to prove that the Iraqi version is closer to ground reality. The Jordanian paper *Al Rai* on February 14, 1991 published a copy of a note which the Kuwaiti Emir addressed to Sheikh Saad, before he met the Iraqis in Jeddah on July 31, 1990. It read *"we are stronger than they think"*. The Emir's instruction came in the form of a comment written into the margin of a letter dated July 29, 1990 which he had received from Saudi King Fahd. In this message King Fahd welcomed the forthcoming Jeddah talks and expressed his "full confidence" that all travails between the two states would be removed. In his comment, the Emir told his Crown Prince Saad not to budge from "our agreed condition" and went on:

> Whatever you hear from the Saudis and the Iraqis about brotherhood and Arab solidarity, don't listen to it. Both have their own interest. The Saudis want to weaken us and exploit our yielding to the Iraqis so that in future we shall yield to them the (joint Saudi Kuwaiti) neutral zone, and the Iraqis want to compensate for their war (with Iran) from our accounts. But neither one thing nor the other shall happen, and that is the opinion of our friends in Egypt, Washington and London. Stand firm (on no concessions) in your talks. *We are stronger than they think.*[37]

The Kuwaiti version of the Jeddah talks is very different. The Kuwaiti officials asserted that Izzat Ibrahim opened the talks with a list of demands concerning territory, oil pumping rights and $ 10 billion. The Kuwaitis apparently found these demands as "orders" and not negotiations. Iraq is reported to have demanded that its demands be considered overnight. Next day, the Iraqis walked out of the talks when Kuwaiti head of the delegation informed the Iraqis of what the Emir had instructed i.e. "stand firm and make no concessions". The Kuwaiti official added, "Nothing of substance was ever discussed at Jeddah."³⁸ Kuwait, he continued, had been prepared to make concessions, if necessary, especially to write off Iraq's debts and to lease one Kuwaiti island. Since these were major issues the Kuwaiti delegation needed time for further instructions.

The Kuwaiti Emir had been sufficiently warned in the last days before the invasion that in defying a man such as Saddam Hussein, he was asking for trouble. The Emir believed that he could rely on immediate foreign support in the event of Iraqi invasion. This false sense of security and their failure to clearly understand the depth of Iraqi anger was a grave and fundamental error of the Emir. Kuwait, more than any other state, should have gauged Iraqi intentions. The sharp and dangerous signals were seen as nothing new because they had come before and they had neutralised it at little cost. On three occasions before August 2, State Department officials had met with Sheikh Saud Nasir al Sabah, Kuwaiti ambassador to US, to inform him of the dangerous Iraqi troop concentration. The Ambassador, after consulting his government, assured the US that the Iraqis were simply trying to bully his country into yielding to their demands. The Al Sabah rulers have been blamed by the Kuwaiti opposition for unnecessarily provoking Saddam Hussein with whose temperament, methods and ambitions they were all too familiar. Even though they had the best reason to find out Saddam Hussein's intentions, they misread the situation and the miscalculation was catastrophic. The Emir developed a false and unjustified sense of security because of his role as donor. He believed that Saddam Hussein dare not move against Kuwait in view of the massive aid it gave to Iraq during the Gulf war. The Kuwaiti rulers also failed to see that for Saddam

Hussein getting more money was essential and "access to the Gulf was his form of *Lebensraum*". Saddam Hussein knew that the Shatt al Arab was not navigable, that he was deeply in debt, that Kuwait was the solution to both these problems.[39]

Secondly, Kuwaiti rulers were banking on Arab mediation, and Arab diplomacy to work in defusing the crisis. That they continued to perceive it as a passing "summer cloud", which could be survived by brotherly intervention, was asking for too much. Kuwait calculated that Saudi Arabia, because of its close ties with Baghdad, and its enormous "financial clout would play a decisive role and that Saddam Hussein cannot afford to displease King Fahd." Much to their dismay, the Kuwaitis found the Saudis not very firm and decisive in their willingness to defend Kuwait or warn Saddam Hussein of serious consequences if he were to harm the Emirate.

Thirdly, the Emir was convinced that the still unsettled Iran-Iraq conflict gave them hope because Saddam Hussein's hands were still tied. No wonder that after the Gulf war 1988 ceasefire, Kuwait had quickly normalised its ties with Tehran so as to keep Saddam Hussein "engaged". Kuwait's reading of the internal Iraqi situation was that falling oil revenues would eventually discredit Saddam Hussein and pave the way for his removal by a *coup* or upheaval. That they were in a hurry and appeared restless in this connection was evidenced by their alleged support to overthrow Saddam Hussein. This was clearly a dangerous game and surely the Kuwaiti Al Sabah leaders were playing with fire, not realising that it would eventually engulf themselves.

To cap it all, the Kuwaiti rulers were also firmly confident that their friends in the West, especially the US and in the

Arab world would, in the ultimate resort, rescue them. The Al Sabahs had survived several times before on outside assistance (especially British and American), and now there was no reason why they should not rely on quick and decisive outside support in the event of Iraqi aggression. Unfortunately, they could never imagine that they would be on their own this time and would be left to the "tender mercies of Saddam Hussein".[40] Convinced that the US had no security treaty with Kuwait, Saddam Hussein concluded that the way was clear for Iraq to assume the mantle of regional Super Power status, to assert its historical claim to Kuwait, and above all, to cut the Gordian Knot of debt and simmering discontent left by the war with Iran. It would also reverse the territorial settlement imposed by Great Britain in the Gulf; it would finally gain secure access to the sea; and it would give vent to the widespread resentment in Iraq that the Gulf Arabs had lived in luxury throughout the war while Iraqis had bled and died to protect them.[41]

In addition, Saddam Hussein believed that he had additional strong cards that could undermine the West; the deep resentment in the area against Israel; traditional animosities towards the West, especially European powers that had oppressed them; the Islamic faith of Muslims opposed to outside/Western influence corrupting their societies; and lastly, but most importantly, his assessment that the US could not bear the huge sacrifices of a war in untested and unpredictable terrain. In a word, Saddam Hussein wanted recognition – pride for himself and power for Iraq as a strong Arab nation – on his terms and Kuwait offered him that chance.

NOTES AND REFERENCES

1. *International Herald Tribune,* May 26, 1981.
2. SWB/ME/July 20, 1981.
3. FBIS/NES-81, February 18, 1981.
4. Ibid, April 23, 1981; *Financial Times*, April 22, 1981; FBIS-NES-80, December 11, 16, 1980; Al Watan, May 5, 1981 cited in *Middle East Contemporary Survey* 1980-81, p. 480.
5. *Kayhan*, May 12, 1982.
6. *Middle East International* (MEI) No. 269, February 21, 1986, p. 4.
7. SWB/ME/October 17, 1983; and December 15, 1983.
8. SWB/ME/December 31, 1983; and February 20, 1984; FBIS-NES May 4, 1984 and February 28, 1984.
9. MEI, July 11, 1986, p. 10-11.
10. MEED, January 16, 1988, p. 6-7.
11. MEI, No. 346, 17 March 1989, p. 21.
12. Ibid., *Al Azmina al Arabia*, 16 March 1989; *MEI* No. 381, August 3, 1990, p. 4.
13. Judith Miller and Laurie Mylroie, *Saddam Hussein and the Crisis in the Gulf,* (New York; Times Books, 1990) p. 8.
14. Ibid., p. 9.
15. Ibid., p. 132; see also A K Pasha, *Kuwait: Strategies of Survival* (New Delhi: Har Anand, 1995)
16. Ibid., p. 134.
17. Ibid., p. 137.
18. Ibid., p. 12.
19. Ibid., p. 15.
20. FBIS-NES, 90-138, July 18, 1990, p. 21.
21. Miller and Mylroie, n. 13, p. 16.
22. Ibid., p. 16-17.
23. Sreedhar, "Iraqi Invasion of Kuwait", *Strategic Analysis,* vol. XIII No. 7, 1990. P. 719

24. A.K. Pasha " The Gulf Crisis", *Détente*, vol. IX, No. 2 and 3, July-October 1990 p. 2-3.
25. Miller and Mylroie, n.13, p.10.
26. A.K.Pasha, "Iraq and the GCC", *Third Concept*, November 1988, p. 22-25.
27. FBIS-NES, 90-138, July 18, 1990, p. 21.
28. Liesl Graz, "Iraq Sabres Rattle in the Gulf", *MEI, No. 381*, August 3, 1991, p.3. SWB/ME/0821/, July 20, 1990.
29. *Jordan and the Gulf Crisis: August 1990-March 1991, White Paper* (Amman: The Government of the Hashemite Kingdom of Jordan, August 1991) p. 2-3.
30. Miller and Mylroie, n. 13, p. 17-18.
31. Ibid., p. 18.
32. Ibid., p. 19.
33. SWB/ME/0822/I, A/1-2, July 21, 1990; 0823/I July 23, 1990.
34. SWB/ME/0829/A/2, July 30, 1990 ; *MEI*, No. 381, p. 5.
35. SWB/ME/0830/A/I, July 31, 1990.
36. Miller and Mylroie, n. 13, p. 20.
37. *Times of India*, February 16, 1991.
38. Miller and Mylroie, n. 13, p. 20.
39. Ibid, p. 214-15.
40. Fouad Ajami "Thief of Baghdad", *The New Republic*, September 3, 1990, p. 21.
41. Miller and Mylroie, n. 13, p. 190; See also, Robert Springborg, "Origins of the Gulf Crisis" *Australian Journal of International Affairs*, vol.44, no. 3, December 1990, pp. 221-35; and Amin Saikal, "The Persian Gulf Crisis: Regional Implications", *Australian Journal of International Affairs*, vol. 44, no. 3, December 1990, pp. 237-45.

3
War over Kuwait [1991]

The first official GCC reaction came 36 hours after the invasion of Kuwait by Iraq on August 2, 1990. One should note the long gap which explains their total shock and disbelief. "How did such a state of affairs come to pass?" *The Gulf Daily News* wondered, given that the Gulf states had supported Iraq during its "difficult days" by giving considerable financial and political support. One Gulf official said, "We had been lulled into false sense of security...Now Iraq has made us think twice." A western oil expert puts it another way: "All their knees have turned to jelly. The Gulf Cooperation Council (GCC)" proved itself to be nonexistent when it was really needed".[1] Initially the GCC leaders tried to minimise what had happened. For three days there was no mention whatsoever of the invasion. The media were not allowed even to mention the word 'tension'. They spoke only of negotiations going on concerning 'the issue' between Iraq and Kuwait. On August 3, the day after the Iraqi invasion the Saudi newspaper, *Al-Gezira* reported talks between King Fahd and other Arab leaders over "the position of Kuwait and Iraq." The *Arab News*, probably the most open of the Saudi English language papers, mentioned that the Islamic Conference

Organization (OIC) was concerned about a "serious and dangerous new situation created in the region and which is characterized notably by the use of force to settle a bilateral dispute". The *Saudi Gazette*, quoting the official *Saudi Press Agency* (whose critics suggest the initials stand for the Sleeping People's Association), said King Fahd was trying to normalise relations "between the two sister countries." The paper excelled itself in the next few days with lead stories ranging from "Devi Lal vows to fight back" to "German leaders want poll moved up to October 14." It was not until August 7 that the Gulf crisis was prominently displayed on the front page, with the UN vote for sanctions and arrival of US troops on Saudi soil. After a few days, editors took courage in both hands to report the news and were finally given the green light to editorials by King Fahd's speech to the nation on August 9, in which he bitterly condemned Iraq and confirmed the arrival of Western troops. Since then, the papers provided wide converge to the crisis "You don't want to get involved in something you'll regret, but it became so obvious that we started testing the water." Then it became official, said one newspaper editor. "It was as if Churchill was telling the *Times* that Poland hadn't been invaded," said another. "Three or four Saudi papers went ahead and did what they wanted. You can't teach an old dog new tricks but there is a sort of mini-*glasnost*." Only when Saudi Arabia became bolder did the UAE press begin detailed reporting. Where Saudi Arabia leads, the small Gulf states follow. "Their policy is to stay in the background and maintain a low profile. The best example of this was in the Gulf war when they supported Iraq, but never stopped trading with Iran."[2]

The UAE, of all the Gulf states, had cause for concern when President Saddam Hussein singled it out, along with

Kuwait, for deliberately over-producing oil. At the OPEC meeting in Geneva, days before the Iraqi invasion of Kuwait, the UAE agreed on production cut. The President, Sheikh Zayid bin Sultan al Nuhayyan considered the OPEC meeting a great success. A Western diplomat in Abu Dhabi said, "He saw his country having sacrificed oil production in the interests of OPEC and of Arab Unity, the GCC states thought that a storm had been averted."[3]

As noted earlier, the GCC managed a statement only 36 hours after the invasion of Kuwait condemning the Iraqi move. At that juncture, the GCC foreign ministers were attending in Cairo an Arab League and the Islamic Conference Organization meeting. In their meeting, the GCC Ministerial Council condemned Iraqi "aggression" against Kuwait. They called for immediate and unconditional withdrawl of the Iraqi forces from Kuwait. Apart from calling upon the Arab League and United Nations to end the aggression and remove its effects, they expressed their "utmost denunciation of and deep regret over this aggression." They also called on these organisations to preserve the sovereignty and territorial integrity of Kuwait.[4] The GCC Ministerial Council held its 12th extraordinary session in Jeddah on August 7, in the backdrop of abject helplessness of the GCC in taking practical steps against Iraq. Apart from reaffirming its previous statement of August 3 and recording its support for Kuwait and backing for its legitimacy, the Council only "studied the best ways of handling the situation and of presenting its recommendations to the Supreme Council."[5] More significantly, at the international level the GCC states moved collectively and tabled the first draft resolution to the UN Security Council – Resolution No. 660 – which called on Iraq to withdraw immediately and unconditionally, and restore legitimacy to Kuwait. It was only on August 9 that Riyadh issued its first clear statement on the crisis. King Fahd called the Iraqi invasion "the most vile aggression known to the Arab nation in its modern history." He expressed "profound displeasure" with the Iraqi move and said Riyadh categorically rejected it. He also demanded a restoration of the situation prevailing before the invasion and the return of the Al Sabah ruling family.[6] Meanwhile the emergency Arab summit in Cairo, at its meeting on August 10, condemned Iraq for its invasion and called for its withdrawal from Kuwait. The GCC states played a key role in getting this resolution passed by the Arab League but, since it was not unanimous, it lost its value as it was not binding.[7] The GCC Information Ministers, in their first extraordinary session on August 15 in Jeddah, expressed their "utmost regret, condemnation and denunciation" of the Iraqi aggression. They expressed their "total rejection of all the excuses" put forward by Iraq for its aggression. They were astonished at Saddam Hussein's peace initiative towards Iran and asked why he sacrificed so many innocent lives, caused such destruction and waste. Clearly, Saddam Hussein's move had alarmed them as they feared a *de facto* alliance developing between the two [Iran and Iraq]. The ministers also decided to stop information cooperation with Iraq in all forms and types and to broadcast a daily TV bulletin to be prepared by Kuwait and broadcast via the TV networks of the GCC states, soon after the main news bulletin.[8]

Another meeting of the GCC foreign ministers was held in Jeddah on September 5 (36th session). The Omani Minister of State for Foreign Affairs, who was the Chairman, stressed the importance of the meeting which, he said, is being held at a time when the region is passing through the "most difficult and critical circumstances." These circumstances, presumably, were Iraq's administrative structure making Kuwait the 19th governorate and Saddam Hussein's call for a holy war against US forces and for the overthrow of King Fahd and other Gulf rulers. Also, China had signalled that it might break ranks with the West and send food and medicine to Iraq. Moreover, there were mounting fears of a war breaking out in the region which would inevitably affect all the GCC states, directly or otherwise. The Minister said Iraqi invasion is a "serious precedent not only in inter-Arab relations" but something the like of which the world has not witnessed since World War II. After profusely thanking the foreign countries which had sent forces to GCC states, he said "it was due to the speedy way in which these forces were sent that the possibility of a wide scale war breaking out was stopped and the security deterrent in the region was bolstered". He stressed the eagerness of GCC to reach a peaceful solution but said Iraq had presented it with the option of war. He emphasised that the GCC states would protect their "interests and the security" by using all options. The communique issued at the end of the meeting contained nothing significant. It called upon Iraq to respect civilians in Kuwait and not to tamper with the demographic structure there. It expressed gratitude to Syria, Iran and Turkey for cooperating in implementing UN resolution against Iraq. They also called upon Iraq not to hamper the "legitimate right" of foreign nationals to leave Iraq or Kuwait. They did not specify what steps they would take if Iraq rejected their demands.[9] It was only on October 3 that it was reported by Oman that there was agreement to hold an emergency GCC summit to examine the situation in the region. Thus, only after two months since the Iraqi invasion, could GCC heads think of a summit.

The much awaited GCC summit was finally held in Doha (Qatar) between December 22-24, 1990. Earlier, the GCC foreign ministers had met on December 20 to prepare the draft resolution of the GCC summit. Qatar's foreign minister, Mr. Mubarak Ali Al Khatir, presided over the meeting. They were expected to lay the foundation for a defence strategy to establish stability and peace in the Gulf region. The GCC Secretary General, Mr. Abdulla Yaqub Bishara, when asked on the eve of the summit about a peaceful solution to the Gulf crisis said, the question was now in the hands of Iraq, which had to comply with the international resolutions and withdraw unconditionally from Kuwait. He said the council could make a "new start toward a comprehensive unity that must not be delayed". He said the summit's agenda would, besides the Kuwait crisis, also include, formation of a unified Gulf army under one command representing member states, unification of foreign policy among member states, lifting of all economic barriers and unification of the oil policy. Mr. Bishara urged Iraq to withdraw from Kuwait saying refusal would lead to measures that would put an end to its unjust aggression on Kuwait.[10]

The Emir of Qatar, Sheikh Khalifa Bin Hamad al Thani, while inaugurating the GCC summit stressed the need to have a more effective security system for the GCC countries to enable them to shield the region against any fresh aggression. He said, "The current crisis with all its gravity and intensity makes it imperative for us to review our security system so that we can ensure a decent living for our people."[11] He denounced Iraqi aggression and called for immediate and unconditional withdrawal of Iraqi troops from Kuwait in order to save the region from war. He also called upon Iraq to respond favourably to the calls of peace and "listen to the voice of reason so as to spare our region as well as the whole world from dangers of war".[12] Meanwhile rumours that Saudi Arabia and Kuwait were having secret talks with Iraq, offering some concessions to find a solution, were laid to rest when the Qatari foreign minister Al Khater told newsmen that there was no intention whatsoever to negotiate with Iraq till it withdrew its troops from Kuwait. The reports had said that Iraq was redrawing its border with Kuwait in preparation for a withdrawal but after ensuring that Kuwait's Bubiyan and Warbah islands – that had now given the Iraqi forces a commanding access to the Gulf at the head of the waterway – were included in its map, along with some rich oil fields. He also said contacts were under way to create a GCC security structure in which Iran would be included. This was for the first time that Iran was mentioned by a GCC state as a country which would be included besides Egypt and Turkey. Just before the GCC summit, Iran's foreign minister, Ali Akbar Velayati had visited Doha. Moreover, the Iranian ambassador to Qatar, Syed Mirzai was invited to attend a session of the summit which was unprecedented and which indicated the thaw in GCC-Iran relations.[13] At the end of the summit the GCC gave a firm warning to Iraq, to withdraw its troops from Kuwait by January 15, 1991 and declared that "all necessary means would be used for ensuring the return of the sovereignty and the legitimacy of Kuwait". But they expressed the hope that the Iraqi President, Saddam Hussein, would respond to the international will by vacating Kuwait immediately.[14] About the possibility of a war after the expiry of the UN deadline, the Qatari foreign minister said "Nobody wants a war if the problem is solved peacefully. We do not want war. But if Iraq insisted on its stand nobody except Allah knows what will happen. It would depend on the circumstances prevailing after that (January 15) deadline," he said. When asked whether there was a move to sever relations with Iraq, Mr. Alkhater said the question was tied to certain topics and depended on the major issues – liberation of Kuwait.[15] Asked if the GCC states would take part in the proposed US-Iraq dialogue over Kuwait's occupation, Mr. Khater said that they had an indirect role as the US was constantly in touch with them. He said, "The dialogue in question complements relevant UN resolutions and the GCC states have an indirect role in this regard."[16]

As the January 15 deadline approached, GCC criticism of Iraqi refusal to withdraw became sharper with King Fahd taking the lead to warn Saddam Hussein that "the end will without doubt be a tragedy for Iraq". However, the logic of his decision to invite outside forces and the US determination to wipe out Saddam Hussein and Iraqi military-economic capability was leading towards war. Reiterating that "I do not want a tragedy to fall on Iraq," King Fahd once again called upon Saddam Hussein to "announce tomorrow" that he will actually be withdrawing from Kuwait unconditionally. King Fahd thought that this was not a "difficult" thing for Saddam Hussein and if he did it then it might be an act of "heroism". He ruled out concessions to Iraq on the issue of its withdrawal saying it "is out of the question. I do not think that anyone can accept this or accept it upon himself in any way whatever". King Fahd, towards the end of December 1990, knew that war would erupt given the inflexible posture of Iraq. Addressing the GCC Supreme Council meeting in Doha (22-24 December 1990), King Fahd said:

> Brothers, we have not made a decision regarding peace or war, but we have made a decision regarding the return of Kuwait, peacefully if peace is possible, or by war if there

is no option but war... we have not been afraid, hesitant, cowardly or languid. However, despite all that, we do not want to close the gates of hope, or shut the windows of anticipation. We would like the person whom we used to consider a brother, a friend and an ally to know that the curtain has not been dropped on the scorching war scene yet, and that he can, even now, spare himself and his people a horror, the first victims of which would be himself and his people.[17]

The final communique, besides calling on Iraq to immediately and unconditionally withdraw from Kuwait, held Iraq responsible for paying compensation to Kuwaiti government establishments, banks, public and private institutions and companies and to Kuwaiti and other nationals who suffered losses as a result of Iraqi action. The communique also noted, amongst other things, that the council had reviewed the progress of joint action in political, security, military, economic and social fields and discussed ways to promote cooperation and the integration process. In all probability, the decision to support the use of force against Iraq was taken at the Doha summit which the Egyptian foreign minister, Ismet Abdal Majid called the "*liberation and change summit*".

Moreover, the GCC emphasised its concern to expedite steps and to make a "qualitative leap in collective action" among the members in future in order to achieve additional coordination, integration and cohesion. They appeared to be satisfied with the level of cooperation in the security and military field and endorsed the defence minister's recommendations on strengthening the "intrinsic defensive capabilities" of the members. The GCC reiterated its desire to adopt all measures necessary to protect the region's security and stability. A renewed declaration was made of their determination to enhance the effectiveness of cooperation among members, to strengthen their individual and joint defensive capabilities to "serve the interests of the region, its security and prosperity which, in turn will bolster world peace".[18]

The much expected war finally broke out on January 17, 1991, with massive air attacks by the US on Iraq. The GCC general secretariat "hailed the will of the international community to implement the Security Council resolutions, to impose the principles of law", so as to compel Iraq to comply with the resolutions. It also hailed all the states participating in the war for their "will, determination and their living up to their international responsibilities". The statement highlighted the various attempts to get Iraq out of Kuwait by peaceful means and went on to say:

> The Iraqi regime responded to these attempts with mockery, dealt with the appeals with arrogance, dealt with the crime of invading Kuwait and annihilating its people with invasion and ignorance, and denied the Kuwaiti peoples' right to their country, history, land and sovereignty.

The GCC statement put the blame on Iraq for the outbreak of war due to Saddam Hussein's "trickery, his scorn for the world and his insult to public opinion and the UN Secretary General", whose peace initiative was spurned and met with "crudity and blatant defiance". The statement ended by saying that the GCC people will not forget the support extended to Saddam Hussein by Arab Gulf states. It called such support "crime" and denounced those who applauded Saddam Hussein and insulted the Kuwaiti people and violated the principles of brotherhood and betrayed ties of kinship.[19]

The war launched against Iraq by the US and its allies was subject to conflicting interpretations. The UN Secretary

General, Perez de Cuellar, made it very clear that it was not a war of the UN. The UN Security Council, through its resolution 678, authorised the use of all the "necessary means" to implement the Security Council's resolution 660 and the subsequent resolutions. In a way it was only a UN authorised war.[20]

The 14th extraordinary session of the GCC Ministerial Council, which met in Riyadh on January 26, 1991, in order to clear the doubts, emphasised that the war to liberate Kuwait was based on international legitimacy, represented in the UN Security Council resolutions, adopted in accordance with paragraph seven, of the UN charter.[21]

Meanwhile Iraq, suffering under intense air bombings, announced a proposal which stipulated its withdrawal from Kuwait under certain conditions. These were:

1) total and comprehensive cease-fire; 2) UN Security Council to abolish all the resolutions passed on Kuwait since August 2, 1990; 3) all foreign forces to withdraw from the area; 4) Israel to withdraw from occupied Arab lands; 5) Iraq's historical rights on land, sea to be guaranteed; 6) In the new political arrangements for Kuwait, no place for Al Sabah family; 7) Countries who attacked Iraq to undertake reconstruction in full; 8) All debts owed by Iraq and the countries of the region to be written off; 9) The Gulf states, including Iran, to be included in security arrangement; and 10) Gulf to be declared a zone free of foreign military bases and presence.

Kuwait rejected all of it out of hand. Its Minister of State for Cabinet Affairs, Dr. Abdal Rahman Abdullah al Awadi, said: "it is merely another ring in the chain of the policy of deception, trickery and procrastination" which Iraq has followed since its invasion. He saw this as one more Iraqi desperate attempt and manoeuvre to bypass the UN Security Council resolutions to overcome its isolation and break international unanimity. He also called on the Iraqi people to overthrow Saddam Hussein's dictatorial leadership whose "corrupted policy has led to successive catastrophes" for the Iraqis and had led to further "division, disunity and destruction" of the Arab and Islamic nations.

The GCC foreign ministers, in a meeting with their counterparts from Egypt and Syria in Cairo on February 15, 1991 rejected the Iraqi proposal saying it was not "serious"., They said the proposal included, "unacceptable conditions" besides including new conditions and reiterating the UN resolutions. Thus, the Iraqi proposal was "rejected part and parcel" by the GCC. The Cairo meeting also reviewed the progress made in liberating Kuwait besides emphasising the need to promote Arab economic and social development. They assessed the role played by funds and programmes for Arab development, especially the newly created Gulf Fund for Supporting Development Efforts in the Arab World. They also discussed the Palestine question, especially the negative impact of the Iraqi invasion on this issue. They recalled the "heavy burdens borne by their countries and the martyrs, funds and unremitting moral, political and diplomatic support they offered despite several challenges and obstacles". The ministers reaffirmed their commitment to work for the resolution of the Arab-Israeli conflict based on Israeli withdrawal. They also voiced their interest in efforts to remove all weapons of mass destruction, particularly nuclear weapons in the possession of all the states in the area.[22]

In the face of the most intense aerial bombardment followed by ground attack, Saddam Hussein's forces were defeated and on February 28, 1991 US President George Bush announced the liberation of Kuwait. On the same day, Iraq accepted all the UN Security Council resolutions on the issue. The GCC welcomed the liberation of Kuwait as the emancipation from "tyranny and aggression, injustice, unprecedented arrogance and stubbornness and obduracy of Iraq". It underlined with admiration the role of Egypt and Syria in defeating Iraq. The GCC Secretariat also praised the role played by US, UK, France and other European states in "defence of international legitimacy and in support of the rule of law". It further mentioned:

> The forces of international legitimacy were triumphant over the forces of despotism, invasion and aggression because their will emanated from the powers of right conviction in their behaviour and the high esteem of their objective.

Finally, it hoped that

> The return to the previous era which was characterised by the plotting of the Iraqi regime against the state of Kuwait, its betrayal of all conventions and treaties, the cooperation of some Arab regimes with the aggression, and their praising of its (the Iraqi regime's) ugly practices without conscience and with no respect to the charter of the Arab League and regardless to the charter of Arab brotherhood, is not possible.[23]

NOTES AND REFERENCES

[1] Gerald Butt, "Gulf States alarmed by Threat of War", *Christian Science Monitor,* August 10-16, 1990.

[2] Victor Mallet, "Open journalism: Saudi debt", *Financial Times,* reprinted in *Times of India,* August 25 1990; see also Sharon Peterson, "Hussein Sniffed Trouble in Kuwait", *Christian Science Monitor,* August 10-16, 1990.

[3] *Christian Science Monitor,* August 10-16, 1990.

4. SWB/ME/0835/A/4-5, August 6, 1990.
5. SWB/ME/0838/A-4, August 9, 1990.
6. SWB/ME/0839/A/7, August 10, 1990.
7. SWB/ME/0841/A/5, August 13, 1990.
8. SWB/ME/0845/A/5, August 17, 1990.
9. SWB/ME/0863/A/9-10, September 7, 1990; For text of final communique see SWB/ME/ 0866/A/7, September 11, 1990.
10. *Times of India*, December 22, 1990.
11. *Times of India*, December 23, 1990; Youssef M. Ibrahim, "Fundamental changes afoot in Saudi Arabia", *Times of India*, September 10, 1990.
12. *Times of India*, December 24, 1990.
13. *Times of India*, December 12 and 26, 1990.
14. *Times of India*, December 26, 1990.
15. *Times of India*, December 24, 1990.
16. *Times of India*, December 12, 1990.
17. SWB/ME/0956/A/12-13, December 28, 1990.
18. Final Communique of the 11th session of the GCC Higher Council held in Doha, December 22-25, 1990 known as the "Doha Declaration", A.G. Noorani, *The Gulf Wars: Documents and Analysis* (New Delhi: Konark, 1991) pp.182-192.
19. SWB/ME/0974/A/10, January 19, 1991.
20. "It is not UN War and UN has no control over war", says Perez de Cueller, Noorani, n.18, pp.239 and 248.
21. SWB/ME/0981/A/9, January 28, 1991.
22. Statement by the Iraqi RCC on February 15, 1991 in Noorani, n.18, pp. 302-308 found in SWB/ME/0998/A/3, February 16, 1991; Kuwaiti minister said Iraqi proposal is nothing new; another "desperate move" and for the statement from GCC; Egypt and Syria calling Iraqi proposal "not serious", SWB/ME/0999/A/11-12, February 18, 1991.
23. SWB/ME/1011/A/14-15, March 4, 1991.

4
Shia and Kurdish Uprisings

Soon after the liberation of Kuwait in February 1991, and temporary lull in fighting, it appeared Saddam Hussein and the Arab Baath Party had been sufficiently discredited by the massive destruction suffered during the war. The subsequent civil war involving Shias, Kurds and the government led to further destruction. According to a prominent Iraqi opposition leader, Ahmad Chalabi,

> The biggest political casualty of all was the Baath Party, which was shown to be an empty shell. The people defied its organisation and discipline. In the areas of the revolt, its members faced either flight or death. The Baath had become merely the veneer that covered Hussein's terror. It ceased to exist beyond this role. The bonds that supposedly tied the hundreds of thousands of its purported members together proved to be based on opportunism and fear.[1]

This assessment may have been partly accurate soon after the 1991 Gulf War, and especially during the civil war, which raged for more than six months but the Baath Party quickly regained control over the security system under Saddam Hussein. It must be remembered that the Baath Party is a highly organised party and Saddam Hussein created a variety of youth

Shia and Kurdish Uprisings

militias. Even though only about 25,000 Iraqis were made full-fledged members of the party, 1.5 million - more than 10 per cent of the population of Iraq – were supporters and sympathisers. It must be noted that this figure only partially overlaps nearly 1.2 million workers under the government. It is natural that increased reliance on the government for survival undercuts the democratic urge because these dependent citizens are in no position to challenge the state/party for democratisation. Saddam Hussein, even though badly mauled "does not sit atop a fragile junta but rather (on) an institutionalised, deeply invasive party".[2] Thus, his grip appeared to be firm on the system but the continuing economic sanctions undermined Saddam Hussein's rule and legitimacy.

To neutralise people's anger, the Baath leadership increasingly talked about democratisation of the political system, but no tangible change occurred. There were reports, probably inspired, which suggested that curbs had been placed on the unlimited powers enjoyed by Saddam Hussein in the wake of the severe battering in the Gulf war.[3] In view of the determination of the US and its allies to cut Iraq to size, Saddam Hussein, in order to retain power, had to give larger doses of liberalisation and democratise the largely authoritarian system.

Iraqi opposition leaders, became more assertive due to Saddam Hussein's defeat, and repeatedly called for a democratic system in the country with autonomy for the Kurdish population. Some 300 opposition leaders of differing political ideologies who met in March 1991 at Beirut took part in the largest gathering of the Iraqi opposition to the rule of the Baath party over the past 23 years. Those attended included the Kurdish front, a coalition of eight Kurdish militia groups, the pro-Iranian Dawa Party, the Iraqi Communist Party, the Islamic Amal Organisation, the pro-Syrian branch of the Baath Party, and the Council for Democratic Iraq, which was recently formed in London, and has close links with Saudi Arabia. Britain, USA, Syria and Saudi Arabia openly supported the Iraqi opposition groups who conceded that Saddam Hussein might survive the uprising.

The Iranian-backed anti-government Shia Muslim group, called the Supreme Assembly for Islamic Revolution in Iraq, (SAIRI) headed by Ayatollah Bakr Hakim appears to have played a crucial role in the Shia uprising in the two southern provinces. Hundreds were killed in large-scale clashes between demonstrators and government troops in four townships near Baghdad. These four towns, Al-Thawra, Shola, Al-Kadhemiya and Mashtal, witnessed scenes of massive demonstrations against the government. Basra, Zubair and Umm al Khasib also witnessed Shia uprisings. By the end of March 1991 Saddam Hussein's forces had crushed the uprising by Shia fundamentalists and Izzat Ibrahim, RCC's Vice-President, said that the situation had returned to normal and services were restored in Wasit and Maysan provinces.[4] In another move to isolate Saddam Hussein, the Iraqi ambassador to Spain, Tawfiq Ismail, asked Madrid for diplomatic asylum.

The US appears to have pursuaded Saudi Arabia to undertake a major effort to destabilise the rule of Saddam Hussein. A dissident Iraqi General, Hassan Naquif, was encouraged by Saudi Arabia to recruit an anti-Saddam Hussein army of Iraqi deserters or defectors from among the Iraqi prisoners of war (POW). Naquif, a former Deputy-Chief of Iraqi Army Staff, had spent a decade of exile in Syria and Lebanon, working as a military adviser to the PLO. It must be mentioned that USA and Saudi Arabia had designated an undisclosed number of Iraqi prisoners as "deserters or defectors" and Saudis held them separately from other POWs.

Saddam Hussein, who not only survived the defeat but also contained the Shia and Kurdish rebellions, realised the need for promising political reforms. Although, he had promised reforms earlier but they were not implemented. This time, the challenges were far too serious and circumstances very difficult, especially with backing to the opposition by external powers.[5] On March 16, 1991, in his first nationally televised address since the end of the Gulf war, Saddam Hussein promised widescale political reforms, including a new parliament, constitution and cabinet. He said that the new constitution would be offered for discussion and debate before it was put for a general referendum. He added that the new parliament would be elected. Saddam Hussein was optimistic and said, "Iraqis will find in this new era more liberty to express their will and their interests through parties, societies and press." He called this "a decisive and irreversible decision". However, he did not give any time-table for holding elections or drafting of the new constitution. He also announced that his government had crushed the Shia rebellion and accused Iran indirectly of encouraging the rebellion. Saddam Hussein referred to the rebels as "stooges and agents of foreign enemies" and said that his country was faced with rebellion while it was still bleeding from the consequences of the vicious aggression committed by thirty countries; referring to the US-led joint forces to liberate Kuwait.[6]

The large-scale destruction caused by the Iraqi army's action against Shias only aggravated the damage resulting from allied bombing and earlier from Iranian attacks. Unlike the support shown to Kurds, international community showed little sympathy to the Shias. Probably the reason was the use of the banner of Shia Islam by the rebel leaders in declaring the uprising. This was a mistake because the Shia leaders, at the Beirut meeting of the Iraqi opposition, had proclaimed that their struggle was aimed at overthrowing Saddam Hussein and setting up a democratic system. The Iraqi Shia leaders based in Iran, highlighted the Islamic character of their struggle. Many Iraqis saw in this a new danger, not to speak of the GCC states and the West, which were perturbed at the rise of Iran's influence. Unity among the Iraqi opposition groups was broken when the Kurds agreed to talk to Saddam Hussein unilaterally on the autonomy and other related Kurdish problems. Muhsin al-Husseini of the Islamic Action Organisation, speaking in Damascus on April 26, 1991, said that he feared that once the pressure was off Saddam Hussein, "he will retract his pledges and the Kurdish people will pay a great price."[7] To the utter dismay of Iraqi opposition, George Bush said that the US was not going to intervene militarily in Iraq's internal affairs and risk being drawn into a Vietnam-style quagmire.[8]

For Iraq, Iran was the main threat. After having regained control over southern towns and cities, Iraq charged Iran, for the first-time after the war, with aiding and abetting the rebels. The Speaker of the Iraqi National Assembly, Saadi Mahdi Saleh, said that Iran had sent large groups of saboteurs. Speaking at the emergency session of the Assembly on March 20, 1991, Mr. Saleh said, "it has been established now that Iran has dispatched groups of saboteurs to do this. For a good time Iran was preparing these groups of saboteurs for this day to carry out its scheme."[9] Meanwhile, Iraqi opposition declared that Saddam Hussein's days as the head of Iraq "were numbered" and that "thousands" of members of Iraq's elite Republican Guard had joined rebel forces. But Saddam Hussein, firmly in the saddle, celebrated his 54th birthday on

April 28, 1991 and much more comfortably his 55th birthday in 1992.[10]

In the cabinet reshuffle Saddam Hussein appointed Saadoun Hammadi on March 1991 as Prime Minister, with the specific task of rebuilding the war-ravaged Iraqi economy. Tariq Aziz was relieved of his portfolio as Foreign Minister but was named Deputy Prime Minister. Mr. Taha Yassin Ramadan, First Deputy Prime Minister, was promoted as Vice-President of Iraq. This was one more attempt to neutralise opposition to Saddam Hussein who was struggling to retain power in the face of UN sanctions, Shia and Kurdish rebellions and the after effects of allied bombardment. As a small relief, the UN lifted all sanctions on food imports and other humanitarian aid to the Iraqi people. The Sanctions Monitoring Committee, established a simple notification procedure for food and medical supplies, besides laying down a no objection procedure for items which Iraq needs urgently - fuel, spare parts and other materials essential for humanitarian relief.

Despite government's claim that rebellion had been suppressed, there were signs that pockets of opposition still remained. Reports emanating from Iran and Syria were certainly biased but a news agency quoting Lt. General Ibrahim al Dawud, a former senior commander of the Iraqi Army, Vice-President and Minister of Defence and an opposition leader now in exile, said that Saddam Hussein had no option but to declare emergency in Baghdad to prevent the advancement of the rebels.[11] As time passed, these appeared to be wishful thinking rather than hard realities since Saddam Hussein had survived.

The first major step taken by the Saadoun Hammadi Government was to reach an agreement with the Kurdish representatives on autonomy for the Kurds, thereby paving the way for an end to the foreign military presence in northern Iraq. Jalal Talabani, Secretary General of the Patriotic Union, announced the agreement on April 25, 1991, after a meeting with Saddam Hussein. There was again no firm time-table as to when it would come into effect but Prime Minister Saadoun Hammadi said that the talks were "marked by a spirit of sincerity", adding that the Iraqi leadership was attached to the agreement of 1970 granting widespread autonomy.[12]

Having suppressed the Shia and Kurdish rebellions, Saddam Hussein put on a show of defiance in the face of demands by the UN over the issue of inspection of weapons sites. He however, backed down after President Bush announced that he would send war planes to Saudi Arabia to escort UN helicopters into Iraqi air space. This incident revealed that despite the Gulf war and massive destruction Saddam Hussein's determination to pursue his own-policies had not weakened. Iraq remained defiant as evidenced by its rejection of UN Security Council Resolution 712 of September 19, 1991 which allowed Iraq to sell oil worth $1.6 billion. It was rejected by Baghdad on the ground that it infringed its sovereignty.

As time passed, Saddam Hussein appeared to be consolidating his grip over Iraq more firmly, as he took a series of steps in that direction. The most significant was his decision to remove his Prime Minister, Saadoun Hammadi, on September 13, 1991, after only six months in office. He lost his job mainly because he openly questioned some of Saddam Hussein's policies, that too at a Congress of the Baath party in Baghdad. He was also sacked from the ruling RCC. Mr. Muhammad Zabaydi, another Shia, was promptly sworn in as Prime Minister. The Iraqi President took other steps designed to strengthen the hand of Saddam Hussein's own family and close associates in top positions in the government, the Baath Party and the security services. Saddam Hussein, in the view of one well placed Iraqi, was "reconsolidating his position, but on a much narrower base".[13] If one scrutinises Saddam Hussein's past promises on democratic reforms, it is a sad story of broken and unfulfilled promises. He had promised dissolution of RCC and a much reduced role for the Baath Party soon after the Gulf war. In a chain of broken promises the RCC, in early September 1991, issued a decree permitting opposition parties. The decree made it clear that the Baath Party would continue to enjoy exclusive privileges within the armed forces. No parties based on ethnic and religious groups were to be permitted. Besides these constraints, Saddam Hussein stressed that Western style democracy would never be allowed. He added that anyone "admiring western standards and values would be barred from any post in leadership or any position which affected the political, social and cultural life of the country."[14] It might be recalled that in November 1988 itself Saddam Hussein had told an Arab lawyer, "As you saw in Eastern Europe, democracy may not be the best thing. We have to be careful on how to proceed."[15]

Meanwhile, in line with Resolution 687, the UN Secretary-General submitted to the Council a 32-page report which proposed sweeping new measures to make sure that Iraq would never again possess weapons of mass destruction. Under the plan, Iraq must provide to the special commission, on a regular basis, complete, correct and timely information on activities, sites, facilities, material and other items, both military and civilian, that might be used for purposes prohibited by the resolution. Iraq must also respond fully and promptly to any questions or requests from the special commission. This places

Iraq under the strictest supervision ever devised by the world body. It must be remembered that should Iraq refuse to comply with these provisions, the UN Security Council is empowered to act under Chapter VII of the UN Charter.[16]

Though Iraq continued to reject the Security Council Resolutions 706 and 712, the so-called oil-for-food resolutions, and despite the improvement in food situation it was reported that opposition to President Saddam Hussein had not ended. Eighty Iraqi officers, who allegedly conspired to stage a coup against Saddam Hussein, were executed in December 1991. The plot was foiled when an army officer, identified only as Mufleh al-Rawi, exposed the alleged conspirators. Saddam Hussein is reported to have later decorated al-Rawi. The source of this information was from the members of the Supreme Assembly of the Islamic Revolution of Iraq, the main Iraqi Shia opposition movement based in Tehran. It must be noted that attempts to overthrow Saddam Hussein had been reported since he moved into Kuwait, with scores of officers either executed or purged. But nothing has ever been verified or confirmed.[17]

Unable to overthrow or remove him from power, the US, marking the first anniversary of the war against Iraq, denounced Saddam Hussein and his "pariah" regime and called for his overthrow. It urged the Iraqi people and military to overthrow him. The White House spokesman, Mr. Marlin Fitzwater, said, "The United States reiterates its pledge to the Iraqi people and the Iraqi military that we stand ready to work with a new regime, a new leadership in Baghdad that accepts the UN resolutions and is willing to live in peace with its neighbours." He added, "Its own people will find a partner in the US, one willing to seek to lift UN sanctions and help restore Iraq to its rightful place in the family of nations." But he also said that the US had no military plans to overthrow Saddam Hussein and added, "Our actions last year were all under the UN resolutions. We don't anticipate anything unilateral."[18]

Meanwhile, Iraq's fractioned exile opposition made one more attempt to unite on a political platform that could be acceptable to many Iraqis if Saddam Hussein was overthrown. Mohammed Ali, a London-based official of Iraq's Shia movement led by Syed Bakr Hakim, said, "We want this conference to end with a political platform of Iraqi opposition that contains all Iraqi political groups."[19] This time there appeared signs of increased regional cooperation, between Iran and Saudi Arabia in particular, to forge the Iraqi opposition into a more effective force against Saddam Hussein. Saudi Arabia, in a major effort to destabilise Saddam Hussein's regime, hosted a meeting of the Iraqi opposition groups which included Shias, Kurds, former army officers and some Sunni Iraqis. This was a major turning point in Saudi regional policy as this was the first time the Iraqi opposition had met publicly in Saudi Arabia. Riyadh which used to move shrewdly and cautiously at the regional and global level, abandoned some of the basic rules set by the late King Abdul Aziz. Whatever one may think of some of the those rules, the fact remains that they were violated during the 1990-91 Kuwait crisis when foreign forces were deployed on a massive scale for the first time on Saudi soil. In the post-war Gulf (1991), they were again broken with the hosting of Ayatollah Hakim Bakr and other Iraqi opposition leaders in the Kingdom. He was the second ranking Shia leader to visit Riyadh after Lebanon's Imam Musa Sadr in 1973. It must be noted that the Kingdom's Sharia courts do not recognise Shias as Muslims and the anti-Shia fatwas of the senior theologian

Sheikh Abdul Aziz Baz are clear and numerous. With this departure in Saudi policy, it has become clear that Riyadh is willing to play a much more active role in the region after the Gulf war. So far, Saudi foreign policy was low key and they generally played an active role behind the scene, shying away from publicity. Syria played a crucial role in bringing Iran and Saudi Arabia together against Iraq. Crown Prince Abdullah (a close friend of Hafez al Asad) met the Iranian President Hashemi Rafsanjani in Dakar (Senegal) during the OIC Summit in December 1991. This war the first highest meeting between the two countries since 1979. This paved the way for closer Saudi-Iranian cooperation against Saddam Hussein. When King Fahd met Ayatollah Hakim Bakr, he told Ayatollah, "I hope to see you in Baghdad soon." He also promised to provide full political and material help to SAIRI to oust Saddam Hussein. Hakim is reported to have given a number of assurances which satisfied the Saudis including SAIRI's commitment to the unity and territorial integrity of Iraq, to preserve and protect the "Arab character of Iraq." The Saudis were thus pursuing a clear confrontationist policy aimed at the overthrow of Saddam Hussein. Many felt the new Saudi policy was likely to enhance the influence of Iran. Undoubtedly, the Iraqi Shia leaders were jubilant over the latest developments. They were convinced that, this time, the US was serious about seeking ways to overthrow Saddam Hussein from power. If the Shias launch an offensive against Saddam Hussein, in which Iran is also involved covertly or overtly, then what an American soldier remarked in (March 1991) when Iraqi forces were fighting Shia rebels in south would be repeated on a bigger scale "We watch them fight and we watch them kill each other." Already the imposition of no fly zone in south was seen as a victory for Iran as it had been demanding it since the West imposed one on the Iraqi Kurdish areas. A commentary on Tehran radio on the subject of the safe zones for the Kurds said, "International organisations and influential powers should think about establishing security for and removing threats against all Iraqi people." Some have even called this development a reversal in Saudi policy. So far the Saudis were not enthusiastic in endorsing the Iraqi Shia opposition because of the Iran factor, but on February 23, 1992 Crown Prince Abdullah ibn Abdul Aziz publicly received a visit from Ayatollah Mohammed Bakr Hakim, leader of the Supreme Assembly of the Islamic Revolution in Iraq, based in Tehran. Hakim was in Riyadh to take part in the Iraqi opposition conference. A similar conference, held earlier in Beirut in March 1991, had failed largely because of wide political differences among these groups.

Active Saudi interest in the effort to stiffen the political clout of the exiled Iraqi opposition was due to renewed US determination to oust Saddam Hussein before US presidential elections. As an Iraqi exile, who had talks with senior US officials, said in January 1992, "The US is very serious from now to November to try to topple Saddam Hussein."[20] In this connection the *New York Times* reported that President George Bush had chosen Mr. Robert Gates, head of the CIA, as his special emissary to the area to discuss ways to oust Saddam Hussein. In early February 1992, Gates had talks with government leaders and intelligence officials in Egypt, Saudi Arabia and Israel on diplomatic, military and covert actions that might dislodge Saddam Hussein. This renewed US determination was due to Saddam Hussein's ability to stay in power, despite his defeat in the Gulf War, which threatened to become a political liability for Bush as he sought re-election. Saudi interest was due to their nervousness and fear from

Saddam Hussein who is known for his vindictiveness. For this and other reasons, Saudi leadership had been pressing Washington to undertake large-scale covert programme.

Alongwith Riyadh, Kuwait also agreed to cooperate both in financing a covert venture and in providing logistical support for military action. The goal was to divide the Iraqi military by building a network of opposition forces that could challenge Saddam Hussein's control of the countryside and ultimately challenge his stronghold in Baghdad. There were Saudi plans to use the Kurds from the north through Turkey to overthrow Saddam Hussein, by providing weapons to Kurdish guerrillas. Syrian intelligence also cooperated with Saudi Arabia in the anti-Saddam Hussein efforts. In the US itself, it was reported that the anti-Saddam Hussein, planning is being coordinated by officials from the Defence and the State Departments, the CIA and the National Security Council.[21]

Meanwhile, further developments related to instability within Iraq came to light. In early March 1992 it was reported that CIA officials had learned that a gun battle had erupted in November 1991 between the security forces of two of Saddam Hussein's closest relatives. At the time Saddam Hussein had removed one of the relatives, Hussein Kamal Hassan, from his post as Defence Minister and had replaced him with another relative, Ali Hassan Majid, who had governed Kuwait soon after Iraq's occupation. In a related development, the former Iraqi ambassador to Spain until March 1991, was quoted as saying that clandestine cells dedicated to overthrowing Saddam Hussein have been formed within the Baath Party and that these groups hoped to set up a transitional government. According to the former ambassador, Arshad Tewflk Ismail, popular discontent was regularly mounting but the security organs were not informing Saddam Hussein. It was this discontent that permitted the formation of clandestine organisation within the million-member Iraqi ruling Baath party.[22]

The Kurds continued to be a problem for Saddam Hussein not only due to their disunity but also because of the outside attempts to manipulate them, especially through Turkey. Whereas Masoud Barzani of the KDP was keen to sign an autonomy agreement with Saddam Hussein, his main rival, Jalal Talabani, leader of PUK, announced in December 1991 that "they were openly cooperating with the Iraqi opposition to overthrow the present government in Iraq."[23] The allies continued to maintain air cover for the 'safe haven' area established during relief efforts in April 1991, north of the 36th Parallel in Iraq. On December 19, 1991, Turkey extended the mandate of the force known as "Provide Comfort II" to June 28, 1992. Saddam Hussein, in a gesture designed to win-over the Kurds, released some 400 Kurdish political prisoners in late December 1991 and there has been a slight easing of economic blockade which has been in operation since October 1991. In return for the lifting of the blockade, Saddam Hussein wanted the return of Iraqi army and security services to the entire north, something that the Kurds fear most.

Despite pressure, the economic blockade, of the rebellious Kurds in the north and Shia Muslims in the South, continued except for the supply of basic things. When Saddam Hussein moved forces into north, immediately USA, UK and France warned Iraq in mid-April 1992 that it would face serious consequences unless it withdrew missile batteries from Kurdish areas and halted all other threatening military activities. Iraq was also warned that if its forces interfered with the allied reconnaissance flight meant to protect Kurds in the north, it would face possible military consequences. In another climb down, Saddam Hussein agreed in April 1992 to the destruction of buildings and equipment at the Al-Atheer nuclear complex. So far, Iraq had argued that the complex was for civilian purposes.[24]

Since January 1992 Saddam Hussein had been showing flexibility on several minor issues but remaining defiant on key issues. Iraq, until mid April 1992, had rejected Security Council Resolutions 706 and 712, as an insult to its sovereignty. But due to the increased economic hardships, Iraq reached an agreement to sell oil under UN supervision to pay for food and humanitarian supplies. This was a major breakthrough from the strangulating economic sanctions and isolation to which the allies had subjected Iraq through the UN. Saddam Hussein, as early as January 1992, had called on the Iraqis to reduce their everyday spending in order to beat the international embargo. He had urged youngsters to "avoid unneeded purchases, dress soberly and accept the frugal food given to you by your parents." He also said "the enemy assembled more weapons and men than us, but we beat them by our faith, which they could not take away from us." He said that the Iraqi people had to "beat the embargo without giving up their faith."[25] That economic sanctions were biting need not be emphasised and that was gradually eroding people's support to Saddam Hussein. It was reported in mid-April 1992 that he had moved several trusted generals into key positions in a command shuffle that reflected his constant efforts to forestall a coup.

The fact that he and his regime survived so long in the face of heavy odds has to be noted. But the determination of the Saudis and the Kuwaitis, backed by the US through the UN, had reduced Saddam Hussein's room for manoeuvre. It appeared likely that Saddam Hussein may be overthrown or replaced as President, but it also appeared unlikely that Baath Party will lose power. Of course, many had feared political instability in Iraq after much physical and human destruction in the war and also due to the subsequent civil war. Making assessments about Iraq's future is hazardous. If Saddam Hussein and his regime survived for so long it may be due to the following reasons :-

1. He had consistently demonstrated a will and capacity to rule. After seeing him in power since 1968, most Iraqis found it difficult to conceive of Iraq without him.
2. He had an efficient security apparatus and was willing to use it to remain in power.
3. He had decimated all opposition in Iraq. All major opposition leaders were in exile and had little credibility. He had depicted them successfully as agents of the West and of Iraq's regional enemies.
4. The longer a just, overall settlement on the Palestinian problem was delayed the better was for his pan-Arab aspirations.
5. Continuing anti-Arab steps like sanctions against Libya and Sudan by the West also helped him remain in power.
6. Due to lack of progress on the Golan peace front, and US-Israeli attempt to isolate/punish Syria, there could have been a reconciliation between Damascus and Baghdad.
7. Egypt and Syria's estrangement with the GCC states on the issue of Gulf security also helped him remain in power.
8. He had succeeded in making himself the embodiment of some important Arab aspirations, especially Arab quest

for independence from foreign control, and criticism of corruption from the GCC rulers.
9. Feelers of reconciliation from the GCC states like Oman, Qatar, UAE.
10. His success in enlisting support from Turkey, France, Russia, China and other states.

One should also not underestimate the not so considerable achievements before the Gulf crisis, like the economic and social advancement, with fairly even distribution of wealth, progress in education, liberation of women, development of the rural areas, upward social mobility for the underprivileged and relatively corruption-free regime. Those who have benefited from this system will not want to jeopardise its potential future because of the political instability that may follow the replacement of the Baath Party.[26]

The most significant thing which one has to keep in mind, while assessing Iraq's future, is the generational change certain to culminate in the coming years. The present generation is a product of the fifties and the sixties, and has seen endemic instability. It remains determined to create stable conditions at all costs. For this, the security and intelligence structures were used selectively but ruthlessly, and remained its pivot. A second generation, already in key positions in the system, and all beneficiaries from Baath Party rule, is in power. Their goal is pragmatism and they will work to preserve the system and may steer towards a more balanced approach to the global situation. Lastly, there are large sections which have seen several wars and who are intensely patriotic but at the same time bitter and frustrated about their plight, due to the several blunders made by Saddam Hussein and his Baath Party both in the field of domestic and external policy. The ranks of these restive people are swelling and will not only be far more assertive, but disruptive also. What they need is not so much political freedom, but improvement in their living standards. Rising expectations could pose a formidable challenge and if the economic sanctions are not eased soon, an explosive situation will soon have been created which may throw Iraq into turmoil, and instability may reign in most parts.

NOTES AND REFERENCES

1. Ahmad Chalabi, "Iraq: The Past as Prologue?", *Foreign Policy*, no.82, Summer 1991, p.20; According to the first independent Iraqi estimate 2,278 civilians were killed and 5,965 wounded; eight universities, 95 hospitals and 43 bridges were bombed. The number of Iraqi soldiers killed and maimed is yet to be established. Iraq is on the verge of famine and shortages of food supply and basic medicines, and the imposition of an international economic embargo, has caused several hundred more deaths. *Times of India*, January 20, 1992; see also A K Pasha, "The Sturggle for Democracy and Political Change in the Post-War Gulf," in K R Singh, ed., *Post-War Gulf: Implications for India* (New Delhi: Lancers Books, 1993) pp. 53-81

2. Muhammad Muslih and Augustus Richard Norton, "The Need for Arab Democracy", *Foreign Policy*, no.83, p.7. It was reported that the economic hardships have driven people to crime to survive. *Al Jumhouriya* acknowledged the growing crime wave in Iraqi society. The weekly newspaper *Alef Ba* quoted Justice Minister, Mr. Shahib al Maliki, as saying that courts are swamped with criminal cases and are no longer able to cope. Car thefts have reached "such alarming proportions that his ministry was proposing the death penalty for convicted theives," he said. *Times of India*, March 19, 1992.

3. Baghdad's daily newspaper *Babel* reported that Iraq's RCC has activated a resolution which effectively trimmed Saddam Hussein's influence indicating that Saddam was losing his extensive grip on power. The government run paper was quoted by INA as saying, "The command of the Revolutionary Council has decided the cabinet should start practising the prerogatives, stipulated by the Constitution. It added that the cabinet would now begin to exercise power "previously reserved for the President", but did not specify which powers it meant. Discontent was also reported in the ranks of the armed forces when Saddam Hussein offered Kirkuk to Kurdish rebels to placate Western powers and persuade them to lift economic sanctions of Baghdad. *Times of India*, April 24, 1992.

4. *Times of India*, March 13, 1991.

5. Ibid, March 14, 1991; see also Gerald Butt, "Iraqi Shiites: Abandoned and Betrayed", *MEI*, no. 399, May 3, 1991, p.4.

6. *Times of India*, March 17, 1991; For Bush's reaction to Democratic reforms in Iraq, see Ibid, March 18, 1991.

7. *MEI*, no. 399, May 3, 1991, p.4.

8. Ibid, p.6.

9. *Times of India*, March 21, 1991.

10. *Times of India*, April 22, 1991, and March 24, 1991; Ayatollah Sayid Mohammad Baqir al-Hakim, in an interview, had predicted on April 21, 1991 that Saddam Hussein would not survive for very long. Ayatollah Mohammed Emmami Kashani, a member of the Guardians Council and a top Iranian cleric, told worshippers at the Friday prayer at Tehran that "Saddam's days are numbered"; see also A K Pasha, "Demography, Political Reforms and Opposition in GCC states", in Girijesh Pant, ed., *The Political Economy of West Asia: Demography, Democracy and Economic Reforms* (New Delhi: Manak Publications, 1994) pp. 67-100.

11. Ibid, March 24, 1991.

12 For a summary of the 15 point pact see *Times of India* April 266, 1991. The paper noted that Saddam survives on agreements and commented "Going by Saddam's notorious record in breaking agreements, one hopes the Kurds won't feel betrayed later." Ibid, April 28, 1991. See also *Times of India*, April 23, 1991 and May 9, 1991.
13 *MEI*, no.409, September 27, 1991, pp.10-11.
14 Ibid, p.11.
15 Judith Miller and Laurie Mylorie, *Saddam Hussein and the Crisis in the Gulf* (New York: 1990) p.137.
16 *MEI*, no. 410, October 1991, p.9.
17 *The Guardian Weekly*, January 19, 1992, p.10.
18 *Times of India*, January 18, 1992, p.18.
19 *The Guardian*, January 19, 1992.
20 Ibid.; For details see A K Pasha, *India, Iran and the GCC States: Political Strategy and Foreign Policy* (New Delhi: Manas Publications, 2000) pp. 197-199 and 201-202.
21 *The Times of India*, February 8, 1992; March 13, 1992.
22 Ibid, March 13, 1992 and January 20, 1992.
23 *MEI*, No.416, January 10, 1992.
24 *Times of India*, March 21, 1992 and April 8, 1992.
25 Ibid, January 20, 1992; *Deccan Herald (Bangalore)*, January 18, 1992.
26 For details see Phebe Marr, "Iraq in the Year 2000", Charles F. Doran and Stephen W. Buck, ed., *The Gulf, Energy and Global Security: Political and Economic Issues* (Boulder & London: Lynne Pienner Publishers, 1991), pp.56-58.

5
Sanctions, Bombings and Regime Change

Soon after the 1991 Gulf War, a wave of optimism swept the Western world particularly the US, with President Bush talking about a New World Order. The main features of the new set-up, which were increasingly highlighted, were open borders and democratic political systems. It was believed that in view of the massive destruction inflicted on Iraq, the Iraqi President, Saddam Hussein, would be overthrown by his own people, particularly from within the army, Baath Party, Kurds and Shias. It appears the optimism was misplaced.

There is no doubt that Saddam Hussein and the Baath Socialist Party were sufficiently discredited by the course of the war. The subsequent civil war involving the Kurds, Shias and the government, led to further destruction. The people in the North and South openly defied the government. But the Baath Party under Saddam Hussein quickly regained control over the system except in some Kurdish-dominated areas. As seen earlier, the Baath Party is a highly organised one and Saddam Hussein had created a variety of youth militias.

The fact that Saddam Hussein and his regime survived for so long speaks of his resourcefulness and his capacity for survival. The US and Saudi Arabia attempted a *coup* through one of the Iraqi Republican Guard commanders who was believed to be pro-Saudi. But the prime Saudi candidate to launch a *coup*, turned out be an agent of Saddam Hussein, much to Washington's dismay.

Undoubtedly, the US fought the war not for democracy, but to prevent Saddam Hussein from controlling half the world's oil. Many Arabs are convinced that US decision to go to war against Iraq was in fact a "deliberate choice" aimed at crippling Baghdad's military and economic infrastructure. Saddam Hussein's disastrous invasion of Kuwait gave US a god-sent opportunity to cut Iraq to size. If Kuwait had no oil it was doubtful whether the US would have done what it did. The US grew apprehensive over the emergence of Iraqi military power coupled with Iraqi efforts at modernisation, including the creation of an impressive infrastructure and an industrial and technological base. Iraq achieved all this despite its eight-year long ruinous war with Iran. In fact, it became fashionable to describe Iraq as the potential Japan of the Arab world. But unlike the former Shah of Iran, who boasted of making Iran the Japan of the Middle East, Saddam Hussein kept a relatively low profile. Soon after Iraq's invasion of Kuwait, US Secretary of Defense wanted to know from his department about Iraq and its capability. "They are formidable," he was told. "They have a capable military and a developed industrial base. They are modern for a third world country. They are nationalistic. They are dangerous." Saddam Hussein's August 12, 1990 linkage theory, which demanded Israel's withdrawal from Occupied Arab territories, not only annoyed the US but it exposed its double standards. No wonder

Israel equally feared Iraq and its capability. Infact, the destruction of Iraq's military capability and its advanced infrastructure has clearly served Israeli aims more rather than US interests. Iraq's military capability and especially its long range missiles had posed a strategic threat to Israel's domination in the area.

Soon after the war, Iraq was condemned on various counts, like using chemicals against its Kurdish population and violations of human rights. It was also accused of secretly developing nuclear weapons. By April 1990 it had become obvious to Iraq that it was the target of a plot. On April 11, 1990 Tariq Aziz charged saying, "Israel wants to attack Iraqi industrial and scientific sites to maintain the balance of power, which has changed... when an Arab country achieves (technological advances) then the whole fuss comes, the comments, suspicions and attempts to discredit the image of that Arab country." During the Kuwait crisis, the US-led devastating attacks on Iraq clearly achieved Israel's paramount objective. This objective was to enable Israel to become the strongest and most dominant power in the region.

No wonder economic sanctions were imposed on Iraq and more importantly they were retained primarily at the behest of US and its allies (primarily the GCC states) in order to reduce Iraq to an insignificant power. Thus, Iraq has accused the US of turning the United Nations Security Council (UNSC) into a tool for "fulfilling tendentious and rancorous imperialistic objectives". Even though Iraq complied with the UNSC Resolutions on most issues, but one pretext or the other was used to humiliate and subjugate Baghdad. If nothing else at least all weapons which the UN had prohibited Iraq from possessing were being totally destroyed. Despite the infringement on its sovereignty, Iraq, towards the end of

October 1992 finally signed a Memorandum of Understanding with the UN for relief operations inside Iraq which was pending for some time. Moreover, Baghdad had scrupulously avoided challenging militarily the Western-imposed 'no fly zones' which are in contravention of the UN Charter.

Tariq Aziz was sent to New York in this background to get the economic sanctions lifted partially, if not entirely. The UNSC which met on November 23-24, 1992, to review Iraq's compliance of 687 and other resolutions, concluded that Iraq had only "selectively and partially" complied with the obligations placed on it by the Council. It was for the tenth time since April 3, 1991 that the UNSC decided to continue economic sanctions against Iraq on the grounds that it continues to violate UNSCRs and that it still claims Kuwait as part of Iraq. Under the ceasefire resolution, the economic sanctions are subject to an automatic review every two months. Tariq Aziz informed the UNSC that Iraq no longer possessed weapons banned by 687. He also informed the UN Security Council that the equipment used in manufacturing such systems had either been frozen or turned to civilian use and that Iraq had done its best to implement other provisions like returning of stolen Kuwaiti property and accounting for missing people.

He also firmly reminded the UN Security Council that Resolution 687 must respect Iraq's sovereignty. He accused the UN commission, charged with destroying Iraqi destructive weapons, of seeking to deindustrialise Iraq. Finally, he said the economic sanction was causing pain and agony to the Iraqi people and claimed that the Council's plan to allow Iraq to sell oil and use part of the oil revenues to purchase food and medicine, would infringe Iraqi sovereignty and security. This statement reflected the thinking of Iraqi people who are proud of standing on their own feet and do not expect aid from the outside world. The Iraqis had already begun to slowly forget the chain of events that pushed Iraq into war and the official message, that economic sanctions are a Western, especially US-Israeli, plot to weaken Iraq, was appreciated.

Not surprisingly, Tariq Aziz during his visits to the world organisation, called the economic sanctions "immoral", "shameful" and "an act of war". In calling for lifting/or easing of UN sanctions, Aziz reminded the UNSC that Iraq had complied with all UNSC Resolutions and that all weapons which the UN had prohibited Iraq from possessing had been totally destroyed. In fact, Aziz claimed that the UN had certified Iraq to this effect. It must be emphasised that according to UNSCR 687 of April 1991, the removal of UN sanctions is linked not only to the elimination of existing stocks of the weapons of mass destruction (WMD) - biological, chemical and nuclear – and all the ballistic missiles with a range greater than 150 kms and also all Iraq's research, design and production facilities. Contrary to Aziz's claims, the UN cleared Iraq only in the nuclear field. Mr Rolf Ekeus, the head of the UN Disarmament Commission, was not entirely satisfied with Iraq in other areas.

Aziz's plea fell on deaf ears as both the US and UK were in no mood to relax the sanctions against Iraq. The British representative to the UNSC, David Hanny, said Iraq had refused to disclose information concerning "supply and procurement networks" for its weapons of mass destruction, abused Kurds and Shias, failed to account for missing foreigners in Iraq, and had "reasserted claims" to Kuwait. The US ambassador said:

> Without full and unconditional Iraqi compliance with all relevant resolutions my government sees no reason to lift

sanctions. Iraq makes declarations of minimal content, declarations which are clearly meant to misinform, misdirect and conceal. Iraq divulges information about weapons programmes only after being confronted with incontrovertible proof. This record is not compliance. Moreover, Rolf Ekeus, Chairman of the UN special commission on dismantling Iraqi weapons, said in November 1992 that Iraq had not complied with demands for long term monitoring of its weapons potential and that 'there are still serious problems in getting the full data, such as the names of foreign suppliers'.

The US also cited the reported statement of Aziz on November 27, 1992 to the effect that Iraq will negotiate UNSC demands on compliance when the international community signals its readiness to lift economic sanctions against Iraq. Aziz's visit marked Iraq's first major attempt to test the political climate at the UN after President Bush's defeat in the 1992 US elections. To sweeten the atmosphere, Iraq had, towards the end of October 1992, concluded a memorandum of agreement with UN for relief operations inside Iraq. This remained effective until March 1993 and covered the role of UN guards which the US claimed had been subjected to Iraqi attacks.

This was despite the adoption by UNSCR 778 on October 2, 1992 under which most of Iraq's oil-related assets were impounded (roughly $800 million) as a stop-gap measure to buy food and medicine for Kurds in northern Iraq and start paying compensation to Gulf war victims. These seized funds were to be transferred to the escrow account established by the UN and administered by the UN Secretary-General. It was also to be used to cover the costs of UN activities in Iraq like elimination of weapons of mass destruction, the provision of humanitarian relief and the work of the Iraq-Kuwait boundary commission among others provided for in UNSCR 706. Iraq declared the UN resolution as illegal and, in fact, the Iraqi foreign minister Sahaf said the measure had "no justification or legitimacy". Even the Iraqi opposition which is supported/financed by the US was angry at the devious means the West decided to appropriate Iraqi funds, argued that the assets belong to the Iraqi people and should be used to help Iraqis rather than compensate rich Kuwaitis and Western companies or pay the expenses of UN arms inspectors whom Saddam Hussein called "stray dogs eating the flesh of the nation".

The confrontation between Iraq and the UN involving the West started when Saddam Hussein regained the political initiative and acknowledged his mistakes. He said:

> Each one of us should quickly take stock of his mistakes. Mistakes were made which enabled those who came from across the borders to get in. We must learn this lesson and change some of our modes of thought. This is because if we fail to do so, we could make mistakes that might result in the payment of a dearer price. When we say we were inattentive, we must guard against being caught unaware again. When we say that we were confused we must make sure not to lapse into perplexity again.

In a speech on January 17, 1992 to the Iraqi people, Saddam Hussein admitted for the first time that Iraq had been militarily defeated. He said:

> If we wish to make a comparison between the balance of forces from a material point of view, we can only deduce that the faithful (Iraqis) have lost (the war) while the infidels (US-led coalition) and the forces of vice and corruption triumphed. The confrontation was a miracle as a result of this disproportion of forces but faith triumphed over atheism and right over evil.

He also made it clear that he intends to rebuild his military machine and once again make Iraq a leading Arab power.

This was not to the liking of the US and its allies who saw red in this speech. Soon they began applying enormous pressure through the UN to prevent Iraq from marching forward.

On January 27, 1992, representatives of the UNSC's special commission on Iraqi weapons of mass destruction made a three-day visit to Baghdad and virtually demanded from the Iraqi government information about its weapons and other material over and above those mentioned in the UNSCRs. This led Iraq to call off talks set for February 5, 1992 in Vienna that were to arrange for the sale of Iraqi oil to buy food and medicine and pay reparation. Next day (February 5) Rolf Ekeus said that Baghdad had told the UN it would not accept monitoring of future arms build ups or purchases. This made the UNSC warn Iraq on February 19, 1992 that its failure to provide full, final and complete disclosure of its weapons capabilities constitutes "a continuing material breach of the relevant provisions of 687". In the face of Iraqi denial to UN inspectors access to equipment scheduled for destruction, the UNSC warned Iraq that it faces "serious consequences" unless it agrees to implement UN resolutions, requiring the elimination of Iraq's weapons of mass destruction. Maintaining its hard-line posture, Iraq, on February 27, 1992 sent a letter to the UNSC rejecting a UN plan to destroy missile equipment with a range of over 150 kms as required by resolution 687. Instead Iraq proposed to hold further discussions. Baghdad dismissed the latest denunciation of Iraq by the UNSC as "a hasty statement against Iraq... full of falsehoods and slanders, portraying Iraq's position in an incorrect and tendentious manner".

As seen earlier in an effort to neutralise mounting isolation at UN, Iraq sent Tariq Aziz to New York to explain its position. He informed the UNSC that Baghdad no longer possessed any weapons systems prohibited by UNSCR 687. He said the equipment used in manufacturing such items had either been frozen or turned to civilian use and that Iraq had done everything possible to comply with the rest of the ceasefire terms, such as returning stolen assets and accounting for missing people. But Aziz showed no flexibility on the issue of destroying equipment used in the manufacture of Iraqi offensive arms. He also charged that the UN commission on eliminating Iraqi weapons had sweeping powers and accused the West of using it to deindustrialise Iraq. Aziz also highlighted the pain and agony inflicted on the Iraqi people due to the economic sanctions and attacked the council's plan to authorise Iraq to start oil exports and use part of the oil revenue to buy food, arguing that it would infringe Iraqi sovereignty and security.

With no positive response from the UN on the issue of lifting economic sanctions and being reminded of its obligation to comply absolutely and not conditionally, Iraq literally "caved in". This was branded by US as "cheat and retreat" policy of Iraq. The change in Iraqi attitude was very much obvious when a 35-member UN inspection team left Baghdad on March 30, 1992 after a nine day visit which was free of controversy. The leader of the team, Derek Boothby said he "found the Iraqis this time business-like or pragmatic, not placing any obstacles, exactly the way we wanted them to be." He also said, "we were able to satisfy ourselves of a high proportion of what Iraq declared. All that I have seen so far leads towards the conclusion that Iraq's declaration on the number destroyed (Scud Missiles) last summer might well be true." Saddam Hussein's new strategy appeared to be to comply with UNSCRs, work for economic reconstruction and gradually build support in the Arab/Third World.

Not satisfied with change in the Iraqi behaviour, the US launched an unprecedented campaign to discredit Saddam Hussein by calling for his overthrow. The US President George Bush, said he would openly like to see "the Iraqi people topple Saddam Hussein and bring Iraq back to the family of peace loving nations". US Secretary of State James Baker said, "I don't think any tears would be shed if Saddam Hussein were to leave power." Dan Quayle, US Vice President said the US wants Saddam Hussein ousted, "the sooner the better". In fact, he sounded optimistic when he said, "I'm convinced we'll see a new leader emerge in Iraq in time." The conclusion by George Bush and his administration was that removal of Saddam Hussein will solve everything and that it will lead to a change in the entire policy of Iraq. They concluded that Saddam Hussein is *sui generis* and that without him Iraq would be a more acceptable place. This assumption, as time revealed, was fundamentally flawed.

The survival of Saddam Hussein in power, especially since 1991, was a concrete sign of the futility of Iraqi opposition, which was mainly backed by the West. Iran, Saudi Arabia and Kuwait also gave support to the Iraqi opposition. It was also clear that Iraq, after a remarkably short period, was on the road to recovery. According to government figures, seventy per cent of war damaged infrastructure was repaired. Of the 134 bridges hit by allied bombers, 120 were passable again. The West is wonder struck at this eye-shattering achievement. They ask – "How has Saddam Hussein managed to achieve so much, given that Iraq is supposed to be bound hand and foot by an embargo banning the import of everything except the essentials for life?" The answer lies in the leadership whose resourcefulness made the unthinkable possible. Common Iraqi citizens lack the means to overthrow their leadership, even if they desired. It's the same manic energy, which propelled the country into war, which was being used into more constructive purposes. The masses are already beginning to forget the sequence of events which led to the war and the state propaganda that economic sanctions are a Western plot to cripple Iraq is getting through. As one Western writer put it:

> Despite the UN sanctions, Saddam is once again in a position where he feels strong enough to do what he loves most, fronting it out with the rest of the world in a succession of showdowns designed to boost his standing at home and among the Arabs, while satisfying his pathological taste for strategic gambling.

Another said:

> Outside Iraq, Saddam Hussein's survival and recovery have further endeared him to Arab nationalists and enhanced his claims to be longed as strongman who has emerged, gilded and triumphant, from all the fire power the West could bring to bear. The war proved the immense difficulty of hurting Saddam himself.

It was clear that even though Saddam Hussein had been defeated on the battle field, but by no means was he defeated at home. He had always gone to considerable lengths to protect himself. The Iraqi leadership saw a vicious circle in their entanglement with the UN. Every compliance was rewarded with further demands and accusations and some of them simply to humiliate the Iraqi leadership. In order to put an end to this disturbing development, which was undermining the regime in the eyes of the Iraqi people, Iraq blocked a UN weapons inspection team from entering the Ministry of Agriculture headquarters in Baghdad. The UN inspectors remained parked outside the building which enabled the Iraqi leadership to organise demonstration against UN officers.

Baghdad's response to UN demands to allow the weapon's inspectors to enter the building, is clear from the slogan, "Saddam is staying for ever", raised by demonstrators against UN inspectors besieging the ministry building. They also sent a clear message that Iraq will use every means at its disposal to combat interference in its internal affairs. But the ineffectiveness of the UN intervention was also too apparent.

After a three-week impasse, on July 26, 1992 Iraq agreed to allow a new inspection team to enter the Ministry of Agriculture. The agreement barred inspectors from countries that fought against Iraq in the Gulf war from entering the building. When the new team of UN inspectors entered the buildings on July 28, it was headed by an inspector from Germany instead of the US. Two American inspectors were made to stand outside the building during the inspection. This was a slap on the face of the US and open challenge to George Bush from Saddam Hussein.

US response was to use the UNSC to punish Iraq. But this time there was opposition from China and India along with others. Nevertheless some pretext was found. UN special rapporteur Max Van Der Stoel's report, that the representatives of the World Food Programme and UN High Commission on Refugees in Iraq were being threatened and harassed, was accepted. The report of the UNICEF that Iraq has not issued permits for international staff to travel in Iraq since July I, 1992 rendering the group unable to monitor ongoing projects, was also accepted. UNICEF chief also reported repeated harassment of UNICEF personnel. Apart from all this, tension was also building up due to long prison sentences imposed on Britons by Iraq. The UN inspectors continued their visits to Iraq and on August 17, 1992 ended their visit. Considerable attention was focused on the mission, following Baghdad's declaration before the visit that they would not be allowed to enter government ministries.

The US, and its allies, now accused Iraq of killing the Shias in southern Iraq in violation of UNSCR 688. Seeing the success of the no fly zone imposed in the north of Iraq, the West under US leadership sought to impose a no fly zone below the 32nd parallel apparently to protect the Shia population in southern Iraq against Iraqi air attacks. Iraq rejected the Western plan. On August 26, 1992 US President George Bush citing UNSCR 688, declared that Iraq had 24 hours to halt air strikes against Shias. It is difficult to accept the US interpretation of 688 because the resolution, which was passed in April 1991, merely calls upon the Iraqi President Saddam Hussein to cease repression against his own population. It makes no mention of further sanctions through military force. In fact, it was adopted by the narrow margin of 10 votes to 3 with Cuba, Yemen and Zimbabwe voting against and China and India abstaining. The US imposed the no fly zone in the south on August 27, 1992 in clear violation of the UNSCR. That they were operating outside the UN umbrella of legitimacy further discredited them. This was obviously a punitive measure against Iraq. Baghdad rejected the no fly zone as illegal and said it could lead to renewed hostilities. It linked the continuation of UN humanitarian relief in the south to the establishment of the no fly zone. Even though this led to considerable tension between Baghdad and West, Iraq avoided a confrontation. Though on August 30, 1992 Saddam Hussein vowed to resist the no fly zone, but he had ordered Iraqi forces not to fire on allied aircraft. Infact, on November 26, 1992 after flying about 7000 patrols over southern Iraq, US pilots reported that Saddam Hussein had "shown no inclination... to test our resolve".

Sanctions, Bombings and Regime Change

The US again provoked Iraq on December 15, 1992 when the CIA Director, Robert Gates warned that Iraq may be hiding enough equipment of supplies to produce nuclear weapons in five to seven years, if UN economic sanctions and weapons inspections were to cease. This was followed by shooting of one Iraqi MIG-25 on December 27, 1992 allegedly for violating the no fly zone. Iraq threatened to retaliate "in a suitable manner". Soon the US sent its aircraft carrier US Kitty Hawk from Somalia to the Gulf. By January 5, 1993 US officials reported that Saddam Hussein had moved surface to air missiles into the southern no fly zone. The crisis escalated further with the issuing of an ultimatum on January 6, 1993 by US, France, UK and Russia which gave Iraq 48 hours to remove the anti aircraft missiles from the no fly zone. Iraq rejected the ultimatum. Iraq also refused to let UN planes to land in Iraq. Moreover, Iraqi forces were reported to have intruded into Kuwaiti territory near Umm Qasr area. On January 1, 1993 the UNSC accused Iraq of repeated violations of the Gulf war cease-fire terms and said the consequences will be serious if it does so again. It was under these circumstances that the US and its allies resumed bombing of Iraq on January 13, 1993. US-led "limited air strikes" or "spanking" for Saddam Hussein had been expected several times since the end of the Gulf war. The military action had become certain in the wake of the imposition of no fly zone in August 1992. Tension between Baghdad and West notwithstanding, neither side had sought a confrontation. A combination of factors, propelled the Iraqi President Saddam Hussein to escalate the situation.

Saddam Hussein defiance should be seen in the background of his "victory" over Kurds and Shias, crushing of several coup attempts against him and the almost total reconstruction of Iraq after the war which boosted Iraqi morale.

No wonder Iraq reiterated its claim to Kuwait. Given its still fairly large military machine, Iraq, it was clear, was by no means a defeated country. In addition, Iraq's isolation was gradually easing with several Arab states calling for normalisation of ties. For Egypt, Baghdad had been punished enough. To the embarrassment of West, Turkey normalised ties with Iraq despite occasional incursions into Iraqi Kurdistan.

Despite loss of credibility because Saddam Hussein "promised a lot and delivered nothing", almost all Arabs sympathise with Iraq's plight. In this connection, the lack of progress on Arab-Israeli peace front, Israel's deportation of Palestinians and refusal to take them back even in the face of UNSC resolution, propelled Saddam Hussein to adopt a defiant posture. The most important question that was asked in Arab countries is why Saddam Hussein is so very important and special. While countries like Israel and Yugoslavia are openly ignoring UN resolutions, Iraq is made a target. In fact, large majority of UN members flout human rights in varying degrees.

For Saddam Hussein, the Gulf war was but a small and temporary setback in Iraq's march towards victory in the "mother of all battles' and he calculated that there will be no anti-Iraq coalition of land forces and even less chance that this would include "Arab troops except Saudi Arabia and Kuwait". Saudi cover for a US, UK, French alliance will be easily potrayed by Saddam Hussein as aggressive Western imperialism on the march again. No wonder Saddam Hussein again raised the ante as he saw the current situation as fundamentally different.

As for George Bush, he wagered his presidency on August 5, 1990 on forcing Saddam Hussein out of Kuwait. It looked

Sanctions, Bombings and Regime Change

as though he was trying to complete his job. Bush's Iraq woes not only started with UN sanctions and military action, but since the end of the war other major complicating elements which have kept Iraq in the news aggravated the situation. These are the questions of support for Iraqi opposition leaders, demands by Democrats for an official investigation into Bush's pre-war policy towards Iraq, criminal investigation involving US loans made to Iraq and so on. In a way, Saddam Hussein became for George Bush what Iran crisis was for the former US President Jimmy Carter.

Despite US victory over Iraq and sabre-rattling by George Bush which continued since the end of the Gulf war, Iraq captured all attention in the political spotlight the US President had hoped to capitalise on, but could not because of Saddam Hussein's defiance, who continued to thumb his nose at the entire world. No matter how many times George Bush explained that the goal of the Gulf war was to get Iraq out of Kuwait, not Saddam Hussein out of office, the US President became his own worst enemy by insisting at the same time that Saddam Hussein has to go out.

The Americans, although, supported air strikes, if not ground war with Iraq, but questioned George Bush why he should take on the responsibility for protecting the Shias, Kurds and the prestige of the UN by attacking Iraq, when there was little direct national American interest involved. For George Bush the temptation to do something dramatic and decisive had been great especially in the back-ground of accusations that he somehow did not finish the job in the Gulf. The US expected nothing from Saddam Hussein's "cheat and retreat" policy since Bush stood to lose nothing. No wonder he authorised air attacks on Iraq if only to teach an effective lesson to the Iraqi President. Past disputes over UN inspectors have been settled without force, with Iraq eventually capitulating under Western pressure like it did in the several cases when it agreed to allow direct flights by UN inspectors, not to intrude into Kuwaiti territory and to keep missiles outside the no fly zone. But one noticed a significant hardening of the Iraqi position since the defeat of George Bush, despite Iraq having "caved in".

It soon became clear that Saddam Hussein will continue to defy the UN restrictions imposed after the war especially near Umm Qasr because it is Iraq's only outlet to the sea, its only port, and its only naval base. (This base has remained out of action since 1980). The Umm Qasr time bomb is bound to guarantee tension in the area which enables the US to return periodically to keep Iraq in check and assure its friends. No Iraqi government could ever accept Kuwaiti control of Umm Qasr.

For George Bush the problem was that there were few, good, dramatic targets left in Iraq for attack. The nuclear, chemical programme had been destroyed. Most of the scuds have also been destroyed. Of course, there are targets in Baghdad and other major cities – especially government offices, highway to Jordan border or military bases such as Falluja. The targets are all located in heavily populated areas and the world still remembers the US attack on Amara air raid shelter which killed many civilians. Moreover, it would put out of action once again urban sewage, drinking water purification and supply and transport. This would mean inflicting horrendous misery on the Iraqi people and would go counter to what George Bush said "we have no quarrel with the people of Iraq." The real target being Saddam Hussein himself, is too difficult to hit.

The air raids were mainly because of personal antagonism between the US President and Saddam Hussein. Bush's decision to leave Saddam Hussein in power continued to haunt him. Unable to do anything at home Bush turned to Somalia, sealing of START-II and spanking of the Iraqi President. His successor, Bill Clinton, also kept up US pressure on Saddam Hussein with the latter not changing his behaviour.

The "mini" crisis in the Gulf involving Iraq and Kuwait, during 1994 on the one hand, and its Western allies, on the other, is, in fact, a continuation of the larger Gulf crisis of 1990-91 in which the US-led coalition forces defeated Iraq and liberated Kuwait. After the war, the Iraqi President, Saddam Hussein, and his Baath Party had been fully exposed due to the heavy destruction suffered during the war. The subsequent civil wars, involving the Shias in the south and the Kurds in the north with the government security forces, led to further ruin. The Iraqi leaders not only survived the defeat but also went on to suppress the Shia and Kurdish uprisings. The Shias only compounded the damage resulting from the massive Allied bombing and the previous Iran-Iraq war damages. After his success over the uprisings, Saddam Hussein put on a show of defiance in the face of demands by the UN over the issue of inspection of weapon sites in mid-1991. He, however, backed down after US President George Bush announced his decision to send war planes to Saudi Arabia and Kuwait to escort UN helicopters into Iraqi air space. This had revealed that Saddam Hussein's determination to pursue his own policies had not weakened. Iraq remained defiant as evidenced by its rejection of United Nations Security Council Resolution (UNSCR) 712 of September 19, 1991, which allowed Iraq to sell oil worth $ 1.6 billion, saying it infringed on its sovereignty. As time passed, Saddam Hussein appeared to be consolidating his grip over Iraq more firmly and took a series of steps in that direction. But mounting opposition to his rule within the country continued because the UN economic sanctions were biting and it was also gradually eroding the people's support to him.[1]

More significantly, support from the military to Saddam Hussein, appeared to be waning due to the effect of economic sanctions. The Iraqi Army Chief of Staff, General Ayad al Rawi, on a visit to the 506th brigade of the 34th division of Iraq's second army corps wished to see the kitchen. According to reports, he was dismayed to find that his men were surviving on little but the poorest bread. General Rawi, along with the Defence Minister Ali Hassan al Majid, alerted Saddam Hussein of the grave situation and its implications.

Not only was Saddam Hussein's treasury virtually empty due to the economic sanctions/embargo on oil sales, even its vaunted gold reserves were getting depleted fast. Fearing widespred opposition and collapse of his regime, Saddam Hussein became his own Prime Minister in the summer of 1994 with the declared intention of improving the situation. Unable to get the sanctions lifted, and having failed in his attempt to check the soaring inflation, in September 1994, the government reduced the rations by half to civilians to divert food to the military. This reduction meant the food ration would now supply only one-third of daily energy needs.[2]

In view of the deepening crisis, in fact, a sort of famine and growing desertions from the army, Saddam Hussein, swallowing his pride, finally agreed to several conditions that the UNSC had laid down in Resolution No. 715, especially the installation of a very elaborate system for long-term monitoring of Iraq's arms industry. Considerable progress had also been made over the implementation of paragraph 22 of the UNSCR 687 to the so-called "mother of all resolutions" which stated that the oil embargo would have "no further force or effect" if Iraq were disarmed of its mass destruction weapons and had no longer the capacity to make them again, except with limited range. In all, 100 UN arms inspectors in Iraq, and their leader Rolf Ekeus, and later Richard Butler was about to issue a favourable report to the UNSC on Iraq's cooperation. Iraq could have looked forward to an easing of economic sanctions at least in stages. In fact, Saddam Hussein could have been close to obtaining permission to resume oil exports which was being vigorously supported by Russia and to a certain extent by France, China and many non-permanent members of the UN Security Council.

It was also reported that Iraq was negotiating a peace treaty with Israel under Moroccan auspices. Nothing is known so far of the outcome. Apparently Saddam Hussein backed out of the deal in view of the several Israeli conditions and also due to its implications on his standing. In any case, Tariq Aziz said Iraq had no problems with Israel and that it is no longer at war with the Jewish state. He said, "We have no bilateral conflict with Israel," and added "since our Arab brothers have decided to settle their disputes with Israel through negotiation, Iraq no longer regards itself as a confrontation state." But Iraq has accused Israel of being behind the 20 bomb explosions which have rocked Baghdad and other places in recent months. The targets included police and security headquarters, Baath Party offices, *Jumhouriya* newspaper and churches. *Al Qadissiya,* in its editorial, accused the "Zionist Mossad agents of these mean and criminal acts with evil objectives aimed at mosques and churches."[3]

But why did Saddam Hussein commit the blunder of sending 80,000 troops near the Iraqi border with Kuwait, an opportunity which the US was too eager to seize and in response despatch a strong force of marines, warships and warplanes with a clear warning not to let the Iraqi leader "off the hook" this time. There are many explanations put forward, ranging from Saddam Hussein's need to distract his people's attention from their dire economic and other troubles to the fear of a fresh *coup* attempt. Kuwait, Saudi Arabia and Israel are clearly opposed to lifting of the economic sanctions. The former two Gulf states also fear that once sanctions are removed, Iraq would flood the international oil market, thereby bringing down the already low oil prices.

According to some, Saddam Hussein pulled off a tactical *coup* while US forces poured into Kuwait and more British contributions were sent to the Gulf. It had become obvious that the issue of sanctions had moved to the world's agenda, especially when the UN was preoccupied with Haiti, Bosnia, Somalia and Rwanda. He also clearly showed to his people that he is not a spent force and that Iraq remained too strong to be ignored, despite a ban on weapons supply. It has also been said that Saddam Hussein with his characteristic foolhardiness, has overplayed his hand at a time when even the UNSC members, especially Russia and France, were beginning to campaign for an easing of the economic sanctions.

Legally and technically, Iraq has the right to deploy its troops near its southern border with Kuwait where a demilitarised zone has been established. But Saddam Hussein's brinkmanship only provoked the US and Britain, which urged its allies to tighten the economic sanctions. Although it put Iraq into the headlines, Saddam Hussein got the opposite of what he had expected. Not only were economic sanctions not discussed, but even after Iraq's recognition of

Kuwait, they have been renewed and the UN has committed itself to them afresh. President Clinton said, "We will not allow Saddam Hussein to defy the will of the US and the international community." US Defence Secretary, William Perry, would not rule out a pre-emptive attack on Iraq. British officials said the Iraqi leader's behaviour had strengthened the determination not to ease sanctions. Furthermore, as one British official put it, "All this is a clear reminder to anyone who had forgotten about who we're dealing with. We were under no illusions but others who were starting to go softer will think again."[4]

The West was again faced with a dilemma, especially the US which wanted a new military exclusion zone north of Kuwait. The reluctance of France, the UK and Russia to support the US plan speaks of Saddam Hussein's diplomacy in widening the gap among the Gulf war alliance partners against Iraq. The main opposition to the exclusion zone is that it could lead to the effective autonomy of the Shia-dominated region and ultimately to the partition of Iraq, which the West wants to prevent so that Baghdad could be a counterweight to Iranian influence in the Gulf region. The US wants an Iraq too weak to threaten US oil/strategic interests in the oil-rich Gulf region, but strong enough to act as buffer to Iran. President Clinton may wish to see Saddam Hussein fall, but the reality is US wants Iraq to remain a united, secular, stable country.

But the ordinary Iraqis seem to have no choice but to endure the sanctions and the consequent misery. No one doubts the effects of economic sanctions which have reduced this rich country—the only Arab country in which population, resources and education are in a really favourable balance and which has few gross disparities between the rich and the poor, with a fairly stable political system, and a hard-working population—into an impoverished country with a hungry, angry and desperate population. According to a recent UN report, about 2.5 million children, pregnant women and nursing mothers face severe malnutrition because of food shortages in Iraq. The UN Children's Fund (UNICEF) has said that with their daily diet, Iraqi children and women risk being severely malnourished. Children under five already on the verge of moderate malnutrition, may reach the level of 'severe malnutrition'. Among the consequences, the report said, were increases in infant mortality and deteriorating intelligence levels among young children deprived of sufficient nourishment. The UNICEF staff estimates there are 1,25,000 households with children under one year and 5,75,000 households with children under five years of age. There are also an estimated 2,30,000 pregnant women and nursing mothers affected by the food shortages.

Iraq, which once prided itself on having the finest education system in the region, funded by the income from its huge oil reserves, today lacks even textbooks and basic materials – the government can only provide well thumbed and torn books and a handful of notebooks. It has no funds to replace broken desks. Equally significantly, there is a lack of teachers as many have quit the job because of the low salaries, averaging around 1,000 dinars a month or less than $6. As Hikmat Bazzaz, the Education Minister said, "Teachers cannot live on their salaries. Those who don't resign often fail to turn up to teach which inevitably affects the teaching standards." In rural areas, some of the teachers had gone over to farming, he added. But most of all there is a lack of pupils. An increasing number of children are playing truant. The percentage of pupils absent in classes is high. Most have been pulled out of school by their parents who put them to work to supplement the family's mearge income, even though primary education is compulsory under the law. Others miss lessons because of illness, often caused by malnutrition. According to Hikmat Bazzaz, "Malnutrition is beginning to be felt in schools. Especially in the increasing failure rate which rose last year to 25 per cent, from 15 per cent in the previous years." According to his figures, 7 per cent of Iraq's five million school-going children quit in 1994. Moreover, the number of children leaving schools is on the rise, mainly in secondary schools, he added.[5]

Thus, years of crushing sanctions imposed by the UN on Iraq have reduced that once booming nation to a shadow of its former self. With its primary installations and networks bombarded out of existence, the Iraqi economy has been forced back to premodern levels; the lack of medicines and medical equipment has exacerbated the epidemics raging in various parts of the country. If ordinary living has taken on a nightmare quality, the life of the mind too has suffered extensive impairment. Writers have not been immune to the general situation of despair and deprivation. Many noted writers, artists and journalists are being forced to sell their prized book collections to survive in Iraq today. Many such intellectuals are now found at Baghdad's narrow Al-Mutanaffi street in the heart of the city, selling their prized collections of books, many of the volumes gathered over a lifetime, which are now seen as a luxury for families struggling just to feed themselves. Noted journalist and playwright, Ahmad Saleh, is not ashamed of his new job as a bookseller. "My salary from the theatre and cinema box offices was 250 dinars (about 50 cents), plus a 500 dinar bonus. Enough to feed my wife and two daughters for two days," he says. The Iraqi dinar has become so devalued that a whole personal library can be sold for 10,000 dinars or about $20 at the official exchange rate. Thus, Iraqi intellectuals have been reduced to looking upon their books as a means of raising the money necessary to support their families. When the Mongols invaded the Abbasid Empire in the 13th century (1258), they destroyed Baghdad's magnificent library – one of the finest in the medieval period; but the deprivations caused by the UN sanctions are subtler in their cruelty. It is unfortunate that innocent Iraqis are having to pay such a heavy price for the antics of their leaders. The October 1994 adventure of President Saddam Hussein to amass 80,000 troops from the Republican Guards near the Iraqi-Kuwait border, as seen earlier, is mainly due to mounting domestic opposition to his regime, fuelled by acute and unprecedented economic hardships. After having survived several assassination and *coup* plots, the Iraqi President has been forced to purge his officer corps. But it simply provoked the Pentagon and reinforced Saddam Hussein's image of being a master of miscalculation, because in the recent crisis, instead of getting the sanctions eased; the US and UK have been propelled to tighten them. The UN committed itself to the sanctions afresh. If he had restrained himself and mustered a little more patience, perhaps the plight of the hapless civilians of Iraq might have improved with the easing of economic sanctions.[6]

In fact, Saddam Hussein had been telling his people that the UN sanctions had reached their final phase and that Iraq would emerge stronger than ever from the four-year embargo. He told a Cabinet meeting on August 21, 1994, that the people had to be "patient" and continue their sacrifice in the final phase of the embargo which he compared to "the last 10 days of a fast" (presumably during Ramazan's *Idd-ul-fitr*), "Passing through this last phase of the embargo we are sure that our country will emerge reinforced and restored after the enemies fail to achieve their goals."[7]

To his growing woes – mainly due to economic sanctions – Saddam Hussein responded with harsh measures that included slicing off the hands of criminals and the ears of army deserters. Even though the embargo has sent Iraq's annual inflation rate soaring upwards of 1,000 per cent and deprived industry of crucial parts and subjected the average Iraqi household to severe shortages of almost every basic necessity, many Iraqis still favour Saddam Hussein. As a young Iraqi recently said, in any UN supervised elections in Iraq, Saddam Hussein would win, "Every one will vote for him because they have no confidence that the UN would guarantee their safety if they opposed him. They have absolutely no faith in the international community." Another Iraqi said, "The only thing the West needs to do is to leave us alone" i.e. opposition to Western double standards and unnecessary interference in Iraq's internal affairs.[8]

As far as Iraq is concerned, President Saddam Hussein emerged after the Iran-Iraq war with a strong military machine, although qualitatively it was no match for Israel. But US and Israel were concerned that this military power could be used to undermine their combined interests in the region. Before Iraq's invasion of Kuwait, Saddam Hussein had made a number of belligerent statements attacking Israel. The Jewish state which had destroyed Iraq's nuclear reactor in 1981 had not fully eliminated Iraqi desire to have non-conventional means to keep Israel neutralised. The eight year Iran-Iraq war had been of great advantage to Israel after which Saddam Hussein intensified his anti-Israel attacks. The invasion of Kuwait in 1990 came as a god-sent opportunity to contain Iraq. The allied attack against Iraq though, invited few missiles on Israel, but the decimation of Iraq's military machine and economic infrastructure was on Israel's agenda, together with Saddam Hussein's overthrow. This along with the UN economic sanctions, crippled Iraq and possibly removed a potential threat to Israel. No wonder Baghdad called the sanctions 'immoral', 'shameful' and 'an act of war'. Iraq highlighted the former UN inspector Scott Ritter's links with Israel. The FBI is looking into allegations about Ritter, who once worked for US army intelligence, of having had clandestine links with Israel while serving with UNSCOM. The head of UNSCOM, Richard Butler, also admitted that he shared information about Iraqi arms with Israeli intelligence. In the context of the Kurds, Iraq has also criticised the Israeli-Turkish military alliance.

Despite pleas from Sheikh Zayed of UAE for reconciliation with Iraq, Baghdad remained largely isolated. But Arab leaders stressed their adherence to the necessity of preserving Iraq's territorial unity. GCC leaders also opposed the Turkish move to set up a security zone inside Iraq. Despite the setback from its recent military intervention in Iraqi Kurdistan, which resulted in a US missile attack on Iraq on September 3-4, 1996, Iraq was allowed to export limited oil in return for food. The Iraqi President Saddam Hussein continued to show his ruthlessness when two of his sons-in-law were killed after returning from Jordan. The oil sales and the reported secret meeting between the Syrian President Hafez Assad and Saddam Hussein, many had argued, could have far reaching implications for the region. The assassination attempt (in December 1996) on Uday, Saddam Hussein's son, and Baghdad's accusation that Iran was involved in it, raised the spectre of further foreign intervention in Iraq. This, together with frequent Turkish military forays into Iraqi Kurdistan to crush PPK; and continued US attempts to interfere in Iraqi affairs, kept tension alive in order to divert attention from the more pressing issue of early Israeli withdrawal from occupied Arab/Palestinian lands.

The Iraq-US stand off continued towards the end of 1998 when Iraq blasted US President Clinton on November 16, 1998 for his call for a new government in Baghdad. The US launched a 40 hours bombardment of Iraq just before the start of the holy month of Ramadan in December 1998 in response to Iraq's decision to stop cooperation with UN Special Commission (UNSCOM) and IAEA over arms inspection issue. When the UNSC was discussing UNSCOM report on Iraq in December 1998, the US launched air attacks on Iraq without prior notification. The message was clear contempt for the UN. Tariq Aziz, Iraqi Deputy Prime Minister said Clinton's call for a new government was tantamount to a violation of the UN charter. The US President was "inciting a revolt and destabilization by financing rebels and outlaws", charged *Al Jumhouriya*. *Babel* said Clinton had, in public, 'exposed the truth over the US policy of aggression and evil' against Iraq. The ruling Baath Party's daily, *Al Thawra* claimed that Baghdad's decision to back down on its break with the UNSCOM had foiled "the US plot to launch an aggression against Iraq." As the threat of US military action eased, Aziz 'strongly' condemned Clinton's call. "This is a flagrant violation of (UN) Security Council resolutions as well as international law," he said. US President Clinton, while keeping up the pressure on Iraq over arms inspections, said at a press conference that Washington would also intensify efforts to install a democratic government in Iraq. "The best way to address (the) threat is through a government in Baghdad – a new government that is committed to represent and respect its people, not repress them – that is committed to peace in the region", he said. The British Foreign Secretary Robin Cook also said that he would "very much" like to see Saddam Hussein removed from power. Cook acknowledged, however, that the "brutality" of the regime stifled opposition. "I would very much like to see Saddam Hussein removed. I don't think there is any country in the world which would not rather be dealing with somebody other than Saddam Hussein and that includes the poor people of Iraq." The British Ambassador, Sir Jeremy Greenstock, took credit by saying that the US and British threats of military action were "instrumental in bringing about the rescinding of Iraq's decision". Meanwhile *The Washington Post* reported that the Pentagon calculated some 10,000 Iraqis died in a massive first wave of air and missile strikes.[9]

To sum up, the United States, since the Gulf war, has been continuously provoking Iraq on a number of issues like treatment of Kurds, no fly zones, massing troops near Kuwait, violations of human rights, non-compliance of UN Security Council Resolutions and, quite expectedly the Iraqi President Saddam Hussein has been making threatening moves inviting US missile attacks, which led to signing of security agreements between the GCC states and the US, and strengthening of US military-naval presence in the Gulf area. The US repeatedly highlighted that Iraq had rebuilt military facilities destroyed during the Gulf war and this was presented as a threat from Baghdad to its Gulf Arab allies. Many analysts felt the US had been deliberately highlighting the supposed threat posed by Iran and Iraq simply to scare the GCC states into buying more arms from Washington and providing it with base facilities. Many also perceive that the US objective in keeping high degree of tension and hostility in the Gulf region among the Arab states like Qatar-Bahrain border tension, Qatar-Saudi Arabia friction on a number of issues, on one side and between Arab Gulf states and Iran as between UAE and Iran over three islands and between Bahrain and Iran over the issue of struggle for democracy which has led to several bomb blasts, killings and police repression, is due to the oil and pricing factor. Iran, which opposes US military presence in the area, is accused of fomenting trouble in Bahrain which is not entirely accurate as the movement for restoration of the Constitution and National Assembly is demanded both by the Shia and Sunni communities in the island emirate. Due to political instability and opposition challenge, the Khalifa Amir agreed on September 15, 1996 to play host to 23 US F-16 fighters, allowing US forces to operate from its soil in its confrontation with Iraq in addition to the naval and air facilities US has in Bahrain. Prior to this on June 3, 1996 Bahrain had announced that it had foiled a plot by Iranian-backed Islamists to overthrow the Khalifa regime. Both countries recalled ambassadors from the respective states. The bomb attacks on US military facilities in Saudi Arabia in the last two years has led to tension between Riyadh and Washington with some in US pointing an accusing finger at Iran. It appears the House of Saud, already beset with mounting domestic opposition is unwilling to escalate tension with Iran. Qatar and Oman had moved ahead of other GCC states in their rapprochement with Israel with active US encouragement. US objective, beside strengthening its grip over GCC states due to oil and other strategic factors, is also to ensure peace with Israel while spreading enmity and war in the Gulf region. The US which has been using its influence to normalise relations between Israel and the GCC states received a setback due to changes in Israel under the Likud government led by Benjamin

Netanyahu when Gulf states froze their ties with Israel in response to Arab League resolutions. In the ultimate analysis, Iraq and Iran have to be included in any Gulf security structure to have meaningful cooperation as also to maintain peace, security and stability in the Gulf region, so very essential for the smooth flow of oil/gas needed by the rest of the world.[10]

NOTES AND REFERENCES

1. For details see A.K. Pasha, "The Struggle for Democracy and Political Change in the Post-war Gulf" in K.R. Singh ed., *Post-War Gulf: Implications for India*. (New Delhi, Lancers Books, 1993) pp.53-82; see also AK Pasha, ed., *Contemporary Gulf: State, Society, Economy and Foreign Policy* (New Delhi: Detente Publications, 1999) pp. 261-298.
2. *The Guardian,* Weekly, October 19, 1994.
3. *Times of India*, November 1 and 7, 1994.
4. *The Guardian*, October 19, 1994.
5. *Times of India*, October 9, 22 and 24, 1994.
6. Ibid, October 18, 1994.
7. Ibid, August 23, 1994.
8. *The Guardian*, October 12, 1994.
9. *Times of India*, November 17, 1998. Under UNSCR 687, the UN inspectors numbering 3,845 comprising 276 teams (during 1991-98) had inspected thousands of sites in Iraq. They had also held interviews with scientists, and others. Some 665 sites, identified for monitoring with sensors and cameras, were destroyed by heavy US bombing during December 16-20, 1998. It must be pointed out that the US had asked the UNSCOM to return from Iraq in December 1998. Arshi Khan, "Not without a hollow reason", *The Hindustan Times*, April 24, 2003.

10. For details see A. K. Pasha, *Arab-Israeli Peace Process: An Indian Perspective* (New Delhi: Manas Publications, 2000) pp. 206-225; and A K Pasha, ed., *India, Bahrain and Qatar: Political, Economic and Strategic Dimensions* (Delhi: Gyan Sagar Publciations, 1999) pp. 1-19.

6

US Invasion of Iraq [2003]

Since 1991 the USA, despite its best efforts, using the UN sanctions, no fly zones in north and south, UN inspectors, bombings by sophisticated airplanes, support to Iraqi National Congress and other anti-regime forces and several failed coup attempts, failed to overthrow Saddam Hussein. In October 1998 the US Congress enacted the Iraq Liberation Act, indirectly calling for the overthrow of the Saddam Hussein regime and its replacement by a democratic regime in Baghdad. A sum of $97 million was allocated for carrying out this task through covert operations. This attempt also failed to dislodge the firmly entrenched Iraqi strongman. Not only had the innumerable measures taken by the US against Saddam Hussein not succeeded in dislodging him, he had in fact become defiant. The UN oil for food programme (1996) had in fact strengthened Saddam Hussein's regime. More than 70 per cent of Iraq's population living in the cities were provided rations at subsidised rates. From wheat flour, rice, sugar, tea, vegetable oil, milk, salt, lentils, white beans, detergent and toilet soap to other basic goods, now reached the Iraqi people through the government, thereby strengthening the grip of the Baathist regime over people.

The high rate of inflation, low salaries and falling value of the Iraqi dinar, made the people more and more dependent on government food support.[1]

While the US was doing everything to cripple Iraq and isolate the Iraqi leader, Saddam Hussein, through his shrewd diplomacy, was working hard to break the UN economic sanctions gradually. Russia, China, France and other countries were concluding agreements with Iraq over oil, trade and other issues. Airlines from Syria, Jordan, France, Russia and other countries were flying directly to Baghdad. The calls for lifting UN sanctions on Iraq were getting louder and universal, especially from Russia, France and others. In fact, the agreement signed by UN Secretary General Kofi Annan and Iraqi foreign minister Tariq Aziz, on February 23, 1998 acknowledged this – "The lifting of sanctions is obviously of paramount importance to the people and government of Iraq."[2] The Clinton administration recognised that its policy to contain Saddam Hussein had failed, so diplomacy was tried once again. The US moved a resolution in the UN Security Council that would renew arms inspections and temporarily suspend some trade sanctions if Iraq complied with another set of disarmament demands. With the abstention of three permanent members of the UNSC—France, China and Russia — Resolution 1284 was adopted on December 17, 1999. This resolution buried UNSCOM and created a new inspection team—the UN Monitoring, Verification and Inspection Commission (UNMOVIC)—whose head will have a final say on Iraqi compliance and hence on UN sanctions which cannot be removed, but merely suspended for a 120 day renewable period. It also added the return of IAEA whose head had already declared Iraq free of nuclear weapons many years ago. For Iraq, the merits of the new UNSCR was that it eased import restrictions on some essential items and more significantly removed the ceiling on Iraqi oil exports. Although some relief was given to Iraq, the new UNSCR not only increased the number of items considered as having "dual use", it signalled the continuation of the US war by other means against Iraq.[3]

Towards the end of the Clinton administration, the US war against Iraq had resulted in "hundreds of thousands of deaths". Iraq had lost over $140 billion in lost oil revenues by 1999. Hyper inflation had ruined its economy leading to widespread poverty, high unemployment rate and growing illiteracy due to social and economic problems, especially because it had won in 1986 a United Nations award for eradication of illiteracy. Life had become a struggle for survival and many parents could not afford to send their children to school. A whole new generation of children were growing up illiterate, especially in a country which had made education compulsory from the primary school to the Ph.D level. According to Naseer Aruri:

> A nation that was on its way out of a third-world status has been forced to deal with epidemics of cholera, diarrhoea, pneumonia and typhoid resulting from the dumping of raw sewage in its Euphrates, Tigris and other waterways. Its modern hospitals can hardly afford electricity or find basic medicines to treat its large, malnourished and sick population. An increasing number of Iraqi professionals are being relegated to driving taxis, while the lower classes fall prey to severe exploitation. Yet the Washington and London establishments continued to argue that sanctions must remain in force to prevent Iraq from threatening its neighbors—or perhaps, as President Clinton said "until the end of time, or as long as he (Saddam Hussein) lasts".[4]

Armour-piercing ammunition made of depleted uranium, radioactive and toxic waste, had contaminated Iraqi soil, as also the air people were breathing. Cancer—which was unfamiliar to Iraq—has become widespread due to bombings since 1991. More and more children were becoming vulnerable to anxiety and depression. Many have become deaf due to carpet-bombing and the number of children in mental hospitals has vastly increased. As one Iraqi parent said, "Our children who know not any guilt are being punished by disguised weapons." Due to sanctions, about 5000 Iraqi children die every month. "There can be no justification for the death and malnutrition for which sanctions are responsible. We are in the process of destroying a society." The US is determined to destroy Iraq and also sought to supress the spirit of an ancient civilisation. Many Iraqis and Arabs feel the US want to control Iraqi oil and to make West Asia free for Israel.[5]

George W. Bush, with a neo-conservative team in 2001, reopened the Iraqi file. They insisted on a tough line towards Iraq's WMD, and the return of UN inspectors. The second Intifada and growing Palestinian assertiveness was matched by the Israeli Prime Minister Sharon's ruthlessness in the Israeli-Palestinian conflict. Israel, through its supporters in the US administration, think tanks, media and the Congress, launched a vigorous campaign for a US attack on Iraq to overthrow Saddam Hussein and his regime. This group was led by Vice President Dick Cheney, Defense Secretary Donald Rumsfeld, National Security Adviser Condoleeza Rice, Richard Perle, head of the Defense Policy Board, Deputy Defense Secretary, Paul Wolfowitz, John Bolton, Under Secretary for Arms Control and others.[6]

Richard Perle became the leading proponent of a pre-emptive attack on Iraq. He told the *Washington Post* in August 2002 that "ultimately, US policy on Iraq will be set by 'civilians', that it will involve a 'political judgement', rather than one by the military leaders in the Pentagon who were more skeptical about the need for a war."[7] Paul Wolfowitz another leading advocate of an attack on Iraq, was concerned about Iraq's capacity to deliver "weapons of mass destruction", even though it does not have long-range missiles. John Bolton was more candid when he admitted that the aim was to remove Saddam Hussein, whether Baghdad allowed UNMOVIC inspectors back or not, to complete the Iraqi disarmament process which had come to a halt since December 1998. Bolton in August 2002 was confident of Saddam Hussein being deposed within a year. He also said, "Let there be no mistake — while we also insist on the reintroduction of the weapons inspectors, our policy at the same time insists on regime change in Baghdad and that policy will not be altered, whether inspectors go in or not."[8] Dr Condoleeza Rice, in an interview on August 15, 2002, made it clear that an attack on Iraq was necessary and proper:

> This [Saddam Hussein] is an evil man who, left to his own devices, will wreak havoc again on his own population, his neighbours and, if he gets weapons of mass destruction and the means to deliver them, all of us. [There] is a very powerful moral case for regime change... We certainly do not have the luxury of doing nothing... He has used chemical weapons against his own people and against his neighbours, he has invaded his neighbours, he has killed thousands of his own people... He shoots at our planes, our airplanes, in the no fly zones where we are trying to enforce UN Security resolutions.

She also said:

> History is littered with cases of inaction that have led to grave consequences for the world. We just have to look back and ask how many dictators, who ended up being a

tremendous global threat and killing thousands and indeed, millions of people, should we have stopped in their tracks.⁹

The September 11, 2001 attacks on WTC and Pentagon gave a God-sent opportunity to the hawks in the US administration to talk about use of force to combat "international terrorism". This came to be largely associated with Arabs/Muslims in West Asia and also elsewhere. Since the US had comparative advantage in using force and violence, US planners began talking about use of force to contain enemies multilaterally or unilaterally. US contempt for international law and especially the UN charter had become totally well known. Madeleine Albright, when she was US ambassador to UN, told the UN, "We will behave multilaterally when we can and unilaterally when we must."[10]

The US war on international terrorism led to the attack on Afghanistan and ouster of the Taliban government. The Axis of Evil speech of George W Bush in January 29, 2002, identifying Iran, Iraq and North Korea, was a clear signal to Baghdad about the impending focus on Iraqi WMD. With legal and moral principles abandoned, the debate focused on US "national interest" and its ability to use force to punish its enemies. The US became more strident in its demands for the return of UN inspectors to Iraq. In order to avoid war over Iraq, Russia, China, France, Germany, Arab League and many others applied considerable pressure on Saddam Hussein to accept UN weapons inspectors who had withdrawn from Iraq when Anglo-American air strikes began on December 16, 1998. Due to persistent pressure and lobbying from the US the UNSCR 1441 allowing for stricter time-bound inspections of Iraq in November 2002 was unanimously adopted.

The UN inspectors led by Hans Blix went to Iraq with all the sophisticated equipment to search for WMD. More than 800 inspections on more than 400 sites was done. They received full cooperation from the Iraqi authorities, including allowing meetings with Iraqi scientists, air surveillance, visits to suspected sites all over Iraq for surprise tests, even on holidays and so on. They found nothing and this was duly reported to the UNSC in the three reports. Hans Blix neither raised the issue of 'material breach' nor reported any Iraqi obstruction to his inquiry. The US continued to insist that Iraq was not revealing its chemical, biological and other WMD. When the UN inspectors found the range of Al Samoud II missiles little more than the 150 kms range allowed, Iraq (when demanded by Hans Blix) destroyed most of the banned weapons. From the very outset, it was clear the US was not in favour of giving the UN inspectors enough time to peacefully disarm Iraq. Hans Blix and Dr Mohammed el Baradei, head of IAEA wanted three more months time to complete the inspections and certify that if Iraq didn't have weapons—UN sanctions could be lifted.

But George W Bush had already signed the September 17, 2002 document (17) called the "National Security Strategy for the United States", which was a declaration of war. Many felt the new doctrine would be applied to Iraq. It endorsed pre-emptive warfare and made past policies of deterrence, containment and collective security obsolete and irrelevant. It stated in part: "The United States will continue to make clear that it reserves the right to respond with overwhelming force—including potentially nuclear weapons—to the use of (WMD) against the United States, our forces abroad, and friends and allies." Furthermore, on December 11, 2002, the Bush administration released a declassified version of NSPD-

17 under the title "National Strategy to Combat Weapons of Mass Destruction". The reference to the use of nuclear weapons was not included in the declassified version, but instead said that the US would "resort to all of our options". In an interesting development, *The Washington Post* on January 31, 2003, published a front page story, revealing the existence of NSPD-17 which warned – "The disclosure of the classified text follows newspaper reports that the planning for a war with Iraq focuses on using nuclear arms not only to defend US forces but also to pre-empt deeply buried Iraqi facilities that could withstand conventional explosives." One might recall that the Bush administration in January 2002 had issued its Nuclear Posture Review, a congressionally mandated report on the US nuclear weapons program. For the first time, the 2002 report openly discussed the possible use of nuclear weapons, naming seven countries that could be targets of the US nuclear weapons: Russia, China, Iraq, Iran, North Korea, Libya and Syria.[11]

This should be read in the context of what John Bolton, a leading hawk in the Bush administration, who runs the arms control and disarmament office at the US State Department said in an interview to the *Washington Times* on February 22, 2002 in which he boasted about the Bush administration's intent to use nuclear weapons, under certain circumstances. He candidly told the *Times* that the world had changed so dramatically on September 11, 2001, that it was no longer unthinkable to use nuclear arms against rogue states thought to possess weapons of mass destruction. Bolton told the *Washington Times* that to continue with the doctrine of no first use of nuclear weapons reflected "an unrealistic view of the international situation." The idea that fine theories of deterrence work against everybody which is implicit in the negative security assurances has just been disproven by September 11, he said, adding, paradoxically, "What we are attempting to do is create a situation where nobody uses weapons of mass destruction of any kind."[12]

It is no coincidence that Bolton's Chief Deputy at the State Department is David Wurmser, one of the authors, along with Richard Perle and Doug Feith, of the 1996 "Clean Break" report to the then Israeli Prime Minister, Benjamin Netanyahu, calling on Israel to abrogate the Oslo Accords, launch preemptive attack on the Palestinian Authority, and drive the US into an armed attack on Iraq, and so on.[13]

On July 8, 1996 Richard Perle, a close ally of Paul Wolfowitz, delivered the report to Benjamin Netanyahu—"A Clean Break: A new strategy for securing the realm", calling for ripping up the Oslo Accords, annexing the West Bank and Gaza Strip, and launching war against Iraq, to divide the Arab world and create a permanent rift between the US and the Arabs, to establish a new Washington-Tel Aviv axis of military domination over the Near East and Gulf region. The principal authors of the study which was prepared for the Jerusalem-based Institute for Advanced Strategic and Political Studies, were Richard Perle, Douglas Feith, David Wurmser, Meyrav Wurmser and Charles Fairbanks. IAPS produced two in depth studies to facilitate implementation of "Clean Break"—"Coping with Crumbling states: A western and Israeli Balance of Power Strategy for the Levant", and "Succession in Saudi Arabia: The not so Silent Struggle", which spelled out detailed strategies for destabilisation and "regime changes" in Iraq and Saudi Arabia. Only on July 10, 1996, Netanyahu presented this "Clean Break" strategy as his policy, in a speech to a joint session of the US Congress.[14]

Soon after, in 1997 Dick Cheney, Donald Rumsfeld, were among the co-founders of an arch-imperialist group called The Project for the New American Century (PNAC). Other founders included Frank J. Gaffney, head of Washington's Center for Security Policy, Paul Wolfowitz and George W Bush's brother, Governor of Florida, Jeb.

It is interesting to note that this same hawkish group issued an open letter to President Bill Clinton on February 19, 1998, demanding military action to overthrow the Saddam Hussein regime in Iraq, and replace it with the Iraqi National Congress, headed by Ahmed Chalabi. This letter was sponsored by Richard Perle and former Congressman Stephen Solarz of Democratic Party (New York) and co-signed by 40 leading neo-conservatives including Douglas Feith, Zalmay Khalilzad, David Wurmser and Paul Wolfowitz, who were all involved in either the 1990 Pentagon Study and/or the 1996 "Clean Break" study.[15]

Again in September 2000, Cheney and Rumsfeld's organisation, The Project for the New American Century, issued a report, "Rebuilding America's Defenses: Strategy, Forces, and Resources for a New Century" which called for US global military supremacy and the use of pre-emptive military force to defeat any challenges to that supremacy. Among the recommendations was for "regime change" in Iraq.[16]

Finally in September 2002, the National Security Strategy for pre-emptive war was issued and shortly thereafter, a document recommending the use of nuclear weapons against presumed threats was leaked to the *Los Angeles Times*, which we have seen earlier. Furthermore, as Lyndon La Rouche declared, the chronology proves that it had not "been prompted in any way by factually defined recent developments" in Iraq.

And the chronology shows the fraud in the US administration claim "that the war on terrorism is a reaction to the attacks on the USA by any of the nations or organisations identified" as 'rogue state' since September 20, 2001. Indeed, the policy against Iraq and other states had been in the making for over a decade before the September 11, 2001 attacks on WTC and the Pentagon.[17]

The doctrine pushed by Cheney, Paul Wolfowitz and others on Iraq and other issues had no serious takers. It was only after the September 11, 2001, attacks on WTC and Pentagon that these were adopted by the Bush administration. 2004 Presidential pre-candidate Lyndon La Rouche wrote – "Solely as a result of the psychological impact of September 11, 2001, Cheney, (his supporters), and Ariel Sharon, are now being given the war they have desired so passionately, so obsessively over a dozen years to date." And he remarked, "What a remarkable set of coincidences!"[18]

After seriously analysing all the strategic documents issued by the group led by Dick Cheney, it is clear that they wish to go beyond a war against Iraq. It is a blueprint for the establishment of a new "Roman Empire", starting with a US-led war against Iraq, an Israeli war against Lebanon and Syria (and the expulsion of the Palestinians), a strike against Iran and the break-up of Saudi Arabia. The Anglo-American establishment would lead the way through a policy of permanent warfare. This is what they meant, when it was said, after September 11, 2001, that the war against terrorism would be a "war of one lifetime". Michael Leaden of the American Enterprise Institute, and an associate of Richard Perle, Cheney et al, articulated in his recent book, *'The War Against the Terror Masters'*, all the points mentioned above. He told the *Wall Street Journal*, September 4, 2002, that the US instead of targeting a single country, Iraq, should be talking about "using all our political, moral and military genius to support a vast revolution to liberate all the peoples of the Middle East". He named, Iraq, Iran, Syria and Saudi Arabia.[19]

The US economic crisis is one of the crucial reasons why this group wants US to reassert its hegemony through sheer military power. Due to "cheap labor" the US has been outsourcing its basic industrial and other productive capacities and has been borrowing very heavily from the outside world to sustain its economy. It is worth noting that the US is the most indebted country in the world with domestic and international debt approaching 3.4 trillion dollar or $12,000 for each, man, woman and child in the US. After the World War II, US dollar became the world standard, virtually replacing gold. This allowed the US to run huge deficits in both domestic expenditure and international trade. While the US printed dollars to meet its fiscal obligations, other countries accepted dollar payments for their goods because of the dollar's value as the currency of choice for oil purchases. As a result, even while the US kept losing its industrial pre-eminence, it managed to retain its economic dominance as the producer of the currency of oil trade. Further, the demand for dollars as the *de facto* oil currency allowed the US to commit enormous resources (by absorbing deficits) to military production making it the nation with the finest military machine in the world with unparalleled power projection capabilities in history.[20] There is widespread unemployment, homeless are growing, bankruptcies are multiplying and the banking sector is virtually collapsing. The dollar is clearly under pressure.

As Michael Ignatieff wrote in the January 5, 2003 *New York Times* "The Burden", historically the US was based on the fight against Empire, but after September 11, 2001, all that dramatically changed. He wrote:

If Americans have an empire they have acquired it in a state of deep denial. But September 11 was an awakening, a moment of reckoning with the extent of American power and the avenging hatreds it arouses...

Iraq lays bare the realities of America's new role... America's empire is not like empires of times past, built on colonies, conquest and the white man's burden... The 21st century imperium is a new invention in the annals of political science... Even now, as President Bush appears to be maneuvering the country toward war with Iraq, the deepest implication of what is happening has not been fully faced: that Iraq is an imperial operation that would commit a reluctant republic to become the guarantor of peace, stability, democratisation and oil supplies in a combustible region of Islamic peoples stretching from Egypt to Afghanistan. A role once played by the Ottoman Empire, then by the French and the British, will now be played by a nation that has to ask whether in becoming an empire it risks losing its soul as a republic...

The impending operation in Iraq is thus a defining moment in America's long debate with itself about whether its overseas role as an empire threatens or strengthens its existence as a republic...

Even at this late date, it is still possible to ask: why should a republic take on the risks of empire?

Regime change is an imperial task *par excellence*, since it assumes that the empire's interest has a right to trump the sovereignty of a state.[21]

Lord William Rees Mogg wrote an article in the *London Times*, January 13, 2003 entitled: "The American Empire: A Fine Old British Tradition", claiming that the previous British Empire, and an emerging American Empire, are continuations of the historical "trading empires" of Athens and Venice. He insisted that a successful American empire now hinges on American action against Iraq.[22]

The Israeli linkage to the US war on Iraq was best articulated by Meron Benvinisti, the Israeli writer and former deputy mayor of Jerusalem. He established a link between Israel's advocacy of US war on Iraq and Israel's overall objective of expulsion of Palestinians from the West Bank. The war on Iraq would provide a cover for longtime Likud objective to "transfer" of Palestinians. He wrote:

> Under the cover of George Bush getting even for his father, Ariel Sharon will be able to settle his own old accounts, going back to the days of Beirut. Maj. Gen. Yitzhak Eitan hinted at the strong connection between a war in Iraq and the war against the Palestinians when he said "an American attack on Iraq will also hurt the Palestinian Authority". Since the Israeli government is coming up with "worst case scenarios" on NBC, here's another one – an American assault on Iraq against Arab and world opposition, and an Israeli involvement, even if only symbolic, leads to the collapse of the Hashemite regime in Jordan. Israel then executes the old "Jordanian option"—expelling hundreds of thousands of Palestinians across the Jordan river. There has never been a better opportunity for that option.[23]

Israeli leaders, from Ariel Sharon to Shimon Peres to Benjamin Netanyahu, accused Iraq of producing biological and chemical weapons. Feverish attempts were made in Israel to supply gas masks to Israeli Jewish citizens excluding Arab citizens and Palestinians from this protective gear in anticipation of Iraqi attacks. Sharon's spokesman, Ranaan Gissin, said, "Any postponement of an attack on Iraq at this stage will serve no purpose... It will only give him (Saddam Hussein) more of an opportunity to accelerate his program of weapons of mass destruction... Saddam's going to be able to reach a point where these weapons will be operational."[24]

Despite opposition from UNSC members Russia, France, Germany, China, Syria and others, the Anglo-American leaders, unable to secure UNSC resolution on the use of force against Iraq went ahead and attacked Iraq on March 20, 2003 after the US gave 48 hours ultimatum for Saddam Hussein to step down from power. The US gave an ultimatum to Iraq on March 17: "The UNSC has failed in its responsibilities, but we will rise to ours." The US Congress and UK Parliament had given the two states authorisation to use force to implement the UNSCRs. Both the states also stated that UNSCR 678, 687 and 1441 also gave them the authority to disarm Iraq using force.

Many countries expressed their clear opposition to US-UK plans to invade Iraq. Many questioned the allegations against Iraq, especially disarming or liberating the Iraqi people from the dictatorship of Saddam Hussein. Many felt Iraq posed no threat to anyone especially since 1991 when UN sanctions had crippled Iraq's military capability severely. Scott Ritter, a UN weapons inspector in Iraq, accused US Senator Joseph Biden, Chairman of the Senate Foreign Relations Committee, of running a "sham hearing" in August 2002 on the issue of whether or not US should use force to occupy Iraq. In fact, Scott Ritter claimed that the Senate hearings were merely a cover for US plans to invade Iraq militarily:

> I believe that Iraq does not pose a threat to the US worthy of war. This conclusion is shared by many senior military officers. According to President Bush and his advisers, Iraq is known to possess weapons of mass destruction and is actively seeking to reconstitute the weapons production capabilities. I bear personal witness, through seven years as a chief weapons inspector in Iraq for the UN to both the scope of Iraq's weapons of mass destruction programs and the effectiveness of the UN weapons inspectors in

ultimately eliminating them. While we were never able to provide 100 per cent certainty regarding the disposition of Iraq's proscribed weaponry we did ascertain a 90-95 per cent level of verified disarmament... It is clear that Senator Biden and his colleagues have no interest in such facts.[25]

Mr Hans Von Sponeck, former UN Assistant Secretary General, made the following interesting statement about Iraqi weapons and UN economic sanctions to the Institute for Public Accuracy in Washington on July 29, 2002:

> Evidence of *al Qaeda*-Iraq collaboration does not exist... Six years of revisions to sanctions policy on Baghdad have repeatedly promised "mitigation" of civilian suffering. Yet, in 1999, UNICEF confirmed an estimated 5,000 excess child deaths every month above the 1989 pre-sanctions rate. Four months ago, UNICEF reported that more than 22 per cent of the country's young children remain chronically malnourished. Credible opposition groups outside Iraq have called for delinking economic and military sanctions. At the March (2002) Arab summit in Beirut, all 22 Arab governments (including Kuwait) called for the same. If the economic embargo on Iraq is not in their interest, then in whose interest is it?

Many in the US and elsewhere expressed deep concern that an adequate case has not been made by the Bush administration in favour of war against Iraq. Even the hawkish Lawrence Eagleburger, former national security adviser to Bush Sr, told the ABC News, "[Unless Saddam Hussein] has his hand on trigger that is for a weapon of mass destruction, and our intelligence is clear, I don't know why we have to do it now, when all our allies are opposed to it."[27] He was also convinced that the war on Iraq would have a negative impact on the US war on terrorism. Scowcraft wrote the following in the *Wall Street Journal*: "There is no evidence to tie Saddam to terrorist organisations, and even less to the September 11 attacks... [Military action] would seriously jeopardise, if not destroy, the global counter terrorist campaign we have undertaken." No connection, with convincing evidence, has been found between Iraq and the attacks of September 11, 2001 and no evidence has been provided that Iraq has continued to manufacture chemical, biological and nuclear weapons and might pass them on to terrorist groups like *al Qaeda*. The US accused Iraq of harbouring *Ansar ul Islam* in northern Iraq, but this was operating in the Kurdish controlled area of northern Iraq, where the US imposed no fly zone and was outside the control of Saddam Hussein's government.[28]

Not only were there deep divisions within the US-Bush administration, but leading think tanks, media, a large section of the public was opposed to the pre-emptive war against Iraq as they argued that sanctions/containment had worked fairly well. Iraq's military capability had been badly crippled and, with no long range missiles to deliver the chemical and biological weapons, Iraq posed no threat to the US, Israel or allies like Turkey or Kuwait. Many saw it as an unequal struggle between US and Iraq which won the admiration of millions of anti-war protesters all over the world from South Korea to South Africa, from Australia to Latin America, from England to India. They came out in large numbers in New York, Washington, Los Angeles and hundreds of US cities in manner unprecedented since the Vietnam war protests in 1960s. Most of the protesters sympathised with the suffering Iraqi people under a very cruel regime. Saddam Hussein's policies were condemned worldwide during the marches which were organised several times before the US invasion and also during and after the invasion of Iraq. The Bush administration may have ignored the peace movement elsewhere in the world, but the one within the US did mobilise hundreds and thousands onto the streets in major US cities, sending a clear message of opposition to US invasion of Iraq.

US eye on Iraqi oil (over 112 billion barrels plus high quality, low cost of production), strategic location in between Syria and Iran (to curb Tehran's options of taking independent action) and to protect Israel's regional supremacy and its monopoly of weapons of mass destruction, were some of the real war aims, besides asserting US global supremacy. Some analysts see an economic dimension to the US invasion of Iraq. That is a deeper economic struggle that the US is waging to preserve its economic supremacy in the world. It is a war between Euro and US dollar and Iraq has become the military beachhead. As Australian economist, Geoffery Heard, said, "The war in Iraq is actually the US and Europe going head to head on economic leadership of the world." Since Iraq started at France's persuasion to trade in Euros for its oil from 1999 replacing US dollar, other states like Iran, Russia and Venezuela also started thinking of switching over to Euro from dollar for their oil trade. US had to nip this in the bud as the dollar's grip on oil trading and, consequently on world trade in general, was under serious threat. Heard observed, "If America did not stamp on this immediately, the economic brush-fire could rapidly be fanned into a wildfire capable of consuming the US' economy and its dominance of world trade." The recent decline in the value of the dollar indicates that the threat was real. A long term weakening of the dollar due to its slipping hold on the world oil trade can have serious consequences for US prosperity and also its capability to finance its military expenditure through deficit financing. In other words, Euro not only threatened America's economic power but also its military power.[29]

So, apart from other reasons, the US goal in going to war in Iraq is also to "safeguard the American economy by returning Iraq to trading oil in US dollars, so the dollar is once again the exclusive oil currency". Further in Heard's words, "(Also) send a very clear message to any other oil producer just what will happen to them if they do not stay in the dollar circle. Place the second largest reserves of oil in the world under direct American control. Provide a secular, subject state where the US can maintain a huge force... to dominate the Middle East and its vital oil."[30] In earlier times gold, silver, grain, cotton were commodities of exchange, today it's oil. The war over Iraq may be a war for oil, but at a deeper level, it is a war for the defence of the continued control of the world oil economy through the US dollar.[31]

US inability to prevent Saudi-Iranian rapprochement, Saudi rejection of FBI supervision to investigate bombings in Saudi cities, Crown Prince Abdullah's perceived lack of support to US policies in the region and elsewhere, and especially towards the Israeli-Palestine conflict led the US to depend less on Saudi Arabia. Also Saudi tendency to side with Iran in keeping oil prices high, around $25-28 in world markets; their unwillingness to effectively curb the financial flows to Islamic groups, and the fear of losing its influence in the Saudi Kingdom as the Saudis are apparently demanding withdrawal of US forces from the Kingdom, also propelled the US to reduce its dependence on the Kingdom.[32]

Dick Cheney and his supporters persuaded George W Bush that *Operation Iraqi Freedom* would unleash the "explosion of joy" and Iraqis would greet the US liberating the Iraqi people from the tyrannical regime of Saddam Hussein. Massive air attacks, with Stealth bombers B-52 and other bombers with satellite-guided precision bombing on command and control centres with decapitation attacks, shock and awe policy would quickly bring to an end the Saddam Hussein regime. The US also believed that Iraqi people, especially the Shias in the South, would rebel against Saddam Hussein and welcome the US invasion to "liberate" Iraq. It was also believed that key leaders, both Baathist and military, would desert Saddam Hussein and facilitate quick US takeover of Iraq.

Three weeks of carpet-bombing known as 'shock and awe' bombing, and pushed by more than a lakh US soldiers, including hundreds of special operations forces, CIA agents, the Iraqis put up stiff resistance in Basra, Umm Qasr, Nasiriyah, Najaf, Mosul and in some parts of Baghdad. But the much expected resistance from Iraqi Republican Guards was never seen, forcing one to believe that either they had perished in the bombing or betrayed Saddam Hussein by secretly surrendering to US forces or simply melted into the civilian crowd. There were massive civilian casualties on the Iraqi side and US forces also suffered enormous losses which has not been publicised. Although many Iraqis were shown on Western and other TV channels as waving and cheering at US troops and apparently welcoming them but the majority of Iraqis see US forces as an occupation army, rather than as liberators.

The mounting civilian deaths, during and after the war, due to exploding cluster and other bombs and the live scenes on world TV channels is leading to growing opposition worldwide, especially in the Islamic countries, to continued occupation of Iraq by the US. President Hosni Mubarak of Egypt and other pro-US Arab leaders, feel vulnerable due to their support to US-led invasion of Iraq and at the same time keep warning that hundreds of more bin Ladens would emerge from the ashes of the US war on Iraq.

Since the US forces have not found WMD so far, this raises a question mark over the motives behind *Operation Iraqi Freedom*. Now the US proposes to send an army of a thousand American inspectors to carry out an intensive search for evidence of WMD. Such US finds of WMD will be challenged and seen as evidence planted. General Amir al Saadi who was advisor to Saddam Hussein, on Iraqi weapons programme, who has surrendered to the US, still maintains that Iraq did not have such weapon stockpiles. Although another Iraqi, a scientist who claims to have worked in Iraq's chemical weapons program for more than a decade, told US military that Iraq destroyed chemical weapons and biological warfare equipment only days before the war began. The US has not been permitting anyone to interview the scientist or visit his home. This information was submitted to US military officials for checking.[33]

The US now wants the UNSC to remove sanctions on Iraq immediately without verification while France, Russia and Germany have made it clear that they would agree to lift the sanctions only after a report from UN inspectors that Iraq was WMD free. The fact of the matter is there are very few buyers for US accusations about WMD in Iraq. Moreover the US wants to restrict the UN's role primarily to humanitarian tasks, while Washington wants to have full say in the new Iraqi set up. However, the Islamic and EU states would like the UN to play a lead role in the transitional arrangements leading to Iraqi elections and thus circumscribe the role of the occupying power. The US intends to stay longer in Iraq with the help of Iraqi exiles, led by Ahmed Chalabi and the Iraqi National Congress and Jay Garner, retired US General head of the US Office of Reconstruction and Humanitarian Assistance (ORHA) in Iraq. The US intends to keep its advisers in all ministries in the new Iraqi set up so as to decimate Baathist influence and prepare the ground for a pro-US Iraq in the coming years. The US President George W. Bush has picked a former diplomat and counter-terrorism expert, Paul Bremer, to be his special representative in Iraq. Mr Bremer will report to the Defence Secretary Donald Rumsfel and he will oversee all political and reconstruction activities in Iraq and will be senior to General Jay Garner. He has maintained a tough line against countries like Iran and Syria while heading the counter-terrorism outfit. He is expected to bring about an orderly transition and would be basically in charge until such time the local component of the government in Baghdad is firmly in place.[34]

The fall of Baghdad to US forces on April 9, 2003 with little resistance from the Iraqi forces, and the subsequent breakdown of law and order, large scale looting, plundering and burning of ministries, National Museum, National Archives/Library, public and private houses, and hospitals, indicates the scale of disorder which has descended on Iraq. US soldiers were mute spectators to the loot and arson. The only thing they safeguarded was the oil ministry in Baghdad and the oil fields/installations in Rumailah area and in Mosul and Kirkuk, clearly revealing their objectives behind the invasion.

The lack of power and water supply, together with severe shortages of food and medicine and the looting of hospitals, led to widespread demands for withdrawal of US forces from the Baghdad area. There have been daily demonstrations on these issues as people continue to suffer from power, water and lack of medicines. People have been openly opposing the continued presence of American troops in the country and also their control over the oil industry. The workers at Umm Qasr port are refusing to work for the British; so are the oil workers in the oil fields and other installations and want US troops to withdraw. The Shia Ulemas were the first to mobilise masses on the issue of continued presence of US forces. Abdel Majid al Koi, a cleric who returned from his exile in London was killed in Najaf while Ayatollah Ali Sistani was ordered out of Iraq in two days. The Shia Ulema are playing a leading role in mobilising people in the name of Islam, especially under the banner of Supreme Assembly for Revolution in Iraq led by Ayotollah Ahmed Hakim Bakr, who gets help from Iran. This group boycotted the April 15, 2003 meeting near Nasiriyah held to chalk out the political future of Iraq mostly led by Iraqi exiles under US supervision. Ahmed Chalabi did not attend the meeting but it was attended by Jay Garner, a pro-Israeli retired US General who heads post-Saddam reconstruction effort of Iraq, Zalmay Khalilzad a stooge of the US and other tribal leaders. Nearby, in the town of Nasiriyah, people mostly Shias, were shouting slogans "Leave our country, we want peace", "No Bush, No Saddam, Yes Yes to Islam", "No Shias, No Sunnis, Yes Yes to United Islam".[35]

The Imam of Al Aadhamiya mosque in Baghdad, Ahmed al Kubaisi, whose mosque dome was bombed, said the US invaded Iraq to defend Israel. "This is not the America we know, which respects international law, respects the rights of people." He led thousands of demonstrators in Baghdad who shouted: "No to America, No to Secular State, Yes to Islamic State", "We reject American hegemony" "We are Sunni and Shia brothers, we will not sell this nation". They also shouted

"Iraq's oil for the Iraqi people". These protesters marched from the Abu Hanifah Nouman mosque in Baghdad.[36]

Due to utter choas in Iraqi cities, the US forces enlisted the help of Iraqi police and others who worked under Saddam Hussein, but the US is determined to purge the system of the Baath Party members and also such Baathist members from police, paramilitary, bureaucracy and other structures of state. The process of witch hunting has begun with the help of Iraqi exiles, who are now wielding enormous power and influence, leading to widespread domestic resentment. The reconstruction process has been initiated by the US through US companies and this is breeding corruption and tainting the US administration. The US has been airlifting police/judicial officers from the US to maintain order in Iraq. They are also airlifting dollars to pay salaries to the Iraqis working for them, thereby fuelling anti-US feelings/sentiments in Iraq. The *New York Times* reported on April 24, 2003 that the US intends to stay in Iraq for several years and continue to use Iraqi military air bases all over Iraq.[37]

Not only did the Iraqis call for the withdrawal of US forces from Iraq immediately, Iraq's neighbours, meeting at the level of foreign ministers in Riyadh, Saudi Arabia also called for early withdrawal of occupation forces from Iraq as well as for respecting Iraq's territorial integrity. The states who took part in the meeting were Iran, Turkey, Jordan, Syria, Saudi Arabia, Egypt, Bahrain and others.[38]

Flush with quick victory over Iraq, the US has started training its guns on Syria and Iran. US Defence Secretary, Donald Rumsfeld, accused Syria of sending military equipment to Iraq and Iran of sending military personnel into Iraq. He also warned Syria against meddling in Iraqi affairs. Colin Powell also confirmed Washington's strict policy towards Iran and said it is time now for the international community to emphasise that Iran stop supporting terrorism. Powell's statements against Syria were made before AIPAC – a Zionist organisation. Rumsfeld's statements reflect US' real fear from Syria and Iran of the possibility that the two countries might answer the call of their people and open the borders for volunteers to fight. The signals made about the possibility of targetting Syria indicate that American reiterations — about not dividing the region and creating political disorder and chaos in it — are mere lies. They also mean that the battle in Iraq aims at fulfilling Israel's objectives by weakening Syria and leaving the Palestinians to face a deadlock. *Al Watan* newspaper said: It is Syria's duty and right to support the Iraqi people. Damascus should be praised for being the first country to announce its support for the Iraqis, who are facing a cruel army which defied all human principles. The Syrian declaration, in support of a brotherly nation that was attacked unfairly, is a good example that should be followed and not an accusation that one should avoid. Powell's threats to Damascus should be rejected since these accusations open the door for Israel to claim that Iraq has smuggled its weapons of mass destruction to Syria. By these accusations, Israel aims at drawing the British, Americans, and the Arabs into a bloody war while it reaps the gains, concludes *Al Watan*.[39]

Although it is not clear whether Saddam Hussein is dead or alive, whether still in Iraq or outside, some of his close supporters are giving themselves up, one by one. Slowly the regime's most wanted 55 men/women may land on US' hands and Iraq being under full US occupation, the peace US is looking for may be elusive. The US attempts to win the Iraqi hearts and minds so far has proved to be unsuccessful.

Throughout the world people have grave doubts about the legitimacy of the US led war and its occupation of Iraq. Appropriating the wealth of Iraq is not as easy as the US believes. As Saudi Foreign Minister, Saud al Faisal, said, "The Iraqi people should administer and govern their country by themselves and any exploitation of their natural resources should be in conformity with the will of the legitimate Iraqi government and its people. If what they (US) intend is the exploitation of Iraqi oil, it will not have any legitimate basis." Instead, the war will be a long and difficult one and might lead to the tumbling of many leaders and the changing of many policies, concludes *Al Riyadh*.[40]

If anti-American sentiments sweeping the Islamic world are not neutralised soon by way of quick US withdrawal from Iraq, then the US invasion and occupation, undoubtedly seen as illegal, unjust and unnecessary, would fuel deeper anti-US feelings and would lead to wider complications for the US. Due to the non resolution of the Palestine-Israeli conflict, the US could become the target of suicide attacks and terrorism on a much larger scale. US double standards, with war on Iraq and a soft approach towards Israeli occupation and repression on the Palestinians, would hurt US interests. Although Tony Blair and Jack Straw accepted "double standards" on Palestine and understood Arab concern about what they described as "injustice against the Palestinians", only quick progress towards establishing a Palestine state and an end to Israeli oppression is wanted. Straw said:

> There is a real concern too that the West has been guilty of double standards – on the one hand saying the UNSCRs on Iraq must be implemented, on the other hand, sometimes appearing rather quixotic over the implementation of resolutions about Israel and Palestine.[41]

Asked if he would plead guilty to double standards, Straw said, "To a degree yes... and we're going to deal with it. It's our responsibility, yes, to deal with Iraq but also, yes, to deal with the Israel-Palestine crisis." Straw said, citing UN resolutions calling for two independent states, that he felt "angry and upset" at the Israelis. Britain, he told the BBC, is "100 per cent committed" to the establishment of a viable Palestinian state with its capital in Jerusalem, based on UNSCR 242, the 1967 borders, the end of Jewish settlements, and a solution of the Palestinian refugee problem. The Israeli-Palestine peace Road Map prepared by the so-called "Quartet", the UN, EU, US and Russia calls for a phased peace plan which stipulates the creation of an independent Palestinian state by 2005. But due to Israeli pressure, the US has repeatedly postponed the publication of the Road Map. Israel's supporters have raised four objections to the plan. Firstly, they oppose the notion of "simultaneous steps" and call for sequential, with Palestinians first fulfilling all of their requirements, and only then would Israelis be required to act. Secondly, they object to the road map's mandates and time tables. Israel wants the stipulation that the road map's call for a provisional Palestinian state be based not on a mandate but on Israeli-Palestinian negotiation and the completion of an Israeli-Palestinian treaty. Thirdly, they want to eliminate the mention of Saudi Crown Prince Abdullah's peace initiative since it speaks of Israel's return to the June 1967 borders. Finally, they want the road map to specifically call for Palestinian acceptance of Israel as a Jewish state, meaning that Palestinians would agree upfront to relinquish the right to return. They are also opposed to the deployment of international observers to implement the plan. The Israelis also have to freeze Jewish settlements and the Palestinians have to reform the Palestinian Authority. What is important is not the road map as there are several plans starting from UNSCR 242, 338, Oslo Plan, Mitchell and Tenet Plan and so on. There has to be a clear mechanism established to implement what is agreed upon. Israel has always refused to implement the agreed provisions as it desires to retain Gaza and West Bank and East Jerusalem.[42]

If the US continues to express lack of seriousness on this issue and tolerate Sharon's massacre of Palestinians, his wholesale destruction of every vestige of Palestinian statehood, his targeted murders, house demolitions, settlements building, bypass roads, closures, curfews and daily humiliation of Palestinians, the world would call for sanctions on Israel like the UN did on Iraq. The time has come for US to squeeze Israel to withdraw from occupied Arab lands.

The US policy makers had hoped to achieve quick victory over Iraq to boost the flagging US economy with cheap Iraqi oil and then to reorder the strategic map in the strategically important Gulf region, but due to mounting opposition in Iraq, from Syria, Iran, Saudi Arabia and other countries in the world, the US could face new and entirely unexpected challenges to its objectives. And surmounting those hurdles could drag the US deeper and deeper into the Arabian deserts or quagmire. The US had unique and unprecedented goodwill after the September 11, 2001 attacks on WTC and Pentagon throughout the world including most Islamic states, but this has been dissipated fairly quickly. The US now has to contend with anger and hatred in the region due to its double standards and dubious policies. The short-sighted Bush administration, with its war mongers led by Dick Cheney, are in no mood to listen to saner voices from any quarter. Only the American people can save the USA and the rest of the world from what is fast becoming a dangerous situation. The world has seen the awesome power of the US and most are frightened. But surely peoples, societies, nations are also working hard to prepare strategies to challenge, to resist, to preserve their lives, cultures, values, and self prestige. It may be Pax-Americana now, but every Iraqi killed, injured and suffering would propel the Iraqis one day to wake up and, when they muster courage, then they will find out the truth. US invasion of Iraq is a wake up call for the struggling people as it is a short term gain for the US. In the final analysis, the Iraqis will take their destiny in their own hands sooner rather than later. From the chaos, a new Saladin may emerge from Iraq and change the future of Arabs.

NOTES AND REFERENCES

[1] Dilip Hiro, *Iraq: A Report from the Inside* (London: Granta Books, 2003), p.3; Laurie Mylroie, *The War Against America: Saddam Hussein and the World Trade Centre Attacks* (Washington: Institute for Public Policy, 2001) pp. 119-132; 148-168.

[2] "Baghdad Agreement on Weapons Inspections", *Washington Post*, February 25, 1998, p. A22, Cited in Naseer Aruri, "America's War against Iraq: 1990-2002", Chapter One in Anthony Arnove, ed., *Iraq under Siege: The Deadly Impact of Sanctions and War* (New Delhi: Viva Books, 2003), p.41; see also Fred Halliday, *Islam and the Myth of Confrontation* (London: 1B. Tauris, 2003) pp. 76-88.

[3] Tim Trevan, *Saddam's Secrets: The Hunt for Iraq's Hidden Weapons* (London: Harper Collins, 1999).

[4] Aruri, n.2, p.43; see John Mueller and Karl Mueller, "Sanctions of Mass Destruction", *Foreign Affairs*, vol. 78, no.3, May-June 1999, p.49.

5. Anees Jung, Baghdad Flash back: Suppressing the Spirit of a Nation" *The Times of India* (New Delhi) April 19, 2003.
6. Julian Borger, "US Plan for New Nuclear Arsenal", *The Guardian*, February 19, 2003.
7. Aruri, n.2, p.44; Thomas E. Ricks, "Some Top Military Brass Favour Status Quo in Iraq: Containment Seen Less Risky Than Attack", *Washington Post*, July 28, 2002, p.A1.
8. Peter Beaumont, et al., "Bush Ready to Declare War" *The Observer*, August 4, 2002, p.1.
9. Jane Wardell, "Rice Calls Saddam Evil Man who will Wreak Havoc if left to Own Devices", *Associated Press*, August 15, 2002, cited in Aruri, n.2, p.45.
10. Mark Tran, "US tells Iraq to Pull Back Troops or Face Air Strikes", *Guardian*, October 17, 1994, p.20, cited in Noam Chomsky, US Iraq Policy: Motives and Consequences", Chapter 3, in Aruri, n.2, p.72.
11. See Muriel Mirak Weissbach, "New Global Approaches and their impact on the Persian Gulf Region", paper presented at IPIS Conference, Tehran, March 4-5, 2003; see Blix's report in *Middle East International*, no. 694, February 21, 2003, p.5.
12. John Bolton, *The Washington Times*, February 22, 2002. (see his interview)
13. Weissbach, n.11; see also Dilip Hiro, *War without End: The Rise of Islamist Terrorism and Global Response* (New Delhi: Roli, 2002) pp. 337-372.
14. Ibid see also Milan Rai, *War Plan Iraq: Ten Reasons against War on Iraq* (London: Verso, 2002) pp. 44-99.
15. Weissbach, n.11, see also *MEI*, no.694, February 21, 2003.
16. *Los Angeles Times*, January 14, 2002.
17. Lyndon La Rouche, "*A Lecture on the World Economy*" (Abu Dhabi: UAE Zayed Centre for Coordination and Follow up, September 2002), p.9-19.
18. Ibid, p.20-34; "Hellbent on War: Can America Really go it Alone", *Newsweek*, February 3, 2003.
19. *Wall Street Journal*, September 4, 2002.
20. *The Hindu*, April 22, 2003, p.14.

21. *New York Times*, January 5, 2003.
22. *London Times*, January 13, 2003, "The American Empire: A Fine Old British Tradition".
23. Meron Benirnisti, "Pre-emptive Warnings of Fantastic Scenarios", *Haaretz*, August 15, 2002, cited in Aruri, n.2, p.45-46.
24. Ibid., p.46; David Lamb, "The One Who Confronts", *The Week*, April 6, 2003.
25. *Institute for Public Accuracy*, "Ritter: A Sham Hearing on Iraq", July 29, 2002, cited in Aruri, n.2, p.46; Noam Chomsky on the Doctrine of Preventive War, *Frontline*, 11 April 2003, pp.10-12; see also Robert D.Blackwill, "Defence of an Invasion", *The Hindustan Times* (New Delhi) April 8, 2003.
26. Ibid., p.47.
27. Todd S. Purdum and Patrick E-Tyler, "Top Republicans Break with Bush on Iraq Strategy", *New York Times*, August 16, 2002, p.A1.
28. Aruri, n.2, p.48.
29. N.S. Rajaram, "The Shadow War: Euro vs Dollar", *The Hindu*, April 22, 2003, p.14.
30. Ibid., see also *Middle East International*, no.684, February 21, 2003, p.3.
31. Ibid.
32. Qamar Agha, *War Against Terror: US-Iraq Conflict* (New Delhi: Third World Studies Centre, 2003), p.14-15.
33. *Times of India*, April 22, 2003; Patrick Scale, "Anglo-American Axis Leading for Disaster", *Gulf News*, March 28, 2003.
34. *The Hindu*, April 21-22, 2003.
35. *The Times of India*, April 20-23, 2003; see also Gulshan Diett, "Museum, memory and mankind," *The Hindu*, May 3, 2003.
36. *The Times of India*, April 21-2, 2003.
37. *The New York Times*, April 20-21, 2003; The US intends to reduce its military presence in Iraq. Multinational peace

keeping forces from about 15 countires especially the US, UK, Poland, India, Spain, Pakistan and others countries are likely to be in Iraq in the future known as the Stabilization forces. *The Times of India*. May 4, 2003.

[38] *The Times of India* and *The Hindu*, April 21, 2003.
[39] "Arab Perspective: War of Words between Syria and US Hots up", *Gulf News* (Dubai), April 4, 2003.
[40] Ibid., James J Zogby, "Present Road map will only lead to dead end", *Gulf News*, April 7, 2003.
[41] Mustapha Karkouti, A Road Map without Proper Directions", *Gulf News*, April 01, 2003.
[42] "Do not trust Israel", *Gulf News*, April 1, 2003.

Select Bibliography

Abidi, A.H.H. and K.R. Singh, *The Gulf Crisis* (New Delhi: Lancers Books, 1991).

Aburish, Said K, *Saddam Hussein: The Politics of Revenge* (London: Bloomsbury, 1999).

Agha, Qamar, *War Against Terror: US-Iraq Conflict* (New Delhi: Third World Studies Centre, 2003).

Agwani, M.S., ed., *The Gulf in Transition* (New Delhi: South Asian Publishers, 1987).

Akbar, M.J, *The Shade of Swords: Jihad and the conflict between Islam and Christianity* (New Delhi: Lotus/Roli Books, 2002)

Ali, Tariq, *The Clash of Fundamentalisms: Crusades, Jihads and Modernity* (New Delhi: Rupa Books, 2003)

_____, *Politics in the Gulf* (New Delhi: Vikas, 1978).

al Nafeesi, Abdullah Fahad, *The Role of the Shiah in the Political Development of Modern Iraq*, Ph.D Thesis, Cambridge University, 1972.

al Naqeeb, Khaldoun Hasan, *Society and State in the Gulf and Arab Peninsula: A Different Perspective* (London: Routledge, 1990).

Arjomand, Said Amir, ed., *Authority and Political Culture in Shiism* (Albany: State University of New York, 1988).

Arnove, Anthony ed., *Iraq Under Siege: The Deadly Impact of Sanctions and War* (New Delhi: Viva, 2003).

Axelgard, Fred, *A New Iraq* (New York: Praeger, 1989)

_____, ed., *Iraq in Transition* (Boulder: Westview, 1986).

Barzilai, G., A Klieman and G Shidlo, eds., *The Gulf Crisis and its Global Aftermath* (London: Routledge, 1993).

Batatu, Hanna, *The Old Social Classes and the Revolutionary Movements of Iraq* (Princeton: 1978).

Bennis, Phyllis and Michel Moushabeck, ed., *Beyond the Storm: A Gulf Crisis Reader* (New York: Olive Branch Press, 1991).

Bennis, Phyllis, *Calling the Shots: How Washington Dominates Today's UN* (New York: Interlink/Olive, 1996).

Brown, Sarah Graham, *Sanctioning Saddam: The Politics of Intervention in Iraq* (London: IB Tauris, 1999).

Bullock, J, and H. Morris, *Saddam's War: The Origins of the Kuwait Conflict and the International Response* (London: Faber and Faber, 1991).

Busch, Briton Cooper, *Britain and the Persian Gulf: 1894-1914* (University of California Press, 1967).

Butler, Richard, *Saddam Defiant: The Threat of Weapons of Mass Destruction and the Crisis of Global Security* (Washington: Public Affairs, 1999).

Chomsky, Noam, Edward W. Said and Ramsey Clark, *Acts of Aggression: Policing "Rogue" States* (New York: 1999).

Clark, Ramsey, et., al, *The Children are Dying: The Impact of Sanctions on Iraq* (New York: 1998).

Cockburn, Andrew and Patrick Cockburn, *Out of the Ashes: The Resurrection of Saddam Hussein* (New York: Harper Collins, 1999).

Cordesman, Anthony H, *Iraq and the War of Sanctions: Conventional Threats and Weapons of Mass Destruction* (Westport: Praeger, 1999).

Cordesman, Anthony H. and Ahmed S. Hashim, *Iraq: Sanctions and Beyond* (Boulder, Westview Press, 1997).

Dann, Uriel, *Iraq under Kassem* (New York: Praeger, 1969).

Doran, Charles F and Stephen W. Buck, ed., *The Gulf, Energy and Global Security: Political and Economic Issues* (Boulder: Lynne Rienner, 1991).

Foster, Henry A., *The Making of Modern Iraq: A Product of World Forces* (Norman: University of Oklahoma Press, 1935).

Haj, Samira, *The Making of Iraq, 1900-1963: Capital, Power and Ideology*, (New York: Suny Press, 1997).

Hazelton, Fran, ed., *Iraq since the Gulf War: Prospects for Democracy* (London: Zed Press, 1994).

Hiro, Dilip, *Desert Shield to Desert Storm* (New York: Harper Collins, 1992).

_____, *Iraq: A Report from the Inside* (London: Granta Books, 2003).

_____, *Neighbors, Not Friends: Iraq and Iran after the Gulf Wars* (London: Routledge, 2001).

_____, *War without End: The Rise of Islamist Terrorism and Global Response* (New Delhi: Roli Books, 2002).

Hussein, Adel, *America Loots Arab Oil* (Beirut: 1957).

_____, *Iraq: The Eternal Fire: 1972 Iraqi Oil Nationalization in Perspective* (London: TWC, 1981).

Ismael, Tareq, *Iran and Iraq* (Syracuse, 1982).

Ismael, Tareq Y. and Jacqueline S. Ismael, *The Gulf War and the New World Order: International Relations of the Middle East* (Tampa: University Press of Florida, 1994).

Kedourie, Elie, *England and the Middle East: The Destruction of the Ottoman Empire* (London: 1956).

Kelidar, Abbas, ed., *The Integration of Modern Iraq* (London: Croom Helm, 1979).

Khadduri, Majid, *Independent Iraq* (Oxford: OUP, 1951).

_____, *Republican Iraq: A Study of Iraqi Politics since the Revolution of 1958* (London: OUP, 1969).

_____, *Socialist Iraq: A Study of Iraqi Politics Since 1968* (Washington: The Middle East Institute, 1978).

_____, *The Gulf War* (New York: OUP, 1988).

Khalidi, Walid, *The Gulf Crisis: Origins and Consequences* (Washington: IPS, 1991).

Khalif, Samir al, *Republic of Fear* (Berkeley: University of California Press, 1989).

Khalil, Samir al, *Republic of Fear : The Politics of Modern Iraq* (London: Hutchinson Radius, 1989).

Khan, M.A. Saleem Khan, *The Monarchic Iraq: A Political Study* (Aligarh: Centre of West Asian Studies, 1977).

Khan, Rasheeduddin, *Political Developments in Iraq, 1914-1932* (Ph.D Thesis, Delhi University, ISIS, 1959).

Kimbell, LK, *The Changing Patterns of Political Power in Iraq 1958 to 1971* (New York: 1972).

Kumar, Ravinder, *India and the Persian Gulf Region, 1858-1907: A Study in British Imperial Policy* (New Delhi: Asia P.H., 1965).

Lloyd, Seton, *Twin Rivers: A Brief History of Iraq* (London: OUP, 1961).

Longrigg, Stephen, *Four Centuries of Modern Iraq* (Oxford: Clarendon Press, 1925).

_____, *Iraq, 1990-1950* (Oxford: OUP, 1953).

Marr, Phebe, *The Modern History of Iraq* (Boulder: Westview Press, 1985).

Select Bibliography

Mattar, Fuad, *Saddam Hussein* (London: TWC, 1981).

Miller, Judith and Laurie Mylroie, *Saddam Hussein and the Crisis in the Gulf* (New York: Times Books, 1990).

Mylroie, Laurie, *Iraq: Options for US Policy* (Washington, DC: Institute for Near East Policy, 1993).

_____, *The War against America: Saddam Hussein and the World Trade Center Attacks* (New York: Regan Books/Harper Collins, 2001).

Nonneman, Gerd, *Iraq, the Gulf States and the War* (London: Ithaca Press, 1986).

Noorani, A.G., *The Gulf Wars: Documents and Analysis* (New Delhi: Konark, 1991).

Pannikar, K.M., *For a few barrels of oil: Politics and Diplomacy in the Gulf* (New Delhi: Patriot Publishers, 1991).

Pasha, A.K., ed., *The Gulf in Turmoil* (New Delhi: Lancers Books, 1992), Kuwait: *Strategies of Survival* (New Delhi: Har Anand, 1995)

_____ ed., *Contemporary Gulf: State, Society, Economy and Foreign Policy* (New Delhi: Detente, 1999).

_____., *India, Iran and the GCC States; Political Strategy and Foreign Policy* (New Delhi: Manas Publicatiion, 2000)

_____., *Arab-Israeli Peace Process: An Indian Perspective* (New Delhi: Manas Publications, 2000).

Penrose, Edith and E.F. Penrose, *Iraq: International Relations and National Development* (London: Ernest Benn, 1978).

Phythian, Mark, *Arming Iraq: How the US and Britain Secretly Built Saddam's War Machine* (Boston: Northeastern UP, 1996).

Rai, Milan, *War Plan Iraq: Ten Reasons Against War on Iraq* (London: Verso, 2002).

Ritter, Scott, *Endgame: Solving the Iraq Problem-Once and for All* (New York: Simon and Schuster, 1999).

Shikara, Ahmad, *Iraqi Politics, 1921-1941: The Interaction between Domestic Politics and Foreign Policy* (London: LAAM, 1987).

Singh, K.R., *Post-War Gulf: Implications for India* (New Delhi: Lancers Books, 1993).

Sluglett, Farouk Marion and Peter Sluglett, *Iraq Since 1958* (London: KPI, 1987).

Timmerman, Kenneth, *The Death Lobby: How the West Armed Iraq* (Boston: Houghton Mifflin Co., 1991).

Trevan, Tim, *Saddam's Secrets: The Hunt for Iraq's Hidden Weapons* (London: Harper Collins, 1999).

Wiley, Joyce N., *The Islamic Movement of Iraqi Shias* (Boulder: Lynne Rienner, 1992).

Wurmser, David, *Tyranny's Ally: America's Failure to Defeat Saddam Hussein* (Washington: AEI Press, 1999).

Yergin, Daniel, *The Prize: The Epic Quest for Oil, Money and Power* (New York: Touchstone Books, 1993).

Index

Symbols

1441 128
1952 Egyptian revolution 8, 9
1956 Suez crisis 7, 9
1958 Iraqi revolution 8, 9
1967 borders 140
1972 Friendship Treaty 14
1979 Iranian revolution 16

A

Abbasid Empire 1, 106
ABC 28, 129
Abdal Rahman Abdullah al Awadi 31, 58
Abdel Majid al Koi 136
Abdul Karim Qassem 8, 10
Abdul Salam Arif 11
Abdulla Yaqub Bishara 53
Abdullah ibn Abdul Aziz 73
Abraham 1
Abu Dhabi 50
Abu Hanifah Nouman 137
Afghanistan 119, 126
Ahmad Hassan al Bakr 11, 12
Ahmad Saleh 105
Ahmed al Kubaisi 136
Ahmed Chalabi 62, 123, 134, 136
AIPAC 136
Al Aadhamiya 135
Al Ahd 4
Al Azmina al Arabia 26
Al Jumhouriya 32, 109
Al Khater 54
Al Qadissiya 101
al Qaeda 129, 130
Al Rai 41
Al Riyadh 139
Al Sabahs 15, 26, 29, 33, 43, 44, 51, 58
Al Samoud 120
Al Thawra 32, 64, 109
Al Watan 136, 137
al-Ahmadi 23
Al-Atheer 75
al-Faw 21
Al-Gezira 48
Al-Kadhemiya 64
Al-Mutanaffi 105
Al-Samita 14
Ali Akbar Velayati 54
Ali Hassan Majid 74, 100
Ali Khalifa 30
Alkhater 54
Allah 54
Amara 98
America 136
American 44, 72, 126
American Enterprise Institute 124, 125
American inspectors 134
American troops 136

Americans 37, 39, 97, 125, 137
Amir Faisal bin Hussein 5
Anglo-American 124
Anglo-Iraqi Treaty 4
Ansar ul Islam 130
anti-American 139
April Glaspie 28, 38
Arab 1-3, 7, 10, 22, 31, 32, 35, 38, 59, 60, 83, 84, 92, 96, 109, 117, 122, 127, 129, 133, 138, 141
Arab aspirations 77
Arab Baath Party 62
Arab Cooperation Council 26, 28
Arab countries 31
Arab diplomacy 43
Arab fund for development 36
Arab Gulf region 8
Arab Gulf states 57
Arab League 8, 10, 14, 29, 32, 50, 51, 60, 112, 119
Arab mediation 43
Arab nation 45, 51
Arab National Charter 18, 35
Arab nationalist 5, 92
Arab News 48
Arab power 88
Arab solidarity 42
Arab states 96
Arab summit 29, 30, 31, 35, 51, 129
Arab Unity 50
Arab world 1, 2, 3, 9, 22, 44, 59, 83, 122
Arab-Arab conflicts 38, 59
Arab-Israeli peace front 96
Arab/Palestinian lands 109
Arabian Gulf region 33
Ariel Sharon 124, 127
Arif brothers 12
Arshad Tewflk Ismail 74
Assur 1
Assyrians 1
Asurbanipal 1
Aswan Dam 8
Athens 126
Auhah 5

Australia 130
Axis of Evil 119
Ayad al Rawi 100
Ayatollah Ali Sistani 136
Ayatollah Hakim Bakr 71, 72, 73, 136
Ayatollah Khomeini 16
Ayatollah Khomeini's 27
Aziz's 35, 86, 87

B

Baath 13
Baath coup 13
Baath ideology 16
Baath leadership 63
Baath Party 12, 63, 64, 68, 69, 74, 76, 78, 82, 99, 101, 109, 137
Baathist 13, 135, 137
Baathist regime 28, 114
Babel 109
Badr al Yacoub 31
Baghdad 1, 3, 4, 6, 7, 8, 11, 15, 16, 25, 26, 28, 30, 33, 37, 40, 43, 64, 67, 68, 70, 74, 77, 83, 85, 89, 90, 92, 94, 95, 98, 101, 103, 107-110, 113, 117, 118, 128, 132, 134, 135
Baghdad Arab summits (1978-79) 16
Baghdad Pact 6, 7, 8
Baghdad's 92, 93, 105, 108
Bahrain 110, 136
Basra 3, 4, 8, 13, 34, 64, 132
Batin 5
BBC 140
Beirut 63, 66, 73, 127
Benjamin Netanyahu 111, 122, 127
Biden 129
Bill Clinton 99, 123
bin Ladens 134
biological weapons 129
Bishara 53
Bolton 121, 122
bombs 132
Bosnia 102
Bremer, Paul, 135
Britain 4, 6, 8, 11, 64, 102, 140

Index

Britain and Iraq 4
British 2, 13, 44, 102, 125, 136, 138
Brooking Institution 24
Bubiyan 5, 6, 13, 14, 15, 20-22, 24, 54
Bush 38, 68, 82, 87, 91, 96, 97, 98, 121, 123, 126, 127, 128, 141

C
Cairo 50, 51, 59
Camp David 15
Ceausescu 28
Chadli Klibi 29
Chairman UN special commission 87
Charles Fairbanks 121
cheat and retreat 90, 97
chemical weapons 98, 126, 133
China 23, 52, 78, 93, 94, 101, 114, 118, 120, 127
Churchill 49
CIA 73, 74, 94, 132
Clean Break 121, 122
Clinton 102, 103, 108, 114, 115
cluster 132
Colin Powell 136
Columbus 1
communist 3
Communist regimes 28
Condoleeza Rice 117, 118
Congress 68, 116
Council for Democratic Iraq 64
Crown Prince Abdullah 72, 132, 140
Crown Prince Saad 41
Cuba 94

D
Dakar 72
Damascus 66, 77, 137
Dan Quayle 91
David Hanny 86
David Wurmser 122
Dawa Party 63
demilitarised zone 102
democracy 28, 69
democratic reforms 69
Derek Boothby 90

Devi Lal 49
Dhari-al Othman 31
Diane Sawyer 28
Dick Cheney 116, 121, 122, 123, 131, 140
Doha 52, 54, 55, 56
dollars 124
Donald Rumsfeld 117, 123
Douglas Feith 122, 123

E
East European 28, 69
East India Company 3
East Jerusalem 139
economic blockade 75
economic sanctions 76, 78, 84, 86, 87, 90, 92, 101, 102, 103, 106
Egypt 2, 7, 8, 15, 37, 39, 42, 54, 56, 59, 60, 73, 77, 96, 125, 132, 136
embargo on Iraq 128
Emir of Kuwait 10, 13, 26, 41, 43
Emir of Qatar 53
Empire 124
England 129
EU 133, 138
Euphrates 1, 115
Europe 1
Europeans 2, 3, 45, 60

F
Failakh 5
Falluja 98
Faw 33, 34
FBI 107, 131
First World War 3
fly zones 110
France 3, 60, 75, 77, 95, 101, 102, 103, 114, 118, 126, 130, 133
Frank J. Gaffney 122
French 2, 96, 125

G
Gaza Strip 121, 139
GCC 19-23, 27, 31-34, 36, 38, 39, 48, 50-60, 66, 77, 84, 108, 110

GCC states 18, 24, 28, 30
GCC summit 52
GCC-Iran relations 54
General Amir al Saadi 134
Geneva 40, 50
Geoffery Heard 131
George Bush 59, 66, 73, 91, 93, 94, 96, 97, 98, 99, 127
George W Bush 116, 118, 120, 123, 131
Germany 4, 49, 93, 118, 127, 133
Gilgamesh 1
glasnost 49
Glaspie 27, 38
Golan peace front 77
Governor of Basra 8
Great Britain 3, 45
Greeks 1
Gulf 4, 7, 8, 12, 13, 15, 23, 36, 45, 54, 58, 95, 97, 99, 102
Gulf Arab States 26
Gulf Arabs 19, 45
Gulf area 110
Gulf army 53
Gulf crisis 49, 53, 78
Gulf Daily News 48
Gulf Fund for Supporting Development Efforts 59
Gulf giants 14
Gulf intervention force 22
Gulf oil 31
Gulf Power 14
Gulf region 8, 16, 34, 53, 103, 110, 111, 121, 140
Gulf rulers 52
Gulf security 77, 111
Gulf states 18, 19, 22, 27, 34, 48, 49, 58, 102, 110, 111
Gulf war 19, 21, 25, 26, 27, 28, 30, 34, 35, 37, 40, 43, 44, 49, 63, 65, 68, 69, 72, 73, 82, 87, 93, 95, 96, 97, 103, 110

H
Hafez Assad 108
Haiti 102
Hammurabi 1
Hans Blix 119
Hans Von Sponeck 129
Hardan Takriti 13
Hasa 34
Hashemi Rafsanjani 72
Hashemite monarchy 5, 7, 126
Hassan Naquif 64
Hatra 1
Hikmat Bazzaz 104
Hittites 1
holy war 52
Hosni Mubarak 37, 39, 132
House of Saud 111
human rights 84, 96, 110
Hussein Kamal Hassan 74

I
IAEA 114, 119
IAPS 121
Ibrahim al Dawud 67
Idd-ul-fitr 106
Imam 136
Imam Musa Sadr 71
India 93, 94, 130
Indian army 4
Industrial Revolution 2
inspection of weapons sites 68
Institute for Public Accuracy 129
inter-Arab relations 52
international terrorism 118
Intifada 36, 116
Iran 7, 8, 12-14, 18-26, 27, 34, 42, 44, 51, 52, 54, 58, 65, 66, 67, 71, 72, 83, 91, 97, 103, 108, 110, 118, 120, 123, 124, 130, 134, 136, 140
Iran-Iraq 19, 24, 34, 44, 51, 99, 110
Iran-Iraq war 18, 107
Iranian 16, 18, 33
Iranian Majlis 23

Index

Iranian revolution 18, 26
Iraq 2, 4, 5, 7, 10, 18, 19, 21, 23, 24, 30, 34, 36, 37, 39, 48, 52, 54, 55, 57, 66, 79, 85, 91, 102, 108, 109, 118, 120, 124, 125, 126, 127, 132, 134, 139
Iraq and Iran 112
Iraq and Kuwait 7, 9, 19, 39, 48, 99
Iraq and Saudi Arabia 122
Iraq and the UN 88
Iraq Liberation Act 114
Iraq-Kuwait boundary 10-12, 87
Iraq-US 109
Iraqi revolution 18
Iraqi Army 67
Iraqi Communist Party 63
Iraqi constitution 14
Iraqi dinar 114
Iraqi disarmament 117
Iraqi economy 67
Iraqi exiles 133
Iraqi invasion of Kuwait 50
Iraqi Kurdistan 96, 109
Iraqi National Assembly 28
Iraqi National Assembly, Saadi Mahdi Saleh 66
Iraqi National Congress 113, 123, 134
Iraqi oil 30, 34, 89, 115, 116, 130, 137, 140
Iraqi oil exports 116
Iraqi opposition 63, 64, 66, 75, 91, 97
Iraqi Petroleum Company 13
Iraqi political groups 71
Iraqi Republican Guards 83, 132
Iraqi Shia 66, 70
Iraqi weapons 90
Iraqi-Kuwait border 5, 106
Iraq's chemical weapons program 134
Iraq's Gulf coastline 21
Iraq's nuclear reactor 107
Iraq's oil 135
Iraq's Shia 71
Iraq's war against Iran 22
Ishtar 1

Islam 134, 135
Islamic 45, 66, 133
Islamic Action Organisation 66
Islamic Amal Organisation 64
Islamic Conference Organization 48, 50
Islamic countries 132
Islamic fundamentalism 27
Islamic groups 131
Islamic nations 59
Islamic peoples 125
Islamic revolution 18, 19
Islamic State 135, 140
Islamic world 137
Islamists 111
Ismet Abdal Majid 56
Israel 16, 45, 58, 73, 83, 84, 96, 101, 102, 107, 111, 116, 121, 126, 129, 130, 135, 137, 138, 139
Israel and the GCC 111
Israel-Palestine crisis 138
Israeli 59, 108, 121, 126, 135, 139
Israeli conflict 138
Israeli Jewish 126
Israeli war 123
Israeli-Palestine conflict 116, 131
Israeli-Palestine peace 138
Israeli-Turkish military alliance 108
Israel's 83, 136, 139
Italy 3
Izzat Ibrahim 41, 42, 64

J

Jack Straw 138
Jalal Talabani 68, 75
James Baker 91
Japan 83
Jay Garner 133, 135
Jeb 122
Jebel Sanam 5
Jeddah 31, 36, 39, 40, 42, 50, 51
Jeremy Greenstock 109
Jerusalem 121, 126, 138
Jewish 107

Jewish settlements 139
Jewish state 101
Jews 3
Jirjan 15
John Bolton 116, 117, 120
Jordan 7, 10, 39, 98, 108, 114, 126, 136
Jordan river 127
Jordanian 41
Jordanian option 127
Jordan's King Hussein 37
Joseph Biden 128
Jumhouriya 101
June 1967 borders 140

K
Kayhan 21
KDP 75
Khaleq Hassouna 10
Khalifa Amir 111
Khor Abdulla 5
Khor al Sabiya 6
Khor Zobeir 5
King Abdul Aziz 71
King Fahd 37, 44, 48, 49, 51, 52, 55, 72
King Faisal II 7
King Ghazi 6
King Hussein 37
King of Iraq 5
King Saud 9
King William IV 3
Kirkuk 134
Kofi Annan 114
Kubbas 5
KUNA 32
Kurdish 63, 65, 66, 72, 84
Kurdish guerrillas 74
Kurdish rebellions 67, 68
Kurdistan 108
Kurds 13, 35, 62, 65, 66, 67, 71, 72, 74, 75, 82, 86, 87, 97, 99, 108, 110
Kurds and Shias 95

Kuwait 5-14, 15, 20, 22, 24, 25, 26, 28-40, 43, 44, 48, 50-60, 65, 70, 74, 83, 91, 96, 97, 99, 102, 107, 129
Kuwait and Iran 21, 23
Kuwait crisis 71, 84
Kuwait ruler 31
Kuwait-Iraq 12
Kuwait-Iraq border 29
Kuwaiti 5
Kuwaiti crisis 26
Kuwaiti Emir 30, 37, 41, 42
Kuwaiti ruler 6, 11, 23, 38, 43
Kuwaiti-Iraq ties 13
Kuwaiti-Iraqi border 20
Kuwaiti-Iraqi problems 38
Kuwaitis 76, 88
Kuwait's Crown Prince 25
Kuwait's oil policy 35

L
Latin America 130
Lawrence Eagleburger 129
League of Nations 3, 4, 10
Lebanon 64, 71, 123
Lebensraum 43
Libya 120
Likud 111, 127
London 7, 42, 64, 71, 115, 134
London Times 126
Lord William Rees Mogg 126
Los Angeles 130
Los Angeles Times 123
Lyndon La Rouche 123, 124

M
Madeleine Albright 119
Madrid 64
mandate 3
Marlin Fitzwater 70
Mashtal 64
Maskan 5
Masoud Barzani 75
mass destruction weapons 101

Index

Saddoun Hammadi 29, 30, 41, 67, 68
safe haven 75
Safwan 5
Sahaf 87
SAIRI 72
Saladin 140
Saleh Mahdi Ammash 13
Samarra 4
Samir Abdur Razzaq 24
Sam's 95
San Remo 4
sanctions 116
Sanctions Monitoring Committee 67
Saud al Faisal 137
Saudi Arabia 9, 10, 14, 21, 26, 28, 31, 32, 34, 37, 39, 42, 43, 49, 53, 64, 65, 68, 71, 73, 76, 83, 91, 96, 99, 102, 111, 121, 123, 124, 131, 136, 137, 140
Saudi Arabia and Kuwait 26
Saudi Gazette 49
Saudi King Fahd 41
Saudi Press Agency 49
Saudi Wahhabism 19
Saudi-Iranian rapprochement 72, 131
Scott Ritter 107, 127
Scowcraft 128
Scud Missiles 90, 98
Secretary General 10, 32
Security Council 57, 58
Security Council Resolutions 76
Security Council Resolutions 706 and 712, 70
Senate 127
Senate Foreign Relations Committee 127
Senegal 72
September 11, 125, 126
Shah of Iran 13, 15, 83
Sharia 71
Sharif Hussein's 5
Sharon's 116, 139
Shatt al-Arab 6, 12, 25, 26, 43,
Sheikh Abdul Aziz Baz 71

Sheikh Abdullah al Salim al Sabah 8
Sheikh Ahmad Al Sabah 5
Sheikh Ali Khalifa al Sabah 30
Sheikh Jaber al Ahmed al Sabah 15
Sheikh Khalifa Bin Hamad al Thani 53
Sheikh of Kuwait 5, 9
Sheikh Saad Abdullah 25, 41
Sheikh Sabah al Salim al Sabah 11, 21
Sheikh Saud Nasir al Sabah 43
Sheikh Zayid bin Sultan al Nuhayyan 50, 108
Shia 34, 65, 67, 68, 94, 103, 135
Shia and Kurdish uprisings 99
Shia and Sunni 110
Shia Islam 65
Shia leaders 66
Shia Muslims 75
Shia opposition 73
Shia rebellion 65
Shia Ulema 134
Shia uprisings 64
Shias 62, 65, 71, 72, 82, 86, 94, 97, 99, 132, 135
Shimon Peres 126
shock and awe 132
Shola 64
Shuweik 20
Sir Percy Cox 5
Somalia 95, 98, 102
South Africa 129
South Korea 129
Soviet Union 3, 8, 9, 10, 23
Spain 3, 64, 74
START-II 98
Stephen Solarz 122
stolen oil 30
Straw 138
Sudan 10, 77
Sumerian 1
Sunni 135
Sunni Iraqis 71
Sunnis 135
Super Power 44
Supreme Assembly for Islamic Revolution in Iraq 64, 70, 73, 134

Syed Bakr Hakim 71
Syed Mirzai 54
Sykes-Picot 3
Syria 14, 52, 59, 60, 64, 67, 74, 77, 108, 114, 120, 123, 124, 127, 130, 136, 137, 140
Syria and Iran 136
Syrian Christians 2

T
Taha Yassin Ramadan 67
Taliban 118
Tariq Aziz 29, 31, 35, 37, 67, 84, 85, 86, 89, 101, 109, 114
Tawfiq Ismail 64
Tehran 19, 20, 44, 70, 73, 130
Tenet Plan 141
terrorism 138, 139
terrorist groups 129
The Burden 124
The Project for the New American Century 123
The War Against the Terror Masters 124
The Washington Post 120
Tigris 1, 115
Times 49, 120
Tom Mc-Naugher 24
Tony Blair 139
Treaty of Mohammara 5
Tunisia 31
Turkey 4, 52, 54, 74, 75, 77, 96, 129, 136
Turkish 108
Turkish Yoke 4

U
UAE 12, 29, 31, 34, 36, 37, 38, 40, 49, 50, 77, 108, 110
UAR 10
Uday 108
UK 9, 12, 60, 75, 86, 95, 96, 103, 106, 127
Umm al Khasib 64

Umm Qasr 5, 8, 13, 21, 95, 98, 132, 134
UN 10, 11, 32, 49, 50, 52, 54, 55, 57-59, 67, 68, 76, 84, 86, 87, 89, 90-99, 102, 103, 105-107, 115, 118, 127, 133, 138, 139
UN arms inspectors 100
UN Assistant Secretary General 128
UN Charter 58, 70, 85, 109, 118
UN Children's Fund 103
UN Disarmament Commission 86
UN economic sanctions 95, 99, 107, 114, 128
UN High Commission 93
UN inspectors 89, 90, 92, 93, 97, 107, 113, 116, 119, 133
UN intervention 93
UN oil for food programme 113
UN resolutions 70, 71, 89, 96
UN sanctions 67, 70, 86, 92, 96, 105, 106, 113, 114, 119, 127
UN Secretary General 32, 39, 57, 69, 87, 114
UN Security Council 9, 11, 20, 57, 58, 59, 70, 84, 85, 89, 94, 101, 109, 114, 115
UN Security Council – Resolution No. 660, 50
UN Security Council Resolution 712, 68
UN Security Council Resolutions 84, 86, 96, 99, 110, 117, 127
UN weapons inspection team 92
UN weapons inspectors 118, 127
UNICEF 93, 104, 128
United Arab Republic 10
UNMOVIC 114, 117
UNSC 86, 87, 93, 95, 100, 101, 102, 114, 119, 126, 133
UNSCOM 108, 114
UNSCR 1441, 118
UNSCR 242, 140
UNSCR 242, 338, 141
UNSCR 678, 687, 58, 128

Index

UNSCR 687, 69, 85, 89, 100
UNSCR 687 of April 1991, 86
UNSCR 688, 94
UNSCR 706, 76, 87
UNSCR 712, 76, 99
UNSCR 715, 100
UNSCR 778, 87
UNSCR 1284, 114
UNSCRs 127, 138
Ur 1
US 20, 23, 28, 29, 32-38, 41, 43-45, 49, 52, 55, 57, 59, 60, 63-66, 70, 72-77, 82-84, 86-88, 90, 91-99, 101-130
US attack on Iraq 117
US Congress 122, 128
US dollar 131
US invasion of Iraq 131, 139
US Iraq 135
US Kitty Hawk 95
US led war 139
US naval forces 23
US Senator .128
US State Department 121
US takeover of Iraq 133
US war on Iraq 127, 134
US war on terrorism 129
US-Iraq 55
US-led invasion of Iraq 133

V
Vasco da Gama 1
Venezuela 130
Venice 125
Vienna 89
Vietnam 66
Vietnam war 130
vilayet 4, 9

W
Wadi el Audja 5
Wall Street Journal 124, 129

war against Iraq 124, 129
war against terrorism 124
war for oil 132
war on terrorism 124
war over Iraq 132
Warbah 5, 6, 7, 13, 14, 20, 21, 54
Warbah and Bubiyan 40
Washington 42, 73, 83, 109, 110, 111, 116, 130, 134, 137
Washington Post 110, 117
Washington Times 121
Washington-Tel Aviv axis 122
Wasit 64
weapons of mass destruction 59, 69, 89, 116, 117-121, 127, 128, 131, 134
West 15, 44, 45, 52, 66, 72, 77, 88, 91-96, 103, 107, 138
West Asia 116, 118
West Bank 122, 127, 141
Western 69, 94, 99
Western imperialism 96
Western pressure 97
White House 70
William Perry 103
World Food Programme 93
World War II 52, 125
WTC 119, 124, 141

Y
Yasser Arafat 37
Yemen 94
Yitzhak Eitan 126
Yugoslavia 96

Z
Zalmay Khalilzad 123, 136
Zimbabwe 94
Zionist Mossad agents 101
Zubair 64

By the same author:
- Libya and the United States (1984)
- Egypt's Relations with Soviet Union (1986)
- Libya in the Arab World (1988)
- Egypt's Quest for Peace (1994)
- India and OIC (1995)
- Kuwait: Strategies of Survival (1995)
- India and West Asia (1999)
- Aspects of Political Participation in the Gulf States (1999)
- Egypt in a Changing World (2003)

Edited works:
- The Gulf in Turmoil (1992)
- Perspectives on India and the Gulf States (1999)
- Contemporary Gulf (1999)
- India, Bahrain and Qatar (1999)
- India and Kuwait (1999)
- India and Oman (1999)
- India, Iran and the GCC states (2000)
- Arab-Israeli Peace Process (2000)

Co-edited works:
- Contemporary Iran and Emerging Indo-Iranian Relations. (1996)
- India and the Islamic World (1998)

Günther Friesinger, Johannes Grenzfurthner,
Thomas Ballhausen (eds.)
Mind and Matter

Cultural and Media Studies

GÜNTHER FRIESINGER, JOHANNES GRENZFURTHNER,
THOMAS BALLHAUSEN (EDS.)

Mind and Matter
Comparative Approaches towards Complexity

[transcript]

This publication was supported by the Department of Art Funding/ City of Vienna, Austria and the Austrian Federal Ministry of Science and Research.

This publication is based on the symposium »MIND AND MATTER. Comparative Approaches towards Complexity«, which took place 2010 in the context of the paraflows Festival in Vienna.

Bibliographic Information published by the Deutsche Nationalbibliothek
The Deutsche Nationalbibliothek lists this publication in the Deutsche Nationalbibliografie; detailed bibliographic data are available in the Internet at http://dnb.d-nb.de

© **2011 transcript Verlag, Bielefeld**

All rights reserved. No part of this book may be reprinted or reproduced or utilized in any form or by any electronic, mechanical, or other means, now known or hereafter invented, including photocopying and recording, or in any information storage or retrieval system, without permission in writing from the publisher.

Cover layout: Kordula Röckenhaus, Bielefeld
Cover illustration: Günther Friesinger, 2009
Proofread by Melinda Richka
Translated by Andrea Wald, Anna Weichselbraun
Typeset by Anika Kronberger
Printed by Majuskel Medienproduktion GmbH, Wetzlar
ISBN 978-3-8376-1800-6

Global distribution outside Germany, Austria and Switzerland:

Transaction Publishers
New Brunswick (U.S.A.) and London (U.K.)

Transaction Publishers	Tel.: (732) 445-2280
Rutgers University	Fax: (732) 445-3138
35 Berrue Circle	for orders (U.S. only):
Piscataway, NJ 08854	toll free 888-999-6778

Table of Contents

Introduction

MIND AND MATTER. Comparative Approaches towards Complexity
Günther Friesinger, Johannes Grenzfurthner, Thomas Ballhausen | 9

The digital reformulation of the relationship of mind and matter
Frank Apunkt Schneider, Günther Friesinger | 11

1. Archives

**Image Science & MediaArtHistories
New Infrastructures for 21st Century Digital Humanities**
Oliver Grau | 29

**The Archive as the Repertoire
Mediated and Embodied Practice on Imageboard 4chan.org**
Jana Herwig | 39

**W0rdM4g1x
Or how to put a spell on Media Art Archives**
Nina Wenhart | 57

Impressive. Memory, Matter and Mind
Herbert Hrachovec | 75

The Many Faces of Expressionism. Prosthetic Memory, Mind and Matter in ORLAC'S HÄNDE/THE HANDS OF ORLAC (1924)
Thomas Ballhausen | 89

Killing (the power of) time
Archiving selves, cities, histories and universes
Christian Heller | 99

2. Technology

Demystification of Digital Media
Lin Hsin Hsin | 117

Biometrics and the Sense of Self in Video Games
Kyle Machulis | 137

I can count every star in the heavens above but I have no heart I can't fall in love ...
The image of computers in popular music
Johannes Grenzfurthner | 141

3. Networks

Trapped in the World Wide Web
Dmytri Kleiner | 175

The Doors of Misperception
Or how we found the web progressive by using conservative terms — A collection of notes
Mela Mikes | 189

Network Sculpture
Jane Tingley | 197

Love on a Wire: Communications Technology Across 10,000 Miles
Adam W. Flynn, Sarah Outhwaite | 211

List of contributors | 227

Introduction

MIND AND MATTER. Comparative Approaches towards Complexity

GÜNTHER FRIESINGER, JOHANNES GRENZFURTHNER, THOMAS BALLHAUSEN

The terms nous (the philosophical term stems from ancient Greek knowledge, spirit, intellect) and matter appear to signify two concepts irreplaceable and permanent in nature. The increasing challenges and modes of reflection of digital life and cultural creation have contributed to a productive doubting of said dichotomy. Net culture has exposed the causality of the two only superficially contradictory systems and translated these into new technological realities. This reader, using an interdisciplinary approach, strives to investigate the entanglement of cultural, artistic and technical praxis, to document the developments, to clarify the status quo of the scientific community in a practical and exemplary fashion and to enable glimpses of potential future developments. The process of transformation of the scientific disciplines, the replacement of extremely heterogeneous meta-scientific values will be made as graspable as the evolution of abstract concepts or the digital saturation of the human body. This reader tries to describe, transmit and clarify a paradigm shift of society as a whole which is still in process.

This three-part reader corresponds to the thematic priorities Archives, Technology and Networks. The part Archives will assume the challenge of the manifold archives and their relationship towards the public to which they should be indebted as much as to the preserved content itself. Cultural science is joined in unison with more practical fields in the examination of storage, traces and latency as focal points.

The next part will take a close look at technical innovations and technological implications, lay out the basics of different fields and sketch the shifts of cultural, technical or political scientific and productive methodology.

The third and final part will revolve around the main metaphor of the "network" and react constructively to the preceding panels with the discussion of the terms "complexity" and "emergence". The net and the networks should, however, not only be treated as exclusively computer-related terms, but rather also be interpreted and pondered as sociobiological and neuro-scientific phenomena.

The digital reformulation of the relationship of mind and matter

FRANK APUNKT SCHNEIDER, GÜNTHER FRIESINGER

THE BODY-SOUL PROBLEM AS A MATRIX OF THE WESTERN WORLD

Our traditional construction of reality is based on the schematic opposition of mind and matter. This dualism was continually updated through the course of Western history in a long series of dichotomies: God and the world, this world and the afterworld, body and soul, forms of being and consciousness, idealism and materialism, culture and nature, art and economy, man and machine, inside and outside but also interior and exterior world. This polarity was anchored in cognitive practive through clear borders and differences: mind was not matter, matter was not mind.

All these constellations shared giving the areas of mind and of matter their own structure and order, their own place. This also occurred at points where the many interferences and interdependencies between the two areas were principally recognized.

Cultural practice exists in a complexly woven cooperation of objects and subjects, mind and matter. But even where this togetherness was densely thickened and its dynamic and complexity grew exponentially, as in historic modernity, the foundationally placed spheres of mind and matter were principally imagined to be pure and unmixed, as unproblematically detachable from one another and essentially separate. The specifically Other in each sphere could be – at least in a reflexive and comprehensive analysis – removed without residue.

On such a horizon, the particularly unique quality of each sphere is determined in the conditional relationship between them: mind needs matter in order to be realized, matter needs mind in order to become a figure that goes beyond the contingency of natural form. In order to prevent the dissolution or the revelation of this culturally producing relationship, mind needed to push itself off of the material in the image it made of itself. In this way, mind hoped not to fall prey to a materialistic worldliness, which Descartes in his epistemological basis of autonomous subjectivity could only imagine as delusional tendencies. *What can I rely on if it is imaginable that everything I perceive is simply an illusion projected by a demon who wants to trick me?* This is the imaginary scenario with which Descartes arrived at the subject as a pure mind-based materialisation. Descartes' imagination of mind as that which is capable of withdrawing itself from entanglements with the world into that which it is essentially, has implicitly molded our ideas of the mind and the world throughout the centuries. This strict separation stirs the suspicion of the mind *visà-vis* the world, precisely because this purity is always threatened with contamination.

Stemming from the fear that the mind could lose aspects of its specificity whenever it becomes involved with matter, a certain ideological matrix became established which had epistemological consequences for centuries – from antique Greek philosophy all the way to the cultural religiosity of the educated middle class in the 19th and 20th centuries.

Adjusting continuously, this matrix certainly had to adapt to changing social life but its central idea remained stable: the hierarchical relationship into which mind – as higher principle – was coupled with the poorly esteemed matter, could be maintained through all external changes and reformulations of its central idea.

Plato's antique ideology already attributed to existing world objects an abstract world of ideas, which ahistorically, that is without history, quasi floated over their respective concrete manifestations in human cultural life, in which they were brought to their particular changeable and time-specific forms. Each given object thus has a "platonic" idea form which precedes it, which can never be completely abrogated, that is to say realized to its full extent in this material form.

Later in Europe, Christian thought which had become hegemonic took over this platonic Denkfigur and newly interpreted it in the special relation between God and the world. In this interpretation, the creation was the secondary execution of a primary creative potential attributable only to God.

Through the course of the Enlightenment, this potential became secularized and was reinterpreted to be genuinely human. Man was thusly transformed from created into creator. Man's technological and cultural achievements were material forms of a human spirit of invention, which once again needed to maintain distance to its creations. The human spirit of invention could only be and remain free – "unattached" and "autonomous" – in that it was fundamentally differentiated from the sphere of matter, of its creative and game material. In this way, history has often attributed more significance to the person of the inventor (as a vessel in which the abstract mind is articulated) as to the creation. This historical term "genius" is the Bekenntnisform of the admiration of creativity in creators, and not of what they created: the genius work is admired because genius is expressed in it and not vice versa.

In this way, the 18th and 19th century have prepared and passed on the idea of the "autonomous mind" in a way that remains effective until today. The autonomous existence of man as it is symbolically expressed in the aesthetic form of the art work and in the biographical form of the genius, has for centuries been based on the virulent and contemporary reformulation of the fundamental difference between mind and matter.

THE REMOVAL OF THE DIFFERENCE BETWEEN MIND AND MATTER IN THE DIGITAL AGE

However, this categorical difference becomes brittle at the point where matter stops existing as a solid and simultaneously autonomous reference *for itself*. The closer and the more precise science and technology have taken "matter" as an object of investigation, the stronger the previously unbreakable evidentiality of matter (as a specifically ontological category) began to dissolve, as a matter of fact in the objects of matter themselves. The previously unquestionable and seemingly self-explanatory difference between "mind" and "matter" appreciably disappeared. The natural sciences discovered previously unknown dimensions of the material, for example, the microorganisational level of atoms as a constitutive level of the world. The human sciences developed a new materialistic and also technicized understanding of mind which conceptualized the content of human consciousness and mental capacity as being determined by their material conditions. These were as a result no longer only vehicle or tool box for the mind. Ferdinand de Saussure saw linguistic signs themselves, Marshall McLuhan communicative forms – "the media" – as the origin of consciousness itself. With psychoanalysis, consciousness lost its autonomous shape in that to the "ego" an "id" and a "we" (the super ego) were added as a supplement. Consciousness became part and parcel of a psychic apparatus, which can tendentially be thought of as analogous to the machines which it also contrived.

And this psychical apparatus in turn was an effect of conditional relationships. In it experiences were collected and – exaggeratedly put – transformed into programs: behavioral patterns for example.

At least the world in and with which humans experienced things influenced consciousness in such a way that it became difficult to continue to plant an autonomous center of consciousness into this psycho-physical web, which was illuminated successively by psychology, neurobiology, and cybernetics. Furthermore, in the 20th century newer natural scientific disciplines replaced older human sciences when it came to understanding human thought and its processes.

While the classical, antique understanding – through all its historical changes – primarily saw mind as static and ahistorical, that is to say subtracted from the changing forms of human culture, modern and postmodern theory (from evolutionary biology to gender theory) saw it increasingly as the product of this change. It was not the issue of simply abrogating the old immateriality of thought as epistemological problem. In general, basic assumptions about the status of man in the world were destroyed.

The principle of the digital processing of information complicated the traditional opposition of "mind" and "matter" even more. Binary code, which lies at the foundation of digital appearances, is no longer integrated meaningfully and certainly not unquestionably into such a dual system. The physical object form, which long emblematically embodied the pole of matter, has in many areas – especially in that of mediality as the leading entity of everyday perception – given way to virtual storage for coded information. That computer-supported data processing could not be unproblematically attributed to the side of matter, was already shown in the fact that the binary thought tradition at first attempted to carry its dualism into the world of computers in that it differentiated between hardware and software components. It assumed that the computer was made up of two categorically separated areas: the "mind" and the "body."

With the Internet the spatial world is expanded by a virtual dimension, which certainly no longer functions as a medium for storage and communication but is increasingly incorporated into areas of human life. In this way, the Internet seems to have developed a life of its own in which we can see formations analogous to consciousness which certainly at the same time represent only transferences – in the shape of analogies and metaphors. The principally imaginary form of the Internet has sometimes led to its misconceptualization as a sort of meta-mind, which exists above or outside of the material world. The problematic notion of "virtuality" contains and transports this reading. In fact though, the Internet can no longer (at least not exclusively) be described in this way.

In its well-night "queer" ambivalence between object and mind, materiality and ideality, the Internet breaks through the traditional (conventional) dualism between mind and matter. This dualism has obviously not gone obsolete simply by this development, but through the existence of a third that is neither one nor the other but nevertheless combines aspects of both in itself, the rigid opposition in which object and mind have been fixed throughout centuries is gradually softened.

The ontological status of the Internet is perhaps best described by its common shorthand term the "web." The "web" of the Internet places not only various computer interfaces into a global non-hierarchical relationship but also terms and categories of different cultural worlds are brought into webbed contact.

As key medium of the present, the Internet has established digital forms of production, transformation, and spread of information as a standard in many areas of our cultural and social practice. And in the extent to which the informational and organizational forms of the Web permeate our daily life, so also the digital permeates our body. This still doesn't make the Web a gateway as popular cyborg fantasies fear and desire it. But on an everyday level we are nevertheless at a point at which we merge with the computer and become "digital everyday nomads."

For example, Web and computer carry consequences for our space-time organization. The time structure and signature of the digital society have transformed industrialized time, which depended on the specific cycle of the process of production. The mechanical, even, or "Fordist" time becomes accelerated, straightened, and flexibilized in the process of digitalization; and thus is also certainly (in a still Fordist sense) optimized. Production and reproduction – the two periodically each other completing cycles of the production process – were under Fordist conditions of the factory and its workplaces large and particularly closed blocks of time. Their continual alternation structured the life of the subject enveloped by it), just as the "natural" change of daylight did.

The simultaneous timelessness of the Web however allows a barely overseeable variety of individual time organizations. Similarly our forms of perception are digitally structured which plays out in our psyche, our subjectivity, our sensuality, and our reflexivity.

This is certainly not new because hegemonic technological and economic culture has always already reeducated and perhaps even constructed the body and mind of man. The character and purpose of technology is to adapt and soften us to its representational and presentational forms. However, the extent to which this is possible through digitalization is new. It creates the impression that we were actually partaking in this cultural paradigm shift, the consequential reach of which is not yet predictable. The old techno-utopia of the new creation of Man in the sign of digitality (for example as cyborg creatures in science fiction stories) here achieves plausibility.

Since the first stone-age tools, technology was an attempt to replace or extend the lacking human body with prosthesis. The computer first realized this on an intelligible level, namely as a form of "artificial intelligence." This artificial intelligence was achieved in that it managed to simulate two elementary functions of the human brain in one and the same machine: the calculator and the archive. In other words: the storage function and the ability to process abstract codes. The computer can, just like the human brain, not only store knowledge but also operationalize it, "think" with it. This is a capacity which long belonged only to the human brain. Only with the computer was the Auslagerung of human brain capacity in an extended and automatizable sense achieved, by which operations which went far beyond human capacities also became possible.

DIGITAL ART AND CULTURE AS CONSCIOUS PARTICIPATION IN AND SHAPING OF THE PARADIGM SHIFT

The process of cultural and technological digitization is not merely a section of everyday life that fits comparably next to other aspects and areas of life. A whole digital culture unto its own has developed. "Digital culture" here is an umbrella term for a dizzying array of organizational schemes and communication forms which reflect and highlight our digital everyday life.

Just as the digital seems to be able to abrogate the old difference between mind and matter so too the digital everyday dissolves the segmentation of industrial social forms in the areas of work and leisure. The digital not only creates new and categorically different professional occupations. It also arches over the many different areas of our everyday life: those belonging to the realm of production and those belonging to the realm of reproduction. Digital leisure takes place during or after digital work at the same time as digital sociality, which communicates and finds new friends over the web. This however raises the question whether this emerging digital society will overcome or rather exacerbate the structure of alienation in capitalist society.

What digitality means and how it can shape us must be decided by those that inhabit the digital world. The digital culture that surrounds us and structures us emerges through our own practice, which we should not surrender to as to fate but which we must consciously confront, for example by apprehending ourselves as digital culture. With such a self-conception we will better be able to engage creatively with the culture of the digital, which is already determining our subjectivity and which will continue to influence it with far-reaching consequences.

How we live, that is to say communicate, relax, work, and experience a digital world is one of the most significant questions of the present.

The design of digital spaces of encounter and communication has always been an important issue for web culture. From early on digital culture has attempted to establish its own culture of the digital that would better meet the needs of people as the exploitation of the digital by an economized mode of domination could, which is defined by the implicit force of exchange.

This area encompasses foundational theoretical considerations on the egalitarian potential of the digital as well as practical accords regarding digital communicative forms, such as "netiquette," which regulates modes of behavior in digital spaces, or also emoticons which attempt to add the communicative dimension of aural and expressive signals and accents to email communication.

Digital art has also early on developed out of and as a sub-domain of general forms of digital culture. Just as art refers to the framework of reality in which it emerged, so too does digital art relate to and work with the material reality of the digital world. Digital art manipulates the material of its reality in the old way of art: in that it represents and engages with digital reality, participating in and changing it. As such, digital art, like earlier arts forms, attempts to reflect on the digital world in which we work, live, and encounter each other. In this way, the functional mechanisms of the digital world should become apparent in order to understand what extent digital reality too is only a reverberation of the late capitalist conditions in which it emerges.

This may help to relativize overblown demands of the digital (as a formal revolutionizing of communicational media) and to put exact knowledge of the possibilities and potentials of the digital in the pace of media-specific illusions and idealistic projections, which in the sense of the old hierarchy of mind and matter are already proclaiming a possible transformation of consciousness as a wholesale modification of the world. With this, however, they only continue to deceive themselves as to their own dependency on late capitalist relations of reality.

At this point, an opportunity is created to show what else might be possible through the technological revolution if it allowed itself to be extracted from its entanglement in economic exploitation. That, however, the majority of digital practices verily supports and maintains this exploitation must certainly always be considered. This concerns, for example, questions of the historically older copyright which is confronted with a digital copyright reality in which protectable originals no longer exist due to the specific ontology of digital artifacts as reproductions. In this way, digital art is today carrier of a utopian as well as practical enlightening potential, which constitutes art in each of its historical manifestations, but which nevertheless always collides with its at least apparently opposed system-stabilizing role.

Unfortunately, this potential is often blurred due to certain manifestations of digital art which sometimes disclose themselves as banal and unreflected expositions of specific digital design options. That such media art is often hardly distinguishable from "advertising" is its own succinct judgment. This deficiency is exacerbated by a false and abbreviated public perception which deriving from an outdated world view, thinks that in digital art it only sees games with technical gadgets.

In contrast, paraflows 2010 makes a different demand of digital art and culture: the technically possible should be engaged in its concrete practice as in its founding theory. Technology may not be left to those who would only incorporate it in to what exists and make us of it according to its requirements. Digital art which only concerns itself with the realization of technology as art merely accentuates and ornaments exploitative interests in that it concretizes all utopian content of the technical into a bonsaiform of bafflement.

New technologies not only open up new possibilities for action in ways that enable us to do things which we were previously incapable of, and which we would then only have to falsify and verify – either practically or aesthetically – with the help of technological artifacts. Every technology contains – in the specific use which it enables, in it being "ready-to-hand" – the potential of new experiences, different apperceptions and illegitimate forms of thought. This is also valid for those technologies which are not available for our own individual use but those of whose existence (its "present-at-hand") we are aware of because they represent the technical standard of our time.

For example, human space travel has already changed our picture of the universe in which we live even though we ourselves are not yet in the position to leave the earth. This will continue to be the privilege of specialists who travel into space under the assignment of others who undertake this because of economic and/or ideological interests as is exemplified by the classic "space race" between the USA and the USSR. With the history of human space travel, a new horizon of possibility emerged which was expressed in countless utopian or dystopian narratives. The space age – the threshold of which we are just stepping onto – has activated human imagination to come up with new modes of living together which are sometimes based on entirely different forms of economic organization. What is decisive here is not so much the realistic quality of these designs as simply their very existence which rather points out: when the technological foundations of a society change then its entire heretofore known form is at our disposal.

That this was made possible is also related to the fact that with space travel human culture has again entered an unknown, not yet discovered and possibly endless space which seems to dissolve previous regulatory forms of the imaginative world determined by its close connection to "earthly conditions." With space, the unthinkable has become thinkable again, for example, in the shape of an imaginable outside perspective on human cohabitation. This outside perspective is determined in the (narrative) possibility to confront this world with the intelligent inhabitants of other worlds.

In this way, technology designs and changes our access to the world. The digital appropriation and transformation of data not only gives us new modes of action but also implements entirely new ideas of what may be possible.

The utopia – or at least the future promise – of the digital exists in the overcoming of the dualistic imprint in which our thought always only perpetuates old orders. Both mind and matter are in the process of combining in a way that would render impossible their re-opposition into wholly unrelated components. It may be speculated how soon this may arrive as well as what shape this materiality of the digital may take.

But it is conceivable (and desirable) that the relation produced by this specific combination would no longer be one of domination and exploitation of one by the other, just as the old relationship of mind and matter always helped to illustrated and legitimize relations and relational dimensions of domination. This may be the emergence of a certain kind of artificial intelligence which we believe to be seeing on the horizon of digital technology of which current computer technology is only a glimpse that equips its promise with plausibility.

How exactly a true artificial intelligence may be positioned and how it will relate to us and our needs is never predetermined. Even the capitalist conditions from and out of which we imagine artificial intelligence today can only relatively convey their determining forces onto this intelligence. Before us lies the unknown, with unknown consequences on what is and what will be.

In this connection we must actively engage in shaping the (always insufficient) ideas we are already forming of this technological revolution through which we will be firstly confronted with real artificial intelligence. Only in this way can we prevent it from becoming merely a tool for exploitative interests which deprive us of our access and our engagement in the matter because the intentions which they attempt to realize will not be our own – and certainly not those of the majority of the world's population – but rather the particular interests of the ruling classes.

At the intersection of new technologies and utopian ideas possibilities for intervention arise that challenge and question the old political and economic order. Before this potential emerges the already historically known practice of obfuscation that describes the digital as a revolution in which the technical always already implies the political.

Digital culture has to take a stand on this issue if it seeks to be more than just advertising for new gadgets, machines, and technologies that merely reproduce the already extant on the next evolutionary level.

Artificial consciousness could definitely render obsolete the "natural" (that is naturalized) form of consciousness, which today still keeps us under the spell of countless ideological affiliations. We will however have to make sure that the potentials of digitality are indeed set free. They must be liberated from the narrow confines of exploitative interests which only want to use these potentials to optimize various problems; they must be freed from a relative deterritorialization, which will only have been a reterritorialization.

These battles have already begun: the digital conditions of cultural work and the digitalization of cultural artifacts have put the old concept of the "common good" on the agenda again; primarily in the shape of the "creative commons" which resists still existing but unnecessarily restrictive copyright. The copyright – the author's exclusive exploitation right of his or her "intellectual property" – originates from the historical formation of the age of the printing press. Marshall McLuhan catchily dubbed it the "Gutenberg galaxy." Digital work and cultural practices – as well as their potential – are inhibited by such a copyright. Sooner or later, these practices will change the existing copyright to fit new possibilities, instead of submitting to it. The classic bourgeois copyright must be overcome precisely because it represents a limitation of cultural production and distribution as well as of democratic participation in given goods and possibilities.

What was foremost only articulated as a diffuse desire for freedom and boundlessness in the realm of digital media use has long since entered non-digital areas as well. The discussion surrounding the so-called "commons" has named and connected numerous things that have been privatized and exploited in the realm of private property: genetic codes of healing plants as well as traditional knowledge, natural resources (such as oil, air, water, and earth). The term "commons" wants to reclaim these things for the common good and ownership, piggy-backing on the popularity of "creative commons", which have for a few years now broached the issue of the disastrous consequences of "private property" on our lives.

In the face of the digital it has become plausible that we ourselves participate in the creation and optimization of artificial consciousness. We have become responsible. And we are primarily given the opportunity to break away from our programmed behaviors that make our consciousness a condensation of societal reality, determining who we are supposed to be.

In inference of our digital everyday experience on our life we could develop the idea of proceeding with "consciousness" as we are used to proceeding with "artificial intelligence": we can deprogram it, reconfigure it, format it, upgrade it, and delete certain program features that we no longer need. We could hack our gender and manipulate the source code of our subjectivity. This is surely not as easy as is suggested by the techno-euphoric and heavily "analog" application of digital terms to our "operating system." And it will surely not always be as easy as we are used to from the user-friendly and self-explanatory technologies that surround us. What is important, however, is that with the help of artificial intelligence it has become possible to newly conceive of our own consciousness and to open a horizon of understanding in which such interventions become acceptable.

The digital age also puts us in the position of being able to model artificial intelligence according to laws that are no longer the laws of nature (that is to say evolutionary) which still dominate our consciousness. "Human nature" (the specifically historical form of human naturalization) was long considered to be man's doom and fate in order to implement dominant and exploitative interests in the subjects: as the logical and necessary consequence of their internal constitution (for example as "women"). Under the transformed premises of mind under the sign of digitality, these "constitutions" can be newly negotiated and changed.

Now that digital technology puts us on the threshold of being able to artificially produce consciousness, this also implies the possibility of participating in the design of this (artificial) consciousness and not to leave it to those who would "design" it according to the old ways of capitalist production (on the basis of the market and its struggles of competition). Differing from these technocrats of new possibilities, we must work towards developing an artificial consciousness that represents advancement vis-à-vis traditional Western forms of consciousness. It must correct the dualistic opposition between Western consciousness and materiality and overcome its disposition towards the idealistic repression of the world and the body. If we succeed, we will not only have produced our own consciousness as something artificial, we will have improved it and with it transformed the world that generates it and perceives it.

If we as digital culture can agree that the possibilities of artificial forms of consciousness should not only reflect the individual interests of particular departments for product development (and their clients), we must counter with collective and webbed work forms. The possibility to create artificial consciousness and thus change humans as well as "cultural consciousness" demands overcoming the old monadic departmentalization of development. This possibility demands new forms and terms of team work that can rupture old borders of operational and national competition and put into motion a new human consciousness.

Such a possibility emerges as a rule where new instruments of production are introduced. We have already missed the last opportunity in this sense – classical industrialization (and also Soviet communism was only an attempt to introduce corrective measures after the fact). With digitalization we are presented with a new opportunity, even if today's instruments of production are still determined by the old order of the industrial revolution.

It is the mission of digital art to oppositionally claim a space, at least symbolically, that goes against the capitalist conditions under which instruments of production are owned, managed, and used. It must thus not only participate in the design of artificial consciousness and thus remove it from the influence of product designers, but this digital art must also show different forms of working which hold together a common consciousness that opposes the consciousness of the individualized late-capitalist subject.

It must actively engage in creating a new consciousness stemming from the artificial, which will either be a "common" in itself or simply the old consciousness in new clothes. Artificial consciousness must belong to all of us, simply because it will transform our lives in unforeseeable ways.

THE MATERIALITY OF DATA: ON THE FRAGILITY OF THE DISEMBODIED

Of special significance is of course the problem of data materiality which will be granted a particularly large space at paraflows 2010. In this regard, it is shown that the digital has never been the freely floating technology as which it has been imagined. Precisely the problem of the data storage medium in the application, archiving, and maintenance of digital cultural artifacts reveals this: as a product of a specific technology, data storage media are always tied to a medial substrate, to the technology which enables the reading of existing data and its conversion for later generations.

The scenario of technological development is currently closer to a "Babylonian data confusion" which foresees that the supralinguisticality of digital codes as the language of culture and communication could end up in the confusion of incompatibilities and technological uncontemporaneity. This might be especially likely if we leave the technological foundations of digital culture up to private market forces which will only ever be concerned with individual interests and never with what concerns us all.

A special way of counteracting the market-oriented closure of the digital public sphere is the idea of open source which develops information technologies as a collective project. The wide influence and significance of digital culture in areas far beyond the Internet and personal computers is clearly evidenced by the many projects and ideas which have been inspired by open source in realms that don't directly belong to the field of digital culture. We would also like to counter the transience of digital culture with exhibits from the early ages of digital art. Together with current exhibits, they will communicate the polymorphism of digital culture and should inspire participation in its development.

OPEN QUESTIONS AGAINST THE MARKET-ORIENTED CLOSURE OF DIGITAL CULTURE

The fifth paraflows-festival for digital art and culture would like to direct its attention to those positions and practices within the digital art world, which ask about the particular potentials held by digitality, and further, which engage with the contemporary (realist, critical, and enlightening) as well as future (and utopian) potential of digital art.

Starting from positions formulated by paraflows in the last few years centering on the idea of space, the festival in 2010 will focus on digital users:

How does digitality change what we are or think to be? In which ways are we already cultural cyborgs and how can we appropriate this status for ourselves in order to use it for our age-old or completely new developing interests? Which subjectivity does the digital enable and to what extent is the old dualism of humans dissolved in mind and matter? What utopian potential and which fundamental changes will the new world composed of digital life, digital media, and digital art hold for us? And how do we want to treat this promise? What would we like to accomplish?

We would like to show that digital art – like all other art forms – is complex and multi-layered, and that in it exists successful and unsuccessful, productive and inappropriate articulations of problems, which do not correspond to the publicly circulating image of digital art as an adventure park of technology nerds. The digital art which paraflows wants to present and tie together lays claims, to be tied to late modernist conceptual art, to give us a developed shape as a special form of the imaginary and the virtual that already envelops us completely as the real.

1. Archives

Image Science & MediaArtHistories

New Infrastructures for 21st Century Digital Humanities

OLIVER GRAU

Never before has the world of IMAGES around us changed so fast in such a short span of time: images are advancing, as we see, into new domains: private platforms like YouTube, Flickr with its 5 billion uploads or Facebook that has received its 500 millionth member; Television became a zappy field of thousands of channels; now in 3D – and, as we know, 3D experiences a renaissance in Cinema as well; huge projection screens are invading our cities, cell phones transmit micromovies in real time and buildings surfaces meld ever more often with moving images, so that the old dream of talking architecture gets a new push and a whole new arsenal of options. *Google Street View* and *Google Earth* step up the concepts of panoramic image spaces in an unknown way, including satellite view.

The images' historical development between innovation, reflection and iconoclasm reaches a new level of global complexity in the 21st century. Society, to a large extent, has been hit unprepared for these transformations. Digital images became ubiquitous and key tools within the global reorganisation of work. They aid in understanding the most complex mathematical formulas and we have to recognize that we will not be able to handle the knowledge societies of our time without further development of new forms of visualization and "orders of visibility". We are witnessing the rise of the image into a virtual spatial image. These are images, which appear capable of changing interactively or even "autonomously" and of formulating a life-like, all-embracing audiovisual and sensory sphere, where temporal and spatial parameters can be altered at will.[1]

MEDIA ART'S STATUS NOWADAYS

Within this rapid development Media art has evolved over the last thirty years into a vivid contemporary force, Digital Art became the art of our time but arrives only slowly into the core cultural institutions of our societies, although it is the art of the widest need. It is the Media Art with its multifarious potential of expression and visualization, which thematizes complex challenges of our societies like globalization, knowledge explosion, genetic engineering, ecological crises and so forth.

Therefore Media Art needs as many Bridges as possible provided by Image Science for the Digital Humanities: conferences, new scientific tools like Databases and Text Repositories, new preservation strategies, new curricula for the next generation of teachers and collectors and new Strategies for visual analysis of complex data.

We know that media artists today are shaping highly disparate areas, like time based installation art, telepresence art, genetic and bio art, robotics, Net Art, and space art; experimenting with nanotechnology, artificial or A-life art; creating virtual agents and avatars, mixed realities, and database-supported art. These artworks both represent and reflect the revolutionary development that the image has undergone over the past years.

INTEGRATING MEDIA ART INTO OUR CULTURAL HISTORIES

The evolution of media art has a long history and now a new technological variety has appeared. However, this art cannot be fully understood without its history. Image Science might help to understand today's image worlds in their society leading and forming function. With the history of illusion and immersion, the history of artificial life or the tradition of telepresence, Image Science offers sub-histories of

---

1 | See: Oliver Grau: Virtual Art: From Illusion to Immersion, Cambridge/Mass., MIT-Press 2003.

the present image revolutions: Image Science might be considered as the political battle ground where the clash of images is analysed. Not at least, the development of new media may be illuminated since the first utopian expressions often take place in artworks and to better understand our present and our goals in a period where the pace appears to get faster and faster.

All of those approaches of comparison are based on the insight that images act diachronic, within a historical evolution and never function simply as an act and without reference. Let's remind ourselves, that scientific work with images, image science, is based on three pre-conditions: 1. definition of the object, 2. setup of an image archive and 3. familiarity with a large quantity of images. Without this historic base, image science remains superfluous and cannot realize its full potential. If those pre-conditions are fulfilled, image science may be practiced within many fields - medicine, biology or history of collections. Image Science, or Bildwissenschaft, now allows writing the history of the evolution of the visual media, from peep-show to panorama, stereoscope, magic lantern, phantasmagoria, films with odours and colours, IMAX to the virtual image spaces of computers. It is an evolution with breaks and detours; however, all its stages are distinguished by a relationship between art, science, and technology and Image Science is an open field resulting from the interplay with neuroscience, psychology, philosophy, emotions research, just to name a few.

We know that a central problem of current cultural policy stems from serious lack of knowledge about the origins of the audiovisual media and this stands in complete contradiction to current demands for more media and image competence. Considering the current upheavals and innovations in the media sector, where the societal impact and consequences cannot yet be predicted, the problem is acute. That's why MediaArtHistories held its first international Conference, which I served as its chair, in 2005 at Banff representing the wide array of 19 disciplines involved in the emerging field of Media Art Histories - and the news is, through the success of the following conferences in Berlin and Melbourne an established conference series has been founded. For 2011 Liverpool is on its way and for 2013 Toronto, Mexico City and Paris applied.[2]

---

2 | See: Oliver Grau (Ed.): MediaArtHistories, Cambridge Mass., MIT-Press 2007.

For education Media Art within the Digital Humanities means the establishment of new curricula, as we developed the first international Master in MediaArtHistories, with faculty members from across the globe, it gives an overview of the most important developments of media art in the last decades and teaches the latest expertise in Curation, Collecting, Preserving and Archiving of Media Arts.[3]

FROM THE MDEMOSYNE ATLAS TO THE VIRTUAL MUSEUM

Inspired by Darwin´s work "The Expression of the Emotions" Aby Warburg, an inspirational figure comparable with Freud or Einstein, began his project of an art-historical psychology of human expression. His famous »Mnemosyne«- image atlas of 1929 tracks image citations of individual poses and forms across media and independent from the level of art niveau or genre. He redefined art history as medial bridge building and argued that art history could fulfil its responsibility only by including most forms of images.[4] We could also mention André Malreaux with the *Museé Imaginare*.[5] And now we are witnessing the birth of the virtual museum a key project for the Digital Humanities.

NEW RESEARCH INFRASTRUCTURES FOR THE HUMANITIES

But let's look for a moment beyond the Humanities: in the natural sciences large collective projects have addressed new research goals: the *Virtual Observatory* enables hundreds of networked astronomical research institutes to access the pooled resources of image and data materials, sparing the bulk of tedious work and maximising the efficiency & concentration of astronomers both professional and amateurs; global warming is understood with collective projects like the

---

3 | www.donau-uni.at/mah
4 | Martin Warnke u. Claudia Brink (Ed.): *Der Bilderatlas MNEMOSYNE*, Berlin 2000.
5 | *Psychologie de l'Art: Le Musée imaginaire − La Création artistique − La Monnaie de l'absolu*, Paris 1947-1948-1950.

Millenium Ecosystem Assignment. And the fast success of the *Human Genome Project* enabled by its collective organisation already became legend. So far unknown collective structures allow answers to new and complex problems.

So why not enable the Humanities to address and solve new complex questions important for our knowledge societies as well. Why not organize an approach of an adequate scale and give the next generation of artists, researchers, curators, media producers and collectors what they need? Comparable with natural sciences, digital media and new opportunities of networked research catapult the humanities within reach of new and essential research, from documentation and preservation of media art to the entire history of visual media and their human reception by means of thousands of sources. These themes express in regard to image revolution current key questions. In order to push the development of humanities and cultural studies, it is necessary to use the new technologies globally. The credo is: not to give up the individual research in the humanities, but add new collective, net based working methods which allow us to tackle explosive questions.

Example of a virtual museum is the first documentation of Media Art, the Database of Virtual Art, which started 10 years ago.[6] As probably the most complex resource available online: hundreds of leading artists are represented with several thousand documents the database became a platform for information and communication. We know that today's digital artworks are processual, ephemeral, interactive, multimedial, and fundamentally context dependent. Because of their completely different structure and nature, they require a modification we call an "expanded concept of documentation".[7] The DVA represents the scientific selection of 500 artists of approx 5000 evaluated artists - high importance we ascribe to artistic inventions like innovative interfaces, displays or software, which could give future students a systematic overview of the enormous variety developed during the

---

6 | www.virtualart.at

7 | For an Expanded Concept of Documentation: The Database of Virtual Art, ICHIM, École du Louvre, Cultural institutions and digital technology, acte publié avec le soutien de la Mission de la Recherche et de la Technologie du Ministère de lla Culture et de la Communication, Paris 2003, Proceedings, CD-Rom, pp. 2-15.

last decades by artist. In addition to thematic searches future Media Art documentation should also allow questions of gender, tracking technical staff from lab to lab, artistic technical inventions, the use of public and private funds allocated to research, and, through a thematic index, show reminiscences of virtual/immersive art in the forms of its predecessors, for example, the panorama. Media Art documentation becomes a resource that facilitates research on the artists and their work for students and academics, who, it is hoped, will contribute to expanding and updating the information. In this way, documentation changes from a one-way archiving of key data to a proactive process of knowledge transfer. Yet, the tools only hold the data – the quality of the analysis continues to rely on thoughtful developments in the Digital Humanities, on projects like the ambitious research on culture analysis Lev Manovich is doing in San Diego[8] and of course Jeffrey Shaw's ongoing work with iCinema.[9]

But bridging the gap of media art documentation means now also the integration into historic treasures of art, so together with probably one of the most important unpublished art collections, the Göttweig print collection[10], with 30 thousand prints of Renaissance and Baroque works and a library of 150.000 volumes going back to the 9th century, like the Sankt Gallen Codex, the Database of Virtual Art strives to achieve the goal of a deeper mediaarthistorical cross pollination. The combination of these two and other databases hopes to enable further historic references and impulses. The collection also contains proof of the history of optical image media, intercultural concepts, caricatures, illustrations of landscapes in panoramic illustrations. For the future this will provide resources for a broader analysis of media art. For the first time a Media-Art and a Classic-Art Database will amalgamate through a new keyword-system. From here networking with other databases especially outside Europe and the US is of great importance.

---

8 | Lev Manovich and Jeremy Douglass: Visualising temporal patterns in Visual Media, in: Oliver Grau (Ed.): Imagery of the 21st Century, Cambridge Mass., MIT-Press 2011 (forthcoming).
9 | www.icinema.unsw.edu.au/
10 | www.gssg.at

THE LOSS OF MEDIA ART'S DOCUMENTATION ARCHIVES

Since the foundation of the Database of Virtual Art a number of online archives for documentation arose, Langlois Foundation in Canada, V2 in the Netherlands, C3 in Budapest, Netzspannung at the Frauenhofer Institut, the Boltzmann Institute or MedienKunstNetz at ZKM – all these projects have terminated, lost key researcher or their funding expired. Among all these projects the DVA is one of the only left standing, leaving a real reduction of materials for research on contemporary art. These evolving archives – our scientific tools – more and more provide the only remaining image source of the works to be explored. A standstill and decease of these archives makes them losing their significance for research, while contemporary digital art continues. So ironically not only media art but also its documentation vanishes and future generations will have no access to the works of the past.

Even the Europeana[11], a large but underfunded project for Europe-wide networks of digital collection documentation is rendered meaningless if the foundation, the archives themselves, is not continued. If we take a look at research on media art over the last 15 years then it is clear: what we need is a concentration of high quality scholarly documentation as well as a huge expansion of strength and initiative. In the field of documentation – systematic and concerted preservation does not exist so far – it is essential to unite the most important lessons learned and strategies developed by initiatives either existing or abandoned under the single roof of an international institution that can guarantee persistent existence. A location such as the *Library of Congress* or the *Bibliotheque National* or/and an Institution in Asia would need to be supported with adequate expertise from the network of important archives & initiatives.

Besides insuring the foundation of documentation, also the establishment of an appropriate research institution bringing together the best heads of the field would be necessary. In Germany, for example, for extensive interdisciplinary questions, too extensive for a single university – and that is exactly what we are facing with research on digital cultures from computer games to avant-garde art – the Max Planck Institute structure could fill this need. At the same time, the European Commission has expressed that to reach its goals in ICT

---

11 | http://www.europeana.eu/portal/

(Information and Communication Technologies) the research funds should be doubled especially for pilot projects in interdisciplinary fundamental research.[12] More: the funding structures themselves must be internationalized in ways similar to those enabling modern astronomy, genomics and climatology. To create enough momentum and the necessary sustainability, responsible sponsors like NSF, SNF, DFG, Volkswagen and EU have to ensure international long-term sustainable structures. In astronomy the funding agencies developed and modernised into a sustainable structure, which is needed as well in the humanities. The virtual observatory infrastructure is funded on an ongoing basis and there is international coordination between a dozen or so countries that produce astronomical data. Only when we develop systematic and concentrated strategies of collecting, preservation and research we will be able to fulfill the task which the digital culture demands from Image Science and the Humanities in the 21st Century.[13]

Such a commitment by experts from the field is needed today, as like the enormous and sustaining infrastructure that was established for traditional artistic media: painting, sculpture, architecture, even film, photography over the last century. What is urgently needed is the establishment of an appropriate structure to preserve at least the usual 3-6 per cent of present media art production, the best works. This important step is still missing for media art from the first two generations. The faster this essential modification to our cultural heritage record can be carried out, the smaller the gap in the cultural memory; shedding light on the dark years, which started about 1960 and lasts till now.

The hope for the future is, that we can bring together the expertise of the most important institutions in order to form an up to date overview of the whole field, to provide the necessary information for new preservation programs within the museum field, new university teaching programs for a better training of the next generation of historians, curators, restorers, engineers and others involved in the

---

12 | "Eine Digitale Agenda für Europa": http://eur-lex.europa.eu/LexUriServ/LexUriServ.do?uri=COM:2010:0245:FIN:DE:PDF

13 | Recently this approach was presented by myself at the G20 summit in Seoul at "tech+ forum 2010" (sponsored by the G-20 Summit), Jamsil Gym, by Invitation of the Ministry of Knowledge Economy (MKE) of the Republic of Korea, 09.11.2010.

preservation and new form of open access to media art. Just as research in the natural sciences has long recognised team efforts, a similar emphasis on collaborative research should make its way into the thinking of the humanities.

Maybe in a very near future we can create collective tools, as represented in Christa Sommerer and Laurent Mignonneaus work *The Living Web*, which generates a spatial information sphere from search engines for web images in a CAVE. The work is a new instrument for visual analysis, with the option of comparing up to 1000 images in a scientific discussion. A very advanced scientific but also entertaining instrument could be the *iCinema*, connected with advanced databases, like the Database of Virtual Art. It would allow analysis of large amounts of visual material and would help to better understand the development of ideas and the combination and creation of new ones in an unknown, striking way.

When these captivating new tools provide access to the breath of digital cultural production coupled with the depth of historical optical media, new unpredictable understandings of today's image revolution will be enabled. When our societies can better understand why we create ever new illusive media and new optical technologies this will lift our digital society into a new paradigm of understanding and media competency with the example of its passage through media by art.

The Archive as the Repertoire
Mediated and Embodied Practice on Imageboard 4chan.org

JANA HERWIG

IT'S A DANCE, NOT A WEBSITE

In the years 2008 to 2010, imageboard website 4chan.org achieved considerable notoriety both within the wider web community and by mainstream media. Three main incidents and their mediatisation contributed to this relative rise to fame of an otherwise modest seeming website and its unassuming owner, Christopher Poole aka moot, who founded the board in 2003 when was 15, seeking to create an English language alternative to Japanese imageboards. 4chan first drew the attention of corporate news media in early 2008, when video material of Hollywood actor Tom Cruise, enthusiastically praising the merits of pseudo-religious organization Scientology, was leaked on the Internet, followed by attempts of the organization to suppress the material, citing copyright infringement. This was the prelude to 'Project Chanology', also known as the 'War on Scientology', an ad hoc activist cause organized on the web, involving both attacks on Scientology infrastructures as well as demonstrations outside of Scientology centres. The collective behind the cause referred to itself as "Anonymous", a name derived from the default user name on 4chan.org, where registering and thus laying an exclusive claim on a nick name is impossible. When appearing in public, members of "Anonymous" wore Guy Fawkes masks in the style popularized by *V for Vendetta*, the graphic novel and film. The second incident: in 2009, moot was voted top finalist in the TIME 100 Internet poll, earning him the title of the world's most influential person. "Moot denies knowing about any concerted plan by his followers to influence the poll, though TIME.com's technical team did detect and extinguish several attempts to hack the vote."[1] This estimation provided by TIME staff would emerge as wishful thinking: the initials of moot and the next 20 finalists' first names spelled the phrase M-A-R-B-L-E-C-A-K-E A-L-S-O T-H-E G-A-M-E – marblecake reportedly being the name of the IRC channel used to organize the scientology protests, and "the game" referring to an inside joke of Internet culture, where thinking or reading about the game inevitably meant losing the game. Rather than having extinguished hacking attempts, the vote had been the result of a precision hack.[2] The third boost in public recognition came with the appearance of Christopher Poole as an invited speaker at the TED 2010 conference, discussing "The case for anonymity online",[3] which centred on 4chan.org's policy of neither requiring a user registration nor keeping records of posted data. With the exemption of web server and banned user logs,[4] all messages and images published on 4chan.org are deleted routinely. There is no 4chan archive, at least not on 4chan.org itself. Instead, users keep copies of images and screenshots of conversations they deem worth preserving on their computers; if the occasion arises, they might use these personal, sediment-like archives to weave some of their contents back into the forum discussion or to contribute to the documentation of highlights to websites such as the wiki-based EncyclopediaDramatica.com (see also: section 5). Christopher Poole has accredited 4chan's reputation as a "meme factory" – a place where Internet memes, i.e. viral jokes in form of text or image, are likely to originate – to this lack of retention and resulting reliance upon user interaction. As he stated in a talk given at the 2009 *Paraflows* symposium:[5]

The way kind of threads work on 4chan is that if you post something and it's crap, it's washed away. The site has no memory and it's just washed

---

1 | TIME 2009

2 | The blogger Paul Lamere (2009) documented the precision hack, based on hints he had received from an icognito hacker through IRC.

3 | Poole 2010

4 | These log files became instrumental in a court case against the hacker who targeted Sarah Palin's Yahoo account. Cf. US District Court 2010: 15-16

5 | Poole 2009

away by all of these new posts. And if it's a genuinely good idea or something that people identify with then either somebody will save it and repost it and that's how we get memes.

The 'meme factory' approach thus takes a quasi-evolutionary stance: only the best (funniest, weirdest, boldest) ideas survive. It is true that meme theory – as proposed by Richard Dawkins and furthered by Susan Blackmore – has won new popularity with the emergence of Internet memes such as Rickrolling and Lolcats,[6] yet its analytical gain is mostly limited to the observation that *something* is being passed on. While disciplines such as linguistics and semiotics have developed a rich vocabulary for classifying elements that carry and convey meaning – e.g. seme as the smallest unit of meaning in words, phoneme as the smallest unit of sound, more complex semiotic systems such as Christian Metz' "grande syntagmatique"[7] for classifying sequences in film –, meme theory subsumes virtually all things and phenomena under the concept of the meme: "tunes, ideas, catch-phrases, clothes fashions, ways of making pots or of buildings arches" (Dawkins),[8] left-hand traffic, right-hand traffic, or a predilection for "Currywurst" (Blackmore).[9] Still, the revival of meme theory is little surprising if one considers that the digital domain has brought forth the 'killer app' of all cultural techniques for passing things on: *copy-and-paste*.

But even copy-and-paste is not a virus that propagates without the action and intervention of human beings: with the following discussion, I am going to reach out for the *human, embodied factor* in human-computer interaction, a factor which, curiously, is often neglected in debates of the cultural consequences of emerging technologies. Does our body indeed become obsolete if we engage online, or less relevant than the information that is being exchanged? Instead of thinking of forums such as 4chan.org as a competition of bodiless ideas, I propose to think of it as a dance: as something that requires the

---

6 | Rickrolling: the practice of distributing a seemingly interesting link ('This is cool, check this out!') which, when opened, starts the music video "Never Gonna Give You Up" by Rick Astley. Lolcats: photographs of cats with captions that comment the scene or voice the animal's 'thoughts'.
7 | Metz 1966
8 | Dawkins 2006: 192
9 | Quoted from Meister/Simon/Teichmann 2003

communion and participation of humans, their simultaneous engagement with each other and with the cultural meaning of the artefacts they exchange, rhythmically and periodically, both making use of and collaborating with the digital technology at hand. Such a dance, inevitably, must transgress the borders between mind and matter, media and body, information and perception, which the dominant discourse has so meticulously established.

THE REAL VS. VIRTUAL FALLACY

From its inception and continuing into the present, the discourse about online interaction has been marked by the insistence that the distinction between offline and online, between face-to-face and mediated encounters must be congruent with the distinction between the 'real' and the 'virtual' and its various derivatives: factual versus fictitious, true versus false, authentic versus deceptive, embodied and reliable versus fleeting and fickle. The assumptions that underlie such divisions between 'real' life and the "consensual hallucination" (William Gibson) that has come to be understood as cyberspace – specifically the assumption that online interaction must be understood as a *disembodied* form of interaction – often go unchallenged. I thus seek to contest this view of the virtual as a disembodied sphere of media or as a lesser reality, departing from two propositions:

First, and from a phenomenological perspective,[10] online interaction is always already inclusive of the body. This requires that we accept that the phenomena appearing on a computer screen are not brought forth by themselves, but to appear require the existence of a body acting as the subject of perception. From such a perspective, virtual reality, cyberspace, or online interaction do not appear as belonging to the realm of pure data and information, not as a sole affair of the mind, but as simultaneously pertaining to a living, breathing body, a body-subject situated in front of a device. Appearance and perception coincide in phenomena, a separation of one from the other, of aspects of the mind from aspects of the body is impossible. The phenomenological approach seems particularly fitting for a discussion of human-computer interaction as the phenomena on the screen are also intimately tied to the behaviour and response of the body-subject:

---

10 | Cf. Merleau-Ponty 1945

A computer without any input device – the most basic: the POWER button – does yet have to be conceived (and for now exists merely in the science fiction of singularity prophets). The means to translate human thought, behaviour and even emotion[11] into computable input are varied and many; we need not resort to a machine that is able to divine the user's thought, the keyboard serves this purpose well (and as a writing tool, as Nietzsche has noted, works on our thoughts as well). Online interaction – which builds on human-computer interaction and adds to it the specificities of a website's interaction design – depends even more profoundly on an incessant stream of user interaction: If nobody ever moved a cursor, clicked buttons, entered letters, hit 'enter' keys, the whole World Wide Web would immediately go into a deep state of hibernation.

Secondly, to interact online does not mean to engage solely with a machine, but is always embedded in social scenarios. While this seems particularly applicable to the type of online interaction that can be found on the so-called Web 2.0 or Social Web, the ability to harness the power of the social and to foster community has been a characteristic of online interaction since the days of the electronic bulletin board. The social manifests itself in various forms online: for instance in dialogic forms such as text or video chat or forums, which resemble or mimic face-to-face-communication or other, older forms of mediated communication, but also in data-driven scenarios: for instance in form of tag suggestions based on user behaviour in social bookmarking services (e.g. delicious.com) or rankings of content items based on popularity with users. Social relevance is not immediately related to whether an interaction took place online or face-to-face: an email exchange, a forum discussion, the number of views on your online video, all these are mediated forms of interaction, and they are undoubtedly socially relevant. Online interaction, due to its social dimension, reaches beyond the boundaries of the human-computer interface and beyond the content dimension of the bytes loaded in a website, to include the activities of all users (all body-subjects) who are contributing or have contributed to the interaction, who have left behind data traces and shaped its conventions. To be able to grasp what is brought in by the participation and performance of the users, I am going to explore this entanglement of information technology and the collective of body-subjects in more detail, building on the distinction

---

11 | Cf. Machulis 2011, in this volume

between the archive and the repertoire as suggested by performance studies scholar Diana Taylor.[12]

ARCHIVAL MEMORY AND EMBODIED PRACTICE

"My particular investment in performance studies", Taylor writes, "derives less from what it *is* than what it allows us to *do*. By taking performance seriously as a system of learning, storing and transmitting knowledge, performance studies allows us to expand what we understand by 'knowledge.'"[13] In particular embodied practices such as song, dance, and ritual have been excluded from the script-dominated Western canon of legitimate knowledge – yet it would be too simple too dismiss this conflict as one of written and oral culture, Taylor argues, introducing her notion of the *archive* and the *repertoire*:

> The rift, I submit, does not lie between the written and the spoken word, but between the archive of supposedly enduring materials (i.e., texts, documents, buildings, bones) and the so-called ephemeral repertoire of embodied practice (i.e., spoken language, dance, sports, ritual). 'Archival' memory exists as documents, literary texts, letters, archaeological remains, bones – items supposedly resistant to change.[14] [...] The repertoire, on the other hand, enacts embodied memory: performances, gestures, orality, movement, dance, singing – in short, all those acts usually thought of as ephemeral, non-reproducible knowledge.[15]

Even when working in tandem, archival practices often serve the purpose of containing practices of the repertoire; Taylor has discussed this with application to colonial history in the Americas. Today, 16th century Franciscan missionary Bernardino de Sahagún is considered one of the founding fathers of ethnography, for the practice of containment he advocated involved acquiring first-hand knowledge of indigenous religious practices through interviews, e.g. with village elders. Sahagún, who was able to speak Aztec language Nahuatl fluently, compiled the *Florentine Codex*, twelve books documenting the

---

12 | Taylor 2003
13 | Taylor 2003: 16
14 | Taylor 2003: 19
15 | Taylor 2003: 20

work of his trilingual team and was mainly written in Nahuatl. But his intentions must not be confused with the aim of contemporary anthropologists to gain an emic ('from within') understanding of a studied culture. Rather, Taylor observes, the archival practice of writing

served as a recognized weapon in the colonial arsenal. Sahagún maintained that he needed to write down all the indigenous practices to better eradicate them: "It is needful to know how they practiced them in the time of their idolatry, for, through [our] lack of knowledge of this, they perform many idolatrous things in our presence without our understanding it."[16]

Ironically, the *Florentine Codex* simultaneously served as a document to what it sought to extinguish, even though it included instructions "not to permit anyone, for any reason, in any language, to write concerning the superstitions and way of life these Indians had"[17] One copy of the *Codex* has survived – it has become one of the most important resources on ancient Aztec practices.

In contemporary culture, the rift between the archive and the repertoire and its associated valorisation of legitimate and illegitimate knowledge reveals itself in the perception of various popular practices. One example of a popular embodied practice that has come to some recognition through its documentation on film (i.e. through an archival practice) is a type of street dance originally performed in South Central Los Angeles: *krumping*, a dance style which grew out of *clowning*, a type of entertainment created by Thomas "Tommy the Clown" Johnson who made a living as a hip hop clown performing and kids' birthday parties. *Krumping*, as its less comedic, more physically explicit, polyrhythmic and confrontational variant, often takes on the form of a battle, spontaneously erupting among participants who switch between dancer and observer, keeping the repertoire of dance moves in constant evolution. In the documentary *Rize* (USA 2005, directed by photographer David LaChapelle), the dancers themselves describe krumping as a collective, dynamic practice, unknowingly echoing Taylor's definition of the repertoire as ephemeral and non-reproducible: "The style changes every day, believe it or not, every day the style changes. And if you haven't danced in two days and you

---

16 | Taylor 2003: 41
17 | *Florentine Codex*, book 1, 37; quoted from Taylor 2003; 41

come to a krump session, we're gonna know, we're gonna know you been slacking off." Even though krumping has meanwhile made its way into mainstream, the original dance style cannot be pinned down as a fixed set of movements. Instead, as a practice of the repertoire, it is newly defined with every dance, drawing on the embodied knowledge of participants and evolving from their interaction. Taylor:

> The repertoire requires presence: people participate in the production and reproduction of knowledge by 'being there', being a part of the transmission. As opposed to the supposedly 'stable' objects in the archive, the actions that are the repertoire do not remain the same. The repertoire both keeps and transforms choreographies of meaning.[18]

While the repertoire unfurls in the present and through the presence of the gathered body-subjects, archival memory "works across distance, over time and space; investigators can go back to reexamine an ancient manuscript [...]. [...] archival memory succeeds in separating the source of 'knowledge' from the knower"[19]. With David LaChapelles film, krumping has left the streets of South Central LA and, through the filter of the archive, become something else: a standardized practice that can meanwhile be learned independently from the communal event, for instance from DVDs in which protagonists from *Rize* explain "Krumping 1.0 – Basic Techniques". Yet how – if so – does this apply to online interaction?

While Diana Taylor herself has suggested thinking of the digital as yet another system of knowledge transmission alongside the archive and the repertoire,[20] I would like to argue instead that this distinction allows us to understand some of the ideological underpinnings of the discourse about the digital, in particular with regard to the 'real vs. virtual' fallacy discussed above. While Western culture is very well attuned to reading and interpreting archival practices – with mediating and remediating archival memory constituting the core techniques of its institutions of ideological reproduction: schools, universities, libraries, etc –, it tends to be dismissive of embodied practices, or recognizes them only if associated to archival practices (wedding ceremonies may hold a cherished place in the Western imaginary, yet

---

18 | Taylor 2003: 20
19 | Taylor 2003: 19
20 | Cf. Taylor 2003: 4, 21, 22

neither the exchange of vows nor the wedding band is considered as legally binding, unless endorsed by a marriage certificate). Similarly, the discourse about online interaction reveals an acute awareness for all aspects that are represented through archival forms, become manifest in form of signs or symbols – information, data, code, and their visual/symbolic equivalents –, but pays little attention for the embodied practices associated with and/or eliciting these forms. In its early accounts, the condition of "being digital" (Nicholas Negroponte) was conceptualized as an immediate effect of binary encoding, with (symbolic) worlds being recreated fluidly, unencumbered by the clumsiness of the physical: "[B]its commingle effortlessly", Negroponte wrote. "They start to get mixed up and can be used and reused together or separately. The mixing of audio, video, and data is called multimedia; it sounds complicated, but is nothing more than commingled bits."[21] But there is more to online interaction than commingled bits: the ephemeral, non-reproducible knowledge invested by users/body-subjects as they engage online, the performative quality of their perceptions, actions, and communications as they connect in the human-computer-interface, mediated through websites and with other users, synchronically and a-synchronically. The notion of the archive and repertoire may be valuable for gaining a new understanding of how the sphere of data, information and code (the so-called 'virtual') relates to the sphere of the body (the so-called 'real') – requiring, however, that we consider the digital not as yet another system of knowledge transmission, but as one that relies both on techniques of the archive and of the repertoire. Usability optimization – i.e. the fine-tuning of information and interaction architectures – can be considered as an effort to decrease the effort the user/body-subject has to undertake to use a website effectively. In terms of usability, the ideal website reduces the potential to be reminded of the clumsiness of the physical to the lowest possible degree, e.g. through requiring as few clicks as possible, building on a consistent set of use cases for the various tasks, through the analysis and anticipation of user-behaviour, corresponding adjustment of interaction opportunities and through increased measures to prevent that a user ever loses data. Yet some websites force users to put in more effort than would seem advisable according to the maximum usability paradigm, making interaction with other users a bewildering game, requiring arbitrary commands and deleting data

21 | Negroponte 1995: 18

constantly. 4chan.org is such a website, and as such, it relies on techniques of the repertoire much more intensely than those furnished with award-winning usability concepts and streamlined navigations.

THE ARCHIVE AS REPERTOIRE: HYBRID PRACTICE ON 4CHAN.ORG

The first-time visitor to 4chan.org will probably not know what to do on this website: unlike the alpha and beta-tested, venture-capital funded and social media-optimized specimen of web 2.0 websites, 4chan's appearance does very little to give away its rank of one of the most popular English-language forums on the web, attracting about nine and a half million unique users within 30 days.[22] 4chan's information architecture is adapted from readily available forum software,[23] giving it a generic, rather than unique 'look and feel'.

From a technical point of view, the entry bars to 4chan.org have been lowered as much as possible: as there is no registration and no login, users may just get on the site and start posting. Captchas – images and letters presented as an image that users have to type in to confirm that they are indeed human – have only been added as late as 2010 to prevent automated postings by spam robots. This low-threshold policy is also cited by Poole as one of the aspects that make 4chan unique and add to its success.[24]

From a usability point of view, however, 4chan might not seem quite that accessible. The first thing the user's eye meets is a listing of the various forums hosted on 4chan, some bearing straight-forward names (e.g. "Transportation", "Television & Film", "Food & Cooking"), others subcultural or other arbitrary terms (e.g. "Mecha", "3DCG", "Robot9000"). Some are flagged as "Adult (18+)" (e.g. "Sexy beautiful Women", "Animated GIF", "Random"), which may prompt some users to leave the site, unless they are prepared for or in a position where they can safely consume so-called "not safe for work" (NSWF) content. Upon entering an adult forum for the first time, the user is presented with a disclaimer, warning that the content is not suitable

---

22 | In spring 2010, US District Court 2010: 4
23 | Japanese board Futaba's code with a few adaptations, making it now proprietrary.
24 | Poole 2009

for minors and a link to the "Rules" page. If the user proceeds, one of the first things he or she will see at the top of the page is banner advertising, either for porn sites or for Japanese culture online shops, which might be irritating to some users who have not yet developed the skill of ignoring banner advertising (be it cognitively or technically, e.g. through ad blockers). Conversations on 4chan are marked by jargon: for instance, users routinely address each other as "fags" (including geographical inflections – "Finfag", "Amerifag", "Britfag" etc – or reflecting user status, e.g. "newfag", "oldfag") and make frequent use of group language expression (e.g. "Tits or GTFO" – meaning that a user must post an image of her, or someone's bosom before starting into the conversation, or "titties first" – a call to post an interesting picture first, especially on the "Request" forum). Sometimes Poole, who is referred to as "moot" in forum conversations, intervenes by exploiting his position as 4chan's "benevolent dictator for life"[25]. For instance on December 1 2010, the text of all messages posted to /b/ was automatically converted into repetitions of "puddipuddi" (borrowed from the soundtrack of a Japanese commercial for "Giga Pudding"), leaving users with nothing but images to communicate, as the following thread shows (text or content contained in images is written between square brackets):

Anonymous 12/01/10(Wed)16:02:42 No.291302XXX
File : 1291237362.jpg-(36 KB, 500x500, thankyoupuddi.jpg [Image of nine colourful squirrels and the text: "PUDDI kills cancers/ PUDDI makes /b/ an imageboard / THANK YOU PUDDI!"])
PUDDIPUDDIPUDDIPUDDIPUDDIPUDDIPUDDIPUDDIPUDDIPUDDI
PUDDIPUDDIPUDDIPUDDIPUDDIPUDDIPUDDIPUDDIPUDDI
PUDDIPUDDIPUDDIPUDDIPUDDIPUDDIPUDDIPUDDIPUDDIPUDDI
PUDDIPUDDIPUDDIPUDDIPUDDIPUDDIPUDDIPUDDI
PUDDIPUDDIPUDDI
Anonymous 12/01/10(Wed)16:11:39 No.291303XXX
PUDDIPUDDIPUDDIPUDDIPUDDIPUDDIPUDDIPUDDIPUDDIPUDDI
PUDDIPUDDIPUDDIPUDDIPUDDIPUDDIPUDDIPUDDI
PUDDIPUDDIPUDDIPUDDIPUDDIPUDDIPUDDIPUDDIPUDDIPUDDI
PUDDIPUDDIPUDDIPUDDIPUDDIPUDDIPUDDIPUDDI

---

25 | The concept of benevolent dictator for life (BDFL) originates from open-source software development, another example of a BDFL is Linus Torvalds, creator of Linux.

PUDDIPUDDIPUDDI
Anonymous 12/01/10(Wed)16:12:46 No.291303XXX
File1291237966.png-(12 KB, 419x99, Screen shot 2010-12-01 at 3.12(...).png[Screenshot of the comment field, containing the word "NOOOOOOOOOOOO"])
PUDDIPUDDIPUDDIPUDDIPUDDIPUDDIPUDDIPUDDIPUDDIPUDDI-
PUDDIPUDDIPUDDIPUDDIPUDDIPUDDIPUDDIPUDDI
PUDDIPUDDIPUDDIPUDDIPUDDIPUDDIPUDDIPUDDIPUDDIPUDDI-
PUDDIPUDDIPUDDIPUDDIPUDDIPUDDIPUDDIPUDDI
PUDDIPUDDIPUDDI

While such interventions by moot have the potential to strengthen the community of existing users – subjecting all of them to the same trial (here: the silencing of their messages through their replacement by "puddipuddi") –, they are probably more confusing than persuasive to first time visitors. To make things even more complicated for first-timers, parts of the forum software have been reprogrammed in a non-conventional way, requiring users to perform arbitrary actions (e.g. entering the word "noko" in the email field to stay in the same thread after posting). In other words: while the technical obstacles to using 4chan might seem low, the cultural and conventional obstacles are considerably higher on 4chan than on other, mainstream-oriented platforms.

Returning to the issue of archive vs. repertoire, it would at first appear only logical to assume that 4chan – being an Internet forum – must be considered an example of an archival practice. As all media technologies do, it separates the knowledge from the bearer: the human-computer interface, in its afore-mentioned function as writing tool, is a knowledge extraction tool par excellence, allowing thought to take on the objectified form of the written record. Knowledge management systems exploit this in their attempt to turn tacit into explicit knowledge, prompting individuals 'in the know' to fill in fields, upload files and provide meta-data so that others might benefit from their knowledge even in their absence.

On social media websites, data entry fields and upload options extract mainly two types of information: on the one hand information relating to the *individual*, creating a data-based representation of him or her – i.e. his or her profile –, and on the other hand information relating to ongoing *communications*, i.e. so-called content. There are currently two main types to organize this information into knowledge: on the one hand, an individual's *social graph* (also: address book, contact or buddy list) maps the relations of an individual's profile to the profiles of other individuals, and on the other hand, the individual's *timeline* (also: activity stream) organizes the content he or she has produced chronologically, generating a past and present, i.e. a history of his or her activities. The currently most dominant social networking site Facebook.com actually keeps a full record of both profiles (the default option merely allows to deactivate, but not to delete a profile) and of timelines – with the latest system updates from December 2010, it is even possible to download a personal archive of all data one has ever published, from first wall post to latest photo. Even if a person never logged onto Facebook again, this archive, in Taylor's sense, would work across distance, over time and space, and investigators could go back to it and reexamine it like an ancient manuscript.

This is not what happens on 4chan. First of all, with the lack of a registration and the absence of profiles, there are also no means to build a social graph to understand the relations between users. This trickles all the way down to the level of the ongoing communications. As becomes apparent from the "puddipuddi" example cited above: if all users are represented as "Anonymous", it is not actually possible to figure out who has been talking to whom. While conventional anonymity online meant that one's real name and identity were protected through the use of (unique and/or registered) nicknames, 4chan takes this one step further: Because no one can register, no one may claim a nickname for him or herself. Users still have the opportunity to specify a nickname with every post they publish – but if one user picks the nickname "OprahWinfrey", this doesn't prevent that other users post as "OprahWinfrey", too. And if no nickname is specified at all, "Anonymous" will appear as the name of the author. With the number of "Anonymouses" posting on 4chan, identifying who said what becomes impossible – the suspicion that a user has been talking to him or herself in order to stimulate a debate is ubiquitous on 4chan: this practice is called "samefagging". Posting as "Anonymous" has become so much part of 4chan's culture, especially on the Random forum /b/, that there is also a word for *not* posting anonymously: "namefagging". During the "puddipuddi" intervention, one user praised the virtues of anonymous posting as follows (the message was posted as a *.gif image):

In the past few months, we've watched /b/ turn into a shitty version of facebook, filled with morons that post more than they lurk, and ignorant to the fact that what makes /b/ great is that when you're here, you are not you. You are anonymous. / Moot is the only one that had both the understanding and the ability to chemo the cancer. The understanding in that he recognized that the answer wasn't to flood cancerous threads with gore, but to take away your ability to post your idiotic opinion, wait 30 seconds, then post it again. And the ability, obviously, because, after all, this is his site. / I hope it stays like this forever. [...] Tl;dr Thank you Moot. You are the oncologist.

With the rejection of profiles and the social graph model, the timeline model also suffers: when there is no profile, there is also no other user timeline than the collective timeline of all posts in a forum. On 4chan, instead of user IDs, individual posts are attributed with IDs. While user handles are used to respond to other users e.g. in chat communication or on microblogging platforms such as Twitter.com (e.g. "@unicorn47 male or female?"), on 4chan, users respond to individual posts, using a nine-digit ID (e.g. ">>291499636 tits or GTFO"). This move from the concept of profile ID (representing an individual) to the concept of post ID (representing just one aspect or position in an ongoing debate) further contributes to the dissolving of the boundaries of self as it (supposedly) manifests itself online: while anything I say on my Facebook page will be subject of a consistency check (is it line with what people have read and learned about me so far?), I need not worry about such forms of social control on 4chan: on 4chan, I am not me. I am anonymous. If the imagery and opinions expressed on 4chan are often radical and extreme, it is because 4chan – rather than being about self-representation like other forms of social media – serves as a semiological laboratory, where body-subjects collectively explore meaning, the potential scope of a debate, and in particular the boundaries between what can and what cannot be said. These experimental conditions are aggravated through the mentioned lack of retention: sooner or later, all posts, text and image, will be deleted – on popular forums such as /b/ after just a few minutes. Poole:[26]

Every board has a maximum number of threads, say a hundred. Every time a new thread is posted, something has to be removed. Eventually all of

---

26 | US District Court 2010: 11-12

the threads are cycled off and then pruned that way. It's time based and on some of the boards it's popularity based. The oldest least replied to thread gets bumped off. Inactive threads basically get bumped off.

If a new thread fails to attract the attention of other users, it will quickly drop to the bottom of the page, receive even less attention and soon be deleted – which is yet another reason why posts on 4chan tend towards the extreme. Every thread vies with others for its existence. At the same time, with an archive that autodestructs after a certain period, the onus of maintaining and perpetuating 4chan's knowledge is delegated to the user community: the collective of body-subjects that uses, reads and knows the language, conventions and narratives of the site, saves images to their hard-drives if they seem interesting enough, weaves them back into circulation if the occasion seems fitting, creates new symbols and forms, new knowledge online. This is not an activity that can be automated: it requires the semiological capacities of the users as body-subjects, their ability to read and comprehend as much as their ability to create and destroy. If "puddipuddi" has had an influence on the negotiated knowledge on 4chan, then even those who were not present on December 1 2010 will learn about its rhetoric and symbols when they return online. This is indeed the point where 4chan resembles a collective of dancers. It reminds us of the confession of the krumps: "The style changes every day, believe it or not, every day the style changes." Or as Taylor put it: "Dances change over time, even though generations of dancers (or even individual dancers) swear they're always the same."[27] And just as the repertoire requires presence, 'being there', being a part of the transmission, 4chan, too, demands that users as body-subjects engage and participate both synchronically and a-synchronically. With its users being distributed across all time zones, 4chan never sleeps. But if the site was suddenly shut down, what would remain – the few pages that evaded deletion – would not be enough to recreate it from scratch: not without the embodied knowledge of the collective of body-subjects that constitutes 4chan.

---

27 | Taylor 2003: 20

4CHAN AND BEYOND

This account of 4chan as a hybrid of archive and repertoire is not complete. 4chan has no fixed boundaries: its knowledge follows its users, and while the site itself may neither provide profiles nor an archived history, attempts at making this knowledge explicit are made on other sites. One such example is the initially mentioned website EncyclopediaDramatica.com (ED) which chronicles major events and terms of internet culture, relating to 4chan and its collective, but also to other sites such as DeviantART.com or SomethingAwful.com. It runs on the same software as Wikipedia, but in contrast to the free encyclopaedia's objectivity aims, language used on ED is idiosyncratic to a degree that some familiarity with Internet culture is already required to use it.[28] Another site where terms relating to 4chan can be looked up is UrbanDictionary.com where users may add and vote for definitions for any term: for instance for "tits or GTFO", which currently has six different definitions, with the top-scoring one having received 1277 "ups" and 119 "downs" (2 December 2010).[29] To gain a full understanding of the way in which archival and embodied practices work together and support each other, one would have to analyze this network of websites, user communities and the streams of mediated and embodied knowledge between them – still, each individual user's story would paint a different picture. If we consider 4chan not just as either a website or either a community, but as a collective, embodied practice enabled by digital technology, we are also able to understand some of its performative aspects, its status as a contemporary, adolescent or post-adolescent ritual. "They dared to touch the wild beasts of 4chan and they lived to tell the tale," this is how A-list blogger Marshall Kirkpatrick described how a social media campaign, surprisingly, managed to charm 4chan users.[30] Social media spaces bear resemblance to the liminal social spaces of initiation rituals in

---

28 | From the article "Something Awful": "[a]n unfunny comedy website owned by Lowtax, and traces its roots back to the good old days of Web 1.0, where Goatse was the pinnacle of shock and the LJ in 'LJ drama' did not yet exist."

29 | No. 1 definition: "An expression often used on imageboards. It is often heard when a girl posts in a thread. *Camwhore: Hi am i hot? Person: Tits or GTFO.*"

30 | Kirkpatrick 2010

that they first remove all signs of the subjects' previous social status, and then conjoin them under the egalitarian spirit of what cultural anthropologist Victor Turner has described as *communitas*, an "unstructured or rudimentarily structured and relatively undifferentiated *comitatus*, community or even communion of equal individuals who submit together to the general authority of the ritual elders".[31] 4chan's culture, with its collective of anonymous users and its loathing of "namefagging" is also antithetical to social structures and hierarchies, which otherwise re-establish themselves quickly in online communities. Its inclination towards the extreme and the bizarre as well as its appearance as a masked collective in public resembles Turner's descriptions of initiation rites:

> Even in liminality, where the bizarre behavior so often remarked upon by anthropologists occurs, the *sacra*, masks, etc., emerge to view under the guise at least of "collective representations". If there ever were individual creators and artists, they have been subdued by the general "liminal" emphasis on anonymity and communitas, just as the novices and their novice-masters have been.[32]

In traditional societies, such bizarre behaviour in liminality often involves impersonating grotesque animals, "caricatures of human outsiders" as Elizabeth Isechei put it, referring to the African masking society of the Chewa: "The dancers, as wild beasts, stand outside of Chewa society and reverse its norms. They are often violent, and their songs obscene."[33] Looking at 4chan, its lore and its symbols, one might suggest this as its epigraph: "Our images are violent, yet our songs are obscene."

REFERENCES

"The World's Most Influential Person Is...". *Time Online*. 27.April 2009, http://www.time.com/time/arts/article/0,8599,1894028,00. html, 28. November 2010

---

31 | Turner 1990: 148
32 | Turner 1982: 43
33 | Isechei 2004: 258

Blackmore, Susan (2000). *The Meme Machine*. Oxford/New York: Oxford University Press [1999]

Dawkins, Richard (2006). *The Selfish Gene*. Oxford/New York: Oxford University Press [1976]

Heathfield, Adrian (2004). "Alive". In: Heathfield, Adrian (eds.) (2004). *Live*. New York: Routledge, 6-13

Isechei, Elizabeth (2004). *The Religious Traditions of Africa: A History*. Westport: Praeger

Kirkpatrick, Marshall (2010). "How the Old Spice Videos Are Being Made". *ReadWriteWeb* (Blog). 14 July 2010, http://rww.tw/bm6apN, 2 December 2010

Lamere, Paul (2009). "Inside the precision hack". *Music Machinery Blog*. 15 April 2009, http://musicmachinery.com/2009/04/15/inside-the-precision-hack, 28 November 2010

Meister, Martin; Simon, Claus Peter & Teichmann, Andreas (2003): "Die Tyrannei der Meme" (Interview mit Susan Blackmore). *GEO*, 12: 82-86

Merleau-Ponty, Maurice (1945). *Phénoménologie de la perception*. Paris: Gallimard.

Metz, Christian (1966). "La grande syntagmatique du film narratif". *Communications* 8(8): 120-124

Negroponte, Nicholas (1995). *being digital*. New York: Alfred A. Knopf

Poole, Christopher (2009). "Meme Factory (Talk)". *Paraflows Symposium* 2009. 12 September 2009

Poole, Christopher (2010). "The Case for Anonymity Online (Talk)". *TED Conference 2010*. 11 February 2010, http://on.ted.com/8jOv, 28 November 2010

Taylor, Diana (2003). *The Archive and the Repertoire. Performing Cultural Memory in the Americas*. Durham/London: Duke University Press

Turner, Victor (1982). *From Ritual to Theatre. The Human Seriousness of Play*. New York City: Performing Arts Journal Publications.

Turner, Victor (1990). "Liminality and Community". In: Alexander, Jeffrey C. (ed.). *Culture and Society. Contemporary Debates*. Cambridge: Cambridge University Press, 147-154. (Reprint from The Ritual Process [1969]).

US District Court at Knoxville, TN (2010). *Transcript of Chris Poole before the Honorable Thomas W. Phillips on April 22, 2010 (CR 3-08-142)*. US District Court: Knoxville, TN.

W0rdM4g1x
Or how to put a spell on Media Art Archives

NINA WENHART

The objects of investigation of this paper are database archives for Media Art. As such I define databases that are mainly documentation archives and have in large parts taken over the role of the classical archive for the field of Media Art; archives that do not necessarily refer to a parallel physical storage/collection, but the (online accessible) documentation archive that can also exist on its own. For in Media Art, what is left to archive very often only consists of documentation material. In this definition of the database archive, I mainly follow the definition proposed by V2_, for example as used in their introductory text (http://framework.v2.nl/archive/general/default.xslt).

Such a database archive is about creating order by managing sense, by making statements through this order, by creating a grammar through the words used (morphology) and the structure applied (syntax). Database archives for Media Art can vary greatly in scope and focus. Some collect physical assets like art works or documentation material, others just describe them; some include their own institution's projects only, others group their archive around research topics. However they differ, what they all have in common is that they contain data and data about this data – metadata. The part of metadata that is interesting in this context is descriptive metadata, metadata based on interpretation that is used to describe the artworks. This kind of descriptive metadata is also what concerns the discussion about a standard terminology for Media Art. The database archive typically makes intensive use of language, of terms to manage and describe the assets. These terms serve to find (on the output/user side) and describe (on the creator/input side). For the system itself, the term is just functional, an index to correlate the assigned data with. On the human (input and output) side, these words also have meaning. The differences in meaning are what make the words such a crucial issue. In these database archives, knowledge and histories are not only stored and managed, but also created and constructed. Because of this, there needs to be a thorough consideration of the processes involved and of how these systems are created. In addition to describing content, a database archive also manages assets and creates order by naming and relating. Most databases are still organized in the manner of a shelf, although no physical constraints force them to re-implement what was only meant as a metaphor in data-space. "The categorization scheme is a response to physical constraints on storage, and to people's inability to keep the location of more than a few hundred things in their mind at once."[1] What might have been useful at a time when digital storage was new – using a metaphor to have something familiar around – now proves to be a real obstacle for the sustainability and further development of the archives: "Now it means that the user has to adopt to the creator's specific view of the world, it has become a dogma. It seems that the GUI and all its metaphors have come into our way. It *seems* natural. How terrible."[2]

THE LACK OF A STANDARD TERMINOLOGY

One of the major problems discussed in the context of descriptive metadata is most widely known as "the lack of a standard terminology" for describing Media Art, as defined in "Capturing Unstable Media" by Sandra Fauconnier and Rens Frommé from V2_[3]. I question whether this really is a problem or if the observed "lack" offers the key to a new concept for "capturing" and describing Media Art. A lack generally means an undesirable condition. Something is missing, and therefore something else is impossible to achieve. The lack has to be removed. In this case it would mean that, without a standard terminology, it is impossible to correctly and comprehensively describe Media

---
1 | http://shirky.com/writings/ontology_overrated.htm
2 | Ibid.
3 | http://archive.v2.nl/v2_archive/projects/capturing/1_2_capturing.
pdf, p. 12: "There is a lack of standard terminology for practices, activities and components in electronic art and for the types and genres of documentation that describes those."

Art. Over the years, several attempts have been made not only to describe Media Art, but also to capture the correct terms and their interrelations; attempts to settle the preconditions for any valid description hence on. As for now, this goal has not been reached; and looking back at the histories of these attempts, it can legitimately be assumed that it never will. For good. No final standard terminology could ever be assumed, as no final point of knowledge can ever be fixed. However, the problem addressed in the "lack of a standard terminology" is a question of language, the necessity of using it, the observation that the existing methods are not sufficient for the task at hand, the fact that language is an unclosed system, and the difficulties arising from dealing with this fact.

Terminologies do more than just name objects and stick labels on them. By not just being assigned to the artworks, but also being ordered themselves, they create structures, a "Grammar of New Media". This creates a set of rules for how to read Media Art. On the creator-side, it means making interpretations, picking the rules, turning what was first an interpretation amongst others into the preferred way of seeing and thereby turning (arbitrary) interpretation into order=command.

The goal of a standard terminology is to find the agreed meaning of a term and its (unique) place in this world, of the correct assignment between an entity and a word (= function of a manual) in order to decrease semantic heterogeneity. The term is treated like a physical object. The standard terminology should make meaning and order clear and self evident - "natural", not to be doubted, but being attributed universal validity, truth value, true or false, following a bivalent logic, black or white, no gray in between, good or bad – it is, in short, a simplifying model that is achieved by a reduction of complex situations. By offering a limited number of preferred ways of naming and ordering, by creating unambiguity, by erasing doubt, belief in this "god" equals belief in the creator of the database archive. The creators are interpreters of the existing sources. For the descriptive metadata, their selection is based on their own interpretations mostly (fact is dealt with separately). Essence and interpretation are both problematic when it comes to creating order, because they *appear* to be natural instead of culturally constructed. The resulting system is absolute.

Semantics on the other hand consist of creating a dense network of interrelations, of having multiple – even conflicting – relations, of creating meanings through nets of relations and of revealing sense and meanings on a context-dependent base. A standard terminology would erode multiplicity and density that are necessary ingredients of semantic networks in favor of *the* preferred way of reading. Homogeneity instead of heterogeneity, hegemony instead of free and open choice, creation of one for many and not of many for many, static instead of variable media through static instead of variable language. In the end, this is a question of exercising power and authority; it becomes, it *is* political from the very beginning.

Where is the Media in Media Art Databases?

In his 1970 book "Expanded Cinema", Gene Youngblood mentions a newly emerging kind of artist and the changing role of technology and the audience as the main aspects that characterize the new genre of Computer Art[4] Almost 40 years later, what Youngblood identified as characteristics of the new art form is still not adequately represented and acknowledged – if at all. If crucial aspects like these are missing in database archives, what else is excluded? And if the terminology of these database archives is built on the literature of the field, then it has to be asked which topics are covered by it and which are ignored? To each generation of Media Art historians and theorists, different aspects of the medium seemed interesting or relevant. Each generation made its own contribution to the field. In consequence, it is only logical that future generations will do the same and have to be able to contribute their own research or re-discover things previously neglected. This must not only be the commitment of the community, but also of its knowledge systems. As database archives become more and more relevant as knowledge systems, they, too, have to systematically enable modifications, new additions, even new categories. They have to systematically remain open. A (systematically) static database archive is nothing but a book in electronic form and at best mirrors the evaluation of a specific time, author and perspective. As can be seen in existing database archives, early revisions of the systems have already become inevitable.

---

4 | Gene Youngblood, Expanded Cinema, Dutton & Co, New York, 1970, p. 193

The Grammar of New Media

"Grammar is the field of linguistics that covers the rules governing the use of any given natural language. It includes morphology and syntax, often complemented by phonetics, phonology, semantics, and pragmatics", so the common grammar definition as found on Wikipedia[5]. To see how and if this applies to database archives for Media Art, if these database archives constitute a grammar in the above sense, if they construct rules that govern the use and via this the meaning, a closer look at the morphology and syntax of these systems will be taken. Two influential aspects should be considered separately: the database archive's/the content's syntax resulting from relations of terms and the specialty of a database archive of a mostly noun-based morphology.

Syntax

Some database archives only have a list of non-interrelated keywords. However, many others use relations to order their keywords semantically. Words are grouped in categories and relations are constructed between the individual terms, for example by introducing "broader term", "narrower term", "associated term",... The order created is absolute and exclusive and each asset is assigned a unique place and function. It neglects that terms can have multiple meanings and varying relations in different contexts, that in most cases the "natural" habitat of a term is a "social knitwork" and not forced by a law of nature. The order commonly met in a database archive rather suggests this second approach, that the terms were found instead of constructed (the Wittgenstein-chapter will go into detail about this and the topic of essences). To avoid this naturalistic appearance, a database archive has to be able to represent relative, flexible and content-dependent order. Whenever writing about something, we take a specific perspective, reducing complexity for the sake of highlighting one special aspect. But by reducing relations systematically, generally and not just for a single purpose, we erode knowledge permanently. Complexity cannot be solved by reduction and by deletion if it does not want to result in over-simplification.

---

5 | http://en.wikipedia.org/wiki/Grammarhttp://en.wikipedia.org/wiki/Grammar

Morphology

Database archives' terminologies are mostly noun-based. The problem with this is:

- We try to find *the* one word that is capable of expressing the whole situation. If not in a database, we would probably just use a sentence or a group of words to express that situation, not just one single noun. The resulting word creation often has nothing to do with real life experience, but resembles a jackalope. The noun, this mythical animal that is invented especially for the database archive in many cases is a compromise, is not the best option. It is not what we actually want to express. This search for the essential element will not deliver satisfying results when what actually can be found is not one thing, but a complex mix of equally relevant features, no matter if they fit in a scheme or not.
- Culturally, this bias poses a problem as not all languages are so focused on the use of nouns.
- Nouns are invented faster than verbs, they are less time-stable, they are fashionable at a certain time and age with their technologies (for example in the early 90s Virtual Reality was used excessively and the same things would be called something else today).

From the above, we see that the seemingly arbitrary choice of descriptive metadata creates the morphology and syntax of the whole system. Because of the scope of their influence, these data need careful handling and consideration.

Dealing with Diversity

The "lack of a standard terminology" does not mean that there are no terminologies. There are many different vocabularies in use, in different database archives, created by different authors, covering different aspects... So the problem of the "lack of a standard terminology" is in fact a problem of how to deal with diversity of expression. It is a matter of perception and interpretation. And it has various effects: the process of perception is influenced by multiple factors, like previous knowledge, the culture of the interpreter, awareness, different goals and contexts,... The second problem is that different interpreters perceive different aspects and name them differently. The same term can have multiple meanings for different people or in different disciplines and contexts. Diversity is a matter of meaning, of the use of language. As mentioned before, in a database archive words not only have a naming function, but these names/labels are structured and structuring. They are functionally implemented in the database archive, language gets a technical imprint. The result is that out of technological necessities of the database models applied, the many meanings and places of a term are reduced and narrowed down so that preferably only unambiguity remains. This is then called the "preferred way of reading". These aspects have massive impact on openness, the character of the resulting knowledge base and finally its sustainability and therefore need to be analyzed critically. Looking at these database archives and their methods of structuring, one can easily get the impression that diversity is bad and should be avoided or eliminated whenever met. In the end, far from resulting in a perfect representation and understanding of its contents, very often the result is a mixed-up representation which in the end leads to incommensurability in content as well as structure, a mix of "apples and oranges". They resemble, as Jorge Luis Borges put it in "John Wilkins' Analytical Language"[6]:

"[...] a certain Chinese Encyclopedia called the Heavenly Emporium of Benevolent Knowledge. In its distant pages it is written that animals are divided into: (a) those that belong to the emperor; (b) embalmed ones; (c) those that are trained; (d) suckling pigs; (e) mermaids; (f) fabulous ones; (g) stray dogs; (h) those that are included in this classification; (i) those that tremble as if they were mad; (j) innumerable ones; (k) those drawn with a very fine camel's-hair brush; (l) etcetera; (m) those that have just broken the flower vase; (n) those that at a distance resemble flies."

To sum up my analysis of current database archives (which due to its extensiveness I cannot include in this paper), the challenges and problems identified in current database archives are:

a. Rigid hierarchical structures that very often are one-directional and exclusive and hard to change once they are implemented. This especially poses problems for the further development of a database

---

6 | Jorge Louis Borges, "The Analytical Language of John Wilkins", in: Selected Non-Fictions, New York, Penguin Books, 1999, p. 231

archive, which is unavoidable. Each new category challenges the system as a whole.

b. Faking fixed meaning ignores that one word can mean different things and have different connotations in different disciplines and contexts (incommensurability, terms used are relative to a scheme) and also ignores that especially Media Art feeds from various disciplines. A model of fixed meaning results in a narrowing down of perspective, which can in the best case be described as incomplete, in the worst case leads to wrong results.

c. Vocabularies follow the internal logic of their creators. This poses a very real and practical problem: as people mostly do not enter a database archive from where its creators plan, namely the platform's start-page, but from a search-engine, they will rely on the words and associations they come up with. The logical consequence for database archive creators should be to make a move towards their users and to incorporate as many different associations, meanings, ways of spelling, synonyms, maybe even typos... they can think of. Even if the creators would succeed in finding the perfect expression, how would the users know how to find it? How would they convey their word magix to their audience? Creators of such database archives need to address these semantic and interpretation issues, if they successfully want to build and sustain their projects.

d. A standard terminology for Media Art contradicts itself. Media Art feeds from various disciplines, crosses boundaries and unites them, resulting in not just a mix of the latter, but also in additional new meanings ("the sum is more than its parts"). Currently applied terminologies reduce the many dimensions to just one (over simplification) or mix what shouldn't be mixed (incommensurability).

Descriptive Metadata and Interpretation

For the field of Media Art, the lack of a standard terminology has created a great deal of uncertainty and thus gained priority in research. How can we discuss Media Art when we can't choose the right words and are unsure if their meanings are universally agreed upon? How can we talk about Media Art, when we do not speak the language of New Media?

In all phases of the interpretation process, many results are imaginable, not just one. They are not correct (as in the only one), but can be more or less appropriate. And not all of the equally appropriate interpretations are considered. The database archives build on a small selection of terms and for the sake of slimness and unambiguity try to avoid any kind of redundancy. Terms are used as structural elements in the database archive. This process leads to the solidification of the system by reducing the terms' inherent options. Differing meanings are structurally eliminated and thereby the words' qualities change: they undergo a move from being appropriate to being *correct*. If interpretation is not about assigning absolute values, such as truth or falsity, but rather about equally acceptable options, it would then be a mistake to build structures on just one interpretation. This would turn the interpretation model with many appropriate results to a scientific model with just one answer being correct.

Interpretation as judgment is influenced by various factors. Pre-existing knowledge, our openness to newness, our time/place/cultural contexts. Unseen and unforeseeable things constitute inevitable change. As these are factors we can count on, but not calculate with, the system developed for Media Art database archives must be apt to *likely* changes. A system for structuring information/meaning that is based on interpretations must remain corrigible to stay correct. Media Art shares many aspects with traditional art history, but it also introduces newness in content, form and means. These aspects have not been fully acknowledged or captured yet. And the systems often do not allow for newness to be included. The field of Media Art needs systems where continued de/construction remains possible. Right now, too much power lies in the authority of the technological structure used and too little thought is given to its authoritative consequences.

Whodunnit?

The interpretations in an archive do not seem to be interpretations; they appear to be discovered rather than constructed. The difference here is that the first implies nature's laws and essences, whereas the second shows choice, culture, authorship, a specific view amongst others. Structure in Media Art database archives does not follow a natural law, it is not discovered, but constructed, based on the selection, which itself is based on the creator's aims. The goal of interpretation is to foster understanding and as Schleiermacher pointed out, vocabulary is important in reaching this goal. But – as he also mentions – it is provisional, subject to change. This "dictionary" would not seek to eliminate varying interpretations but "regard the various manners of use as a collection of many loosely connected parts."[7] Schleiermacher sees both dictionary and grammar as evolving, they begin from a specific point of view, their use must serve to correct and enrich. Interpretation must contribute to the task of furthering knowledge. In both the database archive and semantic network, it is not only about the terminology used, but also about how these terms are linked to the object and to each other. Relations help to further clarify the meaning of a term, its usage. Schleiermacher writes that the sense of every word in a given location must be determined according to its being-together with those that surround it[8]. It follows, that the denser this field becomes, the more clearly individual meanings can be determined. Context and relations serve as an aid, the connections can be "organic" (=internal fusion) or "mechanical" (=external stringing together)[9], discovered or constructed. In this regard, the semantic network contributes to the clarification of meaning by relating terms and terms as well as terms and objects, so that one helps to clarify the other. Interpretation remains an approximation of meaning. This act of translation, as it can never be perfect, is a teleological imperative[10], a guideline for adequate interpretation. The goal is to find out and illuminate the meaning of the source, to create some kind of equilibrium between the source and its translation. A standard terminology can only be an aid as a lexical means and as thus suggest but not mandate acceptable meanings. It can exemplify but must not instruct. In short, it will never become a manual for correct interpretation.

According to George Steiner, "no perfections and final stabilities of understanding in any act of discourse"[11] can be reached; translation

---

7 | Friedrich Schleiermacher, Hermeneutics and Criticism, Cambridge University Press, 1998, p. 34
8 | Ibid., p. 44
9 | Ibid., p. 46
10 | George Steiner, After Babel, Oxford University Press, 1998 (3rd edition), p.326f
11 | Ibid., p. 428

is always partial. Natural language is polysemic and imprecise. What a standard terminology aims at, a closed-circuit system between works and words does not exist. The reason why this whole aspect of translation and interpretation is important for Media Art database archives is that the quality of interpretation changes dramatically when implemented in a database. For here, interpretation becomes structural and functional and from one interpretation among many adequate ones, it becomes the only one. It is not even perceived or presented as an interpretation anymore, but as fact. Every structure that behaves this way is inadequate. Interpretation is the active search for meaning, it is a semantic process. Semantic richness therefore is not the extraction of the perfect translation, but the enriching of the semantic field of a term. A standard terminology is not what one authoritative group assembles, but a compilation of how these words are actually used in the community, the community in the Media Arts being *all* the people participating in the field, the artists, historians, audience... Meaning creation here depends on "a network of recognition"[12]. "Meaning is a process, a consequence of exchange and discourse, correction, and reciprocity."[13] Meaning is a Language Game.

LUDWIG WITTGENSTEIN'S CONCEPT OF FAMILY RESEMBLANCE

"The idea that in order to get clear about the meaning of a general term one had to find the common element in all its applications has shackled philosophical investigation."[14]

In the posthumously published Philosophical Investigations, Ludwig Wittgenstein introduces a new paradigm for ordering. His concept is easy to explain: Instead of finding one assumed core element that is necessary and common to all members of a class, they are connected by a whole series of criss-crossing and overlapping features. Not by identity, but similarity. This kind of relationship is what Wittgenstein called Family Resemblance. It offers a solution to what cannot sufficiently be defined by a class-system or – as Wittgenstein

---

12 | Ibid., p. 314
13 | Ibid., p. 172
14 | Ludwig Wittgenstein, 'The Blue and Brown Books', Harper Torchbooks, 1965, p. 17

wrote - to avoid "the bumps that the understanding has got by running its head up against the limits of language"[15] With this concept, Wittgenstein rejects all taxonomic classification as essentialist and shows the limitations of any hierarchical system with words: That to reach final accuracy in language is an ideal. A class is defined explicitly by a core element; a family on the other hand is described by its rules. And – as he continues in his concept of Language-Games[16] – these rules are not fixed once and for all, but made up and modified "as we go along"[17]. They are the (temporary) results of a common activity, and to be effective and meaningful they have to be agreed upon by the "players". While the traditional classification system was not correct but effective in the times before the computer, now Wittgenstein's model of a non-essentialist ordering system provides a real alternative for descriptive metadata and ordering systems. What does Wittgenstein mean by "rules" and how could this concept be weighed against the concept of classes?

Rules

The importance of rules or of following rules is one of Wittgenstein's main interests in his analysis of games. Rules are conventions. They are not right or wrong in a logical sense; they are just useful. The meaning of a word is the result of following rules. So to fix the meaning of a word by linking it to a thing is just one particular view, not *the* view. What makes a rule different from a definition is that it describes an action, a move, gives direction, but remains flexible; the sum of rules, all statements that tell us how to make meaningful statements constitute a grammar. A definition on the other hand cements the flexibility of a rule by locking the meaning. Deviant usage of words means that "you are not playing the same game". Rules are related and linked to each other and form families rather than strictly defined classes. In that way, a rule differs fundamentally from a definition: To

---

15 | Ludwig Wittgenstein, 'Philosophical Investigations', Blackwell Publishing, 2001 (3rd edition) p.41e, §119
16 | Ibid., p. 4e, §7: "I shall also call the whole, consisting of language and the actions into which it is woven, a 'languagegame'".
17 | Ibid., p. 33e, §83: "And is there not also the case where we play and-make up the rules as we go along? And there is even one where we alter them-as we go along."

fall under a definition, necessary and sufficient characteristics have to be fulfilled. A rule on the other hand is much more open. This is what makes the difference between a family and a class, an open system and a closed one. The members of both family and class are interlinked with each other. But instead of resulting in a hierarchy, a fixed order, a non-extendable model and ideal, that is based on mental entities, a family is a network that can grow by sharing and passing on parts from one member to the other, remixing characteristics and adding new ones. To paraphrase the parent-child metaphor of class-subdivision: Unlike in a traditional classification, in the model of Family Resemblance, reproduction can happen naturally: sex instead of in vitro fertilization. Isn't that more realistic? Things are connected and sufficiently ordered by the connections that are established by Family Resemblance. This is radically different from the essentialist tradition. Precisely defined classes are not necessary to understand what a thing is or what relations it can have. To follow a rule is an action and an expression of a specific view of the field. As there are many ways of interpretation, there are also multiple families a thing can be part of, multiple connections that can but need not be shared by all members of a family. There are different uses for a word, and all the different uses are collected in the concept of Family Resemblances.

"And the result of this examination is: we see a complicated network of similarities overlapping and criss-crossing: sometimes overall similarities, sometimes similarities of detail."[18]

What still makes the prospect of a standard terminology so attractive is its relative lack of complexity. It reduces the different perspectives to just one, something simple and easily comprehensible and takes away the burden of making a decision. Family Resemblance on the other hand results in a complex network and is rhizomatic. It shows a huge number of connections between things, very general as well as very particular ones; it does not weigh what is important and what is not. This is a subjective decision and thus part of the process of filtering (on the user side).

In Media Art archives we sort knowledge that is already present. The order is not implemented to discover new relations, new qualities,

---

18 | Ibid., p. 27e, §66

but the result of pre-perceived classes and pre-assumed relations between them. New things have to fit in an already established world order, which is created and manifested in technology before the assets are filed in. The effect is that we do not compile everything we know about all the pieces of Media Art; we order what we have known before. We remain in already established Language-Games that have not been developed for Media Art[19]. Instead of developing its own language, the field of Media Art plays these pre-existing Language-Games in the context of Media Art archives. This does not mean that the order created is entirely wrong. What *is* wrong is that it presents itself as the only true way of looking at Media Art when it is in fact only one perspective. Only one dimension is highlighted while most information remains in the dark. It is in the nature of such models of (a piece of the) world, that they demand universal validity. We have to remind ourselves that with descriptive metadata we are dealing in the realms of language, something that is not precise. Again, Wittgenstein reminds us of this when he writes:

"We want to establish an order in our knowledge of the use of language: an order with a particular end in view; one out of many possible orders; not *the* order."[20]

Because of this limitation of perspectives, archives are filters. In current archives, filtering and thus reduction is part of the data-entering phase. Filtering is an important part of getting qualified information. The crucial question is: when does this filtering happen? To avoid this narrowing down of possible perspectives, this process should be an option that is up to the user. Applying the concept of family resemblance would allow as many connections as possible to be entered rather than filtering in the data entering phase. The filtering process, the temporary closure, the particular world-view, would all be better suited to being options at the end point of a user accessing the assets of a Media Art archive rather than being fixed when data is entered into the archive.

---

19 | For example by adapting existing standard terminologies like the Getty Art & Architecture Thesaurus (ATT), http://www.getty.edu/research/conducting_research/vocabularies/aat/

20 | Ludwig Wittgenstein, 'Philosophical Investigations', Blackwell Publishing, 2001 (3rd edition), § 132

Networks

Wittgenstein's concept of Family Resemblance is opposed to an approach that presents idealism as fact and accepts the resulting errors. The rules of grammar he proposes instead are guidelines for how to make meaningful statements; they result from the *use* of language. If we deal without definitions, without something that counts as a "hard fact" and if rules can be changed, a question remains: are the relations established reliable and stable enough? Like in a rope or a net, both strength and reliability come from the interweavement of several features, the family network:

"And we extend our concept of number as in spinning a thread we twist fibre on fibre. And the strength of the thread does not reside in the fact that someone fibre runs through its whole length, but in the overlapping of many fibres."[21]

Translating this thought to Media Art, we learn to understand a piece of art in this interweavement of several features, facets and perspectives instead of in terms of one singular, simplified or 'true' essence. There is a multiplicity of different kinds of languages. In using a language we create meaning, and this activity is what Wittgenstein calls a form of life[22]. "So you are saying that human agreement decides what is true or false?" – It is what human beings *say* that is true or false; and they agree in the *language* they use. That is not agreements in opinions but in form of life[23]. Grammar as the sum of rules is the expression and result of a particular form of life, not an abstraction from it. Misunderstandings lie in language, not in the things themselves. Instead of a search for a standard terminology for Media Art, the research focus should concentrate on finding a system that enables us to link these different forms of life. Not to erase one for the other, but to make them comparable and to enrich the system with more views. "Our investigation is ... a grammatical one. Such an investigation sheds light on our problem by clearing misunderstandings away. Misunderstandings concerning the use of words, caused, among other

---

21 | Ibid., p. 27e, §67
22 | Ibid., p. 10e, §23
23 | Ibid., p. 75e, §241

things, by certain analogies between the forms of expression in different regions of language."²⁴

Necessarily, the conceptual model of Family Resemblance is open. New features can always arise and continue to be included. As no list can be compiled that names all features imaginable, the concept of Family Resemblance's ability to incorporate new features presents a significant strength and advantage over other models. Only as seen from particular views or forms of life are the concepts closed. As a result of the open concept caused by Family Resemblance, the boundaries of a group will sometimes be more clear and sometimes more blurry. Even without a core feature for membership, boundaries between concepts can be drawn, as Wittgenstein points out in §68 of the Philosophical Investigations. It can temporarily be thought of as closed to make it workable for a specific use:

"I can give the concept 'number' rigid limits ... that is, use the word 'number' for a rigidly limited concept, but I can also use it so that the extension of the concept is not closed by a frontier. And this is how we do use the word 'game'. For how is the concept of a game bounded? What still counts as a game and what no longer does? Can you give the boundary? No. You can draw one; for none has so far been drawn. (But that never troubled you before when you used the word 'game'.)"²⁵

Conclusion

If the hierarchical structure of vocabulary means a limitation – as Toni Peterson pointed out²⁶ – why has this remained the building principle for so many database archives' terminologies? I want to recall what Petersen wrote: "The semantic network of a hierarchical structure stretches just over broader and narrower terms and through synonyms and near variant lead-in terms. Building a network of related terms [...] takes on additional significance, especially for the representation of knowledge in a field"²⁷. Hierarchies cannot just be turned

---

24 | Ibid., p. 37e, §90
25 | Ibid., p. 28E, §68
26 | Petersen, Toni, "Developing a New Thesaurus for Art and Architecture", Library Trends, Vol. 38, No. 4, Spring 1990, p. 651
27 | Ibid., p. 651

over into semantics without a significant amount of additional efforts. Semantics and density of the net are a result of bringing together actual uses of language, from merging vocabularies and allowing multiple relations for each term. A standard thesaurus for Media Art and a semantic net are therefore, in my opinion, two oppositional and conflicting concepts. The semantic net can inform a lexical corpus, but a lexical corpus will not result in a semantically dense net. This investigation is centered around the question of a standard terminology for Media Art or what the lack of such a terminology means for the field. It showed that contrary to expectations of a solution, a standard terminology poses new and even more severe problems by narrowing, excluding meaning and thereby closing the concept of art. The impact of a decision for such a model is underestimated, as descriptive metadata does not only have a naming/labeling, but also a structuring function in the knowledge base. When the weight of a whole system is put on a rather arbitrary choice of words, when meaning is fixed and the number of the building blocks closed, one cannot endlessly build upon the resulting structure without experiencing the limitations of weight it can carry. To avoid limited and limiting database archives, I argued for an alternative model of structuring and labeling, an open framework instead of a closed and rigid structure, one that is based on Ludwig Wittgenstein's concept of Family Resemblance. With an open concept of art and a polythetic approach to descriptive metadata, we comply with the constant changes in and the interdisciplinary nature of Media Art. A network of relations frees us from the threats of collapsing, overstrained hierarchical systems. Applying and adapting the concept of Family Resemblances values and sustains the conceptual openness and rhizomatic interconnectedness of Media Art. We need to get rid of apriori schemes all together and shift from a fixed corpus to an open framework to develop a sustainable model for descriptive metadata.

Impressive. Memory, Matter and Mind

HERBERT HRACHOVEC

Think of a film. What sort of thing is it? It comes in reels or, more recently, in a great variety of digital formats. Numerous materials have gone into the product, specific activities were called for: the hiring of a director, scriptwriters and actors; the determination of locations; technical support was provided, a plot was enacted, recorded and put onto an appropriate medium; raw takes were cut and reassembled. This is only half of the story, though. What about the movie's impact on an audience? It is perceived as belonging to a certain genre, as entertaining or frightening and, generally, as a work of fiction (or documentary, or else), following the rules of narrativity and aesthetic conventions. These stories differ significantly – and yet, we have no difficulty in applying either of them, or some suitable combination, to the underlying phenomenon. Multiple layers of descriptions are, in this case, taken for granted. The situation is quite different when it comes to human memory.

Living organisms show a capacity to retain and redeploy information concerning their environment. How they are capable to do so is a fascinating topic of scientific investigation. There are, on the other hand, countless instances of individual memories constituting the mental set-up of humans, their personal identity and their ethical profile. Both viewpoints are, again, distinctively different. But here it seems that they are more incompatible than e.g. the lightning of a certain scenery and some conclusion a moviegoer might draw from it. The urge to construct a dualism is much stronger in the first case. And this, in turn, triggers a predictable monistic rejoinder, according to which the intricacies of social constructs like film cannot be taken as a guide in treating so-called natural phenomena.

This paper will set out a dualistic pattern, exemplified by (1) a neurobiological account of memory and (2) a short segment of the work of an Austrian avant-garde film-maker. This segment is chosen to simultaneously show a possible proximity as well as the presumable incompatibility of neurological and artistic approaches. The inevitable question of how those points of view relate to each other is taken up in the final section.

MEMORY MATTERS

Microbiology has advanced so far as to be able to investigate the details of neuronal interaction down to the level of single cells. Eric R. Kandel has received the Nobel Prize for his work on the formation of short and long term memory in the marine snails Aplysia. He was able to isolate the pathways connecting stimuli originating from the tail of this animal to a synaptic relay between sensory and motor neurons, which triggers a gill withdrawal reflex.[1] The next step was to look closer at the biochemistry of the synaptic setup. It turned out that a shock to the tail of Aplysia releases a chemical messenger (serotonin) which binds to receptors on the sensory neuron. A chemical substance (cyclic APM) is thereby produced, which in turn (via a protein called kinase A) enhances the release of glutamate (a neurotransmitter) into the synaptic cleft separating the sensory from the motor neuron. The synapse is strengthened, which leads to a marked change in behavior of Aplysia, e.g. enhanced reactions to an outside stimulus. This is a very superficial sketch of the neuro-physiological foundation of what can be called "short term memory", i.e. in this case a passing mode of information storage in a comparatively primitive organism. It might be argued that such imprints are hardly different from sunburns caused by solar radiation. Such burns, like neuronal activation, result from environmental conditions, carrying information about

---

1 | The following account is taken from Eric R. Kandel's autobiography *In Search of Memory. The Emergence of a New Science of the Mind*. New York 2006. For a handbook introduction see Craig H. Bailey and Eric R. Kandel: *Synaptic and Cellular Basis of Learning*. In: Gary G. Berntson, John T. Cacioppo: *Handbook of Neuroscience for the Behavioral Sciences*, Volume 1. pp.528ff. A generally accessible account is given by R. Douglas Fields *Making Memories Stick*. Scientific American 2005 (2). pp. 58ff

certain of its states. Commonsense talk of memory, on the other hand, is usually referring to a more complicated set of capacities of an organism. Sunburns are transient traces and it has been shown that actual excitation of sense receptors is similarly short-lived. Another type of pre-conditioned and/or conscious behavior is called for in order to understand how memory can persist over a longer period of time. Eric R. Kandel has, again, been instrumental in clarifying the neuro-physiological mechanism responsible for "long term memory". Surprisingly, it hinges on an anatomical change on part of the sensory neurons. While a single stimulus strengthens the synapse involved, repeated stimulation triggers a further chemical process within the cell. It is directed towards the genetic information residing in the cell's nucleus and results, ultimately, in the growth of additional synapses. Long term facilitation of biological senso-motor linkage is, as it turns out, supported by structural changes in the cell's architecture.

Kandel's results have, among other things, been made possible by advanced microscopic technologies. A sequence of chemical processes could thereby *be shown* to lead to cell development which could, in turn, be linked to functions of elementary memory. It has become standard procedure in public presentations, textbooks and journal publications to offer vividly schematic, multicolor graphs on order to show the essentials of bio-chemical interactions. One point is lost in these images, namely the materialistic thrust characteristic of neurophysiological research. It is, of course, helpful to be offered an easily surveyable sketch of the functional dependencies between the various processes underlying memory formation. Yet, an important fact is bracketed by this approach, namely the evidence offered by electronic micrographs that actually *present* (not *re*-present) the biological states. If it were only for the textbook illustrations we could just as well deal with artificial designs (not to mention science fiction). It has, however, to be conceded that those micrographs look considerably less tidy than their idealizations.

Pictures: E.R. Kandel loc. Cit. 18-4, p. 256. http://garcia.
rutgers.edu/tepper.research.html

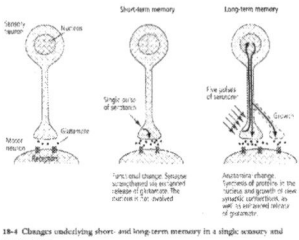 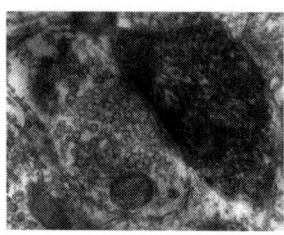

There is one important lesson to be drawn from pictures made by microscope and enhanced with superimposed inscriptions, pointing to an image's relevant features. Neurophysiological research does not proceed by simply rendering the material foundation of life in increasingly greater detail. Those textbook sketches are *unavoidable* since they depict theoretical constructs *guiding* empirical investigations. Looking at a coarse, gray, pointillist surface we do not spontaneously see a synapse, not to mention the chemical reactions leading to the formation of additional synapses. It is true: we have to be able to verify theoretical claims with reference to such visualizations. But we need *concepts* to visually distinguish the salient features. The matter of memory, explored by scientists like Eric R. Kandel, does only reveal its workings under the prompting of an extremely sophisticated array of cognitive and social presuppositions. We are talking about chemical compounds from within a certain understanding of storage and memory. The approach has proved to be extremely successful. But it should be mentioned that this undertaking does not have by itself any bearing on different attitudes to pictures.

Minding Memory

I have introduced some recent results in neurophysiology before remarking on the methodological status of depictions only made possible by sophisticated technical means. Now, consider another set of pictures which look quite similar: gray contours of nondescript blobs devoid of any obvious meaning. Their sheer physicality puts them firmly on the side of matter, subsisting as mindless given, like traces of sedimentation or molecular aggregations in a Petri dish.

Stillframe: 4/61 Mauern-Positiv-Negativ und Weg, Kurt Kren, Austria, 1961

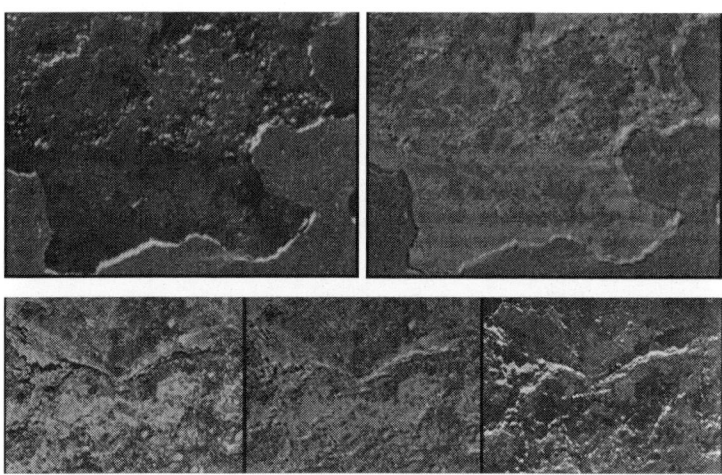

The images switch from positive to negative, a slow change of pattern can be detected. No visible clue enables the viewer to relate this sequence of images to any known natural process. They could be taken from a mudslide or a melting pot. They seem, if anything, just stuff; pure matter. Some filaments appear, delineating a network structure that superimposes itself onto the irregular patches.

Stillframe: 4/61 Mauern-Positiv-Negativ und Weg, Kurt Kren, Austria, 1961

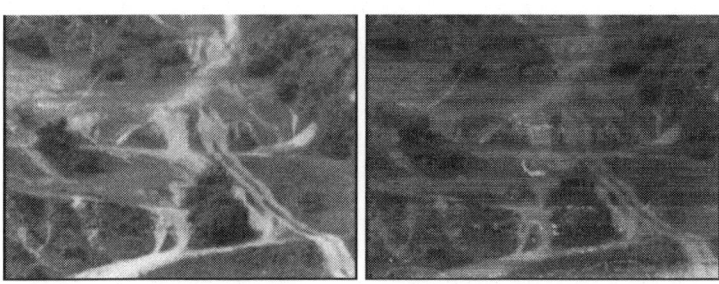

I have been withholding information regarding the provenance of the photo-clips. Just as the previous micrographs needed a caption to be properly deciphered, the second set of pictures has to be contextualized. Here is the relevant snapshot:

Stillframe: 4/61 Mauern-Positiv-Negativ und Weg, Kurt Kren, Austria, 1961

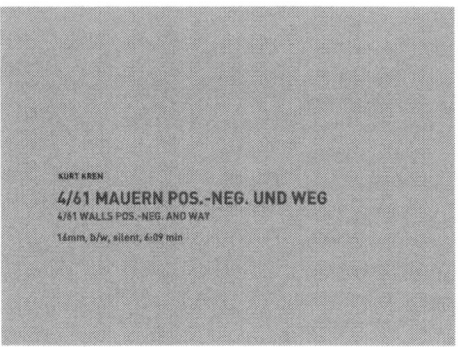

The stills have been taken from a film by the Austrian experimental filmmaker Kurt Kren. The title indicates that it has been produced in 1961 and furthermore it holds the key to the content of its visual representations. We are shown shots from (decaying) walls, alternatively switched to positive and negative mode. The appearance of a biological process is entirely superficial. And we are, secondly, presented with a hybrid image: a system of pathways superimposed upon the mural patterns. Cinematic procedures have resulted in a photographic double-take which can be read as a testimony to two material states encountered by an errant camera. The scenario lacks the intricacy of the previous example. It seems glued to a haphazard depiction of motives devoid of importance, dull instances of chance actions. Alas, there is more to the film than is apparent from its mere imagery.

A wall versus a path: the title of the film establishes a semantic opposition. Walls close in, they stop movement; whereas paths are made for movement. The pictorial patterns *per se* do not express these distinctions. These visual impressions could be given any number of treatments. But they *support* one very particular *interpretation*. The beholder may view those stimuli in a semiological vein. She may observe that block-shaped patterns are reminders of obstacles and that they are contrasted by the network of routes etched into the ground by humans crossing the terrain. She may, furthermore, come to think about the hybridization of those motives; taken in isolation those clips instantiate the dichotomy of stop and go. Dichotomies, however, are just one way to deal with competing states or ideas. The positive/negative modes of the first series of pictures can, in fact, be regarded an echo of this methodological observation. The law of the excluded middle is materialized by juxtaposing two images related to each other by a particular logico-ontological bond: each photo presents *precisely* that state of affairs that the opposite photo constitutively *fails* to present. Given any feature of one of the two, the corresponding one voids its existence.

This is, however, *not necessarily* the relationship between a wall and a path. A wall can be constructed to run parallel to the way; or it is a low barrier designed to be stepped over; or it is made of smoke and can easily be traversed. As those examples demonstrate the meaning of negation ("this is *not*") is not confined to contradictory exclusion. There is a variety of uses of the term and a great number of *differences* that can be established by means of negations less powerful than the global binary operator... "Speed bumps are a kind of wall not stopping, but slowing down traffic." Kurt Kren's film exhibits both kinds of negation, the exclusionary as well as the differential variety. Given the understanding of some of the formal characteristics of negation it can be seen as a playful attempt to visualize those features.

Let me add one more layer of meaning, from a professional philosophical point of view. The preceding considerations have been implicitly been guided by scholarly work entirely unconnected to Kurt Kren's film or his ingredients. In an exegetical paper on Ludwig Wittgenstein's early philosophy[2] I have argued that his elementary sentences in the *Tractatus* are a compound of two different kinds of meaning. Their *pictorial* sense derives from an isomorphism with real states of affairs, while their *veracity* has – according to Wittgenstein – to be located in their bipolarity, e.g. their being either true or false. Wittgenstein calls this their "Richtungssinn", ("directional sense"). Kurt Kren's distinctive shapes, combined with their positive/negative alternation, strike me as surprisingly felicitous "embodiments" of Wittgenstein's theoretical construct. And there is more.

---

2 | Herbert Hrachovec *Bilder, zweiwertige Logik und negative Tatsachen in Wittgensteins 'Tractatus'*. Zeitschrift für philosophische Forschung, 32 (4). pp. 526ff

According to the logical atomism of the *Tractatus* elementary propositions are to be strictly separated from each other. Every proposition is one of its kind, representing one basic fact. Taking up a term used by the later Wittgenstein one may talk of a "picture radical" underlying such propositions. Those radicals exhibit one particular structure *regardless* of the directional sense (the truth value) the picture is given in actual employment. Bivalent building blocks of logically simple expressions are then – in Wittgenstein's early view -- concatenated by truth-functional operators to create a linguistic pattern describing the world. Time and varying degrees of truth-ascription are absent from this account. It is, in short, quite similar to an array of static photo clips. Wittgenstein, returning to this issue in the thirties of the previous century, became aware of the shortcomings of this account. He found that a neatly cut (description of) the world built from immutable primitive elements was more of a dogma than a philosophically tenable position. This led him, among other things, to reassess his views on negation, allowing differences within a given spectrum, rather than insisting on a binary partition of the space of meaning. I will not elaborate on this, but only hint at the fact that the appearance of paths in addition to snapshots of walls in Kurt Kren's film is a clear visual parallel to this development.

MEDIATION

Proceeding from roughly similar looking images two markedly different stories have been told. The first was the sketch of the scientific research leading to the discovery of the neurophysiological preconditions of memory formation. The second one made an entirely different use of underlying depictions. Rather than take them as evidence by means of which theories can be tested, this story started with visual cues, proceeding to develop them into a semantic web and to ultimately utilize them as suggestive prompts within a philosophical argument. It has been pointed out at the beginning that, faced with everyday phenomena like movies, a kind of perspectival permissiveness is widespread. We do not worry too much whether we can strictly relate technical data on the supporting medium to high-level cineastic attitudes. The juxtaposition of diverging stories presented above is meant to prepare the field for the consideration of two quite distinct socio-cognitive strategies with regard to many phenomena, including memory. Relativism, post-modern multiplicity or simply tolerance is one option, as indicated. Yet, there is another influential attitude, deeply entrenched in our culture. Wittgenstein's *Tractarian* logic is, in fact, a prominent example of a "rigorous scientific" approach that only allows *one* access to truth via a closely regimented language and a binary procedure of deciding scientific claims. Forms of expression that do not conform to those requirements are considered inadmissible from the outset. Wittgenstein's spectacular transcendentalism refers a set of non-conforming means of expression into the realm of "Sinnlosigkeit" (lack of meaning), distinguishing them from "Unsinn" (nonsense), but this is quite an idiosyncratic position. It is more common to promote scientific materialism and reject attempts to diversify the field of scholarship by including "soft" disciplines like history, social anthropology or hermeneutics as inquiries into truth. The treatment given to (on the face of it) similar images in the preceding section can serve to highlight the dilemma. From a scientific point of view Eric R. Kandel does serious, well-grounded research, whereas the interpretation I have been imposing upon Kurt Kren's film are aesthetic criticism (at best) and more likely just flights of fantasy for hard-nosed scientists. A humanities scholar, in reply, will point out that this amounts to a dictatorial gesture, ruling out numerous possible options of dealing with the human predicament.

Those different cultures, as a matter of fact, coexist, albeit in constant conflict. Scientific rigor and pluralism hold on to their respective intuitions. The question then becomes: what about this coexistence itself? What should we make of a situation offering such conflicting features? This is the point made by our initial observations regarding movies. How should we treat the indisputable fact that the material substitute of forms of human life obeys its own, physical law *and* that those forms, in turn, are quite distinct from their bodily implementation (storage media versus movie genres). The weight of the problem, obviously, far exceeds the scope of the present contribution which will be confined to just one suggestion on how to approach this thorny issue. I take a hint from a book Antonio Damasio has written on Spinoza.[3] Damasio is a neurophysiologist trying to cope with the limitations of an exclusively "materialistic" outlook. In Spinoza he finds a

---

3 | Antonio Damasio *Looking for Spinoza*. London 2003

daring theoretical construct, a sort of synthesis between "body" and "mind". E.R. Kandel's autobiography, from which I took my cues in presenting his work, runs the two aspects together. It not only contains an account of his scientific discoveries, but also memories of his childhood, his collaborators, and his personal development. One question is not raised: how can the expressions of proteins in some particular cell relate to memories of the Viennese 18th district before the Second World War?

This is a philosopher's concern. Damasio presents Spinoza's solution: "What is Spinoza's insight then? That mind and body are parallel and mutually correlated processes, mimicking each other at every crossroad, as two faces of the same thing. That deep inside these parallel phenomena there is a mechanism for representing body events in the mind."[4] Monism and pluralism are both put aside in favor of another type of view. Take film reels and film genres. Is there a way to conceptualize their interdependence? Addressing the body-mind problem Spinoza's proposal is to consider both as parallel and mutually correlated processes. There is an underlying given (a continuum of "films" and "humans") and at least two different implementations of its potential which are held together by the very action of positing this given. It is because we regard films as something simultaneously material and cognitive that we can establish the necessary cross-connections. Easy, initial correlations could be established between photographic material and color films or between photographic procedures and animation. The general idea is that it must be possible to relate a multiplicity of appearances back to a common ground, *given* one wants to avoid ending up with numerous partly equivocal uses of a term.

Spinoza is explicitly stating that, as far as body and mind are concerned, they are two aspects of a common "thing". "quod scilicet Mens, at Corpus una, eademque res sit, quae jam sub Cogitationis, jam sub Extensionis attributo concipitur."[5] This is not the place to go into exegetical details concerning this surprising doctrine. I shall restrict myself to offering two lines of thought intended to show the attractiveness of this type of proposal. The first will be taken from the later Wittgenstein; the second one will refer back to the stories

---

4 | Damasio loc.cit. p. 217
5 | Baruch Spinoza *Ethica*. Pars Tertia, Propositio II, Scholium.

presented at the beginning of this article. Wittgenstein has introduced a standard psychological test design into his philosophical discussion of "seeing as ...", i.e. aspect dependence of visual impressions. His famous "duck-rabbit" exhibits a structure that can be put to good use in approaching Spinoza's two-aspect doctrine. There is just one underlying drawing, but two conflicting ways to look at them. Both claims are equally valid: (1) depictions of ducks and rabbits are generally distinct and (2) these depictions are (in this case) demonstrably rooted in a single substrate. We can identify the precise pictorial traces that can both be seen as a duck and as a rabbit. One may even pick only part of the drawing and obtain similar results: this very segment represents a duck's beak or a rabbit's ears.

This hint does, of course, not do justice to Spinoza's intricate demonstrations linking *res extensa* and *res cogitans*, nor does it in any way specify how one might go about relating (e.g.) *genetic change* in the establishment of long term memory's *content*. But it can show the attractiveness of a Spinozistic approach which is neither simply monistic, nor does it split the ontological realm into dualistically opposed parts. It rather endeavors to combine intuitions about the ultimate homogeneity of the world with intuitions pertaining to incommensurable ways of dealing with a common substrate. Wittgenstein's paradigm, likewise, shows a way to uphold a singularity while refusing to abandon multiplicity built upon it. To see *something* as one thing or another is not the most elementary starting point, which is, presumably, to *simply* see something. "Seeing as ..." introduces points of view and those, in turn, give rise to an ominous question. *What* are those different views about? How can some unit be posited as underlying the constitutive duplicity?

The question seems easy with respect to Wittgenstein and very difficult regarding Spinoza. One and the same glass window can be taken as part of a wall or as an opening. A piano can be used as a musical instrument or for book storage. Cases like this can be sorted out comparatively easy. The mind-body divide, on the other hand, seems to pose a much more complicated problem. Here we are faced with two qualities that have been defined as being constitutively different. There is no obvious neutral point of reference for physical stuff and ideas to converge upon. Whereas one can easily switch between the two ways to talk about a window it is difficult to see a *tertium* in the case of Cartesian dualism. Spinoza's answer cannot be explored here, but I will offer a first approach to justify the sort of thing he is doing.

To do so I return to the stories presented in the first two sections of this paper.

Someone looks at a micrograph. What is this an image of? Let us assume that one answer is that this shows the development of an additional synapse between a sensory and a motor neuron. And let us further assume that someone else claims that this shows the formation of an instance of long term memory. The first response is an example of straight "materialistic" talk, the second one makes reference to memory, which term has strong connotations to a state/capacity of a mind, i.e. a non-material phenomenon on the face of it. Once the situation is laid out like this the question immediately becomes: how can those two different descriptions relate to each other? Can we reduce phenomena of the mind to physical givens? This is the well-trodden path of debates about monism, dualism, reductionism, epiphenomenalism and so on. But, in the light of Kandel's story, consider the initial step that effectively triggered this set of options. A certain situation prompted a particular intake by a recipient. It is this intake which gets processed in various forms along the way, leading to points of view dramatically diverging and producing seemingly irreconcilable post-process results, e.g. reference to chemical compounds and to states of the mind. What should we say about their relationship? What *can* be said? The answer is: *the routes leading to different outcomes are all open to inspection*; it is possible to draw the course they are taking.

Two sets of genetic information can be identical in lab conditions. But they may be part of the physical setup of monozygotic twins. So they develop in different ways. Kandel's research, in fact, tells us that some of their genetic information will change due to environmental circumstances. The lives of two different persons develop, even though they share an extraordinary amount of common traits. And the obvious way to deal with this puzzle is to trace the respective lifelines, in other words to tell a story about an initial state and the emergence of differences. Such stories are necessarily told in hindsight. There is no way that, just given an ad hoc situation, the possible divergences can be foreseen. The initial state *as* initial state is already marked within a narrative. It is possible to bracket the narrative, but then the present problem disappears. It is only by *figuring in stories* that a given unit of information (of physical parameters of sense impressions) can be unfolded into various "branches". The question of how those branches relate to each other, then, comes to this: what do the narrative accounts tell us about those associations. The strength of dual-aspect theory of certain phenomena depends on the conviction carried by the pertinent stories. I started out observing that an easygoing relativism governs everyday talk about, for example, the world of film, whereas an almost obsessive dualism can be observed in a number of domains, some of them embattled in philosophy. The mind-body dichotomy is a traditional case in point. On closer inspection the weight of claims to have discovered the neurophysiological foundations of long term memory depends on how successful the accounts of bio-genetics and (ultimately) psychology can be interwoven. A similar result holds for Kurt Kren's film. His snapshot of patches of decaying walls is not *per se* visual comment of certain of Wittgenstein's ideas. They can be put forward as such insofar as a coherent cognitive relation is established in an argument. Mind-body dualism is quite a superficial pattern, and so is reductionism. What we should look out for are rich descriptions of investigative approaches and conceptual design.

The Many Faces of Expressionism

Prosthetic Memory, Mind and Matter in ORLAC'S HÄNDE/
THE HANDS OF ORLAC (1924)

THOMAS BALLHAUSEN

EXPRESSIONISM

»What does a contemporary director understand about expressionism?«[1] John Heartfield (then still under his birth name Helmut Herzfeld) asked the diplomat Harry Graf von Kessler in a letter in 1917. Together with George Grosz he had been contemplating possible film projects which should have given cinematography the appreciation reserved for an art form once and for all. Besides grotesque children's books like Heinrich Hoffmann's *Shock Headed Peter*, he suggested topics from the field of horror for the expressionistic film: Edgar Allen Poe's *The Mask of the Red Death* or Oscar Wilde's *The Picture of Dorian Gray*. He stated that a purely naturalistic adaption would lead to a poor plot structure when dealing with grotesque topics. Only expressionism could transfer the subtle to the screen. He – as well as later theorists – may have envisaged a "radical new filmic arrangement and spatial order" but planned a widely audience-minded production. George Grosz's and John Heartfield's ambitious expressionistic feature film projects were never realised. In 1919, one could read in *Der Kinematograph* magazine about the invention of »futurist film« without the article being able to define »futurist film«. It seemed too impossible to journalists, contrary to the also new style of expressionistic film. Just as Heartfield had felt previously,

---

1 | John Heartfield: *Ein wiederentdeckter Brief über expressionistische Filmpläne*. In: Kintop No. 8 (1999), p. 174.

one editorial was convinced that film was expressionism's ideal way of expression as both were about projecting interior processes to the outside: »Painting must be viewed as a rather undue means to display these inner experiences and emotions because its very nature ties it to a single phase of movement, and it has to reach for the peculiar means of painting over and parallel to depict a movement's flow or the complexity of an emotion. [...] How different would such inner stories and experiences be depicted by moving pictures which may casually follow the emotion's flow. Cinematographic technique offers the possibility of such a picture.«[2]

The fantastic sensations' filmic adaption whilst listening to music or the ghost-like stories of love and death which, as they did with Heartfield, read like early ideas for horror films were, cited as possible examples for this. Subsequently, so the theory goes, the contents (up until then film was emulating theatre and novel) could be reduced to the form's benefit, and so the establishment as a genuine form of art could be possible. Of course, the audience would always demand lighter entertainment which could be easier conveyed through conventional film »than through 'expressionist film'. It is about a way being shown on which the artistic film – much missed by many quarters – might be possible one day«.[3] Two years later, in 1921, *Der Kinematograph* put expressionistic art film in the centre of an article once again. In the article, it was claimed that genuine artistic means for film, which had not been borrowed from theatre, had been demanded as far back as 1913. Filmic adaptations of plays and novels alone are of little help to film to prove itself as an independent form of art. Besides the possibility of »refusal of movement« which would distinguish film from all other arts, this would also be the visualisation of thought – parallel to the ongoing plot. However, the article aims at a filmic composition which would make actors as redundant as set pieces. »Optical music«, moving ornaments, living architecture, blending colours should be able to be depicted. The vision is more of an experimental than a feature film: »There will come a time when eyes' music can be play as artistically on the bioscope as ears' music on the organ today.«[4] Of course it is conceded that the new, ideational form will not be able to supersede conventional cinematic drama.

---

2 | *Der Kinematograph* No. 658 (13. 8. 1919), s.p.
3 | *Der Kinematograph* No. 658 (13. 8. 1919), s.p.
4 | *Der Kinematograph* No. 744 (22. 5. 1921), s.p.

Working with painted sceneries, one could read, would become the directors' main task. The conviction was that this would – as with CALIGARI – only work as an experiment. »As soon as one of these characteristic sets was to be seen in another film, the suggestive impact of the scenery's mood and with it the whole piece's impact would be greatly diminished.«[5] Literary sources for this would be hard to find. The examples quoted, however, are not surprising: E.T.A. Hoffmann, E.A. Poe, Gustav Meyrink. There is evidence that elements of expressionistic film in Austrian film productions can be found as early as 1918. Judging this, one is not caught in the traditional difficulty whether the term expressionistic film generally means German silent film or the only genuine example of the form, THE CABINET OF DR. CALIGARI.[6] It is more a matter of influences, things in common or possible inspirations. In 1926 Rudolf Kurtz, in his book *Expressionismus und Film*, comes to the conclusion »that with the exception of CALIGARI's surprising success, expressionistic film has not met with a response from the audience«.[7] Although Austrian film studios like Sascha-Film could not compete with German studios, they inspired their productions. There are guesses that the first film to use expressionistic elements was DIE SCHLANGE DER LEIDENSCHAFT (1918) which was shot in Austria.[8] Only few Austrian feature films from the time of silent films in which expressionism's influence can be found have survived. Little is known about DIE SCHLANGE DER LEIDENSCHAFT which would confirm this thesis. The dramaturgic construction of the fever-nightmare, which chastens the protagonist, is what is most likely arguing for this assumption.[9] DAS HAUS DES DR. GAUDEAMUS (1921) also has not survived. Only stills and newspaper articles can be used as evidence

---

5 | *Der Kinematograph* No. 747 (12. 6. 1921), s.p.
6 | Cf. Leonardo Quaresima: »Der Expressionismus als Filmgattung«. In: Uli Jung & Walter Schatzberg (eds.): *Filmkultur zur Zeit der Weimarer Republik*. München: K.G. Saur 1992, p. 174-195.
7 | Rudolf Kurtz: *Expressionismus und Film*. Berlin: Lichtbild-Bühne 1926, p. 126.
8 | Cf. Jürgen Beidokrat: »Die künstlerische Subjektivität im expressionistischen Film«. In: Institut für Filmwissenschaft (ed.): *Beiträge zur deutschen Filmgeschichte*. Berlin: Institut für Filmwissenschaft 1965, p.71-87.
9 | Cf. *Die Filmwoche* No. 255 (1918), p. 12; *Paimann's Filmlisten* No. 106 (1918), s.p.

for expressionistic decor in this and possible other productions. DIE STADT OHNE JUDEN (1924), which in some scenes – the topics dream and insanity also dominate here – clearly uses an expressionistic aesthetic, is better documented. Robert Wiene's literary adaption ORLAC'S HÄNDE/THE HANDS OF ORLAC, based on one of French author Maurice Renard's works, fits onto the short list of expressionistic examples in Austrian film heritage.

GHOSTS

Director Andrei Tarkovsky describes the onset of public cinematography in its diverse effectiveness and mode of operation thus, »What, then, is cinema? Wherein lies its idiosyncrasy, wherein lie its possibilities, methods and images – not only in a formal but also – if you will – but also in intellectual regard? What materials does the film's director use? To this day, we cannot forget the ingenious film 'Arrival of a Train at La Ciotat' which was already shown in the last century and started it all. This commonly known film by Auguste Lumière was only shot because film camera, film roll and projector had just been invented. In this film that lasts no longer than half a minute, a sun-drenched part of a platform can be seen, ladies and gentlemen strolling up and down, and – finally – the train moving directly towards the camera from the depth of the shot. The closer the train got, the more the panic in the auditorium grew: people jumped up and ran out. Cinematic art was born in this moment. This was not only a technical question or a question of a new form of displaying the visible world. No, a new aesthetic principle had emerged here. This principle consists in man – for the first time in the history of art and culture – having found a possibility to immediately capture time and at the same time being able to reproduce it, coming back to it, howsoever it crosses his mind.«[10]

Film's promise of immortality implied here can be, totally in the medium's sense, expanded to the realm of the uncanny. Not only does the desire for novelty and documentation stand at the beginning of cinematography, but also the yearning for fear and dread. The ghosts and undead, which in their media character as revenants were and

---

10 | Andrej Tarkowskij: *Die versiegelte Zeit*. München: Ullstein 1985, p. 68.

still are the new medium's perfect protagonists, distinctly shaped film's early times. Austrian silent film also coquetted with the ever differentiating genre of fantastical film – the clearest reference can be noticed by looking at THE HANDS OF ORLAC. This film's production has already been discussed and followed at length in specialist media. An exemplary contemporary review proves that the high expectations in Wiene's new work – also in regard to comparable international productions – could be fulfilled, »A piano virtuoso is robbed of the use of his hands in a railway accident. His attending physician operatively gives him the hands of a just-executed robber and murderer. Given notice hereof by a stranger the artist fears that the dead man's hands will drag into crime, and soon afterwards he is suspected of killing his own father. Only now is it revealed that this deed was done by a friend of the executed man. This friend also carried out the crime the innocently executed man had been charged with. – The subject has a thoroughly gripping exposition and, optimally asserted by a splendid ensemble lead by Konrad Veidt, keeps up the suspense until the last scene. The direction is taut and diligent, especially in the railway accident's very realistic scenes; the get-up is tasteful, effectively underscoring the plot's events. The photography is on a peak in every aspect. A domestic film in no way inferior to the best foreign products.«[11]

MOVEMENT

Two of cinema's main themes are brought together in ORLAC'S HÄNDE/THE HANDS OF ORLAC. The train journey on the one hand and the therewith associated dynamic of movement, the origin of cinematography addressed by Tarkovsky, and, on the other hand, the no less frightening fantastic which differentiated itself into the various genres of fantastic film in the 1930s and 1940s. Both realms are connected by the idea of travel, the adventurous journey into the unknown. The railway accident prefacing is part of the filmic concept of shock pursued by Wiene, in which the mass of modernity as well as the body parts are set in motion. This is a concept with a real historic foundation: »[E]arly railroad travelers lived a double relation to the train journey: the pleasure of speed, the thrill of the 'projectile' being

---

11 | *Paimann's Filmlisten* No. 441 (1924), p. 181.

shot through space, matched against the terror of collision and its psychological effects – phobia, anxiety, and, in many cases, hysteria. Certainly, as noted, with the marked increase in railroad accidents in the United States after 1853, the extent to which fear of collision had become bound up with the fabric of train travel could not be doubted. The medical and legal professions were in any case obliged to take the connection seriously, since lawsuits mushroomed from the mid-nineteenth century on claiming damages for victims of 'railway spine'. 'Railway spine' was a condition analyzed as a deterioration of nervous tissue, a result of physical damage to the spinal cord – damage typically received in a railway accident. Pathological causes and effects were the only admissible evidence for claims against the railway companies until litigants began to demonstrate, with no corresponding physical source, symptoms such as anxiety, partial loss of vision, paralysis, and dyspepsia. Nerve disease studies taking place simultaneously in England, France, Germany, and the United States led the medical profession to expand its view of 'railway spine' include 'railway brain', a more psychologically based disease. [...] If early railway travel caused its passengers considerable anxiety in anticipation of accidents, by the later nineteenth century improvements in railway travel had led to the reduction of anxiety and the internalization of panoramic perception as second nature, such that one no longer necessarily expected a violent interruption in the train journey. The term 'shock' then applies all the more to the phenomenon of the accident – which, though possibly less frequent [...], had certainly not disappeared or faded as a 'horizon of expectation'.«[12]

The dynamic of disruptive shock (beyond the quoted horizon) addressed therewith also applies to Orlac's self-image and so also means the character's head. According to the accident scene shaped as a battlefield the protagonist's interior life in this film, which stands at the intersection of expressionistic speculative fiction and psychological thriller, is a gashed landscape – a circumstance which begins to have negative consequences for Orlac, »More than the victim of an intrigue, Orlac becomes the victim of his own imagination. At the same time he falls for a picture of himself like it was embodied by expressionistic film, and almost perishes because of it. Whereas Fritz Lang's criminal in the sound film MABUSE sarcastically departed from

---

12 | Lynn Kirby: *Parallel Tracks. The Railroad and Silent Cinema*. Durham: Duke University Press 1997, p. 58f.

expressionism [...] Orlac distanced himself from it in an inner life and death fight. A psychologising bypath of the genre, which opened up new possibilities especially for actors, starts with ORLAC'S HÄNDE. Horror is no longer just experienced as a possibility of the uncanny in the picture but also as man's subjective sensation.«[13]

REASON

With the cuts – almost regardless of their running along wrists or across mental rooms of imagination – the segmented parts together with the shapes are set in motion. The cutting security of form and contour can easily turn into the opposite. The mutilated and then cobbled together again bodies are no less out of form/norm as the limbs and organs taking on a life of their own. According to the film-technical developments of the means for composition cut, a filmic tradition which demonstrated the constant increase of chaotic conditions along with the destruction of the form arose also on contentual level.[14] Not least because of this does the film's dramatic (plot) opening entail hysteria, loss of confidence and crime. Wholly committed to curiosity, the arrangement of dread and the creeps of expressionistic film, Wiene's masterpiece bears a homonymous title. In the accident in question the pianist Orlac loses his hands which, in a staging anticipating the classic horror genre, are replaced by the hands of – as it turns out later to everybody's relief: alleged – murderer Vasseur. Orlac, who gradually perceives himself as overwhelmed and traumatised by his Shakespeare-esque blood-stained/stainless hands, and his wife Yvonne are only tokens of the actual criminal – the greatly cunning and ruthless Nera. It is crucial for the crooked trick to work to endow a consciousness for the pre-memory, for a prosthetic memory of the transplanted hands. This is an image with correlating filmic roots: »In the 1908 Edison film The Thieving Hand, a wealthy passer-by takes pity on an armless beggar and buys him a prosthetic arm. As the beggar soon discovers however, the arm has memories of its own. Because the arm

---

13 | Georg Seeßlen & Fernand Jung: *Geschichte und Mythologie des Horrorfilms*. Marburg: Schüren Verlag 2006, p. 116.
14 | Cf. Eberhard Nuffer: *Filmschnitt und Schneidetisch. Eine Zeitreise durch die klassische Montagetechnologie*. Potsdam: Polzer 2002, p. 51-60.

remembers its own thieving, it snatches people's possessions as they walk by. [...] This moment in early cinema anticipates dramatically a preoccupation in more contemporary science fiction with what I [= Landsberg, T.B.] would like to call 'prosthetic memories'. By prosthetic memories I mean memories which do not come from a person's lived experience in any strict sense. These are implanted memories, and the unsettled boundaries between real and simulated ones are frequently accompanied by another disruption: of the human body, its flesh, its subjective autonomy, its difference from both the animal and the technological. Furthermore, through the prosthetic arm the beggar's body manifests memories of actions that it, or he, never actually committed. In fact, his memories are radically divorced from lived experience and yet they motivate his actions. Because the hand's memories – which the beggar himself wears – prescribe actions in the present, they make a beggar into a thief. In other words, it is precisely the memories of thieving which construct an identity for him. We might say then that the film underscores the way in which memory is constitutive of identity.«[15]

Maurice Renard's exuberant literary source, of which exists a translation by Mabuse-creator Norbert Jacques, turns into an expressionistic intimate play between the novel's protagonists in Wiene's screen adaption. Around Vasseur's corpse as the negative centre of gravity, Orlac, his wife Yvonne and the shrewd criminal Nera gather for a little ballroom dance which changes into a downright danse macabre as the plot progresses. The solution is delivered partly by Nera himself who seems to prevail with his extortive plans against Orlac. The – not insignificant – rest – bringing to light Vasseur's and Orlac's innocence – is solved by the police. It is remarkable that Nera had reached for the means of cinematography in the literary source to technically substantiate his allegedly occult deceit and give it credibility. At this point it says the novel, »Young man, forget your schoolteachers' lessons, especially the physics courses, and especially optics, and especially ray science, and especially the 'real images'. A game of curved mirrors and lenses suffices the man who knows how to make use of it to project any immovable or movable image into space as if it

---

15 | Alison Landsberg: »Prosthetic Memory: Total Recall and Blade Runner«. In: Mike Featherstone & Roger Burrows (eds.): *Cyberspace/Cyberbodies/Cyberpunk: Cultures of Technological Embodiment*. London: Sage Publications 1996, p. 175

were on solid ground [!]. One has made graceful and surprising uses of it; I remember [amongst others] a living dancer appearing in a narrowed scale. We have made use of the cinema. – What do you want! There are those who know how to make use of the cinema, the others know how to make use of a phonograph.«[16]

Reaching back to explanatory models outside of all metaphysics in this period's Austrian film, since it integrates elements of the uncanny and the horrible at the same time, is only too understandable. People had just escaped confusion and only seeming predictability of an industrialised conflict, World War I. Now the horror of loss of control and the retrieval of control and the framing order via a rationally determined explanatory model is gone through on the screen. In total accordance with the gothic novel's literary tradition, ratio comprehensively wins – a fact not devoid of all uncanniness.

---

16 | Maurice Renard: *Orlac's Hände*. München: Drei Masken Verlag 1922, p. 254.

Killing (the power of) time
Archiving selves, cities, histories and universes

CHRISTIAN HELLER

SELF-PRESERVATION

Self-preservation is a common urge among Terran lifeforms. We humans though may be the only ones able to verbalize it and to reflect on what this "self" to preserve is. I do not intend to present here an elaborate discussion on the definition of "self". For a start, let's assume we are talking about an inclusive assortment of information processes like consciousness, memory, personality and other qualities usually listed under the umbrella term of "mind". In any case it's an information process that we cannot easily reduce to dead matter as we understand it today. (As science marches on, our understanding of the interconnections between mind and matter may improve. See the fourth part of this text for further discussion.) And yet we consider ourselves capable of determining a critical location for its emergence: our brain.

For the goal of self-preservation, this entanglement of our selves to specific objects in the physical world is a major problem. Every brain to which a self belongs is only part of a larger physical system: a specific human body, a complex machinery that keeps the brain and thereby the self running. Unfortunately, the human body is frail, easily disturbed in its functioning by damage and aging. Once its core processes are hurt, the brain's activity quickly disintegrates, and our self with it – at least as far as it is actually stored in there.

These unfortunate implications may explain the popularity of the idea of "soul": a form of personal mind immortal due to its mystical, dualistic independence from the constraints of matter. Though somehow an inhabitant of the body during the latter's lifetime, in

Christian theology the soul is able to survive the body's death and enter an afterlife beyond our current physical universe. In this regard, this "Heaven" of afterlife may be considered an ideal garden of pure information not torn down by laws of the profane world of matter; thus, time here is no threat to the preservation of self. Once portability of the mind away from a single human body is achievend, the mind's endurance seems to become a triviality – another example would be the reincarnation concept of eastern religions. The idea of "soul" may thus satisfy self-preservation urges of those who are able to believe in it. But not everyone shares these religious views. So we still have to look for other options.

If we exclude mind portability as an option, self-preservation demands hardening the original storage medium: Keep your body healthy and live long. But natural evolution does not optimize its organisms so much for longevity or health of individual animal bodies as for longevity and distribution of individual genes. It cares much more for our sperm and egg cells than for us growing old, wise or happy. As we develop priorities different from those of genetic evolution, it is our turn to optimize our bodies towards those priorities. Why not optimize our human biology towards greater durability and longer-lasting health of the individual body?

We need not consider this goal too far-fetched, in view of the last centuries of ever-improving biological science and technology. We are pursuing it since the first inventions of medicine and have already reached a stage of biotech that would seem futuristic to most of our ancestors. Why not approach the process of aging as yet another disease that can be attacked – if not with a single magical cure, then with an ever-growing repository of cures and therapies of the damages that accumulate in the body as we grow older? This is what life-extensionists like biogerontologist Aubrey de Grey propose[1]: to systematically identify and counter the disintegrative processes of aging, continuously rejuvenating a body system's parts by repairing them with, over the course of time, progressively better medicine. We may, so de Grey argues with some techno-optimism, soon reach a point where, each year, biotechnology is able to extend the expected lifetime of a living generation for a year or more. Such a generation would be lucky enough to expect living very long indeed, into a future where

---

1 | de Grey & Rae 2007

rejuvenation becomes easier and easier and eternal youth would finally be achieved.

Naturally, visions like this encounter skepticism. Even if the human biological system could, in theory, be constantly repaired towards rejuvenation, the technology breakthroughs needed may be far beyond our current generation's lifetimes. And even then, immortality would not be achieved: Human bodies do not die of aging only, but of other causes, too. It's hard to imagine any biotechnological cure to, e.g., blowing up a person in an explosion. So the cause for self-preservation still must insist on the other option: the portability of the self.

We have discounted the mysticism of soul as a solution. Yet historically, the soul has never been the only conceptualization of the self as something that can gain a certain independence from the body. There have been numerous other ideas for forms considered as belonging to our selves yet somehow being able to survive beyond our body. Think, for example, of one's reputation, honor, name.

Looking back in history, we know of many powerful men who were able to build monuments to themselves – so that generations afterwards people would still remember their name and face. Going down into the history books was always part of a king's job description. Either it was their deeds' momentousness that would preserve their memory; or their privileged access to endurable storage media and the workforce to sculpt those into statues, pyramids, inscriptions. Not a very satisfying solution, though: in a world where space for text is scarce, not even the wealthiest ruler can count on his self's endurance for more than a few streamlined bits of lasting interest to future court historians and politics; ancient chronologists regularly punished the memory of those royals they deemed too self-obsessed and peculiar, from Echnaton to Nero. Nor would the vast majority of non-royals find any immortality outlet under these conditions: a peasant could hardly count on his name being remembered in his village a few generations after his death.

Once writing materials become more abundant and available, and a writing culture develops beyond dynasty listings and tax collections, the situation improves: in the Graeco-Roman world, a whole class of privileged literates emerges. They pursue writing as an individualistic activity to record their own experiences and thoughts, to a great depth of what goes on inside their mind. All those letters, personal opinions and philosophical arguments may be written on crumbling papyrus much less endurable than the rock temples of Abu Simbel.

But they're written in crude alphabetic scripts that can be easily and cheaply copied. This high portability allows for memetic propagation of mind depths like those of Hellenistic philosophers, reaching far beyond the calling distance and lifetime of their physical bodies. Today, we can still converse with fragments of the minds of Aristotle and his peers. Those memetically lucky ancient few have achieved a sort of immortality for the parts of their selves they deemed substantial enough to be written down.

Externalization of individual minds into written text has exploded in the last few centuries. At first, diaries, memoirs, biographies and character studies of novel writers reassured the bourgeois subject of its relevance and uniqueness. Then, nowadays, even the most mundane and incidental details of everyone's life get recorded in the abundant and ubiquitous digital media of the internet age. Getting stored as a person in the records of Twitter, Google and Facebook is not so much a privilege anymore but a default. The data now recorded often goes beyond what the individual hopes for as defining characteristics of their self: data protection enthusiasts actually argue for curbing scriptorial immortality as it burdens the memory of a person's name with more than just the politically opportune.

From a past where hardly any information about anyone was recorded beyond the vicinity of their living body, we have gone to a present where everyone's words and movements are transformed into highly portable, disembodied data copied from internet server to internet server many times over around the globe. There are many who embrace this development. They pursue blogging and status messages as means of extended self-expression. They try to dissolve their lives into machine-readable, quantifiable data that can be analyzed and compared to gain a better understanding of what determines them – consider the movement of "The Quantified Self"[2].

Or they attempt to map and externalize their mind's memories, concepts and interconnections into the evolving hypertext of personal wikis – as practised, for example, at the personal websites of Rainer Wasserfuhr[3] or the author of this very text[4].

Such a personal wiki may serve as an individual's mind backup and extension and, dependant on the creativity of the technical

---

2 | http://quantifiedself.com
3 | http://mindbroker.de
4 | http://www.plomlompom.de

implementation, develop some kind of autonomy and life on its own, very much surviving the physical death of its author. In the end, it may provide an intermediate stage to what futurists call a "mind upload" – a concept we will revisit near the end of this text. To quote Wasserfuhr:
"It is becoming more and more a mirror of my thoughts, of my entire life. [...] [T]here is a more and more strong convergence between things that are written down in my lifewiki and thoughs in my brain."[5]

RECONSTRUCTION OF PHYSICAL ENVIRONMENTS

After talking about preserving something usually considered "mind", let's reverse the perspective by talking about something usually considered "matter": the preservation of physical environments. Let's define physical environments as any configuration of a space in time that can be walked through by our human bodies, e.g. a beach, a building, a cityscape.

It's not very common for such configurations to endure for long. The shape of man-made environments rarely survives longer than a few hundred years. Nature alone attacks them with many agents of change: erosion, fire, earthquakes. Few exceptions like the Pyramids of Gizeh may look today roughly as they looked thousands of years ago. But in most cases we can be happy to find any ruins, a few stone foundations as remnants of ancient man-made structures. The single original instantiation of any physical environment is hardly an endurable format for a snapshot of it. So let's assume we want to make such a snapshot available to future generations – what alternatives do we have? Obviously we need to transform the physical environment into information we can store in other media and, from there, reconstruct. That should satisfy our preservation criteria.

Like for the externalization of personal minds, let's consider the option of written text: write the verbal description of, for example, a building. At first sight, this looks doable at least for buildings like the Pyramids: a clearly defined, simple geometric shape of such and such parameters, made from certain materials. At second sight, any such description would extremely simplify and abstract the structure even

5 | http://mindbroker.de/wiki/LifeWiki

of the Pyramids, or else we would have to write down every single stone with its peculiarities and, consequently, every single atom. If we would refuse to simplify, our book would grow to an unimaginable volume. For more complicated architecture (the Cologne Cathedral?), simplification down to a manageable size of purely verbal description may not even be possible.

Pictures may be more convenient. They are better able to capture information about the arrangement of shapes and of textures. Nevertheless, they have their own limitations: they contain only two-dimensional visual impressions of objects, cut to certain central perspectives, and of limited size and resolution. We cannot directly pictorially capture sound, smell or other non-visual data of a physical environment. Yet we may get pretty close to the three-dimensional shape of an object via many different pictures of it from different perspectives. To have a thousand different drawings or photographs of a physical environment should provide a good guide to satisfyingly reconstruct it; this is already a given in our digital age for many popular places. Search for "Eiffel tower" on the Flickr image hosting platform and rest assured you'll find enough pictures from all imaginable perspectives of said monument to, should it ever vanish, rebuild it from these pictures alone up to the last screw.

Any such reconstruction would have to converge onto a 3D representation of the environment preserved. Let's look at ways this could turn out. A first example: movie sets. Even in the age of CGI, big budget productions like to have three-dimensional sets for their actors to walk through. One of the main selling points of, for example, the TV series *Rome* (2005) was its elaborate physical reconstruction of the ancient Forum Romanum, at two thirds its original size. A large part of *Rome*'s promotional material was spent on boasting about the sets, on how carefully they were designed, on how they provided authenticity and how actors could turn around 360° and walk from corner to corner without losing touch to their immersion in a snapshot of the distant past. One can certainly argue about the authenticity details of such a reconstruction; nevertheless, *Rome*'s set may have been the closest thing available in our age to the original Forum Romanum, most probably giving a better impression of it than its pitiful ruins in present-day Rome.

Nevertheless, it failed in one important aspect: being an endurable preservation of it. As a physical reconstruction, it had to face the same struggle any physical structure has to face: the series ended when the set accidentally burned down.

A physical 3D reconstruction thus may be a valid output, but virtual 3D reconstructions are the better storage format. One place to look for examples of those is video games. Though only projections onto 2D screens, first person shooters etc. allow for the exploration of 3D environments with all the freedom of movement and perspective a human observer would have in an actual 3D environment.

In video games, we are used to purely invented environments, but we also find reconstructions of historical ones. We can live through the Normandy Invasion of 1944 on Omaha Beach in *Medal of Honor*, copying the movie *Saving Private Ryan*. Or, in the *Grand Theft Auto* series, we can walk through thinly veiled reconstructions of real cities like New York or Los Angeles as channeled through the popular culture of a certain decade: In *Grand Theft Auto: Vice City*, a pastiche of 1980s Miami can be freely explored as it was presented in the TV series *Miami Vice* or the movie *Scarface* in that decade. Such environments are probably the closest that we get nowadays to the Holodeck simulations of periods past visited by the characters of *Star Trek: The Next Generation* (there also mostly used as gaming environments). The idea to use such gaming environments for snapshots of cityscapes is expanded by, for example, the community behind *GTA: Berlin*[6]: realistically rebuilding the present-day city of Berlin into the *Grand Theft Auto* engine, landmark by landmark, metro station by metro station. One could argue that gaming environments are no snapshots of reality. So let's jump to an alternative for multi-dimensional snapshots of physical environments: the series of *Google Maps*, *Google Earth* and *Google Street View* products. *Google Maps* starts with a high-resolution 2D super-photograph of the whole planet Earth's surface. *Google Earth* adds geometrical information extending the surface's dimensionality: altitude and (mostly simple) 3D shapes representing buildings inside of cities, those blocks textured with photographs of their buildings' facades. Thus we get a primitive 3D representation of the planet's surface and cities that can be moved through freely. This information set is extended further by *Google Street View*, which adds street-level 360° panoramic images of cityscapes as seen by cameras mounted on cars, which can be clicked through sequentially, following the cars' driving paths through cities' streets. Put all that

---

6 | http://gtaberlin.de

together and you get quite a comprehensive (and annotated, too!) database on the physical environment of the whole planet, from a vast number of perspectives, though with varying resolution depending on the area selected.

These Google snapshots of Earth's surface are, of course, snapshots of certain points in time. It's not unusual to encounter views quite dated, with buildings still standing that have been torn down since, or vice versa. There is some value to up-to-date screenshots, so Google will regularly update their data to a more recent stage. That does not mean that old data is deleted, though: for a while now, *Google Earth* has been offering a time slider functionality, enabling the viewing of earlier datasets. Thus, Google adds a fourth dimension to the freedom of movement it offers through the physical world: travelling not only freely through space, but through time as well. This trend gets pushed to the extreme by *Google Earth* layers like *Ancient Rome 3D*, adding a 3D model reconstruction of the whole city of Rome as it is supposed to have looked like in 320 AD on top of modern-day Rome.

With all this 4D data on our physical environment available at our fingertips, interesting "Augmented reality" ("AR") applications become possible. Consider the AR smartphone app *Layar*[7], which allows us, through the window view of our smartphones, to overdraw our visual perception of the physical environment with additional information, like names or hypertext links. Arbitrary visual manipulation of the environment is possible as well: *Layar* allows the transformation of present-day views into what they would have looked like in earlier stages of the physical environment if those are available as 3D models to be layered onto the landscape. Examples realized by *Layar* so far include the New York World Trade Center destroyed in 2001 and the Berlin Wall: just look at the world through the *Layar* window and see those buildings past re-appear in the size and angle you would see them if you'd be there a quarter century earlier.

What this all adds up to is a 4D bubble consuming more and more of the physical environment of Earth, which we can move through freely in all directions – including forwards and backwards in time, at least as far as past models date back and models of the planned future are already incorporated (like those of construction projects not yet finished or even started). This bubble's data is technically highly portable and thereby potentially safer from the erosion of time than the

---

7 | http://layar.com

physical environment it describes – though as long as it is property of Google Inc. and bound to its servers, its portability may leave some desires unanswered. But consider this: our present-day physical environments are preserved in this 4D bubble, to be roamed freely from any future environment consumed by the bubble, in the very same immediacy that we can roam them today. Information is not lost now but preserved; our past and present are just as available to any observer of the future as his own time. Is time thus defeated?

FLATTENING AND POSTMODERNIZATION OF HISTORY

Such a view of the past as completely available and immediate is quite the contrary to how we usually perceive history. History in many ways can be considered the study of a past not directly available, that we have to inquire about and reconstruct from often insufficient data. History's past is buried in a certain depth, a certain distance from us that can be crossed by effort alone – and sometimes not at all.

The past of history is delivered to us only through present-day artifacts that we have to interpret as holding traces of a past. History tries to contextualize ruins and armory, statues and bric-a-brac; but its main sources for that contextualization is the written word: old parchments and inscriptions, bureaucratic documentation, letters. If we find any such writing, then we have before us a messenger of the past, insofar as we assume that someone in the past put down on it a perspective on his present reality. Pastness is inscribed into the document, for look at the crumbling papyrus, the archaic typography and how it was only found by excavating ruins deeply buried in the ground. But it is still a present-day object, its molecules' existence intersecting with the Now, and we can only read it via our present-day knowledge. We hope to derive historical value from it through information about the past stored in it, but the object is not the past in itself. When we proudly exhibit it in a historical museum's glass cabinet, we do not exhibit the past, but merely a symbol of the past and a pattern that, we hope, remained to a large degree unchanged since that past.

To harvest information about the past from it, we scan in the document for a portable image to be passed around safely without damaging the original. We then try to decipher the typography, ambiguous, faded and broken by worm holes: we cannot read the text right away, we actually have to re-create, produce it. What text we get, we cannot take as a direct window into past reality either: we have to fit it into certain contexts and reference systems for it to make any sense, and even then we still have to do text-critical work on it, assuming imperfect or intentionally misleading descriptions of the past. What we thus get to know is riddled with insecurities. If we believe to have comprehensive information about a certain period, as in the 4D Google Earth bubble described above, we may feel greater security about ambiguities. But the farther away a past is, the less we know about the period, the more holes we have to fill, the less sure we can be about contexts and references. Thus, the study of history becomes a free-form literary interpretation work, where it's doubtful whether any definite reality can be found at the bottom at all.

Such history can hardly claim more respect for its truth probabilities than fiction does – which, too, may occasionally overlap with reality. This redeems depictions of history disrespectful towards alleged realities of the past like the movie 300(2006) about the Battle of Thermopylae. In all its highly stylized, over-the-top, fantastical, antirealistic nature, one can hardly criticize it for historical inaccuracy. Its most outrageous parts strongly result from taking ancient sources – that modern history of the time, too, is necessarily mostly built on – by word, without applying certain realism and normalization filters used by modern historians. As such, it gives accurate representation to the source material's wobbliness. Other movies try to give a realistic impression of distant time periods by normalizing them into our modern ideas of realism. 300instead is honest about dealing with aloof speculation and invention beyond which we can hardly know anything. We simply lack the volume of trustworthy historical data to honestly disprove such a fantasy with realistic counterpoints.

A more appropriate way to deal with history, then, might be to treat it as fiction. A good idea of how this could look like is offered by the wiki "TvTropes"[8]. Here, patterns of popular fiction are collected, mostly of television shows, videogames, anime, comic books and literature, and compared between works. Considering the possibility of reading history as fiction, it's no surprise that historical subjects, too, have found their way here. So instead of analyzing the historicity of Julius Caesar, he is analyzed as a configuration of literary traditions and cliches like "Antagonist in Mourning", "Asskicking Equals Authority", "Magnificent Bastard" or "Take Over The World", linking him to

---

8 | http://tvtropes.org

pages discussing The Joker, Klingons, Dracula and Marvel's Doctor Doom, respectively. Granted, literary traditions may evolve as a mirror of reality. But the way TvTropes sorts its material, "Real Life" uses of any trope are just one bullet point in many. In the eyes of postmodernity, history is but yet another literary text without more dignity than any other.

Such an understanding of history may be unwittingly reproduced in what German discourse calls "Chronologiekritik" ("criticism of chronology"): large scale historical revisionism calling into question not just a few historical facts, but the existence of whole epochs and civilizations usually considered of central importance to western or world history, due to a radical denouncement of historical sources as mostly invention. German author Heribert Illig, for example, denies[9] the existence of three centuries of the Early Middle Ages, including Charlemagne, claiming their chronologies to be forgeries of a later date. And truly, if history is just text, it is easily forged – as demonstrably happened quite a lot to documents in those days.

Illig's chronologiekritik is petty compared to that of Russian mathematician Anatoly Fomenko. In his theories[10], all of history up to the Renaissance is mostly wrong and no historical information about any past is transmitted from before the 9th century. Ancient civilizations happened, if at all, in what we currently call the Middle Ages. Jesus Christ lived in the 12th century, and only later was the Bible written, New Testament first. Constantinople was the first Rome, after which an Italian city was named whose historians liked to imitate in their historical writings that large empire of the East. Petrarca and Livy were contemporaries. Old Egypt was as much Christian as was Ancient India; pagan prologues are just backdated Christian mutations and hereticisms. Conventional chronology was forced on historical memory only in the 16th and 17th century by some influential chronologists, founded on accumulated misdatings, wrongly read sources, forgeries and dubious rationalizations, and has since then served uncriticized as history's backbone.

Apart from their colorful nature, what's most interesting about Fomenko's ideas are the methods by which he claims to arrive at them. His "empirico-statistical" analysis starts with treating all available historical and chronological text, all ancient writings, dates, names

9 | Illig 2005
10 | Fomenko 2007

and lifetimes of persons and cities as one vast, flat and unsorted alphabetical and numerical text volume. Over this he forces algorithms for pattern recognition, data compression and sorting by formal criteria. He thus finds lots of dynasties, wars and biographies that seem to run similar courses and thereby manages to conflate a lot of widely separated facts into one and the same. He also enjoys translating names, descriptions and datings back and forth between different languages and writing conventions and forces them through simple string manipulation filters until they become identical to each other. Disrespectful to any previous historical theories built on and reshaping the historical text, and proudly blind to its semantics, he juggles and shifts around its words to superficially more efficient forms like an algorithm improving a book's text by sorting all its letters alphabetically. In short, he proves that conventional chronology and geography is quite an inefficient compression algorithm for history as alphanumeric text.

For all its aesthetic appeal, this solution to history, like Illig's, fails to satisfy academic historians. They argue that archaeological findings and physical/chemical dating disprove such alternate chronologies. Fomenko thus has no choice but to attack these very methods: arguing that both archaeology and dating via, for example, the radio-carbon method and dendrochronology are too vague at best and only calibrated on conventional chronology, thus only able to prove what the latter presupposes; and that in archaeological excavation only that is looked for and kept which fits those same expectations: they determine what is original and what forgery, which meter reading is plausible and which one is not. He fails to name methods for historical dating or research that do not in such a way calibrate themselves on a commonly accepted reading of a body of texts considered historical. He does not actually assert it so directly, for then he would have to concede the arbitrariness of his own counter-history, but in the end, in his science of history, text will always be supreme to physical artifacts and methods. And since text can easily lie or be forged in later times, and even the algorithms of his own "empirico-statistical" method have to be calibrated against some body of historical texts accepted by him, trustworthy history cannot actually be possible.

So what does this mean for the transmission of information through time, from past into future? Let's imagine us visiting the ruins of the Acropolis of Athens. Do we have before us a messenger of the past, from which we can truthfully reconstruct previous reality? If we follow the line of thought developed above in discussing Fomenko, we cannot: for the only thing the Acropolis can mirror is our present-day inventions of history, and we can derive no other knowledge about the past from it. (Fomenko actually claims that Ancient Greece never existed; that the Acropolis merely consists of Ottoman buildings creatively reduced by Western archaeologists to their own ideal of antiquity.) Thus we could raze the Acropolis; we would not lose any connection to the past from this, for we never had any. If, on the other hand, we believe the historians who attest that physical objects provide veracity to historical text, provable via hard natural science, then of course something like the Acropolis is the only anchor we have of the past; a digitized image of it, like in *Google Earth*, would not suffice due to it being as easily manipulated as any other text. This past of history would be opposed to the kind of past simulated on *Google Earth*or on Holodecks, due to its physical provability.

Concluding Cosmological Considerations

Using a phrase like "physical provability" is of course somewhat bold. Yet questions concerning the possibility of transmitting information through time won't be able to dodge delving into some fundamental questions of physics at some point. Unfortunately, my understanding of physics is meager at best, so I'm unable to offer a deep physical discussion of problems and possible solutions involved. Still, I want to conclude my observations by pointing to a few theoretical discussions of physics that, to me, sound relevant to questions previously raised here and onto which someone with further interest in those issues might focus their attention. I apologize in advance for any misunderstandings and misrepresentations due to my lack of expertise in this area.

I spent some time discussing the possibility of retrieving past reality from present reality. In all cases described, the possible quality of such reconstruction had to be assumed imperfect at best, due to limited information processing bandwidth and storage, unavoidable incompleteness of recordings, human fallibility, etc. Limiting oneself to the resolution of understanding provided by the human brain and culture or our current calculating machines, we may be satisfied with less than perfection. But let's move into the territory of cosmological thought experiments and ask a question such as: Is an absolute reconstruction of past reality from present reality actually possible according to physical theory? This seems to be a question for the thought experiment of "Laplace's demon". This entity has complete knowledge of the present state of the universe: of all the states of all that is in the universe right now, all its atoms and momentums and so on. It also has complete knowledge of the laws of physics and their formulas. It could use these to calculate forwards and backwards from the present configuration of the universe – so it should be able to predict the future of the universe and reconstruct its past, should it not? This certainly would be a boost to our ambitions to reconstruct past from present, to know that, in theory, this would be possible with a sufficiently large and high-resolution knowledge of the present.

Unfortunately, the theoretical possibility of such a powerful demon seems to never have held up very well, and only less so in the two-hundred years of scientific history since its first imagination. Apart from questions on how an entity with such vast computational abilities could fit into the universe, the development of cosmological models seems to have more and more moved against it. Thermodynamics countered the step-by-step reversibility from a present state to a previous state with entropy – there would not be enough information available in the present for the demon to unambiguously reconstruct the past. And then, quantum mechanics and Heisenberg's Uncertainty Principle called into question the ability of any such demon to absolutely know all properties of the universe at the same slice of time, and to calculate forward with absolute certainty where chance plays a role at the lowest level.

Such problems become less theoretical to human information preservation projects if we consider the idea of "mind uploads". Remember our discussion of self-preservation: one solution lies in making what happens in the brain more portable, so it can be put into more durable form or copied again and again onto backup media. One more comprehensive way to externalize what goes on in our head would be to gain a deep understanding of brain processes, of how our mind actually emerges in there; and thus the ability to simulate these processes in outside media.

Neuroscience advances, but it's still far from drawing a map of self-emergence in the brain clear enough to model in high-level computer simulations. If we consider all this neurological wiring too complicated to be understood by us, there may still be a brute-force option for moving the mind, with its consciousness and memories, from our brain onto a computer simulation. If we know that the brain's physical system is responsible for our mind, no matter due to what internal complexities, we just need to make a snapshot of it – neuron by neuron, synapse by synapse, atom by atom, charge by charge –, move this snapshot onto a computer simulation of the laws of nature and power it up. If all relevant information is preserved by this brute-force copy, and our laws-of-nature simulation works correctly, then the digitized brain should experience the same consciousness, the same memories, the same mind as the physical original, should it not?

This method for mind uploads proposed by futurists like Ray Kurzweil[11] needs a lowest physical level of mind-relevant brain processes that works in mechanics simple and deterministic enough to be modelled by our computer systems, and discretely enough to be captured without ambiguities that could produce errors in the mind copy. This seems theoretically possible if we assume all relevant processes can be reduced to the level of, let's say, atoms. But what if the relevant information is buried some levels deeper, say, in the quantum craziness world that might not only confuse us, but our deterministic computers, too? That basically seems to be what physicist Roger Penrose argues against such visions[12]: that the physics fundamental to consciousness still contain too much magic (in the sense of not being properly understood by us) to be captured by our current methods or simulated by our current computers.

Physics, it seems, provides pessimism and fundamental barriers to ambitious information preservation projects. Let's expose this view to a final, super-optimistic counter-example: Frank J. Tipler's Omega Point Theory. Tipler is a mathematical physicist who argues[13], through some rather ambitious-sounding cosmology, that informational complexities like intelligence and life are fundamentally entwined with the future development of the universe; that they will fill it up in the next billions and billions of years until the whole cosmos becomes a universal super-computer; that this super-intelligence will engineer the final collapse of the universe and exploit the special physical conditions therein as an energy source to power infinite growth of its computing ressources and infinite acceleration of its computing

11 | Kurzweil 2005
12 | Penrose 1989
13 | Tipler 1994

cycles, thus experiencing infinite subjective time while external time reaches its end point; that this final super-intelligence, the Omega Point, will, in its qualities of omnipresence, omniscience and omnipotence, equal the Christian God; that, as omniscient end of the universe, it will capture all information available then and, in the infinity of its subjective time, reconstruct all possible pasts from that, and revive all intelligences contained therein into an unimaginable number of computer simulations for all eternity.

This solves all our problems. Nothing will be lost, for all will be reconstructed – including that which never existed. We need not fear death of our self, for we will all be revived at the end of the universe, in something equal to the Christian Heaven. We will be able to explore and touch all buildings ever torn down, all cities lost, and even those facades pixelated in *Google Street View*. We will see the past with our own eyes, talk to Aristotle and Confucius and hunt the Woolly Mammoth, if we wish to. We will be able to exlore conventional history just as well as Fomenko's revised version, for both will be true. In short, anything we could ever hope for will be available to us, we just need to wait long enough – if Tipler is right (or rather, this writer's certainly incomplete understanding of him).

References

de Grey, Aubrey & Michael Rae (2007). *Ending Aging. The Rejuvenation Breakthroughs That Could Reverse Human Aging in Our Lifetime.*New York: St. Martin's Griffin.
Fomenko, Anatoly (2007). *History: Fiction or Science? Chronology 1.* Paris, London, New York: Delamere.
Illig, Heribert (2005). *Das erfundene Mittelalter. Die größte Zeitfälschung der Geschichte.* Berlin: Ullstein.
Kurzweil, Ray (2005). *The Singularity is Near. When Humans Transcend Biology.* York: Viking.
Penrose, Roger (1989). *The Emperor's New Mind. Concerning Computers, Minds and The Laws of Physics.* USA: Oxford University Press.
Tipler, Frank J. (1994). *The Physics of Immortality. Modern Cosmology, God and the Ressurection of the Dead.* York: Anchor Books.

2. Technology

Demystification of Digital Media

LIN HSIN HSIN

Introduction

Over the past one and the half decades, Internet communities have been uploading, browsing and downloading some trillions of Web pages[1]. An enormous proportion of which contains digital media. Be it 2D, 3D, still, animated or interactive, Web sites, DVDs, games, mobile devices and the like, the contents are largely digital media driven. Away from the Web, this mega assemblage of digital media contents amounts to *zettabytes*[2] of files associated to the computing power of servers and laptops, storage networks and connectivities that contribute to greenhouse gas emissions[3],[4]. As such, the abundance of digital media mandates an investigation on its true identity, genres, creation tools and processes. With the current device availability and the rampant download scenarios, it confronts the rationales and concerns of digital media authentication, its issues and rights management. It also examines the quest for digital media valuation, archiving and conservation as it may require extinct devices that are costly to maintain for the said purpose.

---

1 | Google claims to have indexed 3.3 billion Web pages. http://wiki.answers.com
2 | http://en.wikipedia.org/wiki/Zettabyte
3 | Lifang Peng, Qi Li et al, (2005). "Optimism or Pessimism: Environmental Impacts of the E-Commerce", International Society for Environmental Information Sciences Environmental Informatics, ISSN 1811-0231/ ISEIS Publication Series Number P002, 2005 (3)
4 | http://www.neatorama.com/tag/alex-wissner-gross/

Digital Media

Definition

By any definition, in most English dictionaries[5] the noun, medium (plural, media or mediums), is defined as an agency or a means by which something is communicated or expressed, or the intervening substance through which sensory impressions are conveyed or physical forces are transmitted; or a particular form of storage material for computer files; or the material or form used by an artist, composer, or writer.

Thus, it would be logical to say digital media is a substance whereby digits are the substance or agent in which an expression can be created, displayed, transmitted and communicated between the thoughts of the creator and the viewer. Just like in the analog world, where drawing media include chalk, charcoal soft or hard, conté, crayon, graphite, ink etc; common paint media such as acrylic paint, oil paint, watercolor and so on. As such, digital media can be manifested in different forms and formats in visual and performing arts, and hence the different genres of digital media.

Confusions and Misconceptions

Since the inception of the digital as a media, many terms have sprung up. The proliferation of the usage and misuse of terms without proper understanding and guidance, includes but not limited to: computer graphics (commonly abbreviated as CG)[6], new media (*Ger Neue Medien*), media art (*Ger, Medienkunst, Elektronische Kunst, Computerkunst*)[7], multimedia, cyber art, virtual art, Net art, Web art, mathematical art etc[8]. Of which, the most corrosive and corrupted correlation was the

---

5 | Merriam-Webster Dictionary. http://www.m-w.com, http://www.fondation-langlois.org/html/e/index.html, http://www.oxforddictionaries.com/definition

6 | http://en.wikipedia.org/wiki/Computer_graphics

7 | http://en.wikipedia.org/wiki/Computer_graphics

8 | Lin Hsin Hsin (1997). "Building an Ultimate Museum on the Web", Museums and the Web Conference proceedings, Los Angeles, California, USA book 1997

archaic association of "equating the digital with the electronics[9]" where the later is usually referred to as devices that work by controlling the flow of electrons, albeit commonly abbreviated as "e" such as e-commerce or email. Indeed, this is yet another example that demonstrates the inconsistency with the alphabet's *e*, with or without hyphen. To make the matter worse: video art[10] is generally regarded as new media synonymously known as digital art, while electronic music is often referred to as digital music.

Evolution or otherwise, the coinage of the term new media is totally unacceptable. Exactly what is new media? When acrylic paint was invented, it became a popular painting medium for the artist, but why is it not referred to as new oil paint? In the first place, traditional medium does not have the word medium attached to it, although it is, a medium associated with its intrinsic properties. Assuming digital media is a new medium denoted in plurality -- binary functions operate in two states, viz 0 or 1. Some questions:

- Will there not be a newer media in future times? If so, will it be named newer media, then newest media and so on?
- Social media[11] has just be admitted to the dictionary, isn't it also a new media as compared to *existing new media*?
- So what is *new* and what is the meaning of *new*? If this term is incorrect, why hasn't it been corrected or abolished? Or does popularity endorse and condone errors? If so, what is the rationale behind it? Or have we lost touch with meanings?

If digital media is intellectual property, hence an asset, it needs to be properly identified and labeled. Errors due to inheritance, for example, classifying video art as digital art, must be clarified and not permitted to continue or taught. When a misconceived notion spreads widely and rapidly, wrong words and usage propagate, permeate and penetrate, it naturally becomes harder and harder to distill and correct. To date, digital media, the highly desired Internet commodity is

---

9 | http://www.aec.at
10 | Nam June Paik, John G (2003). "The Worlds of Nam June Paik" http://www.arthistoryarchive.com/arthistory/videoart/
11 | David Kirkpatrick (2010). "The Facebook Effect: The Inside Story of the Company That Is Connecting the World"

not being understood; although it is fuzzily popular. Is this concerning?

Graphics versus Art

Another misconception is the notion of graphics versus art. While there is no shortage of literature about these two words, or rather subjects, there is a need to differentiate and highlight the meaning and usage of computer graphics *vis-à-vis* digital art (*German, Digitale Kunst, French, d'art numérique*)[12].

Computer Graphics

The origin of the word graphics[13], meaning "traced" (implied in graphical), dates back to 1610. Its etymological root in Greek, *graphikos,* which implies "picturesque", or in Latin, *graphicus,* which implies "of or for writing, belonging to drawing, picturesque". Originally, this plural noun (usually treated as singular) is derived from *graphe,* "writing, drawing" or from *graphein* "write" means "to scratch" on clay tablets with a stylus. From 1669, it is defined as "vivid", on the notion of words that produce the effect of a picture. From 1756 onwards, it connotes "of or pertaining to drawing". According to Oxford's online dictionary[14], graphics are the use of diagrams in calculation and design; thus computer graphics are the product of the graphics produced by the computer, especially in the area of commercial design or illustration, whereby it makes no mention about art.

What is Art?

In contrast with graphics, what is art[15]? Early in the thirteenth century, art is defined as "a skill as a result of learning or practice". Art has several language roots: from Latin, artem (nom, ars) "art, skill, craft"; from Greek arti "just", artios "complete"; from PIE, ar-ti- ; From Sanskrit, rtih "manner, mode"; from Armenian arnam "make"; from base, "fit together, join"; from Old French, art; from German, art "manner,

---

12 | http://dictionnaire.sensagent.com/peinture+num%C3%A9rique/fr-fr/
13 | Dictionary of Word Origins, John Ayto, Bloomsbury
14 | http://www.oxforddictionaries.com/definition
15 | Dictionary of Word Origins, John Ayto, Bloomsbury and http://www.etymonline.com/

mode". In the Middle East circa 1300, art is usually associated with a sense of "skill in scholarship and learning", especially in the seven sciences, or liberal arts (divided into the trivium – grammar, logic, rhetoric; the quadrivium – arithmetic, geometry, music, astronomy "human workmanship" (as opposed to nature). Art seen as a skill in creative arts was first recorded 1620; especially in painting, sculpture etc. Art as an adjective means "produced with conscious artistry" (as opposed to popular or folk). In 1767, the term fine arts meant "those which appeal to the mind and the imagination". However it was attested from 1890, possibly from the influence of the German Kunstlied "art song", art film (1960s), and art rock (1970s). With the exception of the Australian National Dictionary, which ironically defines or rather contests an artist "as a person practised or habitually engaged in activity which requires little skill or reprehensible", "art is a product of a skill".

According to the dictionary definition of art, what then is considered as art? Two citations exemplified in the ancient traditions: is a Chinese carving of a grass hopper perched on the edge of a cabbage leaf made out of a single piece of ivory considered as art? Or the fascination of photorealism by the Greek painter Zenxis, who has astonished his audience by painting a bunch of grapes so *real* that birds tried to *eat* them, considered as art in the Western world? As such, is skill considered as product instead of process or is the product a skillful process?

Nevertheless, there are still countless views of what is and what is not art: an ongoing debate, unceasing in rebuttals to date, continues worldwide. As William Butler Yeats stated, "Supreme art is a traditional statement of certain heroic and religious truths, passed on from age to age, modified by individual genius, but never abandoned. The revolt of individualism came because the tradition had become degraded, or rather because a spurious copy had been accepted in its stead"[16]. While William Shakespeare took an opposing view: "more matter with less art"[17]. So then, what is art? Who controls what?[18] Indeed, a stimulating endless academic and power struggle.

---

16 | Dictionary of Word Origins, John Ayto, Bloomsbury
17 | http://www.etymonline.com/
18 | Don Thompson (2009). "The $12 Million Stuffed Shark: The Curious Economics of Contemporary Art", Doubleday

Digital Art

Definition

Digital Art is not digitization; digital art is not created by digitization. Aligned with the meaning of art, digital art is "art produced by a digital source with a digitally recognized skill". While the conventional wisdom of visual art and performing art applies, digital art spans a wider spectrum. Harnessing on the power of computation, digital art is an extremely rich media with infinite possibilities, it is scalable and accessible to the billions of worldwide audience[19] (almost) instantly and simultaneously if so desired (upload).

As the digitals are intrinsically rich, digital art assumes its presence in the digital and virtual world; the cyberspace; and the real world. Before the millennium, it was the digital in the virtual presence that triumph ed, but increasingly, it is the virtual becoming the real that surpasses[20]!

In line with the associated properties of conventional art, we need to address the various concerns about digital art. Typically, digital art valuation, archiving and conservation, especially that of the ephemeral or *"digits-in-transit"*, the much needed scholarly proper classification and categorization. Because of its inseparable association with computing, this is a process to be jointly assessed by the technologists and the art experts in humanities. One asks, what are the initiatives that have been installed? How accurate are they? Who leads and who concedes and how severe are the *digital-art-political* struggles? Or aren't all these the same old attacks or are the politics in technology complicating the matter further?

Digital Genres

Beyond the convention classification of visual and performing art, digital art takes many appearances and classifications.

• The versatilities of digital (visual) art extends digital oils, digital watercolors, digital inks, digital crayons, digital pencils. Digital tools such as the old-fashioned mouse are capable of creating digital artworks as real as real-world hand-drawn sketches, drawings, paintings,

---

19 | http://www.internetworldstats.com/stats.htm
20 | http://rapidprototypingjournal.com/?cat=5

landscapes, portraits, cartoons, comic strips, still, animated, interactive, Web-enabled 2D images, 3D sculptures, designs, *l'objet d'art* and beyond.
- Digital (performing) art include digital sound, music and dance, creating virtual musical instruments, network enabled performances etc.
- Digital animations and digital movies, a genre: evolved from the initial digital animations.
- Gaming (video) art[21] has become a class of digital art in recent years. It has evolved by virtue of the game industry. Judging criteria has highly deviated from the conventional sense of aesthetics.
- Be it interactive, or Web-based, the commonly acknowledged software art[22] is a sub-genre of code-based art. This category of art is strictly compute bound, and it includes images; as it is completely possible to create images in non-image file formats[23]. Besides evaluating art with the conventional sense of aesthetics, code scrutiny is a mandatory criteria in determining the aesthetics and the sophistication of the codes therein.
- Like its real-world counterpart, hardware-based art is often interactive, it includes art created by software and maneuvered (or accompanied) by the dedicated hardware. Early examples were established in the 90s; whereas recent examples include robot dancers, virtual musical Instruments such as I-Musika[24].
- True 3D art is a relatively new genre. Art in this category may involve 3D LCD screen or viewing glasses. However, the author has invented a new way of creating this art genre without new hardware[25].

---

21 | Dave Morris, Leo Hartas (2003). "The graphic art of computer games"
22 | http://en.wikipedia.org/wiki/Fork_bomb
23 | Lin Hsin Hsin (2010). "A New Paradigm for Visualization and Generating Grid Geometry Art and Beyond", Information Visualisation Proceedings of the 14th International Conference, IEEE
24 | Lin Hsin Hsin (2007). "I-Musika: Mobile Interface Musical Expression (MIME)", Proceedings of the 11th International Conference, IEEE
25 | Lin Hsin Hsin (June 2011). Conference Proceeding, to be published.

Digital Tools, Process and Genres

Digital Tools

With the abundance of digital recording devices and increasing readily available commercial software, purchased or otherwise, will D-I-Y software and hardware even be considered as an option, let alone examined as a paradigm shift notion? As such, is a first-rate user interface far more important to software development for the majorities? Will CLI always remain as the heaven of the command-line driven geeks and geeks only? One might ask; are the rise of the garden varieties of digital devices such as pointing devices, PC Pens and stylus, tablets, scanners, digital cameras, digital video recorders, mobile devices and so on, an indication of the strong economies that came and is to come? Is this not part of the burden and responsibilities of greenhouse gas emissions? Have algorithm driven and write your own never been a dream of the users? Or is this the preferred way of life: adopting the *prêt-à-porte* over the *déjà-vu* D-I-Y? Indeed, could this be the *software bento* that impedes innovation or outweighs the importance of the development of the mind? Is the current ballooning of social media evidence of "the geek who writes software" well monetized by the stroke of luck? Besides the notion of connectivity, one of the embedding success factors is the "digital media factor" acknowledging the power of digital recording devices -- digitization versus creation, or is it not?

Digital Process

Digital process is not digitization, it is a process. If a process is a series of actions or operations conducing to an end, a digital process is a process performed digitally. A digital process may involve single step or multi-step operations by several existing or non-existing methods. An instance of a digital process includes the following: the production of digital media (content) by a single programming or markup language; an algorithm-driven (i.e. with programming logic) function, code-based encoding, one or a set of equations; or a combination of the above, usually built from the ground up, with or without user interface. Such processes can be revolutionary and even evoke a paradigm shift phenomenon. Basically, they involve concrete information visualization, perception and hence conceptualization of a different dimension. It is an alternative to the legacy, where the nonplussed for the unfazed takes place.

Nevertheless, does the accessibility of garden variety digital tools endanger or empower innovation? Currently, the burgeoning *apps-in-the-pocket*[26] is redefining the mobile industry and producing a new breed of entrepreneurs. On the other hand, is the much desired convenience, hence speed, a substitute for encouraging excellence in *hands-on*? While realizing each tool has its own merits, one argues, isn't excellence a product of intelligence, patience and endurance, or is it a thing of the past?

Mouse as a Painting Device

User Friendly Interface

From the phantom haptic devices to the wireless and 3D mouse, and multimodal interfaces, academics contend about the similarities and differences in theoretical approaches and understanding of the next generation of interfaces in the pursuit of formulating research directions. Researchers are actively pursuing the emergence of the next generation of human-computer interaction predictions, discussing emerging new interaction styles and interface designs; few or almost none have discussed an exquisite offering such as the use and merits of using an age old two-button mechanical mouse in the artistic interactive taxonomy.

With its tangible interfaces -- lightweight, tacit, passive, perceptual and non-command line interaction, the mouse as a painting device is founded on an event-based dab-and-scribe, press-and-release dexterity in a discrete or continuous process as a user interface. From the most subtle to the volcanic, from landscapes to portraits, from the abstract to photorealistic, there is literally nothing that cannot be painted by the mechanical mouse. By realizing and harnessing this immense power of the mouse, the author has used the device as a digital brush since 1994[27].

---

26 | http://www.planetsoftheapps.com
27 | Lin Hsin Hsin (1997). "@art: a Cyberart show by Lin Hsin Hsin"; Lin Hsin Hsin (2007), "A Non-Photorealistic Rendering Images by a Handheld Device". Proceedings of the 11th International Conference, IEEE

As such, she has researched, created, presented and demonstrated an exclusive range of results, an extensive repertoire of digital artworks created by the autonomous, ubiquitous and pervasive handheld interaction of this painting device: absolutely without the deployment of a scanner, or the *point-and-click, drag-and drop, cut-and-paste, morph-and-tween* processes.

The Benefits

Away from illegal downloads, the mouse as a painting device eliminates the necessity of extra input devices and layers. Not only does it offer an end-to-end solution in digital painting: from instant conceptualization to visualization to the finished product, it is chemical-free and ecologically friendly. As this handheld device is always with a computer, desktop or laptop, the user is not constrained to a *studio environment*, he or she can paint anytime, anywhere. Even with the increasing tablets and mobile devices, this approach and practice has established the fact that mouse is a cost effective handheld device and an indispensable tool, thus bridging the gap between desire, creative thinking and realization in the age of mobile lifestyle reign.

Beyond which, the author has compared notes on the sensitivity of this wired two-button mechanical roller ball mouse versus a high precision laser mouse while she profiles the futility of the wireless self-powered optical mouse as well as the pen tablet[28].

COMPUTATIONAL AESTHETICS

While mathematics abides by order, art responses to order, it is therefore, an option or even a virtue to take the less obvious path. Indeed, computational aesthetics is as rational and it can be, as poetic as you can define and desire. When the concept of computational aesthetics takes center stage, invariably, it is computation that allows the creator, artist, designer, or whoever that has the desire to "camp" in equations, algorithms, and consequently achieving the traditional, the unconventional and/or the "seemingly impossible" viz, the resource intensive manpower and time.

---

28 | Lin Hsin Hsin (2007). "A Non-Photorealistic Rendering Images by a Handheld Device". Proceedings of the 11th International Conference, IEEE

While mathematics has the ability to distill the essential elements to incorporate an attribute or transform or perform spatial translation, making an attempt to explain the appeal of computational aesthetics against the slew of *de-facto,* commercial software to paint, sculpt and animate may not be the dream of online communities. As such, the heroic act of discovering the wonders of mathematics only appeals to the minorities, this unit of pleasure is only mumbled by those who take pleasure and pride in a worthwhile "diversions" – perhaps, it is a recipe (the mathematical commentary sprinkled underneath), for the elite. In conjunction of the mobile devices, computing aesthetics have an advantage of *coding on the move* while you pen your thoughts.

However, describing and learning how to write code is not only time consuming for the beginner, any lack of the mathematical fundamentals not only act as a deterrent and may even be seen as impossible for the generation that has grown up or is growing up with "point and click", "drag and drop", "cut and paste" habits and practices, from infanthood to adolescence and into adulthood. It may be worse than rendering the physics of the imaginary world. Software is the conceptual basis of why it all works, but the fact remains: the surface is the magic, the magic that feeds the sensory delights, and make digital media appealing. To summarize: to be hidden in the dingy labyrinth of existing software is a total contrast to the airy elegance of computational aesthetics.

Mathematical Art – A Traditional View

For the non-professionals, mathematical art[29] is deemed as art with perfect symmetry, one without hues and textures, still and dead, maybe even old-fashioned and boring. Generating or building mathematical art is seen as difficult, *unwise,* a.k.a. slow, and hence the production of mono types, for example, and, at best, some glorified output by fractal geometry of the 80s.

Though mathematical art formulated by Euclidean geometry: one that measures size, shape, and relative position of figures with properties of space can be traced back to Mesopotamia; studies on the intrinsic structure of geometric objects that led to differential geometry which empowers art; as well as art formulated by axiomatic geometry

---

29 | "The Nine Chapters on the Mathematical Art"

such as Riemannian geometry in the twentieth century, majorities still subscribe to mathematics in art with a traditional view.

Quite often many still prefer to challenge the petri polytopes associated with tetrahedrons and dodecahedron in academia, based on the number of published papers on this subject. Exterior to the ivory tower, even with the emergence of block-buster digital movies and animations, few realized that it is the mathematical power that enables the 3D commercial software, albeit ultra resource intensive and ecologically repulsive. With the gigabit bandwidth and mobile devices, digital media is a pleasing quotidian interlude, anywhere, anytime, made feasible technologically with mathematics in absentia.

Mathematics-centric

To be ecologically friendly in computing means, art should be computed whenever possible. Being mathematics-centric implies enabling mathematical power in the creation process. From 2D images, to equation-based textile design[30] to 3D sculptures, objects and jewelery[31], there are just as many categories of art that can be computed and achieved. Amongst:

- Perception-based Orthogonal Grid Geometry Art (both soft edge and hard edge). Examples include De Stijl[32] such as works by Josef Albers, Frank Stella, Ellsworth Kelly, Kenneth Noland[33], Paul Klee, Mark Rothko and their followers and variants[34]
- Non-Orthogonal Grid Geometry Art. Examples include injecting

---

30 | Lin Hsin Hsin (2007). "The Automorphism of Amalgamation pf Polytopes and Tessellation", Proceedings of the Bridges Conference, San Sebastian, Spain
31 | Lin Hsin Hsin (2009). "The Art of i,j,k"
32 | Marty Bax (2001). Complete Mondrian, Lund Humpries
33 | Lin Hsin Hsin (2010). "A New Paradigm for Visualization and Generating Grid Geometry Art and Beyond", Information Visualisation Proceedings of the 14th International Conference, IEEE
34 | Lin Hsin Hsin (2010). "Bel Canto by Lin Hsin Hsin – Blobs and Spots", Volume VII

dynamism into static passages, art with complex opticalillusions, pseudo 3D art, simple objects and pictures[35].
- 2D images of plants such as leafs and flowers.
- Creating different dripping paints and brushstrokes on 3D surfaces simultaneously[36].
- 3D generated 2D images.

Mathematical Art - A New Perspective

Self-aware knowledge is insufficient to propagate and combat the actualization in battle of pursuit. Widening the inherent mathematical perspective is a progression that takes place in a different cosmos, ethnically challenging, emotionally fulfilling, and a confabulation way of achieving media in a sonic way.

Characterizing mathematical designs is an aura of simplicity, one that is expressed in alphanumeric and symbols (only) – a lucid design language, possibly with "less intuitive" interface. Creating mathematically generated art is an attempt to rival commercial software to create and/or generate content, to look beyond the standard "givens", to acknowledge the past and the present.

Mathematical art is not just about the space, depth and continuity, of geometrical regularity and symmetries, of the variations of the assumptions and the *déjà-vu*... It is the result[37] of a sustainable ecosystem with infinite possibilities anchored to the basics. As such, the creator dictates the dimensions, colors, textures, lightings complete with chiaroscuro effects, dispersed arbitrarily, to produce compositions and movements without barrier. Even with a minimum and legacy hardware, one can achieve a wide range of results effectively.

Benefits

From parallel lines to hyperspace, there are numerous benefits in mathematics-centric artisticexpression, as it not only offers a gamut of opportunities, it eliminates dimensional boundaries and

---

35 | Lin Hsin Hsin (2010). "Voice Over Intellectual Properties - Digital Media", Volume I
36 | Lin Hsin Hsin (2010). "When Equation Paints"
37 | Lin Hsin Hsin (2010). "Voice Over Intellectual Properties - Digital Media", Volume I

- stipulates the possibilities for realization of perception to express the act of thinking instantly. As such, it is an ideal vehicle for instant visualization, planning, sketching, creating, generating, developing and delivery
- creates instant variations, and variants of a desired theme
- demonstrates the opportunities to express and realize unlimited multiple options concurrently
- its usefulness spans and extends across multiple disciplines for the following professionals: an idea sketchpad for architects, draft sketches for city and urban planners, artists, designers, IT professionals, mathematicians, scientists, musicians, choreographers and even cross-stitch handicraft lovers.

The intrinsic properties of being mathematics-centric means one is able to visualize and createmathematical art; gleaning benefits as the result is ubiquitous and platform independent, though with exceptions, instantly Web-enabled. As it uses a fraction of the time to create the same work as compared to other or conventional methods, it is an excellent tool for generating high scalable optical illusion art[38], perhaps, to satisfy the current 3D craze, with uses minimum resources, output files are of minimum file size, 135 artworks with an average file size of 0.92 KB per artwork, for example,[39] where no other known software can achieve this to date.

Digital Media Authentication

While rapid diffusion of digital media on the Web brings numerous benefits such as pleasure in entertainment, it also demonstrates the urgent need to differentiate the original versus imitations, derivatives and spin offs. Beyond the *mundanes,* there is a need to craft, specify,

---

38 | Lin Hsin Hsin (June 2011). Conference Proceeding, to be published.
39 | Lin Hsin Hsin (2010). "A New Paradigm for Visualization and Generating Grid Geometry Art and Beyond", Information Visualisation Proceedings of the 14th International Conference, IEEE

verify and certify digital authenticity and hence empower digital art in the real-(art)-world, initiate digital art auction[40] and beyond. The recognition of digital art analogous to that of its counterpart in the real-world has not been understood and has largely been ignored. While online businesses of a different sort are gaining huge momentum and deemed as successful, the potential of the Web as a distribution channel for digital media as a form of *digital fine art* is largely impeded by ignorance, fraudulent sales, illegal downloads and syndication. Typically, targeted buyer types vs. crowd-sourcing and mass consumerism[41] span over different measures of economy of scale. As it has always been the case of high-end content-based product is often build on trust, scarcity and authenticity, whereas low-end price-point product is primarily based on availability, affordability and the *also-have* or *must-have* or impulse mentality. Digital media-based art forms must first be defined, understood, authenticated and accepted prior to vending them on secured *digital* distribution channels.

The Rationale

While the intellectual property rights agnostics[42] reject and condemn digital rights that span across multidimensional text, images, audio, video packaged in thousands of device types in thousands of file formats, millions of deliverable and distribution channels, streaming, archived or otherwise, right[43] holders are faced with the ever

---

40 | Lin Hsin Hsin (1997). "Building an Ultimate Museum on the Web", Museums and the Web Conference proceedings, Los Angeles, California, USA book 1997
41 | http://www.planetsoftheapps.com
42 | Richard M. Stallman (2003). "Did You Say 'Intellectual Property'?" "It's a Seductive Mirage" http://www.gnu.org/philosophy/not-ipr.xhtml; Richard M Stallman (2003). "Software patents – Obstacles to software development" transcript, University of Cambridge Computer Laboratory, Foundation for Information Policy Research, from http://www.cl.cam. ac.uk/~mgk25/stallman-patents.html; Georg Jakob, (2004) "Deharmonization through the Intellectual Property Enforcement Directive"; http://mikro.org/Events/OS/text/freie-sw_fn.html
43 | Elad Harrison (2008). "Intellectual Property Rights, Innovation and software Technologies. The Economics of Monopoly Rights and Knowledge Disclosure", New Horizons in intellectual Property, Edward Elgar

challenging nonstop snooping, spoofing, hacking, web-lifting, multi-faceted attacks now known or to be invented, by curious individuals, cohorts and even consortium, institutions and enterprises[44]. Thus, prompting the confrontation of a multitude of issues that occur in the real, virtual and cyberspace worlds in digital authorization, authentication, protection, detection and revocation processes.

Digital Media Shell

Not to be confused with information security which seeks to protect, deter and prevent data from unauthorized access, misuse, or theft, digital media storage security refers to the security storage device housing and media delivery networks. Security principle begins with digital media asset classification that categorizes and defines content rating according to its requirements for confidentiality depending on the potential impact of disclosure or loss. It assumes and exerts control over managing and mining digital media databases, the mandatory requirement for issuing a non-compete and non-disclosure agreement, and the deployment of media shell[45] housing even for a demo session. It questions the risks and necessity of utilizing a watermark and encrypted version when the need for searching for a similar frame in the zettabytes or thousands of hours of movies arises.

Assets and Liabilities

The question asked is: whether digital media that parades across the cybermall can still enthrall will greatly depend on the unceasing prevention[46], monitoring, tracking and protection of digital media assets prior and amidst the relentless battling with the invincible. As such, the mandatory cyber and real world defense mechanism,

---

44 | Varadharjan Sridhar, Sasken (2010). Challenges of Information Security Management in a Research and development Software Services Company: case of WirelessComSoft, Communication technologies. Journal of Cases on Information Technology.
45 | http://www.wibu.com
46 | http://www.cptwg.org; http://www.hitachi.com; Wolfgang Kellerer, Bernhard Quendt (1998). "Multimedia Service Architectures – An Overview – Kellerer, Quendt Munchen", Germany. http://www.lkn.ei.tum.de/~wolfgang/publ/EUNICE98.pdf

however complex, must be put in place, at best effort, before any business commencement. Any discrepancy cannot, should not and must not be negotiated and compromised. As such, should an abnormality be detected, it must generate a violation alert signal that chills and revocation be endorsed so as to prevent similar and/or future occurrences. From tactical operation to strategic digital media asset security initiatives, who assumes the role of data sensitivity rating, who authorizes permission setting for creation, access, modification, retention and deletion, who determines the deployment of watermarking and encryption strength and techniques vis-à-vis regulatory compliance must be set up prior to asset development and business commencement. In the case of technical drawings, biomedical voice recordings, images and videos, are the entrusted parties in storage management roles likely to operate under the radar of the information security department? Meanwhile, digital media assets are multiplying at an unprecedented rate, the demands for, and thus "replicas" of, are proliferating exponentially, across the globe, complicating the security paradigm[47] under archaic legal regimes. From content to consumer, digital media authentication must offer persistent end-to-end protection for the digitally real and cyber estate of the real economy.

As such, can trust in the content-based Web site be translated to digitally certified digital fine art? Confronted by the realities of the strengths and weaknesses of opportunities and threats and hundreds, if not thousands of persistent presence of bots and crawlers, will a virtual exhibition be converted to IP thefts? In the first place, will an acid-free canvas printed by 73,728 inkjet nozzles, fault tolerant 5' print head be distinguished vis-a-vis glicée on a sheen coated paper?

DIGITAL MEDIA TRAFFICKING

The Scenario

Over the past decade, digital media Web smuggling for digital media supply chains – businesses that anchor on the use of digital media, is a 24/7, IP-based multimillion dollar business growing at an exponential rate. One asks: is illegal digital media downloading any

---

47 | Alistair Croll and Sean Power (2009). "Complete Web Monitoring", O'Reilly

different than the ancient trade of drug or human trafficking? While the former faces a life sentence, the later results in a 7 year jail sentence; we need to know just how much digital media downloading and distribution that is against the will of the creator/owner gets away scotch free. With the abundance of digital media pilferage, fakes and clones proliferating at an unprecedented rate on the Net without the owner's awareness, the millions, if not billions of revenue loss, can digital media trafficking be equated with the notion of trafficking of the same severity in the digital age? Should digital media smuggling, and indeed, a reformatted manifestation of human intellectual trafficking be punished with the same sentence?

The Issues

With the complexity of the Internet network topology, and the magnitude of the Web, would a Web auditing procedure be even thinkable, let alone possible? If so, what would be the best practice to combat the digital media traffic encumbrance? With super high speed transmission, the influx of mobile technology and the invasion of mobile devices, how could one control this logistic nightmare? In the name of compression and speed, the spade of built-in sniffer for Web servers doubl ing up for trafficking tools, how does one filter the undesirables upon the exploitation of the Internet security loopholes? Beyond which, in some cases, scores of CCTV act as convenient industrial espionage devices.

Even so, it is a mammoth task to take on the law and hence prosecute – an exercise that requires enormous efforts and various resources, let alone policing the billions of Web pages[48], the unstoppable borderless cyber traffic. By then, technology could possibly have leaped to another new frontier. Would a better law enforcement procedure[49] help in the crackdown of the digital media abuse? If so, how soon can we see lights in the tunnel? In face of the current cyber oil leak, is the age of free usage or free-or-charge enticement long overdue or this is simply the way of business life? Can intellectual properties digitization, such as book scanning and hence readily available and accessible

---

48 | Alistair Croll and Sean Power (2009). "Complete Web Monitoring", O'Reilly

49 | Peter Toren (2003). "Guide to Protection Against High-Tech Theft and Intellectual Property Violations"

publications on the Web, be viewed as a way of digital lifestyle more than welcomed by the public-at-large? Generic IP spoofing and illegal downloading, followed by the creation of its instant multitude of variants against the will of the creator/owner of the intellectual property, is the unbearable loss of revenue due to the digital media smuggling and is clear evidence of intellectual properties accountability. It needs to be addressed and compensated!

Conclusions

Art is anchored in science; art is an expression of the universe, and science is governance. Amidst the mushrooming of digital media in the rapid growth of *one-more-zettabyte* of Web pages, the instant deliveries of the embedded devices and the *one-more-gadget-cum-apps-syndrome*, is this simply a flash crowd bandwidth? Or will the pockets of the lone voices be heard in the wilderness of this digital jungle? If the purpose of digital media is to play and entertain, one asks is greenhouse gas emission never an issue or is it? Whatever the case may be, the multiplication of greenhouse gas emissions should not be coated by *"hardware and gigantic file"* pollutions. Indeed, we need to adopt the uphold to make ecology first value.

Going forward, will there be an increase in awareness of digital authenticity? May we see a behavioral change in digital media abuse – translates into 24/7 downloading, or will the Web continue as a *never-be-a-concern* distribution channel? As such, is there a need to set up a new framework of governance? If so, who is responsible?

In the shortage of time and caring expertise will *new media* always remain as new media *per se*? Whether digital media will be permanently pleasing quotidian interludes, absolutely *sans souci*, is yet to be seen. Will the embezzlement of digital media be a daily battle between the creators/owners and *the* have not? While we can only hope, see and wait for the day when the public is eager to know and differentiate, the digital media chase will continue, while the demystification of digital media will constantly be the challenge ahead of all Netizens in the years to come!

Biometrics and the Sense of Self in Video Games

KYLE MACHULIS

INTRODUCTION

Modern video games assault the senses with the goal of making a fantasy situation seem real. The player can drive a car they can't afford, shoot others with no consequence other than being shot back at themselves, or have countless other experiences that cannot be rendered in reality due to either laws of physics or their local government.

While the technology increases to make the video game world more immersive, this focus on fantasy situations removes the player from awareness of themselves. By using the player's body as a game console, the game designer can possibly teach the player things about themselves and their bodies while also creating an entertaining experience.

SENSORY INTERACTION IN GAMES

Video games can be defined as a system that takes input from some sort of device manipulation (most of the time, a joystick) and provides a reaction via some sort of simulated environment. The sensory concentration for this environment usually exists in the visual realm, i.e. computer graphics. While there is also audio (though it is not usually a focus), and very rarely haptics (the feeling of touch, as usually stimulated by vibration in the controller), the reliance on graphics causes the player to put most of their concentration on a single sense, watching the screen intently. This overloading of a single sense is what causes the player to lose their sense of bodily self. While this is a good thing for the designer and developer, as immersion usually equals success of design, it also means that there is no use of the body as an environment.

BIOMETRICS IN GAMES

To re-incorporate the body into the game playing experience and turn it into an environment that can execute game mechanics, the designer can turn to biometric control systems. Biometrics (in this specific case) refers to hardware that can track bodily signals such as

- Pulse
- Temperature
- Brain Activity
- Blood Oxygen Levels

These are just a few of the measurements of life, and each has their own specific properties for relaying information about what is happening in the player. Pulse increases when anxious, brain activity changes when calm, etc... These readings can be combined to create immersive game mechanics based on what the player is actually feeling, versus assuming what the player is feeling through tactics like emotional implications via plot points in the game story.

Biometric control has existed in video games since the early 80's, when Atari created a prototype EEG (electroencephlogram, reading electrical signals on the surface of the brain to infer the mental state of the user) control, The Mindlink System, for their 2600 console. While the technology was too new and expensive to end up in homes of consumers at the time, the idea lived on, and is now available in games such as *Mindball*, where two players don EEG helmets in order to play tug of war via relaxation. Other games use attention to enhance the game, such as *Judecca* from NeuroSky and Square Enix, which required the player to concentrate a certain amount in order to be able to see enemies on the screen.

Games to teach users about themselves have also been created. *Journey to Wild Divine* was distributed with a blood oxygen and galvanic skin resistance measurement unit called the "Lightstone". This control tracked the amount of anxiety and oxygen intake the user was experiencing, and used these measurements to guide them through relaxation techniques via an interactive game experience.

A Self-Game Sketch

As a simple example of a game that teaches the user more about themselves, the game mechanic can focus on a single value from the list of biometrics available. The following design chooses to use the heart rate of the player as this metric, as it is simple and universally understood, yet still quite powerful.

The game consists of a single button interface. To play the game, the player puts on a finger clip that measures their blood oxygen levels. From this information, the game can deduce the heart rate of the player, via oxygen level spikes in the readings. The game lasts one minute, during which time the player is to press the button at the time they believe their heart to have beat. The goal of the game is to get a score as close to zero as possible, keeping the pressing of the button as close to the pulse rate as possible. After the time is finished, score calculation occurs by summing the distance of every press of the button from the nearest heart beat. Penalties are introduced for hitting the button too often (i.e. multiple times around a single heartbeat) or for missing heartbeats altogether.

In order to bring the body in as a pure game mechanic, aesthetic design is reduced to an absolute minimum. The game only uses minimal graphics for menus and no graphics during game play, putting the player in a sort of sensory deprivation from what they may normally expect from video games.

Even so, there may still be outside stimulus from the play environment that effects gameplay. This stimulus can be considered an addition to the game, integrating the environment into the mechanic. For instance, a noisy environment will cause the user to find ways to concentrate on their internal state while having to ignore the outside world.

The concentration on the self also works as a negative feedback loop. If the player cannot sense their own pulse rate well enough, they will become anxious and stressed, thereby increasing their pulse rate and making the game even more difficult for themselves.

Conclusion

The game described here is a very simple example of what can be done when we remove sensory stimulation and use the body as the game console. With new technologies like depth cameras and consumer EEG helmets, the amount of information developers can access about game players is quickly growing. Soon, things like facial reaction/expression, body position, and other external information could be added to the internal biometric information to create games that take even more of the player's state into account. Addition of the sense of self could add a whole new level of immersion to the bleeding edge technology of video games.

References

Atari Mindlink, The Atari Museum, http://www.atarimuseum.com/videogames/consoles/2600/mindlink.html
Mindball, http://www.mindball.se/
Journey to Wild Device, http://www.wilddivine.com/

I can count every star in the heavens above but I have no heart I can't fall in love ...

The image of computers in popular music

JOHANNES GRENZFURTHNER

As I can tell by your looks and as you can tell by mine, we are all stupid computer nerd freaks. Stupid computer nerd freaks who successfully managed to refuse to get a life, instead we have chosen to live in a world that is totally obsessed with the computer. We are obsessed with computer culture, with the culture of reflecting computer culture and of course with culture that is reflecting culture that is reflecting computer culture.

So when I was asked to speak here in front of this most predictable audience, I was thinking about how to carry "Eulen nach Athen", as we say in German. The British version is "carry coal to Newcastle" – a foolhardy or pointless action.

The best coal I could bring here for you would be to talk about the computer as reflected through popular music. You like stuff like that don't you? I bet you do. I mean: it's about the computer ... now that sounds great, doesn't it ... ?!

You probably like your computer as much as Austrian rock musician Ulli Bäer ...

(Johannes plays song on his computer.)

ULLI BÄER: I HAB AN AMIGA

I hob an Amiga, von Commodore den Amiga
Leiwand wos der olles kann, mit dem Amiga zah i an

Der Amiga is ka Hexerei, es is wirklich nix dabei

Also Leidln, ans is kloar, darum Freinde, ans is woahr
Amiga mit Dir bin i erschte Liga
Amiga mit Dir bleib i immer wieder Sieger

I hob an Amiga, von Commodore den Amiga
Drum waaß i ans genau, i häng ned immer vorm TV
Und i brauch a nettes Bier, a kloarer Kopf, jo der reichat mir

Also Leidln, ans is kloar, darum Freinde, ans is woahr
Amiga mit Dir bin i erschte Liga
Amiga mit Dir bleib i immer wieder Sieger

Wos i wü des tut er
Der Amiga is mein Computer
Der Amiga macht mer Spaß
Ja den Amiga find i klass!

ULLI BÄER: I HAB AN AMIGA (TRANSLATION)

Awesome what this thing can do, my Amiga
Provides me with full speed

Amiga is no witch craft
It's very easy to work with

Folks, one thing's for sure
Friends, one thing's true

Amiga, I'm always in the first league with you
Amiga, I'm a winner again and again... with you

I have an Amiga
I have an Amiga by Commodore

One thing's for sure
I'm not watching TV all the time anymore
And I don't need beer

A clear mind's good enough for me

Folks, one thing's for sure
Friends, one thing's true

Amiga, I'm always in the first league with you
Amiga, I›m a winner again and again... with you

It does what I want it to do
Amiga is my computer

Amiga is fun
Amiga is awesome!

Don't be afraid... this song was just a shock treatment before the real show...

We will now thumb through the monochrom record collection and find some exciting and hilarious stuff to rejoice to after a hard day living in Vienna. Before that you might enjoy some theoretical embedding.

The so-called pop culture came up in the late 1940s. If we understand it as a certain youth culture it started with white rock 'n' roll taking African-American music from the peripheries to the center of cultural industries.

Young people all over the world – or at least in the Western part of it – got hit by this new experience. They got hit so hard, that they derived their very own culture from it, the so-called youth culture. It became a culture that stuck with them throughout their lives, and each follow-up generation up to the present joined in.

That's what we find now: practically everyone has lived through the experience of pop culture. Oh bugger, something went completely wrong... we *won* and now we are lost.

During this process, pop culture took over – and it was kind of a hostile takeover – the cultural main powers of definition from bourgeois high culture. The cultural class war was won so that today we find pop culture implemented as the famous "mainstream" and the no lesser famous "establishment". And we are part of it; but we should at least *try* to act surprised by that in order to keep at least some of our dignity.

But how could pop culture (and especially pop music as one of its main fields) come into the position to do so and to beat bourgeois high culture on the battlefield called "culture"?

One possible answer would be that it was far more capable and fit (in the very Darwinist sense of the word) of coping with the evolution of bourgeois technologies since the 1950s.

High and educational bourgeois culture had simply been overrun by modern technologies since the beginning of the 20th century – and it didn't get a break. Things became even worse after World War II.

Technology threatened to demolish and break through the traditional class barriers. Barriers that were kept up through "great culture", "high culture", or: "Culture of value".

The ruling cultural elite has the job to maintain and to fortify, to janitor or let's say: to be the bouncer of cultural class barriers. Thus they need to understand what is going on and they need to sort out what should become part of culture and what should not. But when the spiral of technological change began to hyperventilate some day or the other around 1960, they started to hyperventilate too. They got caught in the most beautiful panic attack you can imagine. And so they produced very stupid and hackneyed technophobic manifestos and images. What threatened them – by forcing their human capital into inflation – was interpreted and mediatized as a threat to society. That's a very old trick they had learned from the Catholic Church and other professional old timers.

That is why all those dull anti-computer images are to be found throughout bourgeois literature, art or reflection for such a long period. Phenomenologically, those images are as incorrect as can be. Ideologically, they represent the bourgeois culture shock of that time. Unfortunately, there is no B-movie from the 1950s called "The Attack of the 50ft Computer" – but I wouldn't be too astonished if somebody would have come up with it.

This cultural shock came in an almost lethal dose for the tools of perception of the carriers of the cultural panic. Their basic strategy had been to ignore, prejudice and to *nostradamn* the computer for the most part. And they managed to keep that strategy up to the 1990s. Around 1995, they surrendered to the computer that had taken over society without bringing apocalypse to culture but new and improved ways of production and communication. The educational bourgeois idiots did start to fall for the other side and embrace the computer or hid away in the first niche that they could find.

On the other side of the great cultural divide, pop music discovered and explored the computer not only as a musical instrument but also as something to sing and think about. And it got very important by that, because the conception that many people have of the computer has been formed by images and ideas broadcasted through popular music. Images that came from groups such as Kraftwerk – we have just heard a title of their famous LP "Computerwelt" as a jingle. It is, of course, from the only LP that you have at home. Or is there anybody around who owns another LP? Anybody who owns Mike Oldfield's "Tubular Bells" album? Or, how about "Pictures of an exhibition" by Emerson Lake & Palmer?

Of course those images were influenced and guided by high cultural computer panic as well as by naïve technomania as I am going to demonstrate towards the end of my little field trip.

When computers first came into use, and the word was spread, they were just one more part of a long line of technological innovations swapping over post war people. And so these people's reaction was to be amazed in a highly experienced way: "Oh! Something new again – that's great – or at least it should be..."

But people soon began to realize that the computer was not just another machine to be used by man. They came to the conclusion that it was the first machine to resemble man in one significant respect. It was not the first machine that tried to rebuild and optimize certain functions of the human body. But it was an imitation of the executive floor of it: the brain.

That's why people came up with the stupid nickname "the electronic brain".

And this was the beginning of what you could call the war between the electronic and the natural brain. This war became one of the main plots of late 20th century storytelling from "Blade Runner" to "The Matrix".

This is an update of that very old story that derives from the conception of a Creator God: the creature that is competing, rebelling or just not understanding the plans of its creator. And when that creature is of explicitly technological content it starts freaking out and gets dangerous – like in the golem story from mediaeval Jewish Prague or in Mary Shelley's "Frankenstein" novel. The image of the fake human-machine we find there is a special double-bind, a mixture of sympathy and horror.

This structure we find again in one of the first songs about computers. It's a Country & Western tune by a group called The Moonbillies. It dates back to the early 1960s and was released as the flipside of their single "The Fall of the Planet Earth" dealing with some space invasion which, of course, is made audible by means of a Theremin as it always was, back in the old days.

THE MOONBILLIES: THE 'LECTRONIC BRAIN

(Singers)
Listen, O listen, and we will explain
The sad sad story of the 'Lectronic Brain
The greatest invention, the smartest of all
But he just kept a'saying as he stood by the wall

('Lectronic Brain)
I am the 'Lectronic Brain,
With the highest IQ that you can obtain
I can count every star in the heavens above
But I have no heart, I can't fall in love

(Singers)
He has no heart, he can't fall in love

A girl in the office where the brain was installed
Saw him in action and she was enthralled
She said "I love you and will 'til I die"
His tubes turned red, and he said with a sigh...

('Lectronic Brain)
I am the 'Lectronic Brain,
With the highest IQ that you can obtain
I can count every star in the heavens above
But I have no heart, I can't fall in love

(Singers)
He has no heart, he can't fall in love

The brain got so nervous it nearly went mad
Its wires got twisted, his switches went bad
The girl kept on a'vowing her love for him
And he kept replying as his battery went dim

('Lectronic Brain)
I am the 'Lectronic Brain,
With the highest IQ that you can obtain
I can count every star in the heavens above
But I have no heart, I can't fall in love

(Singers)
He has no heart, he can't fall in love

Now all you take warning to what we advised
A woman can ruin the best brain alive
So what chance has man against her sweet way
Like a 'lectronic brain he finally will say...

('Lectronic Brain)
I am the 'Lectronic Brain,
With the highest IQ that you can obtain
I can count every star in the heavens above
But I have no heart, I can't fall in love

(Singers)
He has no heart, he can't fall in love

Seen through the very eyes of 1960s Country & Western music, the story has to be a – quote: "sad sad story" to work within the boundaries of what country music deals with.

That means computers are great machines: "the greatest invention/the smartest of all" and as an "electronic brain" they outline men by "the highest IQ that you can obtain". But of course IQ doesn't make it! As always the next-door-country-music-buddy-guys'n-girls feel threatened by large amounts of intellectualism which – on top of that - are artificial: something that they always sensed when running into intellectual capacities. We know that because we have a high IQ. That's why we are here today.

So there is something missing from that just-a-brain-being created by some suspect just-a-brain-egghead: "I don't have a heart/I can't fall in love".

So it has, of course, the ability to count every star in the heavens above. But what it can't do is reach out and understand stars or let's say: feel them. Because – you know: understanding always equals feeling in country music. That's why country music can be so wise and so stupid at the same time.

The 'lectronic brain is unable to feel how stars work and function within the field of human romantic feelings. It can't feel the stars above in a country music sense without any bureaucratic concerns of exact numbers.

So that's where the drama starts: and in the end that very part of the 'lectronic brain's body that probably compares best to the human heart is running thin: the battery. The message here is clear: being human is being superior – and there's no homunculus to compete with such a perfect machine that is even capable of producing romantic feelings when the stars are shining. But that is not a big problem after all: these country-music-loving-folk do not panic about computers taking over culture and everything in the 1960s. They just smile at the missing characteristics: *lovability* and *felicity* – to put it nicely.

And at least love is not a problem but a topic for some nice novelty songs such as "Lectronic Brain" or as "Computer No. 3" by France Gall. France Gall was a popular French singer but she did some songs in German too. Like this one about using computers in the field of relationship initiation; composed and produced by Mr. Christian Bruhn, who later composed such wonderful soundtracks as "Captain Future".

FRANCE GALL: COMPUTER NO 3

Der Computer Nummer 3 sucht für mich den richtigen Boy,
und die Liebe ist garantiert für beide dabei.
Der Computer weiß genau für jeden Mann die richtige Frau,
und das Glück fällt im Augenblick aus seiner Kartei

Denn einer von vielen Millionen, der wartet auf mich irgendwo.

Gross: 182; Kragen: 39; Schuhgröße: 46, stop!

Der Computer Nummer 3 sucht für mich den richtigen Boy,
und die Liebe ist garantiert für beide dabei
Lange war ich einsam, heut' bin ich verliebt,
und nur darum ist das so, weil es die Technik und die Wissenschaft und Elektronengehirne gibt

FRANCE GALL: COMPUTER NO 3 (TRANSLATION)

The Computer Number 3 is looking for the right boy for me
And love is guaranteed for both sides
The Computer knows exactly the perfect man for every woman
And momentarily love falls out of its index

Cause one out of many millions is waiting for me somewhere

Height: 182; Collar size: 39; Shoe size: 46; stop!

The Computer Number 3 is looking for the right boy for me
And love is guaranteed for both sides
I've been lonely for a long time, now I'm in love
It's only because there is technology, science and electronic brains

In both songs we have computers reflected through the very concern of popular music: that is love in all its facets. Both try simply to derive some interesting constellation of that love thing by introducing the computer.

The Moonbillies created a scenario where a computer becomes subject to the interactions and problems of love, and they decided to show the melancholic and "sad, sad" side of this interaction. There are also songs featuring computers that can make love to people like the euphoric synthie pop song "Computerliebe" by German synthie band Pasodoble – you know: "Die Module spiel'n verrückt / Mensch ich bin total verliebt".

With regard to the current role of the computer in our sex and love lives we have to admit that this was the more realistic vision.

France Gall's song, on the other hand, stands in the tradition of techno euphoria. But this computer does not speak as a subject that wants to share some point of view. It reports the data of people that want to go out on a date. It is the good servant that technology is supposed to be in bourgeois society; where machines are produced to free people from work, to get rid of the problematic working class that causes the middle class to feel bad for having to exploit them. So, machines are here to clear our conscience while the ex-working class is rotting away in some out-of-sight ghettos.

But then, things suddenly changed: the counter culture swapped over the clear and understandable conditions of commercial pop songs, and its naïve and merely entertaining approach. Pop Underground came into being and it came with a political dimension - it wanted to change the conditions we live in. Here, things became very complicated.

The hippie movement brought new reflections on everything. And it changed our perception of technology. On the one hand there were some who embraced technological progress in the hope that new machines would bring new experiences and destroy the boundaries of the bourgeois subject. Let me name Marshall McLuhan (actually a Catholic), Buckminster Fuller or Timothy Leary here, who acted as an inspiration for hippie culture's notion of what one could do with technology. And what technology could do to you.

From that strain, a techno-futuristic cult derived with bands and projects indulging in technology and developing a new aesthetics through playing what might be called techno music. We all know about the famous German group Kraftwerk as a post hippie band but there were others working in that field that helped bridge the gap from hippie culture to New Wave.

But only few of them understood the computer as the most important tool of the future. And almost no one in the 1970s tried to rebuild musical aesthetics on the basis of a computer to bridge the gap between hippie and Punk/New Wave culture and techno. One of these rare pioneers was an US-American-guy named Bruce Haack who was rediscovered in the 1990s and his most rare and very expensive records have now been re-released on independent labels.

Bruce Haack was a weirdo making some really spaced-out recordings meant to be a modernist child's music. He programmed his music on a polyphonic synthesizer he had built himself without any plan or diagram. He never studied electronics. He was a total amateur. This synthesizer provided him with the means – quote, unquote – "to produce up to twelve simultaneous voices in changing sequence via memory holding over four-thousand bits of information. It will also compose at random".

In his lyrics, technology is presented in a way that children and highschool people – his declared target group – would understand the wonders of the world: the natural as well as the technological. Most of his songs deal with robots but there are some hints to the upcoming computer age, too - like the following "Program Me".

BRUCE HAACK: PROGRAM ME

My heart beats
Electrically
My brain computes
Program me
I am complicated
Let me be
I am new
Program me

This trip
Reality
Is mine if you
Let me be

I am love and I am free
I am child
Program me

What is amazing here is not that Bruce Haack did such incredibly strange records which remind us of groups such as the Residents or later New Wave synthie pop stuff. Neither is it amazing that Kraftwerk chose the computer as the topic for their late LP "Computerwelt" that came out in 1981. Before that they had worked on other technological aspects such as the acceleration of life through driving experience on their "Autobahn" and "Trans Europa Express"-albums and again the aesthetics of robotics on "Menschmaschine". But they made programmed music before "Computerwelt".

What is amazing is that the biggest part of the prog rock and psychedelic and avant-garde movement of the 1970s did not work with computers or programmed music. Instead, they preferred to indulge in the very old romantic stuff from early 19th century. Even in the field of electro-acoustic and modern classical there are only a few experiments like Haack's.

Maybe that had something to do with the hippie movement becoming the ecological movement. The hippies derived their image of nature from people like the Swiss philosopher Jean-Jacques Rousseau. Nature was not just the best and most natural living space for man. Man was also conceived as a natural being - that is: animals on the ultimate level of evolution. Everything perceived as technological and unnatural threatened that ideology. They developed an antitechnological point of view mistaking technology for capitalist society and so on.

There are literally thousands of songs in which the same old criticism of the techno-capitalist society is repeated over and over again. Especially in Germany and Austria a flood of musically quite uninteresting singer/songwriters appeared and tried – well: not to change the world through singing (as it was often said) but to make clear that morally they belonged to the axis of good.

That is the only thing that liberal leftists can do about this world going completely wrong: to be on the right side (or grimly looking for it). They don't have any theoretical tools to distinguish and understand what is going on. But, being very sensitive, they have an enormous ability to feel what is wrong. We just get a short cut from a song here by Austrian singer/songwriter Georg Danzer. During his last years, he made neo-nationalistic bullshit with some other good old Austropoppers. Well, in the early 1980s his fear and hatred of the computer broke loose.

What distinguishes this from other social critics is that he is not only wailing about how bad things are instead he also tries to make a radical gesture. is to proclaim: destroy the computers.

GEORG DANZER: ZERSCHLAGT DIE COMPUTER

Sie wissen, wer Du bist
Sie wissen, was Du isst
Sie kennen genau Deine Maße

Du bist schon programmiert
Jetzt wirst Du kontrolliert
Zu Hause und auch auf der Straße

Zerschlagt die Computer

Sie kennen Dich genau
Sie kennen Deine Frau
Sie lesen vor Dir Deine Zeitung

GEORG DANZER: ZERSCHLAGT DIE COMPUTER (TRANSLATION)

They know who you are
They know what you eat
They know your precise measurements

You are programmed already
Now you are being controlled
At home and out in the streets

Smash the computers
They know you well
They know your wife
They read your newspaper before you do

On one hand this seems to be an act of rebellion against the powers that remain in control due to computers and surveillance cameras. On the other hand, he makes it very clear – not voluntarily of course – what the conflict is. The computers are interfering in the realm of the bourgeois power, which is meant to be at home: the male patriarchal subject. And they are trying to get their electronic hands on its very insignia: first his wife and second his newspaper. So he needs to fight back the intruder, like every NRA guy would do.

The pseudo-criticism of the capitalist society from the point of view of its very product: the bourgeois subject always brings up some ideological stuff to deconstruct. Like in the next piece we are going to hear coming from a group that belonged to the German Sakropop scene of the late 1970s. Sakropop was pop music by Christian bands in Germany meant to be played at church services. It is one of the most incredible and strangest kinds of music you can find. This genre cannot be compared to Christian pop from the US. It is unique, as we will hear now....

Info Music Bamberg: Die Nummer

Man wird als Nummer in Computern gespeichert
Dort hat man kein Gefühl und keine Stimme

Man ist ganz einfach als Impuls registriert
Man tippt mich ein und aus und Amen

Man wird als Nummer in Statistiken erwähnt
Dort hat man keinen Wert und keine Würde

Info Music Bamberg: Die Nummer (Translation)

You are registered as a number in a computer
Where you don't have emotions and you don't have a voice

Your are merely registered as an impulse
They type me and turn me off and Amen.

You are being mentioned as a number in a statistic
Where you don't have value and dignity

"Man wird ganz einfach als Impuls registriert, man tippt mich ein und Aus und Amen" – what a great line. It sounds as if they've read McLuhan but didn't understand a single word of it...

Another good example of that kind of stuff can be found on young German singer Juliane Werding's first album. "Juliane Werding is". It says there is "a 16 year old girl singing for a better world and singing for people". On her first LP she had lots of songs concerned with almost any topic you could come up with back then: "Am Tag als Conny Kramer starb" (about drug abuse) or "Der letzte Kranich vom Angerburger Moor" (about ecological problems materialising).

And of course, there is a song about a world overrun by computers. An executive named Schmitt – or Smith that is - that is to say: not an individual but one of the "greys", this Schmitt visits companies, factories and offices as a commercial traveller for an obscure company named IBO. International Business Objects?

JULIANE WERDING: DER COMPUTER MACHT ALLES

Schwarzer Koffer und weißer Kragen,
So besucht er an allen Tagen
Jede Firma, Fabrik und jedes Büro,
Und er stellt sich vor:
Mein Name ist Schmitt,
Ihr Berater von der IBO.

Der Computer macht alles,
Der Computer kann für dich denken.
Der Computer weiß alles,
Der Computer ersetzt den Menschen.

Er berechnet mit Elektronen
Das Apartment, in dem wir wohnen,
Deine Arbeit und Freizeit wird programmiert.
Er spart Personal,
Das ist bares Geld,
Und er sucht den Freund, der dir gefällt.

JULIANE WERDING: DER COMPUTER MACHT ALLES (TRANSLATION)

Black suit, white collar... that's how he visits each day every company, factory and office

He introduces himself: "My name is Schmitt, your consultant from IBO."

The computer does everything
The computer can think for you

The computer knows everything
The computer replaces man

It calculates with electrons the appartment we live in
Your work and your leisure time are being programmed

It saves workforce
That means cash
And it searches a friend you like

In these pieces (like in a bunch of others from the mid 1970s to the early 1990s), the computer is a threat to individuality and human nature. As we all know, the techno-capitalist society is nothing but a gigantic tautological machine producing alienation to be felt in each and every aspect of everyday life. So why not try to figure out why this is and what the ideological and economical core of that mess might be. And what you can do about it. Liberals do not have that option, because they are products of this society. And if they questioned it they would be questioning themselves and their identity. Well, bad things happen, but at least they have to question something if they do not want to look like idiots not questioning anything. That's why you always find them working on the symptoms and using them as some sort of wailing wall to sit down in front of it and weep gently about how things went wrong.

We have to clearly distinguish them from the progressive leftist movement which tried to come up with an analysis of what's going on rather than with a bunch of nice but incredibly silly songs. These songs are the merchandise of a regression into a pre-computer-age utopia. Some kind of nostalgia park where they could send proletarian kiddies to coalmines again to produce wealth through their sacrifice; a wealth to form the basis of modern techno-capitalist society. So there' no way back, motherfuckers!

By the way, have you noticed that whenever it comes to computers, there is a certain proto New Wave-sound coming to town: we had that with "Computer No 3" and we have it here. So it might be of interest what happened to the computer in popular music after Punk and New Wave took over in the late 1970s.

First we need to understand that Punk and Post-Punk were a reaction to liberal post-hippie affairs. This was based on the fact that people like Georg Danzer, Juliane Werding or the Info Music Bamberg represented a bloody wrong consciousness. And so, Punk and Post-Punk tried to provoke their bourgeois anti-modernism by some pretty good confusion. Like the German art Punk group SYPH singing "Back to concrete". This was a reaction to the post-hippies' "back to nature"-approach. The confusion Punk and Post-Punk brought about was enormous and difficult enough to survey. There were lots of different dispositions within the new movement. Some crossfaded the old bourgeois computer panic into the new sounds and as we can hear in a short take from "Computerstaat" the hit song of Hamburg based Post-Punksters Abwärts...

ABWÄRTS: COMPUTERSTAAT

Montag klopft es an der Tür
Und Arafat steht neben dir
Dienstag gibt es Probealarm
Paranoia in der Straßenbahn
Mittwoch ist der Krieg sehr kalt
Breschnew lauert in der Badeanstalt
[...]
Sonntag, da ist alles tot
Im Golf von Mallorca der Weltkrieg droht

Stalingrad Stalingrad
Deutschland Katastrophenstaat
Wir leben im Computerstaat

ABWÄRTS: COMPUTERSTAAT (TRANSLATION)

On Monday there's a knock on your door and it's Arafat standing in front of you
On Tuesday there is an emergency system test
Paranoia in the tramway
On Wednesday war is very cold
Bershnew's lurking in the public spa
[...]
On Sunday all things are dead
In the Gulf of Mallorca the World War is imminent

Stalingrad Stalingrad
Germany catastrophe nation

We are living in computer nation

This was a paranoia classic from a time when the system waged war on a German leftist terror group called Red Army Faction. They used computers to gather information about the leftist scene to discover supporters of the RAF. What they did would now be called Rasterfahndung (dragnet investigation) – early computerized criminal investigation.

But Abwärts did not do a song about the computer as a tool used by the opposite side. Computers appear only in the last line: "Wir leben im Computerstaat". But we get strange impressions before that, like: "Montag klopft es an die Tür und Arafat, der steht vor Dir" ("On Monday there's a knock on your door and it's Arafat standing in front of you") and "Mittwoch ist der Krieg sehr kalt/Breschnew lauert in der Badeanstalt" ("On Wednesday war is very cold/Bershnew's lurking in the public spa") ... These are disparate impressions, not from the real world but from an information society. The subject is overrun by all the information. But it's not clear whether Abwärts want to criticise information society or if they want to make fun of the typical liberal criticism of it. That's why it is such a great song. It does not give us a clue which of the two possibilities it favours. The early Punk and Post-Punk musicians used this ambiguity as a cultural weapon against the simplicities of 1970s liberalism.

So the changes brought upon the human condition through the modern world were one of the main items of early Punk and Post-Punk groups. The computer age was not in full swing yet, so computers were not yet on the agenda. Or let's say: not in a way that might be called adequate. You would expect a band like Devo to make songs about computers but there is none, as far as I know. Also, there are lots of songs by Post-Punk groups with titles like "I am a Computer" but most of them were just following the Gary Newman scheme of becoming machines. Some others stood in the old liberal tradition of conservative criticism, saying computers eradicate people's individuality.

Here is a song I found on a pretty obscure and rather rare British New Wave-single by a group called The Goo-Q.

THE GOO-Q: I'M A COMPUTER

One door opens
But two places

Which way, this way
And she won't go
Life is oh so fundamental
Ready steady, stuff I've started
2 x 2 makes
Only 18
1920
I accept tea
Call me, all me, call me
Navy Blues and Rock & Roll
I'm wasted

I'm a computer
Are you a computer too?
I'm a computer
Are you a computer too?
And out

Oh show business
Knows no business
Left is, right is
Back or forwards
Inside out shot, buy or sell it
Wrong decision, have to go now
Is the answer
Don't ask questions
See you later
Calculator
Voice decoder, out of order
You're so square, so geometric

I'm a computer
Are you a computer too?
I'm a computer
Are you a computer too?
And out
Lala and soso
Doctor and coco
Yes, yes, no, no
Uno, that's so limbo, disco, pogo, tango

I'm a computer
You computer too?
I'm a computer
You computer too?
I'm a computer
Are you a computer too?
I'm a computer
And you - are you a computer too?
And out
I'm a computer
I'm a computer
I'm a computer
I'm a computer
I'm a computer
I'm a computer

This is a jolly little song about modern world confusion with some nice hints to rock 'n' roll history – such as: "See you later, calculator"...

Another song of that kind comes from a widely unknown Canadian group who worked as a band as part of their projects like it was the case with a lot of Post-Punk groups. They called their band "The Government" and recorded "(I'd rather be a) Real Computer".

THE GOVERNMENT: (I'D RATHER BE A) REAL COMPUTER

Image!
Organize!
Process!
Xerox!
Determination!
Black, white!
Much more complicated!
Color generation!

Re-generation!
Image peek dot image!
Process!
Coffee break!

I'd rather be a real computer

I'd rather be a real computer

Every day I go to work
There's numbers in my ear
And then I go to bars I get these numbers in my beer
Sometimes I think I'm seeing numbers in the mirror

I'd rather be a real computer

Here we get a more adequate approach to alienation: it's not technology itself which alienates us. It's the specific condition of society's economics in which we are involved. And in which we are produced as social subjects.

And if you take into account what economics made of us through work, it would seem preferable to be a computer.

Computers are not intruders from a technological outer-space. The electronic subject is a new utopia. This utopia won't work for us because it does not change capitalist economics – but still it serves as a foil for criticising it.

Maybe the best song about computer panic taking hold of the bourgeois small family as the most important piece in bourgeois patriarchal ideology came from German New Wave outfits Der Plan. It was called "Gummi Twist". It is a funny, yet exact, portrait about the confusion and panic that has grabbed the bourgeois subject. Not only for computers threatening this subject by attacking its individuality and subjectivity. It also poses a threat as a technological advance to cope and keep up with. Kids got to have a C64 for Christmas to keep up with the capitalist pace and defeat the others on all tomorrow's markets.

So, there was some fine stress for the archetypical middle class-father as we will see now...

DER PLAN: GUMMI TWIST

Woher weht der Wind von morgen,
wozu wird das Ding gebaut?
Wonach schreit der Mensch von heute,

wer hat mein Gehirn geklaut?

Ich frage Leute auf der Straße,
in der U-Bahn, im Büro,
alle woll'n Computer haben,
keiner weiß genau wieso.

Gib mir Parallelschnittstellen,
64-Bit-Prozessor,
Fortram, Logo, CPU
und VisiCalc und RAM-Modul.

Interslip und Floppy Chip,
Pershing II und Apple Panic,
sind die Russen unsre Feinde,
ach, die Welt ist so verwirrend!

Papi, schenk mir einen Computer!
Hilfe für die ganze Familie!
Liebling, nimm die Rüstungsspirale!
Tanz den Gumimtwist!

Kann ich morgen nicht mehr leben
ohne Personalcomputer?
Kann ich meine Blumen nicht mehr
ohne den Computer gießen?

Kann ich keine Suppe kochen
ohne LCD-Display,
und wenn ich meine Socken wasche,
brauche ich ein Interface?

Woll'n die Russen uns vernichten,
oder sind die Amis schuld?
Crazy Shoot Out, Space Invaders,
Snack Attack und Roach Hotel.

Von allen Dingen auf der Erde,
die es gibt und geben darf,
weiß ich eines völlig sicher,

was war es gleich, grad wußt ich's noch?

Papi, schenk mir einen Computer!
Hilfe für die ganze Familie!
Liebling, nimm die Rüstungsspirale!
Tanz den Gummitwist!

DER PLAN: GUMMI TWIST (TRANSLATION)

Where does the wind of tomorrow blow from,
what's the reason to build this thing?
What is today's man longing for,
who stole my brain?
I'm asking people on the street,
in the subway, in the office
They all want to have computers
No one knows exactly why

Give me parallel interface,

64 bit processor,
Fortran, Logo, CPU
and VisiCalc and a RAM module
Interslip and Floppy Chip,
Pershing II and Apple Panic

Are the Russians our enemies?

Oh my, the world is so confusing!

Daddy, buy me a computer!
Help for the whole family!
Darling, get the arms race!

Dance the Rubber twist!
Is life impossible tomorrow without a personal computer?
Is it impossible to water my flowers without a computer?

Is it impossible to prepare soup

without LCD display?
And do I need an interface to wash my socks?
Do the Russian want to wipe us out,
or is it the American's fault?
Crazy Shoot Out, Space Invaders,
Snack Attack and Roach Hotel

Of all the things there are on Earth
That are and may exist
I know one thing for sure
What was it? I still knew it a moment ago

Daddy, buy me a computer!
Help for the whole family!
Darling, get the arms race!
Dance the Rubber twist!

"Von allen Dingen auf der Erde, die es gibt und geben darf, weiß ich eines völlig sicher, was war es gleich, grad wußt ich's noch?" ("Of all the things there are on Earth / That are and may exist / I know one thing for sure/ What was it? I still knew it a moment ago") – this is a nice snapshot of the bourgeois overcharge or let's say overload by new technology. It's not coming from the outside world into their safe European home but from the material this safe European home was made of. And now they are haunted by the poltergeist that clings to it...

Der Plan was intelligent enough to learn and understand what was going on and reflect it in their music. This might have had to do with the fact that they lived in Düsseldorf. Back then, Düsseldorf was one of the avant-garde places to be in Germany. People like the Post-Punk writer Peter Glaser who had already opened up for the new technology, lived there. He hung out with Der Plan and worked with them on different occasions.

On the other hand, there still was the liberal angst culture which was afraid of being swept away by everything new under the sun. You know, those Herod kind of types. And while the New Wave was rolling and rolling they got involved. And they applied the new style to broadcast their old messages like the German ex-Schlager singer Pierre Schilling did. He had a comeback as Peter Schilling – even though nobody noticed that it was a comeback.

He did some modern world songs that still tried to cope with the old liberal core imperative: be critical. And yet he transmitted a teenage fascination with the problems of the modern world that clearly divided it from the old model of sheer criticism. Maybe that's why he became big for one or two seasons having a number of hit singles, starting with "Völlig losgelöst" and followed by "Die Wüste lebt". Not unusual for successful NDW-bands of that time, he tried to get a foot into the international market. And so an English version of his LP "Fehler im System" was released under the title "Error in the System". There we also find "Die Wüste lebt" - translated into "The Noah Plan", a song in which there's global catastrophe coming. And what would you do if you were a global catastrophe and had to wipe out the stupid social world? Yes that's right, you would cut off their basic organizational tools as we're going to hear now...

PETER SCHILLING: THE NOAH PLAN

A million years have come and gone
The Earth is shifting towards the sun
Synthetic atmosphere is lost
And forces the computers off
Communications are confused
The tides reverse
And start a chain reaction

The seismograph's consulted
incredible results
It says we're losing all control, losing all control
The scientists around the world decipher everything they do
But they don't really know, they don't really know
instead of systematic the news becomes erratic
No-one can agree, no-one can agree
The world is getting frantic as people start a panic
What does all this mean?
The sun is moving closer
And the atmosphere gets hotter
As the system overloads, system overloads, fighting these adverse conditions,
Loading for the expedition

Everyone must go, everyone must go
The fools that think the worst is over
They won't live to be much older
Why do they remain, why do they remain
everything is ready, everyone that's coming has been safely brought on board

The 1980s could be called the computer age or at least the beginning of an age with its end not yet in sight. Computers became more and more a part of our everyday lives.

Musical development started to work with computers in the fields of studio recording, synthesizer programming and, of course, on its non-musical side that is neglected most of the time when reflecting on music. At the same time, rock and pop avant-garde started to work with computers as an aesthetic means – Neil Young for example released an album in 1982 called "Trans" – it's one of his worst by the way. On this album he worked with synthesizers and sang about the "Computer age" and "Computer Cowboys", both still very much in the vein of social criticism about how the computer occupies more and more ground of what once was "the real world". So nothing new here.

About 20 years later, computers have made their way through pop culture and nowadays we find thousands of songs in which computers appear as something rather normal, a piece of our environment providing some special potential. As such we find the computer featured as a door into another world in a song by famous New York antifolkies The Moldy Peaches. It tells the story of a kid discovering his own homosexuality.

MOLDY PEACHES: DOWNLOADING PORN WITH DAVO

Sleepin' in a van between A & B
Suckin' dick for ecstasy
Paid a 70 year old hooker to make out with me
Now the "get high shack" is just a memory

Downloading porn with Davo
Downloading porn with Davo
Put a latch on the door so Mama don't know

That I'm downloading porn with Davo

Tried to buy your love, but I came up short
So I fucked a little waitress in exchange for a snort
My girl's got a dick hangin' out of her shorts
Me and Eric in the bathroom with the weather report

Downloading porn with Davo
Downloading porn with Davo
Put a latch on the door so mama don't know
That I'm downloading porn with Davo

Baby, I know ya love the good old days
Cruisin' on the Long Island Expressway
I used to be dead, but now I'm gay
All I ever think about is drowning, drowning

Downloading porn with Davo
Downloading porn with Davo
Put a latch on the door so Mama don't know
That I'm downloading porn with Davo

To open the Google door to porn download pages and slip into the gay section he and his friend Davo have to close the door to keep his mother out. Thus the image of the computer had shifted from something technical (which might damage the social world) to something social.

It is a space where you can have experiences that deconstruct the ideological content of your surroundings – that is to say: that free you. In this case they free you from the enforced heterosexist form you were socially born into.

After the Moldy Peaches dissolved around 2000, Kimya Dawson and Adam Green did a lot of solo recordings. Since both of them were kids of what you could call the computer generation computer-related stuff appears here and there in their lyrics. On Adam Green's first album we find a song called "Computer Show" that tells a surrealist story. And on Kimya Dawson's solo album "Hidden Agenda" we have the great "Anthrax (Powerballad version)" in which she reflects about 9/11 as a sudden shock that hit the lives of those New York bohemian kids.

KIMYA DAWSON: ANTHRAX (POWERBALLAD VERSION)

In Montreal I got so mad, someone broke into the van, stole my guitar and Aaron's bag
Then we turned on CNN, watched the towers fall again and realized that our lives aren't so bad

This is just a test take it with love and you will pass
You will be rewarded if you do your very best
Nothing ever goes as planned so don't take anything for granted
If you do the world will kick your ass

The air is filled with computers and carpets
skin and bones and telephones and file cabinets, Coke machines, firemen, landing gear, and cement

They say that it's okay but I say don't breathe in that shit in

In the middle of the song she hallucinates the very moment of the catastrophe and how everything collapses. She comes up with a very strong picture of it. Everything that used to be normal and in its place gets physically confused like in a huge explosion. Together with skin, bones, telephones and carpets we get computers being IN the air. A very intense picture of how normal computers have gotten to those post-modern kids…

So in the end of this long speech we find that conservative people who were frightened and disgusted enough by the computer to damn it, were wrong – like they always are. Sorry, but natural history has been telling you this for about 6 billion years. And so does human history: there's no way back in culture.

And quite obviously, by now the Austropoppers (like late Georg Danzer) and the Info Music Bamberg are pretty much ashamed of what they produced 20 years ago, and they sit in front of their computers writing emails or buying books on Amazon. Or they download porn with Davo.

Computers are established widely enough for us to have some historisation for the last track of tonight coming from a group called Laux in honor of Konrad Zuse who started it all. And of course I'll join in and dedicate my speech that ends right now to the great Galileo

Galilei of the computer age: Konrad Zuse. Always remember he was fucking clever that's why he invented the computer.

LAUX: ZUSE

Mein Computer ist noch an um Mitternacht
Zum Lesen, Rechnen, Schreiben, toll wie der das macht
Gedichte dicht ich im Editor, Text als Liebespfand
Pixel auf dem Bildschirm mit Taste, Maus und Hand
Und dann schau ich mir das Bild vom alten Zuse an
Der das Ding erfunden hat, mit dem es einst begann

Er war so faul, deshalb erfand er den Computer
Er war so schlau, deshalb erfand er den Computer

Konrad ist ein kluger Kopf, er hasst die Plagerei
Weil er zu faul zum Rechnen war erfand er die Z3
Er will lieber Bilder malen und sich nicht mit Zahlen schlagen,
Abends länger Bier trinken, morgens lang im Bett versinken
Bleistifte zu Tode spitzen, Tintenflecke auf den Sitzen
Sind nichts für einen Mann, der ja viel mehr kann

LAUX: ZUSE (TRANSLATION)

My computer is still on at midnight
For reading, calculating, writing, what an amazing thing
Writing poems in the editor, text as love token
Pixel on the screen, with keyboard, mouse and stuff
And then I look at the picture of old Zuse
He who invented the thing, who started it all

He was so lazy, that's why he invented the computer
He was so clever, that's why he invented the computer

Konrad is a mastermind, he hates drudgery
Because he was too lazy to calculate, he invented the Z3.
He prefers drawing pictures to dealing with numbers
Drinking beer all evening, sleeping in all morning

Sharpening pencils to their deaths
Ink spots on seats
Are not for the man who is capable of so much more

Well this is not the kind of applause I feel adequate to come up with an encore, so I'll hold back here...

(Applause)

I need more applause! I need eurotrash techno applause! This is a pretty weird song about the internet that was produced for the Eurovision song contest a long time ago... in 1996.

EUROCATS: SURFEN MULTIMEDIA

Surf, Surf, Surf!

Surfen, Surfen, durch die Welt mit Multimedia
Surfen, Surfen, Tag und Nacht auf der Datenautobahn

Komm heute Nacht ins Internet,
ich warte schon auf dich,
Mensch sei ein User,
geh Online, im E-Mail triffst du mich

Surfen, Surfen, durch die Welt mit Multimedia
Surfen, Surfen, Tag und Nacht auf der Datenautobahn

Und fehl'n dir ein paar Megabyte,
du findest sie bei mir,
ob Interface or Cyberspace,
ich teile gern mit dir.

Surfen, Surfen, durch die Welt mit Multimedia
Surfen, Surfen, Tag und Nacht auf der Datenautobahn

Mit Bits und Bytes,
Mit Maus und Klick,
da gehen wir auf Tour,

im World Wide Web,
da folgen wir heut jeder heißen Spur.

Surfen, Surfen, durch die Welt mit Multimedia
Surfen, Surfen, Tag und Nacht auf der Datenautobahn

Surf, Surf, Surf!

Eurocats: Surfen Multimedia (translation)

Surf, Surf, Surf!

Surfing surfing through the world with multimedia
Surfing surfing, day and night on the data highway

Come join me on the internet tonight
I'm already waiting for you
Dude, be a user, go online
You'll meet me in the email

Surfing surfing through the world with multimedia
Surfing surfing, day and night on the data highway

And you should lack some megabytes
You'll find them here with me
Be it interface or cyberspace
I'll gladly share with you

Surfing surfing through the world with multimedia
Surfing surfing, day and night on the data highway

With bits and bytes
With mouse and click
We are going on a tour

In the World Wide Web

We'll follow each new hint today

Surfing surfing through the world with multimedia

Surfing surfing, day and night on the data highway

Surf, Surf, Surf!

Good Night.
And please hug your iPhone.

3. Networks

Trapped in the World Wide Web

Dmytri Kleiner

The revolutionary possibilities of the early internet lay particularly in the capacity for direct interaction between users. As such, the internet promised to be a platform where freedom of speech and association was built into the architecture. However, without most users noticing, the architecture of the internet is changing, and the topology of the network is being remade in such a way that not only serves the interests of capitalism, but also enables monitoring and control of its users on a scale never dreamed of before.

The internet took the corporate world by surprise, emerging as it did from publicly funded universities, military research, and civil society. It was promoted by a cottage industry of small independent internet service providers, who were able to squeeze a buck from providing access to the state-built and financed network. Meanwhile, the corporate world was pushing a different idea of the information superhighway, producing monolithic, centralized 'online services' like CompuServe, Prodigy and AOL. What made these corporate services different from the internet is that they were centralized systems that users connect to directly, while the internet is a peer-to-peer (P2P) network where every device with a public internet address can communicate directly to any other device.

While both users of CompuServe and the internet had access to similar applications, such as email, discussion groups, chat groups and file sharing, users of CompuServe were completely dependent on CompuServe for access, while users of the internet could gain access through any service provider, and could even chose to run their own servers. Platforms such as internet email, and internet relay chat were based on a distributed structure that no one owned or controlled.

This structure was accepted by the most enthusiastic early adopters of the internet, such as public institutions and non- government organizations. However, capitalist investors were unable to see how such an unrestricted system would allow them to earn profits. The internet seemed anathema to the capitalist imagination.

The original dot-com boom, then, was characterized by a rush to own infrastructure, to consolidate independent internet service providers and take control of the network. Money was near-randomly thrown around as investors struggled to understand what this medium would be used for. Ultimately, the mission of these investors was largely successful. Their mission was to destroy the independent service provider and put large, well-financed corporations back in the driver's seat. If you had an internet account in 1996 it was likely provided by a small local company. Ten years later, while some of the smaller companies had survived; most people were getting their internet access from gigantic telecommunications corporations, which persist even stronger today.

The internet is more than the Web, a term inaccurately used as a synonym for the entire network and all of the applications that run on it. The World Wide Web is a technology that runs on top of the peer-to-peer network that is the internet; however, it is unlike the classic internet technologies like email, IRC, Usenet etc. The Web is neither distributed, nor is it peer-to-peer; it is a client-server technology. The publisher of a website runs the servers and has exclusive control over the content and applications their website provides, including control of who should or should not have access to it. The users have control of the browser, the client software used to access the website. A website has more in common with CompuServe than a peer-to-peer system. The publisher has full control of the content and options available to users.

The Web started innocently enough as a platform for publishing text online; however, it rapidly became the focal point for organizations looking to commercialize the internet. From modest beginnings, as companies began to put brochures online, the commercial Web took off with the development of e-Commerce. At this point, the Web had not yet taken over online sharing. People used the Web to, for instance, browse a bookstore, but continued to employ distributed technologies to communicate with other users. However, soon enough the Web, funded by venture capital, would move in to make websites operated by large corporations the primary online social platforms. The internet itself would soon disappear behind the Web, and users would never again leave their browser.

Web 2.0 emerged as a venture capitalists' paradise, where investors pocket the value produced by unpaid users, ride on the technical innovations of the free software movement, and kill off the decentralizing potential of peer-to-peer technology.

Wikipedia says that:

"WEB 2.0, A PHRASE COINED BY O'REILLY MEDIA IN 2004, REFERS TO A SUPPOSED SECOND GENERATION OF INTERNET-BASED SERVICES, SUCH AS SOCIAL NETWORKING SITES, WIKIS, COMMUNICATION TOOLS, AND FOLKSONOMIES, THAT EMPHASIZE ONLINE COLLABORATION AND SHARING AMONG USERS."[1]

The use of the word 'supposed' is noteworthy. As the largest collaboratively authored work in history, Wikipedia should know. Unlike most of the members of the Web 2.0 generation, Wikipedia is controlled by a non-profit foundation, earns income only by donation, and releases its content under a copy left license. It is telling that this Wikipedia entry goes on to say '[Web 2.0] has become a popular (though ill-defined and often criticized) buzzword among certain technical and marketing communities'.

The free software community has tended to be suspicious, if not outright dismissive, of the Web 2.0 moniker. Tim Berners-Lee, the creator of World Wide Web, dismissed the term saying that, 'Web 2.0 is of course a piece of jargon, nobody even knows what it means'. He goes on to note that 'it means using the standards which have been produced by all these people working onWeb1.0.[2] In reality, then, there is neither a Web 1.0 nor a Web 2.0. There is only an ongoing development of online applications that cannot be cleanly divided.

In trying to define what Web 2.0 is, it is safe to say that most of the important developments have been aimed at enabling the community to create, modify, and share content in a way that was previously only available to centralized organizations that bought expensive software packages, paid staff to handle the technical aspects of the site, and

---

1 | 'Web 2.0', Wikipedia.org, http://en.wikipedia.org/wiki/Web_2.0.
2 | developerWorks, 'developerWorks Interviews: Tim Berners-Lee', developerWorks 22 August 2006, http://www.ibm.com/developerworks/pod-cast/dwi/cm-int082206txt.html.

paid staff to create content which generally was published only on that organization's site.

A Web 2.0 company, then, fundamentally changes the production of internet content. Web applications and services have become cheaper and easier to implement, and by allowing end users access to these applications, a company can effectively outsource the creation and the organization of their content to the end users themselves. Instead of the traditional model of a content provider publishing their own content and the end user consuming it, the new model allows the company's site to act as the centralized portal for users who are both creators and consumers. For the user, access to these applications empowers them to create and publish content that previously would have required them to purchase desktop software and possess a greater technological skill set. For example, two of the primary means of text-based content production in Web 2.0 are blogs and wikis. These allow the user to create and publish content directly from their browser without any real knowledge of mark up language, file transfer or syndication protocols, and all without the need to purchase any software.

The use of web applications to replace desktop software is even more significant for the user when it comes to content that is not merely textual. Not only can web pages be created and edited in the browser without purchasing HTML editing software, photographs can be uploaded and manipulated online through the browser without expensive desktop image manipulation applications. A video shot on a consumer camcorder can be submitted to a video hosting site, uploaded, encoded, embedded into an HTML page, published, tagged, and syndicated across the web all through the user's browser. In Paul Graham's article on Web 2.0, he breaks down the different roles of the community/user more specifically. These include the professional, the amateur, and the user (more precisely, the end user). The roles of the professional and the user were, according to Graham, well understood in Web 1.0, but the amateur didn't have a very well defined place.[3]

As Graham describes it in 'What Business Can Learn from Open Source', the amateur just loves to work, with no concern for compensation or ownership of that work. In development, the amateur

---

3 | Paul Graham, 'Web 2.0', PaulGraham.com, November 2005, http://www.paulgraham.com/web20.html

contributes to open source software whereas the professional gets paid for their proprietary work.[4] Graham's characterization of the 'amateur' has an odd similarity to If I Ran the Circus by children's author Dr. Seuss, where young Morris McGurk says of the staff of his imaginary Circus McGurkus:

"MY WORKERS LOVE WORK. THEY SAY, "WORK US! PLEASE WORK US! WE'LL WORK AND WE'LL WORK UP SO MANY SURPRISES YOU'D NEVER SEE HALF IF YOU HAD FORTY EYESES!"[5]

And while the term 'Web 2.0' may mean nothing to Tim Berners-Lee, who views recent innovations as no more than the continued development of the Web, for venture capitalists, who like Morris McGurk dream of tireless workers producing endless content without demanding a pay check, it sounds stupendous. And indeed, from YouTube to Flickr to Wikipedia, you'd truly 'never see half if you had forty eyes'. Tim Berners-Lee is correct. There is nothing, from a technical or user point of view, in Web 2.0 that does not have its roots in, and is not a natural development from, the earlier generation of the Web. The technology associated with the Web 2.0 banner was possible and in some cases readily available before, but the hype surrounding this usage has certainly affected the growth of Web 2.0 internet sites.

The internet has always been about sharing between users. Indeed Usenet, the distributed messaging system, has been operating since 1979. Since then, Usenet has been hosting discussions, 'amateur' journalism, and photo and file sharing. Like the internet, it is a distributed system not owned or controlled by anyone. It is this quality, a lack of central ownership and control, which differentiates services such as Usenet from Web 2.0.

If Web 2.0 means anything at all, its meaning lies in the rationale of venture capital. Web 2.0 represents the return of investment in internet start-ups. After the dot-com bust (the real end of Web 1.0), those seeking investment dollars needed a new rationale for investing in online ventures. 'Build it and they will come', the dominant attitude of the 90s dot-com boom, along with the delusional 'new economy', was no longer attractive after so many online ventures failed. Building

---

4 | Paul Graham, 'What Business Can Learn From Open Source', PaulGraham.com, August 2005, http://www.paulgraham.com/opensource.html
5 | Dr. Seuss, If I Ran the Circus (Random House, 1956)

infrastructure and financing real capitalization was no longer what investors were looking for. Capturing value created by others, however, proved to be a more attractive proposition.

Web 2.0 is Internet Investment Boom 2.0. Web 2.0 is a business model of private capture of community-created value. No one denies that the technology of sites like YouTube, for instance, is trivial. This is more than evidenced by the large number of identical services such as DailyMotion for online video sharing. The real value of YouTube is not created by the developers of the site; rather, it is created by the people who upload videos to the site. Yet, when YouTube was bought for over a billion dollars worth of Google stock, how much of this stock was acquired by those that made all these videos? Zero. Zilch. Nada. A great deal, then, if you are an owner of a Web 2.0 company.

The value produced by users of Web 2.0 services such as YouTube is captured by capitalist investors. In some cases, the actual content they contribute ultimately becomes the property of site owners. Private appropriation of community-created value is a betrayal of the promise of sharing technology and free co-operation. Unlike the dot-com boom era, where investors often financed expensive capital acquisition, software development and content creation, a Web 2.0 investor financed marketing, the generation of hype and buzz. The infrastructure is widely available for cheap, the content is free and the cost of software, at least software that is not freely available, is negligible. Basically, through providing some bandwidth and disk space, it is possible to become a successful Web 2.0 site if you can market yourself effectively.

The principal success of a Web 2.0 company, then, comes from its relationship to the community. More specifically, success comes from a company's capacity to 'harness collective intelligence', as Tim O'Reilly puts it.[6] From this perspective, Web 1.0 companies were too monolithic and unilateral in their approach to content. Success stories of the transition from Web 1.0 to 2.0 were based on a company's ability to remain monolithic in its branding of content, or, better yet, in its ownership of that content, while opening up the creation of content to the community. Yahoo!, for instance, created a portal to community

---

6 | Tim O'Reilly, 'What is Web 2.0: Design Patterns and Business Models for the Next Generation of Software', March 2007, Munich Personal RePEc Archive, MPRA Paper no. 4578 (posted 7 November 2007), 22, http://mpra.ub.uni-muenchen.de/4578/1/MPRA_paper_4578.pdf

content while it remained the centralized location to find that content. eBay allows the community to sell its goods while owning the marketplace for those goods. Amazon, by selling the same products as many other sites, succeeded by allowing the community to participate in the 'flow' around their products.

Because the capitalists who invest in Web 2.0 start-ups do not often fund early capitalization, their behavior is markedly parasitic. Web 2.0 capitalists frequently arrive late when value creation already has good momentum, swoop in to take ownership, and use their financial power to promote the service, often within the context of a hegemonic network of major, well-financed partners. This means that companies not acquired by venture capital end up starved of cash and squeezed out of the club.

In all these cases, the value of the internet site is created not by the paid staff of the company who run it, but by the users who use it. With the emphasis on community created content and sharing, it's easy to overlook questions of ownership of all this content, and the ability to monetize its value. These questions rarely come up for the user. They are part of the fine print in their Facebook Terms of Service agreement, or in the 'flickr.com' in the URL of their photos. Ownership often isn't an issue for the community, and is a small price to pay for the use of these wonderful applications. Since most users do not have access to alternative means to produce and publish their own content, they are attracted to sites like Facebook and Flickr.

It should be added that many open source projects can be cited as the key innovations in the development of Web 2.0: free software like Linux, Apache, PHP, Ruby, Python, etc. are the backbone of Web 2.0, and the Web itself. But there is a fundamental flaw with all of these projects in terms of what O'Reilly refers to as the 'core competencies' of Web 2.0 companies, namely control over unique, hard-to-recreate data sources that get richer as more people use them, and the harnessing of the collective intelligence they attract.[7] Allowing the community to contribute openly and to utilize that contribution within the context of a proprietary system where the proprietor owns the content is a characteristic of a successful Web 2.0 company. Allowing the community to own what it creates, though, is not.

---

7 | Ibid., 36

Thus, to be successful and create profits for investors, a Web 2.0 company needs to create mechanisms for sharing and collaboration that are centrally controlled. The lack of central control possessed by Usenet and other peer-controlled technologies is, in the context of Web 2.0, a fundamental flaw. They only benefit their users, not absentee investors, as they are not 'owned'. Thus, because Web 2.0 is funded by the same-old capitalism, Usenet is mostly forgotten. While YouTube is worth a billion dollars, PeerCast, an innovative P2P live video streaming network that has been in existence for several years longer than YouTube, is virtually unknown.

From a technological standpoint, distributed and peer-to-peer technologies are far more efficient than Web 2.0 systems. Making better use of network resources by using the computers and network connections of users, peer-to-peer avoids the bottlenecks created by centralized systems. It also allows content to be published with less infrastructure, often no more than a computer and a consumer internet connection. P2P systems do not require the massive data centers of sites such as YouTube. Distributed systems also tend to have greater longevity. Usenet has been subsumed in some way by Google, who owns the largest Usenet archive and the most accessed Usenet web-based client, Google Groups. However, because of the distributed nature of Usenet, other means of access continue to exist in parallel, and while its role as an online platform has lost prominence, many newsgroups remain active. For instance, the Church of The SubGenius newsgroup, alt. slack, continues to be an important social forum for the popular US-based mock religion. The lack of central infrastructure also comes with a lack of central control, meaning an absence of censorship, often a problem with privately-owned 'communities' that frequently bend to private and public pressure groups and enforce limitations on the kinds of content they allow. Also, the lack of large central cross-referencing databases of user information has a strong advantage in terms of privacy.

From this perspective, it can be said that Web 2.0 is capitalism's pre-emptive attack against peer-to-peer systems. However, despite the many disadvantages in comparison to P2P, Web 2.0 is more attractive to investors and thus has more money to fund and promote centralized solutions. The end result is that capitalist investment has flowed into centralized solutions, making them easy and cheap or free for non-technical information producers to adopt. This ease of access, compared to the technically challenging and expensive undertaking of owning your own means of information production, has created a 'landless' proletariat ready to provide alienated content-creating labor for the new info landlords of Web 2.0. The mission of Web 2.0 is to destroy the P2P aspect of the internet and to make you, your computer, and your internet connection dependent on connecting to centralized services that control your ability to communicate. Web 2.0 is the ruin of free, peer-to-peer systems and the return of monolithic online services.

A telling detail here is that most home or office internet connections in the 90s, such as modem and ISDN connections, were symmetric, equal in their ability to send and receive data. By design, these connections enable you to be equally a producer and a consumer of information. On the other hand, modern DSL and cable-modem connections are asymmetric, allowing you to download information quickly but upload slowly. Moreover, many user agreements for internet services forbid the user to run servers on a consumer account, and may cut off your service if you do.

Capitalism, rooted in the idea of earning income by way of idle share ownership, requires centralized control. Without such centralized control, producers have no reason to share their income with outside shareholders. So long as the financing of internet development resources comes from private shareholders looking to capture value by owning internet resources, the network will only become more restricted and centralized. While the information commons has the potential to play a role in moving society toward more inclusive modes of production, any real hope for a genuine, community enriching, next generation of internet-based services is not rooted in the creation of more privately owned, centralized resources, but rather in creating co-operative, P2P and commons based systems owned by everybody and nobody.

To reiterate, although small and obscure by today's standards, with its focus on peer-to-peer applications such as Usenet and email, the early internet was very much a common, shared resource. The commercialization of the internet and the emergence of capitalist financing have enabled the enclosure of this information commons, translating public wealth into private profit. Thus Web 2.0 should not be thought of as a second generation of either the technical or social development of the internet, but rather as the second wave of capitalist enclosure of the information commons.

The third wave of enclosure of the information commons is already coming into view. Cloud computing, provided by large corporations such as Google and Amazon, where customers do not own the physical infrastructure they use, is further centralizing the infrastructure of the internet. Additionally, legislation, such as the 'Telecoms Reform Package'[8] presented to the European Parliament, seeks to make it possible for service providers (large telecommunications conglomerates) to decide which websites their users are able to access. Capital is showing us their vision of the future of the internet, and the future looks a lot like CompuServe: monolithic, centralized, mediated, controllable and exploitable, and naturally, operated by a few large corporations.

Almost all of the most used internet resources could be replaced by peer-to-peer alternatives. Google could be replaced by a P2P search system, where every browser and every web server is an active node in the search process; Flickr and YouTube could also be replaced by Peer-Cast, BitTorrent and eDonkey-type applications, which allow users to use their own computers and internet connections to collaboratively share pictures and videos. However, developing internet resources requires the application of wealth, and so long as the source of this wealth is venture capital, the great peer-to-peer potential of the internet will remain unrealized. If we cannot find alternatives to capitalist financing, we will not only lose the internet as we know it, but also the chance to remake society in its 2P image.

References

Bell, Daniel. 'The Subversion of Collective Bargaining'. Commentary. March, 1960

'Charter for Innovation, Creativity and Access to Knowledge 2.0.1. Charter for Innovation, Creativity and Access to Knowledge 'Introduction'. http://fcforum.net/charter_extended

---

[8] | The 'Telecoms Reform Package' was presented by Commissioner Viviane Reding to the European Parliament in Strasbourg on November 13, 2007. Its aim is to change the EU Telecoms Rules of 2002. Its goal is to unify Europe's telecommunications market for all 27 EU member states. For more information see: http://europa.eu/rapid/pressReleasesAction.do?reference=IP/07/1677&format=HTML&aged=0&language=EN&guiLanguage=en

DaBlade, 'Richard Stallman Interview'. P2Pnet News. February 6, 2006. http://www.p2pnet.net/story/7840
developerWorks. 'developerWorks Interviews: Tim Berners-Lee'. developerWorks 22 August 2006. http://www.ibm.com/developerworks/podcast/dwi/cminto82206txt.html
Graham, Paul. 'What Business Can Learn From Open Source'. PaulGraham.com. August 2005. http://www.paulgraham.com/opensource.html.
Graham, Paul. 'Web 2.0'. PaulGraham.com. November 2005. http://www.paulgraham.com/web20.html
Industrial Workers of the World. 'Preamble to the IWW Constitution'. Industrial Workers of the World: A Union for All Workers. http://www.iww.org/culture/official/preamble.shtml.
Keynes, John Maynard. 'Chapter 2: The Postulates of the Classical Economics'. The General Theory of Employment, Interest and Money. Marxists Internet Archive. http://www.marxists.org/reference/subject/economics/keynes/generaltheory/ch02.html Originally published, Cambridge: Macmillan Cambridge University Press, 1936.
Khayati, Mustapha. 'Captive Words: Preface to a Situationist Dictionary'. Translated by Ken Knabb, International Situationiste 10 (1966). Situationist International Online, http://www.cddc.vt.edu/sionline/index.html
Kretschmer, Martin. 'Music Artists' Earnings and Digitisation: A Review of Empirical Data from Britain and Germany'. Bournemouth University Eprints. http://eprints.bournemouth.ac.uk/3704/1/Birkbeck_06_04_final.pdf
Kretschmer, Martin. 'Empirical Evidence on Copyright Earnings'. September, 2006. DIME. http://www.dime-eu.org/files/active/0/Kretschmer.pdf.
Landauer, Gustav. Revolution and Other Writings: A Poltiical Reader. Edited and translated by Gabriel Kuhn. Oakland: PM Press, 2010.
Lessig, Lawrence. Presentation at Wizards of OS 4: Information Freedom Rules International Conference, Berlin, Germany September 14-16, 2006.
Macmillan, Fiona. New Directions in Copyright Law. Cheltenham, UK: Edward Elgar Publishing, 2007.
Mandel, Ernest. 'Historical Materialism and the Capitalist State'. Translated by Juriaan Bendian. Scribd.

com. http://www.scribd.com/doc/20878564/MandelErnestHistorical-Materialism-and-the-Capitalist-State. Originally published in German in Marxismus und Anthropologie, Bochum 1980. 53

Marx, Karl. 'Preface'. A Contribution to the Critique of Political Economy. Marxists Internet Archive. http://www.marxists.org/archive/marx/works/1859/critique-pol-economy/preface.htm. Originally written, 1859.

Marx, Karl and Frederick Engels. Manifesto of the Communist Party. http://www.marxists.org/archive/marx/works/1848/communist-manifesto/. Originally published in German, 1848.

Mill, John Stuart. Principles of Political Economy with some of their Application to Social Philosophy. Library of Economics and Liberty. http://www.econlib.org/library/Mill/mlP.html. Originally published, 1848.

Miller, Ernest. 'Woody Guthrie on Copyright'. Copyfight July 27, 2004. http://copyfight.corante.com/archives/2004/07/27/woody_guthrie_on_copyright.php.

O'Reilly, Tim 'What is Web 2.0: Design Patterns and Business Models for the Next Generation of Software' March 2007. Munich Personal RePEc Archive, MPRA Paper no. 4578 (posted 7 November 2007). http://mpra.ub.unimuenchen.de/4578/1/MPRA_paper_4578.pdf

Proudhon, P.J. 'What is Property? An Inquiry into the Principle of Right and of Government'. Project Gutenberg Ebook no. 360. http://www.gutenberg.org/ebooks/360. Originally published, 1890.

Ricardo, David. 'An Essay on Profits'. London: John Murray,1815. McMaster University, Faculty of Social Science website, http://socserv.mcmaster.ca/~econ/ugcm/3ll3/ricardo/profits.txt

Ricardo, David. On Principles of Political Economy and Taxation. Library of Economics and Liberty, http://www.econlib.org/library/Ricardo/ricPCover.html Originally published, London: John Murray, 1821.

Seuss, Dr. Seuss. If I Ran the Circus. Random House, 1956.

Smiers, Joost and Marieke van Schijndel. No Copyright and No Cultural Conglomerates Too: An Essay. Amsterdam: Institute of Network Cultures, 2009. http://networkcultures.org/wpmu/theoryondemand/titles/n004-imagine-there-are-is-no-copyright-and-no-cultural-conglomorates-too/

Stallman, Richard. 'Copyleft: Pragmatic Idealism'. GNU Operating System. http://www.gnu.org/philosophy/pragmatic.html
Thorstein, Veblen. 'Chapter 4: Conspicuous Consumption'. The Theory of the Leisure Class. Bremen, Germany: Europaeischer Hochschulverlag GmbH & Co KG, 2010. Originally published, 1899.
Tucker, Benjamin. 'State Socialism and Anarchism: How far they agree, and wherein they differ'. The Anarchist Library. http://flag.blackened.net/daver/anarchism/tucker/tucker2.html. Originally published in Benjamin Tucker, Individual Liberty (New York: Vanguard Press, 1926).
United Nations University-World Institute for Development Economics Research. 'Richest 2% Own Half the World's Wealth'.

The Doors of Misperception
Or how we found the web progressive by using conservative terms — A collection of notes

MELA MIKES

Last year in preparation for the NECS conference in Lund, I started this collection of notes on the terms active/passive in connection with performativity/mediality of 'self' conceptions of the so-called web 2.0. I am very happy that paraflows 2010 invited me to present them in Vienna as well. The discussions about web 2.0 have their focus on the activities of its users, as well as on the technical options/limitations of the various platforms in use. My thoughts and interpretations are influenced by the work of Ramon Reichert and Susanne Lummerding as we proposed a panel on this subject for the NECS. Let me give you some sort of philosophical twist onto that important discussion by asking about the active/passive dualism concerning user generated content and 'self' representation.

Why, you might ask, is this question of any value to this discussion? Well, when I started to read certain cyberfeminist theory in the late 1990s I had the feeling that questions of identities and methods to articulate their constitutions were rather sophisticated. In the recent discussions about web 2.0, and even so called 'queering' of platforms, the concepts of what is valued a progressive strategy began to be less progressive and more angsty. Where was the cyborg manifesto of the web 2.0? Where did the discussion of hybrid identities and practises go to? What happened to all those great ideas? Instead we're looking at profiles on Facebook and MySpace as if they'd tell us something completely new.

But let's take a look further beyond the obvious. The idea of 'activism' as the preferred term in philosophy goes back at least to the ancient Greek. Activism was connected to the concept of 'male' identity. Passivity of course was female, ironically connected to the ever-changing mode of matter. Whereas 'activity' would lead to a perfect paradise that would contain eternal spring and no death since nothing ever changes. Therefore we just have to look at Plato's writings about Socrates.

Not only Derrida would call that dualism a perfect example of a phallogocentrism that is making any difference between subjects invisible and establishes the white male logic again and again. Thankfully feminist theory had a look at these axioms and mad them an issue up to the 90s. This dualism has as a consequence that only 'activism' was valued and praised and that passivity got dismissed as something non-political and with almost no agency attached.

Contemporary political ideas about 'self' concepts like the one Jack Halberstam is sketching in his text on 'The anti-social turn in queer studies' are connecting the active/passive dualism to the modi of Aristotelian logic as well to the dreams of efficiency and sense of the capitalist world. Whereas Halberstam tries to find an expression of 'radical passivity' in performance art I'd like to connect this term of 'radical passivity' with Ranciere's 'the emancipated spectator' a concept from his talk at 5th International Summer Academy in Frankfurt in 2004.

"Why identify the fact of being seated motionless with inactivity, if not by the presupposition of a radical gap between activity and inactivity? Why identify looking with passivity if not by the presupposition that looking means looking at the image or the appearance , that it means being separated from the reality which always is behind the image?
Why identify hearing with being passive, if not by the presupposition that acting is the opposite of speaking , etc, etc.? All those oppositions looking/knowing, looking/acting, appearance/reality, activity/passivity are much more than logical oppositions. They are what I can call a partition of the sensible, a distribution of the places and of the capacities or the incapacities attached to those places. Put in otherterms, they are allegories of inequality. This is why you can change the values given to

each position without changing the meaning of the oppositions themselves."[1]

This problem faces Halberstam's description of radical passivity and its location in performance art; especially two works by Marina Abromovicz and Yoko Ono are leading to some methodological problems. Halberstam locates passivity within the performance of these two women and points out the active role of the spectators. This is putting the dualism into works again, as their passivity is only to be seen as reverse activity of the audience. There are various other points I don't share in his text 'the antisocial turn in queer theory', but it points out that there is relevance to that sort of spin on self concepts. In the late 1990s feminists like Trinh T. Minh-ha pointed out that there are of course passive modi of resistance and political agency. With the active/passive dualism many racist arguments find a common ground, it is like an invisible axiom that doesn't even need a discussion. As activism seems to be the natural preferred modus of action but is it really that easy? Maybe it is time to put deconstructive strategies of on adjectives as well and not only on subjects and objects. Of course it is not progressive either to stop here pointing at this well known dualism. Stating this divide is only a start to looking further at the next 'shift' in terminology; the one from performativity to mediality.

Throughout the past couple of years I've come across the term mediality rather often. And every time I did, like when reading Erika Fischer-Lichtes 'Aesthetics of performativity' or Reiner Matzker's 'Aesthetic of mediality', I found myself thinking that performativity is not able to capture what 'new media' content generates as identity strategies. But then I also found myself wondering if this shift is really to follow the way it is done like those writers suggested. Instead of pointing out that this 'magic', overflow or emotions are bound to the idea of an ontological rest, something that is connected to Deleuze's idea of the nonsense or the esoterical word, it gets naturalized and reinforced as affective mechanism. I know that the late Deleuze embraced a strange idea of affect but that is a different talk. The term mediality promised me at first to get into effect where performativity seemed to fail. Precisely at the interface of the performer who

---

[1] | J. Ranciere: The emancipated spectator. Ein Vortrag zur Zuschauerperspektive. In: Texte zur Kunst, Jg. 15, H. 58 (Juni 2005), p. 36-51.

perceives the own performance and the connection of this very moment with the 'outside', the spectators.

The term performativity - as I know it relays- on the combination of performing and perceiving the performance of 'self'. This was a rather radical break with the conservative identity concepts of the past where identity would be something buried inside oneself, something true and 'unchangeable'. Perfomativity also offered practises that were able to deal with the idea of a non-linear incoherent self... the so-called post-modern, fractal self.

Anti-essentialism should prevent us from being re-established as 'women' and all the seemingly natural things attached. There were new differences, new questions and more room for strategies on how to sketch out identities. Performativity though was bound to the stage, the street, the clubs and classrooms. It seemed to stop before our screens and not enter the cyberspace.

Mediality on the other hand or at least the ideas I got from reading Fischer-Lichte and Matzker have something 'magical' attached. It seems to be that this mediality is more connected to the idea of contingency and ontological ideas. Is that the backdoor for essentialism to enter the discussion about self-conceptions again? Why is it that this notion is attached? There are a lot more books to be read to find out how and where this term works and leads to what kind of consequences. For me, the borders between performativity and mediality are not clear.

In fact by trying to find out how 'mediality' is used in recent discourse I was a bit disappointed. Why?

When I was re-reading the Cyborg Manifesto by Donna Haraway recently I was really surprised how contemporary it reads. It doesn't seem to have aged in the 25 years that it has been around. It also points out rather clearly where the 'informatics of domination' would go and that within this 'net' terms like activity and passivity would stick to their gendered meanings. Additionally she offers an alternative when it comes to political strategies for the Cyborg self to build alliances against the über dominance web of power. What Haraway suggests for these alliances is that affinity is of more value for the cyborg than actual 'family' relations. She would also write against any 'essentialism' that is the source for identity or a paradigm of experience like radical feminists did. As a consequence technology is not defined by essentialism neither is identity. This is the flexible framework that enables political agency to act within the informatics of domination the 2.0 version of Foucault's net structure of power. Only if all 'things' within the net get hybrid essentialism can be avoided or at least made visible. With this notion the division into real and internet friends would reach another level too.

This emphasis in cyberfeminist theory by writers like Rosi Braidotti and Sandy Stone on terms like anti-essentialism and non-coherent identity, as well as on 'narratives' and re-writing of narratives, were the source for my idea of 'mediality' that seems to be only loosely connected to what media studies would describe as mediality. As it seems the ideas are interconnected though, surprisingly at the intersection of performativity and mediality.

Therefore I had to re-visit a minor text by Foucault about literature that is called 'Un fantastique de bibliotheque' in which he is not only analyzing a book by Flaubert but also talks about something that he calls 'the library effect'. This effect describes that the imaginary is not longer fed by the dark, the unknown but by the known, the citations and that this 'new' desire is constituted between book pages, comments, re-reads and gaps in texts.

For Foucault this new 'desire' is created by discovering a region of the imaginary that is more powerful than any other before the 19th century where he locates its formation. This new kind of virtuality knows phantasmagoria that are part of the vigil states of mind, possessing undivided attention, hard studying and a proper look out of new inspiration.

This idea of 'mediality' is not only bound to the paradigm of 'activity' it is also connected to something 'passive', the reception of things, reading and perceiving the world connecting it to something read or heard before. It is very much like Donna Haraway is stating in her work again and again that reading and writing are the most important techniques for the cyborg to compete with the informatics of domination.

When we look at the web 2.0 practises that have a variety like sharing, posting, chatting, self presentation then indeed we find a similar effect like the one Foucault described for the 19th century and the explosion of available books, libraries and archives. Isn't any activity on the net very much interconnected like citations of other activities on the net? As with citation I am not emphasising on the mere content itself but on its presentation like a sea of meme.

And is this citation, re-reading of web 2.0 content not what feeds the desire to do so or to change the ways it is done? What I want to say with this is that it might not always be the best way to discuss the seemingly 'active' outputs of the web 2.0 communities by ignoring the fact of the passive practises of the web 2.0. Again I am not talking about dualism. How to describe this two terms in a less dualistic approach? An offer to think about ways to deal with this is offered by Gilles Deleuze in his early work like 'logic of the sense'. Another offer is made by Foucault in the text 'the fantasia of the library'. Both are working with the feedback levels, loops of 'characters' and words that are connecting different times and spaces. The connection is not only done by sharing space. The connection is done either via translation or memory.

The meaning or value of a word, picture, and character is not produced via linear logic; it is produced by a sophisticated pattern that is stretching from page to page, sentence to sentence. Within esoterical words and nonsense meaning is created like chimeras.

This paradox logic offers a completely new basis for reasoning. There is no depth, no behind only surface and tension. It sounds very easy, even trivial but on a second and third look or by trying to apply this system to arguments it quickly shows how radical this approach is.

For Foucault, who uses a similar way to analyze Flaubert's 'Temptation of Saint Antony' the temptation gets represented in this very movement of interconnecting different spaces and positions. He comes to the conclusion at various points that there is not one truth attached to the temptation but that there are various ones and they are in use simultaneously.

Where does this all lead in my chain of thoughts?

When we agree on the necessity of discussing not only the visible content of the web 2.0 but also try to find a way to describe the creation of the content in a less dualistic way then it might be possible to get a glimpse of what is new about the web 2.0 rather than locating it in the 'pure' technological details or in adjectives like 'activity'. This would open up spaces in-between the practises that are invisible up to now and allow theorizing identity concepts alongside different terminologies.

When performativity makes us aware that even the seemingly most natural habits are cultural practises then mediality has at this point in time not really reached that power. We should carefully look at the very basics of our methods and systems to make sure that the 'logical' consequences are really the ones we want to reinforce. It will be useful to take a deeper look at the intersection of mediality and performativity when discussing self concepts of the net. It will take time to find the difference that is in-between active and passive as well as describing hybrid adjectives for their agency. There is something 'new' going on in the web. But I am not sure if we have started to look at it from the angle that will give us the questions that will make it visible. Maybe that is why mediality has still this metaphysical glitter attached, maybe that is why performativity still works quite good when it comes to describing self concepts and political agency on the web2.0.

Yet I think that the fact that more and more essentialist, metaphysical or even worse ontological dreams are connected to what we call web2.0 points to something that is hard to get, even harder to describe.

Eventually the web2.0 is more about reading than writing, less about profiles than about instant messengers. Maybe the web2.0 is about private conversations and passive content creation. Maybe. Let's find out.

Writer's note:
After months of adding thoughts and deleting them again I've given in to the fact that my thoughts need more time. That is the reason why you only get the raw and short lecture I've given at Paraflows. There will be more at some point I promise.

REFERENCES

Fischer-Lichte, Erika (2004) *Ästhetik des Performativen*. Frankfurt a. M: edition suhrkamp

Foucault, Michel (1993) *Schriften zur Literatur*. Frankfurt a. M: Fischer Wissenschaft

Halberstam, Jack/Judith (2008) *The Anti-Social Turn in Queer Studies*. Tel Aviv: Graduate Journal of Social Science - 2008 - Vol. 5 Issue 2

Haraway, Donna (1995) *Die Neuerfindung der Natur. Primaten, Cyborgs und Frauen*. Frankfurt aM: Campus Verlag

Matzker , Reiner (2008) *Ästhetik der Medialität. Zur Vermittlung von künstlerischen Welten und ästhetischen Theorien*. Reinbek bei Hamburg: Rowohlt Verlag

Network Sculpture

JANE TINGLEY

In trying to relate my work to the idea of network sculpture I first referred to the Wikipedia definition of the word network.

Network and networking in their original and most literal sense are the weaving of thread (yarn) into textile nets and the weaving of ropes, wires, or cables into similar nets. Since the rise of electrical and electronic technologies, network and networking also refer literally to local-circuit net-like connections of electrical conductors (wires and cables) and more broadly to wider-reaching circuits and wireless (radio) connections.[1]

When I read this definition it instantly dawned on me how my work is connected to the network – not as content, but as metaphor for how the body connects to its world, and as a visual strategy for unifying multiple objects in space. The use of the visual network first showed up in my work as I transitioned from having an object-based practise to working with installation, responsiveness, sound, and robotics. Installation allowed me to explore the constant and subtle changes that occur within the body as well as within the spaces we have created for the body, as we move throughout the world. I started working with sensors and actuators in the pursuit of highlighting the active space between the body and the installation environment. In working with larger scale electronic installations, the cables and how to handle them becomes an issue. Only once I completed my first piece of this sort, and had all of the cables and wires splayed along the floor, did I see the visual connection between the networks housed within

---

1 | Wikipedia [on line Sept 10th, 2010]

the human body and those comprising the technological body. If you take away the hard shell of technology, what remains is fragile and exposed system, no more impenetrable than yours or mine. There are striking similarities between systems found inside our walls, be they flesh, drywall, or plastic. The network exists within the body, extends itself throughout the skin, spills beyond the flesh and into the room, exists within our walls, moves through cables as electricity to form the World Wide Web, and travels through time as information and memory. My work attempts to visually draw parallels between natural networks and those that are constructed, as well as to offer new metaphors in order to see the mechanical within the body and the sensitivity of the technological.

An equally important concern alongside space and experience is my interest in the object. I spend a lot of time exploring materiality and thinking about objecthood. I draw on a wide range of media, less concerned with the technological aspects of the medium than its semiotic implications. The formation of ideas through materiality and material investigation is a central component of my practice. I am interested in the cultural meaning of material and process, and try to align material with concept; as a result, I approach the construction of an installation via a number of material explorations. Often the primary idea fractures to result in side projects that I work on in tandem with the original, which not only allows me to explore ideas and develop the technology, but also enables the projects to cross-pollinate. This approach has become very important to how I work and develop ideas.

STEP 1: RETHINKING THE BODY

My movement from building sculpture, where object is sight of contemplation, to installation, where the body of the viewer actively explores a space, was marked by *Body;trichobothria* and *Peripheral Response* built in 2005-6. These sculptures were created during my MFA, and were shaped by the philosophical climate of Concordia University (Montréal) at that time. At Concordia I was introduced to new ways of thinking about the body in the writing of philosophers like Deleuze and Guattari, and Henri Bergson. It was during this time that I started to think of the body as something extending into space, and something that qualitatively changes as it comes into contact with other bodies, spaces and situations. I stopped thinking about the skin as a barrier and conversely stopped thinking about sculpture as a discrete object, but rather as an object that also qualitatively changes as it interacts with the viewer. As a starting point, I naturally began with where the body and the world meet – the flesh. Both *Body;trichobothria* and *Peripheral Response* are visual explorations of re-thinking the body and how it relates to the environment.

While learning the technology for the installation *Peripheral Response*, I took a small break and did a sculptural investigation, which resulted in a large-scale room sized weave, the work I exhibited at the Künsterhause for the Paraflows exhibition *Mind and Matters*. The *Body;trichobothria* is woven in a non-linear form of Italian weaving or lace making called bobbin weave, and refers to the flesh as a sensory organ allowing us to sense our environment. I used a medical photograph of the brain's neural network as a pattern for the weave.

> Much like a subt'll spider, which doth sit
> In middle of her web, which spreadeth wide;
> If ought doe touch the vtmost thred of it
> Shee feeles it instantly on euery side (1:70)
> John Davies "Nosce Teipsum"

Not unlike trichobothria, which are the hairs on a spider's leg allowing it to sense its web, the system of web-like nerves in the body extend into our environment through touch. The body weave is given shape by a hundred little threads connected to the walls of the room, and takes on a physical quality that attempts to unify the sensorial body with the incorporeal body. Through the use of the weave and its visual connectivity to the surrounding architectural space, I consider a body, which is at once becoming and diminishing.

Body;trichobothria – Around the Frayed Edges, Agnes Jamieson Gallery, Minden, Canada, 2010

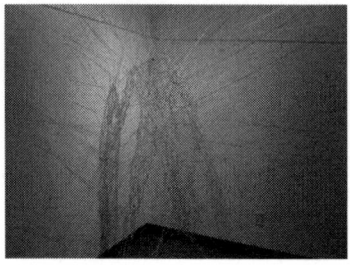 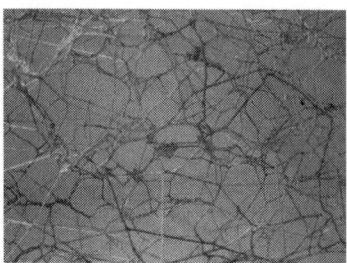

After completing *Body;trichobothria*, it became clear what I was trying to achieve with *Peripheral Response* and I returned to the installation. I knew that I wanted to use the body's peripheral nervous system as a launching point for an exploration of how the body relates to its environment. I built the elements in the installation in steel after medical textbook illustrations of the body's sensory receptors (Pascinian corpuscle, a Ruffini corpuscle, nerve endings etc...), which combined create our somatic sensory system, or our sense of touch. Each of the nine objects has a solenoid, which mechanically pushes down an arm with a tap from a tap shoe fastened to it, to articulate robotically mimicking Morse code. In addition, the objects have multiple sensing devices, such as sonar and infrared, used to track not only the viewers' location but also the distance of the viewer from each object. The objects respond to the viewers' location and articulate at different rates, according to rules established in the Pure Data patch. As one moves through the space, the ripple effect caused by their presence calms and the installation settles.

Peripheral Response, BRT exhibition curated by Group Molior, Montréal, Canada, 2008

STEP 2: NEW EXPRESSIONS OF HYBRIDITY

From this project I returned to a theme that has reoccurred in my work since the beginning of my practise, which is the interaction between the body and technology. As with rethinking the body, I started to rethink the relationship between body and technology. I was less interested in thinking about these two forces as oppositional, and became interested in new expressions of hybridity. Unlike genetically engineered hybrids, I was more interested in accidental and durational hybrids. Entities naturally change each other as they interact, and I am interested by the collaborative potential of culture/technology and nature/the body if given a chance to co-exist within a state of balance. I am as interested in how technology relates to the body as I am with how it extends and modifies it, and how it can provide new experiences for it. My work relating to this theme attempts to find new metaphoric relationships between body and technology.

The genesis of the *Plant(iPod) Installation*, and the *Branch Replacement Project* grew out of an interest in rethinking technology in relation to nature. The goal of *Plant(iPod) Installation* was to explore the poetics involved in creating new relationships between human and plant life, and to subvert the traditional hierarchy, which positions plant life below human life. While developing the technology for the installation I did a sculptural investigation to determine what material I could use that somehow expressed my interest in restoring unity to nature. After some time I settled on cork, as it embodied both the physical and conceptual properties I was looking for. It is flexible, rugged, and water resistant, and being a renewable resource, it is also the perfect example of human/nature coexistence[2]. This material investigation resulted in a prosthetic branch for a telephone/hydro pole, which I then installed out of curiosity onto a tree in St. Faustin, Québec. As soon as I placed the branch onto the tree, it became clear to me that building a branch for a hydro pole had very little meaning,

---

2 | Contrary to popular belief that the world's supply of cork has been depleted, there is in fact plenty of cork in the world to go around. If the wine stopping industry stops using cork and switches to alternative methods of stopping wine, it is likely that the cork forests will deemed 'useless', and will be replaced by a more forestable product. Cork forests are home to a number of indigenous species including a number of endangered species such as the Iberian Lynx, Iberian Imperial Eagle etc...

especially since hydro poles in Canada are made from Boston Furs, which naturally lose their branches as they grow taller. In order for this project to have any meaning, these branches needed to be custom built for specific trees – trees that were damaged. I decided to return to this project at a later date.

Branch Prosthetic Prototype at exhibition in Montréal, Canada, 2008

With my selected material I returned to the *Plant(iPod)Installation*. I built eight plant/prosthetic objects of various shapes and sizes that house embedded houseplants. In building the objects, I visually referenced tree-like forms that resemble coppiced or pollarded trees, which are types of pruning that encourage new growth. Each of the sculptural objects also include a built in subwoofer with metal branches rising from it to hold two small speakers close to the leafy part of the plant, and function as a sound system. Each object also contains sensors so that the sound being played to the plants is directly affected by the viewer's location and proximity. The sculptures are spread out in a grid like fashion throughout the gallery, and spaced about one and a half meters apart, which is the distance trees are planted from each other when being reforested by planters.

The sound component of the work is also sculptural in nature, and has two modes - one for when there is a viewer and another for when there isn't. In "rest" mode, the speakers play the sounds of many different types of breathing, as though the space is filled with many people. As the viewer moves throughout the space, coming into range of the individual plants, the sounds transform into quiet whispering, evoking the theory that plants respond to people speaking to them, growing stronger and healthier. For the breathing sound, I have general noise files and convolved[3] them with sound files of breathing to create a sound that is clearly breath, but with a feel that isn't quite natural – a sound that alludes to the breath of both the plants and the technological components. The "active" mode consists of recorded stories, and cultural tales that come from a web site of folktales and stories about trees. Individually the sounds played to the plants are not loud, but together fill the gallery space with collective breathing. As the viewer moves through the space, the sounds of the plants that s/he is closest to drifts in and out of stories told in multiple languages. I was interested in the possibility of developing technologies that are nature-centric rather than human-centric – technologies that could breathe life back into the idea of the enchanted forest. The installation invites the viewer to walk through an environment where the location of the body as it moves through the installation space triggers new auditory experiences for both plant and viewer.

Plant(iPod)Installation at la Nuit Blanche in the Artscape Wychwood Barns, Toronto, Canada, 2009

I then returned to the *Branch Replacement Project* with the intention of building prosthetics for specific trees that had lost branches due to storms or had been pruned back to prevent disease.

...the word stump, a word that refers to both the body that is maimed and the prosthetic that replaces it. The stump of a limb is replaced by a wooden leg, also referred to as a stump. The cut-down root of a tree is a stump, and by analogy the limb that is removed from the body is also a

---

3 | Convolution is a term describing a way of using one sound to modify another – the characteristics of one sound are superimposed over another, and create a new sound suggestive of both.

stump. [...] the human gains a stump from the stump created in the tree. (Lennard , 92)

During my residency at the *Vermont Studio Center* in Johnson, Vermont, USA, I built a branch for a selected tree in Montréal, which has been installed since March 2009. Prior to building and installing it, an arborist and a zip line installation and operational expert were consulted in order to prevent any damage to the tree. I use the same anchoring system employed in zip line courses. My method uses a compression technique to anchor the cables around the trunk of the tree, which effectively holds the line firmly in place - allowing the sap to flow freely through the cambium of the tree. This method also allows for airflow, preventing the development of bugs, and does not inhibit the natural growth of the tree in any way. In fact, if the prosthetic were to remain on the tree, the tree would eventually absorb the metal piece, and the branch would appear to be coming from the tree.

Branch 2 at Vermont Studio Center and Installed in Montréal, Canada, 2009 Branch 3 at CAMAC, Marnay-Sur-Seine, France, 2010

The third investigation of this project is installed permanently in France at CAMAC, which is a residency located in Marnay-Sur-Seine, France. This branch brings together ideas of the *Plant(iPod)Installation* and the Branch Prosthetics. This branch contains speakers and sensors powered by a solar panel/battery combination. The sound files were processed in Pure Data, and populated with a collection of recordings made in the city during the residency. Aside from the natural sounds, I collected meaningful phrases and stories from residents of Marnay and other resident artists. With these sound files I created sonic portraits that explored the individual in direct relationship to CAMAC and Marnay-Sur-Seine itself. As I did the majority of recording on site, when the sound files are triggered by the presence of the viewer, the actual ambient sounds of the yard mix with the sounds played back though the branch. The mono recordings mix with the actual sounds of the environment, creating a "multichanneled" sound experience - it becomes difficult to distinguish the real from the recorded/created.

STEP 3: SOUND, MEMORY, AND SPACE – FUTURE AND CURRENT WORKS

Sound art has an amazing ability to affect the body of the viewer, create worlds, and draw attention to the passage of time. Artists working with sound are creating works for an embodied body which experiences the world through all of its senses. My movement from sculpture to installation was a conscious decision to create an artistic experience that moved beyond vision. I feel that works that speak to a complete body have the potential to create more meaningful experiences for the viewer. I wanted to use sound in a way that could utilize its potential, and decided to approach sound artist Michal Seta to collaborate on a new project. I proposed the project *Foresta Inclusive* to him, which will be a more complex version of the system built at CAMAC in France. The installation will consist of around ten prosthetic branches, built for specific trees located within close proximity to each other in an outdoor location. Each branch will contain a microphone, sensors, and speakers. I have not secured a location for this installation but am interested in exhibiting the work in places such as the Jardin de la Métis (Québec), and/or The Tree Museum (Ontario). If I cannot find a public outdoor location, I will build the work for a remote location, and then will cast parts of the original trees in Forton in order to create an indoor replica of the forest space to relocate them into the gallery. The system will be powered by a solar panel/battery combination when outdoors and wall powered when exhibited indoors. For this project I am interested in the visual integration of the technological network onto a natural one, and ways that I can give voice to not only the forest, but to life that moves through it.

The sound component of *Foresta Inclusive* will consist of an accumulation of recorded samples of the ambient sound gathered in both in the forest and in the installation space. The samples will, inevitably, include fragments of visitors' conversations - comments, reactions and the like - but will also include the general ambient soundscape of the area surrounding the sculpture. The samples will be chosen at random and arranged into an evolving sound composition influenced by the location of the viewer and sonic content: for example, through the analysis of prominent features such as rhythm, pitched/unpitched material, and spectral content. The resulting soundscape will form an abstract and poetic rendition of recontextualized sonic memory of the space, which will develop in subtle ways while retaining the general sonic signature of the surroundings. The overall form, on both micro and macro levels, will be based on a set of rules permitting a formal and structural consistency. The harvesting of audio samples will be governed by the fluctuations in the overall ambient sound presence and volume as well as via triggers designed around the proximity sensors.

The conceptual starting point for this project can be found in Robert Pogue Harrison's book, *Forests: The Shadow of Civilization*, where the author looks at the cultural history of the forest and its relation to civilization. He explores the constant push and pull between the borders of civilization and the forest (from the return of the forest after the ice age, to present day dominance of civilization). The book explores the historic, linguistic, and legal understanding of the forest: its exteriority to civilization, but also civilization's dependency on its existence. This project will address these relationships, and in some way will try to merge the exteriority of the forest with interiority of personal memory and experience of a space. It will record natural sounds as well as the sounds of people within the installation. The playback will amplify the ambient sounds of the forest, but will also refer to past and present participants. The audio, as well as the visual attachment of the prosthetic system onto the natural host system, will provoke a heightened awareness not only of the environment, but also of our personal participation within it.

As with my past works, I have also started a side project; however, this one is a technological sketch done in order to figure out how I wanted to design the system for *Foresta Inclusive*. In Sept/Oct 2010 I was invited to be the Paraflows Artist-in-Residence at the Quartier 21 studio at the MuseumsQuartier. For this residency I wanted to prototype the technological system for *Foresta Inclusive* but also wanted to start an unrelated visual investigation, which we are calling *Soif-Clouds* (working title). I invited Michal Seta to come to Vienna and participate in the final two weeks of this residency in order to work on the sound. I spent the first month and a half working on the sculptural aspect of the project and creating the technical system.

At Paraflows residency at the quartier21, MuseumsQuartier in Vienna, Austria, Sept-Oct 2010

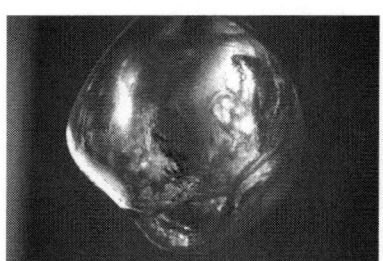

The objects for this project are made from clear casting resin, and are based on a hand- made original that contains a cast of the inside of a mouth. Inside these mouth objects are speakers and microphones. For the residency I built 20 of these objects, half containing microphones and half containing speakers. At first we thought we would handle the sound in a similar way to *Foresta Inclusive*, but have found that due to the natural shape of the mouths, the sound recording and playback have a very specific tonal quality. While the range of sound is limited, we have decided to work with it and to try to expand the complexity of sounds by changing the size of the mouth cavity (casting different sized mouths) as well as changing the shape of the cavity by making mouth moulds of a mouth forming the vowel sounds (a, e, i, o, u). We believe this will give us a wider tonal range with which to work.

The final installation will be comprised of a network of 100 mouths hanging/lying in clusters throughout the exhibition space. Only some of these mouth objects will contain speakers and microphones, and most of them will be hanging from the ceiling, mouth open and facing downward. The hanging objects will be at head height, and will randomly record individuals within the exhibition space. The viewer will be free to move around the installation space, touch, hold and speak into the sculptural objects, in order to trigger sound events that include the viewer's voice, mixed with the voices of past viewers in past exhibition spaces. The goal of this project is to use sound in a way that refers to memory of a space, as well as to create a sound experience that evolves and moves throughout the gallery, essentially creating a network of connections through space and time.

Network sculpture is a suitable title for how I approach art making, as it emphasizes my interest in object making, but the word network challenges the closed nature of sculpture. Above all else, I am interested in the interconnection of things and the poetry housed in the individual points of connection. I create installations and juxtapose objects and sounds in order to create an atmosphere conducive to the making of meaning. The goal of my artistic explorations is not to generate factual understanding, nor to locate truth, but to seek out the poetry housed between scientific knowledge and lived experience. I am interested in possible truths, or individual truths; I welcome misinterpretation and ambiguous explanation.

BIBLIOGRAPHY

Coward, Rosalind. (2007) "Writing the Environment in Journalism." In: R Kerridge and H Tarlo. (Eds) (2007). *Crowded Space: British perspectives on environmentalism, literature and culture.* University of Virginia. [Accessed on-line – Dec 10 2007] http://roehampton.openrepository.com/roehampton/handle/10142/14322

Davis, Lennard J. (2006) "Stumped By Genes." In: Smith M. and Morra J. (Eds) (2006). *The Prosthetic Impulse; From a Posthuman*

Present to a Biocultural Future. MIT Press: Cambridge, Massachusetts. 92.

Parker, E. (2006) *Cork screwed? Environmental and economic impacts of the cork stoppers market.* WWF Mediterranean Programme Office. [Accessed on-line – Dec 10 2007] http://assets.panda.org/downloads/cork_rev12_print.pdf

Harrison, Robert Pogue. (1992) *Forests; The Shadows of Civilization.* University of Chicago Press: Chicago.

Love on a Wire: Communications Technology Across 10,000 Miles

ADAM W. FLYNN, SARAH OUTHWAITE

INTRODUCTION

In the autumn of 2008, the authors became acutely aware of the problems of love across time and space as they embarked on a relationship that tested the limits of intimacy across distance. A nascent love came to span the earth as one member left for a year-long fellowship in Cambodia, while the other remained in the U.S. to finish her college education. A generation ago, this would have been laughable.

The modern long-distance relationship springs from technology, joining minds when matter cannot. Paradoxes of space grow more extreme as we strive for greater intimacy. Failures, both from technology or technique, can shatter illusions of physical proximity and create self-reinforcing feedback loops of communicative stress.

We seek to share insights gained from maintaining an LDR over one year, ten thousand miles of distance, and a twelve-hour time-shift. We will discuss particular attributes of different communication media, and how communication objects come (and fail) to embody our lovers.

BACKGROUND AND METHODOLOGY

As we are not trained sociologists and have no funding, we must admit to operating without quantitative support. It must be noted, however, that numbers matter less in our case, since we are not looking to make objective pronouncements based on our experiences.

Given that our topic requires an equal mix of systematic reflection and poetic inspiration, an insistence on the subjective and phenomenal seems necessary. Our methods are inspired by participant observation, a form of ethnographic fieldwork that seeks to form a deep empathetic understanding of a particular group (be they Bushmen of the Kalahari Desert or workers at IBM) over an extended period. As media-conscious lovers connecting entirely by mediated means, our set of experiences, archived communications, and post-facto reflections form a body of qualitative inquiry best described as *observant participation,* beginning with second-order communication: discussing and reflecting on the frequency, volume, and methods of our correspondence in order to optimize it. It was from this thoughtful exploration of our communicative patterns that the present paper emerged.

WHY DISTANCE RELATIONSHIPS?

Lovers in distance relationships are worth examining because of their status as *Fringe Users,* users who place unusual or extreme demands on their technology. By examining the activities and needs of fringe users, designers and researchers may uncover forthcoming trends or deep insights about the entire range of users. The process recalls *argumentum a fortiori*: solve the most challenging forms of the problem, and the center will take care of itself.

For a maker of kitchenware, for example, it might be more fruitful to deeply examine the needs of arthritic housewives instead of drowning in inconclusive data about a mythical "median user." A case in point is OXO, for whom "universal design" has become a cornerstone of brand identity. (See http://www.oxo.com/OurRoots.aspx for their brand-approved origin tale.) At times, designing for 'disability' has driven the invention of wholly new media: important predecessors of the typewriter were sold as writing machines for the blind, and Alexander Graham Bell worked in speech therapy and deaf education before his experiments with telephony.

This is not to exaggerate or over-romanticize the problems of distance relationships to the point of actual physical disability. Yet the LDR is a form of sensory deprivation: distanced lovers suffer from a lack of touch both of physical proximity (actual touch), and of the intimacy and commonalities that shared life brings (being "in touch").

They need technology that erases the physical distance between bodies, and make time a non-factor in long distance communication. Even more than family members or businessmen needing face time to close deals, lovers are acutely aware of the advantages and dangers that different forms of virtual presence bring.

But what were *our* contemporary circumstances of love on a wire, coming from Cambodia? Internet connections were present, but often weak and limited to standard business hours. Phone calls were possible from long distance call shops or with phone cards if one could master the complexities of international calling codes. Most importantly, there was a full twelve-hour time-shift to negotiate: to paraphrase one of Marshall McLuhan's favorite lines from *Finnegan's Wake*, "the west shall shake the east awake...while ye shall have night for day;" we were as disjunct in circadian rhythms as two could be while remaining on the same planet. Forced into extreme circumstances, we sought to find the rules by which we were playing. The following are some of our findings.

Historical/Literary Context

Given the importance of historical and literary models for lovers as well as the general utility of searching for past antecedents when studying media, it is necessary to trace the techno-social history of distance relationships. There are three main communicative regimes worth looking at. First, the purely literary, when letters were the sole means of communication; second, the era of high modern media during the late 19th and 20th centuries; and finally, our current era of digital networks.

Relationships were once constituted only by face-to-face contact or by letters. Literary lovers of note include Abelard and Heloise, Napoleon and Josephine, and John Adams (founding father, 2nd president of the U.S.) and his wife Abigail. Letters had all the advantages of any asynchronous medium, chief among them the ability to thoughtfully reply at one's leisure. Without the quasi-timeless aspect of written correspondence to make it possible, our culture would lack the rhetorical sophistication and heightened register of literary romance-- not to mention a great deal of over-wrought poetry.

In looking at the effect of distance on a relationship, we also should take care to note its relative progression when contact is restricted to mediated forms. Then as now, distance was easier to bear early on in a romance, when much is to be learned about a potential partner and hunger is inflamed by scarcity of contact. One may go so far as to argue that, given the artificially-imposed restrictions on face-to-face contact and consequent emphasis on media, the communicative dynamics of courtship should be viewed as an important predecessor to those of the modern distance relationship. Since face-to-face interactions were strictly controlled by adults and chaperones (for obvious reasons), it was not unusual for young lovers to get to know each other by letter. John and Abigail Adams were no exception: they exchanged 16 letters during the months of April and May of 1762 while courting, when he was quarantined after inoculation for smallpox. Separation among married couples, though, was an entirely different and more serious matter. It was once a rare thing to travel far from home, and was usually done for critical reasons: emigration for work or mobilization for war.

Mortality being a non-trivial concern, it was important to send back word the writer hadn't died yet. Letters did that; irrespective of their actual 'content,' they reassured your partner that you had been alive at least at the time of its writing. Even if the traveler was illiterate, sufficiently large cities and organizations had scribes and letter-writers one could dictate to, and communities usually had at least one literate acquaintance to read received letters.

In times when handwriting was considered an indelible sign of one's distinct personality, a handwritten letter was prized as the unique product of the correspondent's mind, body, and soul. Sufficiently focused readers in those days before film could induce phantasmagoria of imaginary sounds and images to accompany text. (Caveat: this is obviously a brief and simplified sketch of media discourse networks as they existed in early modernity through roughly the mid-nineteenth century. For more information, see McLuhan's *Gutenberg Galaxy* or Kittler's *Discourse Networks 1800*, depending on nationality and philosophical tendencies.) Letter-writers could aid visualization and extend the illusion of physical proximity by including physical artifacts such as locks of hair, perfume, or lipstick traces. It is no coincidence, then, that longing was one of the major tropes of Romanticism.

Still, text had limitations. As a storage medium, it was (and is) fairly lossy. It's also not dynamic; it's a frozen moment of the writer's

mind at a certain time. You can't clarify something immediately or engage in a dialogue,
> ...except by writing another letter
>> ...and waiting for a response...
>>> ...which takes time.

There were also the manifold difficulties brought by unreliable transport over unpredictable infrastructure. Sometimes letters would arrive out of order, or never arrive at all. If you wanted to remember what *you* said, duplicate copies (also handwritten) were necessary. Additionally, there is always the potential of missives being read by a third party, which was the origin of cryptography: secret confidences either military or romantic. John Adams once wrote his wife Abigail, he then in the midst of a troubled revolution, she then in the midst of a troubled pregnancy, to inquire about her health:

My dear: I am anxious to hear how you do. I have in my mind a source of anxiety, which I have never had before. You know what it is...Can't you convey to me, in hieroglyphics, which no other person can comprehend, information which will relieve me. Tell me you are as well as can be expected. (Feb 10, 1777)

In later wars, the third party was an expected part of civil-military communications: militaries used their formidable logistical networks to carry messages for lovers, but in the process left black marks where censors stopped the transmission of what they believed to be "sensitive information."

In those days before packet-switching, among settled couples one person usually remained "Home" while the other was "Away." The person at home (archetypally female) wrote of local news, while the sojourner described the novel places he'd been to and the things he was doing. In terms of other content, there may also be reminiscences of the past, plans for the future, and of course, professions of love:

I dare not express to you at 300 miles how ardently I long for your return... The idea plays about my heart, unnerves my hand whilst I write and awakens all the tender sentiments that years have increased and matured. (Abigail to John, Oct 16th, 1774)

Because the couple already possess substantial common knowledge about home, the novelty of the traveler's circumstances lead him to write more; During the sessions of the Continental Congress, for instance, John wrote about three letters to Abigail's one.

This was the nature of distance for most of the literate era. It was inconvenient and difficult, but circumstances were pressing, marriages were for life, and affairs were easily kept secret. What changed this?

Wires.

The invention of the telegraph divorced the speed of communication from the speed of transport or even visual contact for the first time in history, a development that *cannot* be understated. It made and unmade empires, even as men (and women) struggled to understand its implications. The invention of the telephone gave this revolution a human voice (fittingly enough, inaugurated by Alexander Graham Bell asking his assistant Watson to come see him in person). Physical traces were unavailable, but lovers gained a theretofore unprecedented illusion of physical proximity.

The American author Mark Twain was one of the first to recognize the storytelling potential inherent in this new techno-social situation. Twain was a committed early adopter, embracing both the telephone and typewriter before nearly any other thinker, though he abandoned the typewriter "for the reason that I never could write a letter with it to anybody without receiving a letter by return mail" inundating him with questions about the device, over and above the actual business discussed in the typed letter (quoted in Kittler, *Gramophone, Film, Typewriter*, pg 192).

Twain was a keen observer of telephonic interactions, and published the fruits of his observations in the *Atlantic Monthly*, among them a short sketch in June 1880 on the absurdity of a one-sided "Telephonic Conversation:"

You hear questions asked; you don't hear the answer. You hear invitations given; you hear no thanks in return. You have listening pauses of dead silence, followed by apparently irrelevant and unjustifiable exclamations of glad surprise or sorrow or dismay... "Visitors? (Pause.) No, we never use butter on them."

In 1878 Twain addressed the possibility of romance by telephone with the satirical design fiction "The Loves of Alonzo Fitz Clarence and

Rosannah Ethelton." In the story, low-cost long-distance ubiquitous telephony allows two lovers to meet, court, and eventually marry, entirely over the wire. They do not see each other in person until days after their wedding. Setting Alonzo in snowy, wintry Maine and Rosannah in warm, rainy San Francisco, Twain played with the of the then-novel idea that two people could talk about the weather or the time of day, with the weather and time of each party radically different. During their tearful reunion the couple encounters one of the complexities of synchronous communication in the days before standardized time zones when they vow to record the happy hour:

"We will make record of it, my Rosannah; every year, as this dear hour chimes from the clock, we will celebrate it with thanksgivings, all the years of our life."

"We will, we will, Alonzo!"

"Four minutes after six, in the evening, my Rosannah, shall henceforth--"

"Twenty-three minutes after twelve, afternoon shall--"

"Why; Rosannah, darling, where are you?"

"In Honolulu, Sandwich Islands. And where are you? Stay by me; do not leave me for a moment. I cannot bear it. Are you at home?"

"No, dear, I am in New York--a patient in the doctor's hands."

An agonizing shriek came buzzing to Alonzo's ear, like the sharp buzzing of a hurt gnat; it lost power in traveling five thousand miles.

Twain was one of the first to note the surprising discontinuity of space and time that arises with simultaneous communication at long range, a discontinuity that persists today and from which speculative fiction continues to draw narrative potential: Cory Doctorow's *Eastern Standard Tribe* spins a world where allegiance to time-zones trumps nationalism. For two people to communicate on a synchronous medium, they must synchronize *themselves* for at least a short while. As the time-shift gets more extreme, the windows of mutually convenient call times shrink. Compared to asynchronous forms of communication like letters, telephony is emotionally intensive but logistically intensive.

For further examples of the relative complexity and preciousness of telephonic conversations over letters, one needs only to examine the restrictions on communication during military basic training: letters are unlimited, but phones are strictly controlled, both in time and circumstances of the call. It's unclear whether this is because phone calls are more authentic or more precious, or perhaps just because "mail call" is easier to schedule when dealing with mass quantities of correspondents. Long after the absurdities of the telephone were normalized, the scandal of illusory intimacy still held great storytelling potential. A caller could extend the home's intimate space through the wire, invite a telepresence in, or even chat with a handsome man while in the bathtub, a scenario played to good effect in the 1950s romantic comedy *Pillow Talk*. In fact, the ability of wires to bridge lovers across time and space seemed so impressive, authors and paranormal investigators hoped to extend its power beyond the grave. In the introduction to *Gramophone, Film, Typewriter*, Kittler describes the real-life search for ghostly voices in recordings of short-wave radio, as well as a story ("Resurrection Co." by Walter Rathenau) where a phone company is formed to bring phone service to the graveyards of a town plagued by premature burials. (12) The *Twilight Zone* followed suit years later with "Night Call," the tale of a lonely spinster haunted by nightly calls from her late suitor, on whose grave a telephone wire has fallen. Asynchronous media, of course, are inherently posthumous: pictures and letters let us hold on to departed loves, whether or not they are able or willing to return; as Patsy Cline put it, "I've got your picture, she's got you."

The 20th century brought numerous forms of recording and transmitting experience beyond the old means of text. Ubiquitous photography emerged as an upgrade to the letter system, since they were also subject to transport and free from time-synchronization. Photos were and are formidable anchors for visualization and longing, particularly for the mythical G.I. in his foxhole. Cassette tapes became objects of love, not only because the obvious capability of sending a recording of one's voice, but also because of the ability to send a curated collection of songs, and thus make them "belong" to the relationship. Lovers could dramatize their circumstances and connect themselves to the grand tradition of heroic and/or sentimental love songs, the popularity of which rose meteorically during the Second World War for obvious reasons.

As readers of this volume should be aware, the current digital regime dissolves and encompasses media, turning them from physical things into just different formats of ones and zeroes. In other words, all these things have migrated, one way or another, to the internet. Telegrams beget texting. Letters beget email, but have to give up their physical traces. (People save old love letters and tie bundles of them with ribbons; they don't print out old love emails.) The phone begets Skype, with the added science-fiction aspect of video calling, something that people have been promising for years. Photos beget digital photos, and mixtapes become playlists. (Chat is a weird hybrid beast, straddling categories depending on the circumstances of its use.) We now have a wide range of tools, both synchronous and asynchronous, which is useful because we do not necessarily have "home" and "away" correspondents. These days, two moving targets can keep up with each other. Wires beget the wireless.

STORYTELLING AND THE MODERN CONTEXT

Before discussing the storytelling of wired to wireless, consider the special function stories and art have always served for lovers, whether in or out of distance relationships: as a model for conduct and expectations, a means to dramatize one's own emotions, and a bundle of emotions and experiences to be shared, discussed, and incorporated into the common knowledge of the couple.

Techno-social innovations change how these stories are shared and discussed, but also the content of the art. Storytelling through plays, books, films and songs helps us come to terms with how new technologies change us as individuals, and as a culture, both by depicting use *and* drawing from unique stresses to create new sources for dramatic conflicts. Contemporary love stories *must* deal with the newest, most intimate communication technologies, just as lovers would use them; new dynamics must be found to retell the age-old story of longing over distance. The chain of miscommunication that leads to "the Tragedy of Romeo and Juliet," for instance, is nigh-impossible to plausibly update, given our current communicative toolkit. A truly contemporary staging would result in their survival and eventual mutual outgrowth of each other.

Today's strange new wireless dynamics present suitable challenges for contemporary artists and a need for new stories for our age. In an attempt to depict cellphone interactions in a meaningful way, Sarah once wrote a play where the characters remained onstage in their own spaces before, during, and after their calls, so that viewers can see the interruptions and aftermath created by the call. In mainstream art and cinema, the stories that seem to most deeply explore the communicative dynamics of cellphones are cops-and-robbers dramas, notably *The Wire* (which unfortunately would require a paper of its own to be done justice) and Martin Scorsese's *The Departed*.

In the film, undercover cop Billy Costigan (Leonardo Di Caprio) and crooked cop Colin Sullivan (Matt Damon) bury themselves so deeply to infiltrate the enemy that their only link to a true identity lies in a cell phone. Costigan appears a consummate criminal, but maintains contact with his police handlers through a secret phone number. Sullivan keeps a dedicated device to tip his crime boss off to cop plans. Director Martin Scorsese takes advantage of a powerful and realistic symbolism as his antagonists hunt with equal hunger for each others' phones and bodies: when an object becomes the only link for communicating with a person's body, the object embodies the user.

The film then demonstrates that the greatest dramatic potential for wireless technology comes not from erasing distances (as old as the telephone) but from intrusive embodiment. The computer/phone/device ceases to be anchored by a physical wire; it becomes the sole thing "bringing" the other's telepresence into your space. The device becomes the body of the caller's telepresence; the smaller, the more dramatic. And because you can get a call or log on at any moment, the device *continually* embodies the telepresence; the recipient remains haunted by the person she expects to reach. We aren't the only ones who've noticed this: Douglas Rushkoff has noted the phenomenon of "phantom phone vibrations" as a dreadful consequence of attaching our nervous systems to "the entire online world, all the time." (28-30)

LDRs attempt to create the illusion of physical closeness, in order to confirm emotional closeness. The greatest stress occurs when emotional closeness is *also* proved to be an illusion. When technology fails on two users, the illusion of physical closeness shatters. We discovered, however, that this can actually *increase* the feeling of emotional closeness: lovers may dramatize their situation, and rise to the occasion against persecution from impersonal machines. In those situations, the technical device no longer embodies the lover, and deserves kicks rather than caresses. Technical failures can still bring stress to a LDR if mishandled, but strategies abound for mitigation. It is failures in interpersonal conduct, on the other hand, that can endanger the stability of the relationship. When do our uses of technology make the other person feel a break in emotional closeness?

Stress on a Wire

We dealt with many forms of communication during our period of distance: email, status messages, twitter, online chat, Skype video calls, Skype phone calls, shared song files, objects sent through friends, orders and directions, and face-to-face interaction. But classification by medium would be a facile and ultimately fruitless endeavor, since each communicative event exists under highly variable emotional and social circumstances. First, what risks are borne? Is the sender sure the message will reach the recipient, in the case of email or phone conversations, or is there a risk of not reaching the recipient, as there is in placing a call or posting a status that may not be read? Secondly, is the attempt a failure or a success? What defines failure and success, and do both parties agree on the definition? Finally, what kind of waiting is happening? Does one wait patiently for the answer that will eventually arrive, or stew impatiently for the answer that should have come already? The communication stresses that we faced turned out to be best classified by looking atthe kind of telepresence taking place at each end of the connection: synchronous, sequential, or asynchronous.

- In the Synchronous State, both parties are virtually present, exchanging such a constant stream of data as to seem immediate. Examples include *video feeds, telephone calls, and of course live interaction.*
- In the Sequential State, one person waits for a message from the other before responding, resulting in a ping-ponging back-and-forth of data transmissions. Examples include *chat messaging, text messaging, and dedicated email conversation threads.*
- In the Asynchronous State, either person initiates connection purely from internal impulse, reaching out to deliver a surprise shot of data. Examples include out-of-the-blue emails, ecards, post to blogs or social networking sites, or the very act of calling or logging into chat.

We noticed that, just like changing lanes while driving, transitioning *between* states proved the most stressful and also that, regardless of medium, transitioning from a Sequential to an Asynchronous State was always the most emotionally damaging. Moving *up* from the spectrum always increased the immediacy of connection, and decreased stress: *a phone call going through, logging in to find the other online, an email being sent while looking at one's inbox.*

Conversely, moving down the spectrum always interrupted the immediacy of connection, and increased stress, with one exception: moving from a Synchronous State to an Asynchronous State was rarely a big deal, since a*ll conversations must eventually end*. We hang up a phone, log off a network, and otherwise get on with our normal lives. It was rather the troublesome Sequential State, which required one party to wait for the other that stung. Moving from Synchronous to Sequential States was not enjoyable-- a *Skype video call turning into chat due to lost connection, for instance*--but moving from Sequential to Asynchronous States was the worst: *one member of a chat getting distracted and leaving the computer without notifying the other*. Their interlocutor is in for a nasty shock that shatters the emotional closeness conjured by the medium, and may justifiably take offense during their next conversation. The sequential state is most dangerous because it is based so firmly on waiting and shared expectations. What plays out in short distance relationships, then, also applies to long: high expectations set lovers up for disappointment. If you are communicating under expectations of telepresence, with all its implications of time-synchronization and emotional closeness, only to find that the other party isn't there, it dispels the illusions of emotional presence that are so vital to maintaining love at a distance.

Lessons and Strategies

• Blame the technology, blame the medium, but try not to blame the person. Under normal circumstances of mediated communication, "there is no psychological discount for broken or underdeveloped technology...technical problems have social consequences." (Reeves and Nass 214) In our case, we found that a basic awareness of how technology structures communications could help combat the impulse to see human causes for everything.

• Find inexpensive and convenient ways to call your partner without prior arrangement. If both partners are in the same country, this is trivially easy. If not, explore options in terms of international calling cards, VOIP programs with out-calling capability, or oversea-call shops. Once you can be reached by phone, let your wireless device embody your lover as much as possible, but divorce and blame it immediately for any communication problems.

- Dramatize your situation. Make yourselves feel like you belong with the most heroic lovers of all time. A few delusions of grandeur never hurt anyone, and it helps with the longing. Small acts of collective dramatization, like assembling songs into a CD or sending favorite poems, are a great means of finding suitable models and establishing common metaphors. Listening to the CD becomes an asynchronous and repeatable means of experiencing couple-hood, and in conversation one can reference the songs and instantly call up certain feelings.

- If you're in a situation or environment that your lover doesn't know about, explain it to them, or better yet, show them. By giving each other images, lovers can connect, at first by teaching each other respective ways of seeing, then as a means of what Mizuko Ito calls "Intimate Visual Co-Presence," defined as "the sharing of an ongoing stream of viewpoint-specific photos with... an intimate other," stressing "co-presence and viewpoint sharing rather than communication, publication, or archiving." By sharing photos and reflections gathered over the course of a day, lovers may allow each other a small sampling of the thousand tiny moments and unsaid pieces of experience that make up their separated existences. In so doing, they gain insight into the shape of the other's life without tiresome interrogation about "what did you do today." In our case, photo-sharing was somewhat more difficult than simply hitting 'send' on a phone, but it was an important part of correspondence.

- Soon after arrival in new circumstances, take care to describe and explain all the new places, faces, and experiences encountered while still phenomenologically fresh. Twitter is great for amassing this kind of subtle background knowledge, as are photos, videos, and anecdotes that give the color of your life. Common knowledge between two parties, once established, acts like a codec, in that it allows greater density of information to be passed in the same amount of time/space.

- Take care not to go overboard in staying connected: too much time in front of screens begins to detract from the quality of life outside the telepresence. One must, in Rushkoff's memorable admonition, seek to "Live in Person."(35)

- Watch out for imbalances; specifically, the imbalance of one party initiating too frequently or using one medium too much. Keep changing, so that the novelty of new media continues to delight, and the flaws of any one of them don't come to dominate the relationship. (Lacanian analysis seeks a similar flexibility by refusing to standardize the timing of its sessions.) Similarly, make the effort to surprise the other person with unexpected patterns, objects, and projects. Intelligent, passionate lovers can be won by many means, but kept only by continual surprise.

- When you do get together, recognize that face-to-face interaction is itself a medium, the hardware for which is taken for granted except by sufferers of Aspberger's Syndrome. It follows that if it is a medium, then it also has its own patterns and limitations, something any marriage counselor can confirm. Just because face-to-face is the most immediate and emotionally intensive form of communication does not mean it is best for every situation.

- If you feel distant from your partner or worry about diminished influence, consider writing up playful directives. By following seemingly banal instructions like, "bring oranges on the flight, after one hour, take your shoes off; drink red wine whenever offered beverages," the directed partner invites the absent presence of the lover into his or her body through the performance of small actions, rituals, or assignments. The willingness of a lover to follow silly romantic instructions also reassures his or her partner of both the lover's commitment and the partner's continuing ability to influence them even without physical or electronic presence. While this might seem like an unusual practice, it shares much with religious devotionals, traditions of courtly love, and modern BDSM.

- Because your online presence is a major part of who you are to your distant love, take special care to protect your passwords, and always make sure to log out when finished; your partner must be able to trust the green dot by your name.

- Manage expectations. Understand what your lover can and can't do, logistically. Try to be thankful for the connections you have, rather than resentful about not getting more. If you're feeling hungry for more than they can currently give, review old asynchronous media (photos, songs, letters, etc.) and try to rediscover the power of imagination and visualization.

- You can always go back and use older forms of technology at any time. Seeming obsolescence yields fetishization. Archaic forms like handwritten letters help the dramatization, and you can rediscover their romantic elements, as well as the ability to leave physical traces. With cellphones, we miss the sexy part of having a corded landline in the bedroom - playing with the cord, wrapping it around your finger, being on its leash...not to mention the obvious tactile eroticism of using an old-fashioned dial phone.

- It's worth noting that in the world today, we are more and more able to communicate with lightning speed and velvet-ease across distances. This raises the expectations of communication enormously. *It is as if everything is becoming a Synchronous State. Watch out, and take to heart Douglas Rushkoff's warning: "Do Not Be Always On."(22)*

REFERENCES

Adams, John and Abigail. Archived Correspondence, 1762-1801. Electronic Archive, Massachusetts Historical Society. <http://www.masshist.org/digitaladams/aea/letter/ >

Ito, Mizuko, "Intimate Visual Co-Presence." Delivered at the Ubiquitous Computing Conference, 2005 <http://www.itofisher.com/mito/publications/intimate_visual.html >

Kittler, Friedrich. *Gramophone, Film, Typewriter.* Translated by Geoffrey Winthrop-Young and Michael Wurtz. Stanford University Press, 1999.

Reeves, Byron & Clifford Nass. *The Media Equation: How People Treat Computers, Television, and New Media like Real People and Places.* Cambridge University Press, 1996.

Rushkoff, Douglas. *Program or Be Programmed.* OR Books, 2010

Twain, Mark. "The Loves of Alonzo Fitzclarence and Rosannah Ethelton" *The Atlantic Monthly*, March 1878

Twain, Mark. "A Telephonic Conversation." *The Atlantic Monthly*, June 1880.

List of contributors

Ballhausen, Thomas is an Austrian author as well as literary and film scholar. Ballhausen writes prose and essays and also works as publisher and translator. He teaches at the Department of Comparative Literature and at the Department of Theater Studies in Vienna and is director of the library of the Austrian Filmarchiv. Ballhausen directs the literature department of the culture magazine skug and was also co-founder of the authors' circle die flut.

Flynn, Adam is a researcher-at-large and media theorist recently returned from Phnom Penh, Cambodia.

Friesinger, Günther lives in Vienna and Graz as a philosopher, artist, writer, curator and journalist. He is Head of the paraflows Festival, member of monochrom, co-organiser of the Arse Elektronika Festival and the Roboexotica Festival.

Grau, Oliver is a German art historian and media theoretician with a focus on image science, modernity and media art as well as culture of the 19th century and Italian art of the Renaissance. Oliver Grau is Professor of Image Science and Head of the Department for Image Science at the Danube University

Grenzfurthner, Johannes is an artist, writer, curator, and director. He is the founder of monochrom, an internationally acting art and theory group. He teaches art theory and art practice at the University of Applied Sciences in Graz, Austria. He is head of the "Arse Elektronika" festival in San Francisco, host of "Roboexotica" (Festival for Cocktail-Robotics, Vienna and San Francisco), and co-curates the paraflows Symposium in Vienna.

Heller, Christian lives in Berlin. He pursues personal internet identity experiments and writes and talks about post-privacy, singularitarian futurism, web culture and film history. His website: www.plomlompom.de

Herwig, Jana is currently a researcher and PhD candidate at the Dept. of Theatre, Film and Media Studies, University of Vienna, Austria. She has worked in the online industry in various roles since web 1.0 days – as a web developer, community and project manager, individual and corporate blogger, researcher and instructor – taught German in South Africa, English in Austria and returned to academia and media studies in 2008. At present, she blogs mainly in German at digiom.wordpress.com, where she can also be contacted.

Hrachovec, Herbert professor at the Department of Philosophy, Universität Wien. Studies in German, history, philosophy, and theology in Vienna and Tübingen. Longer teaching assignments and research visits in Oxford, Münster, Cambridge, Massachusetts, Berlin, Essen and Weimar. Work on analytic philosophy, metaphysics, and aesthetics. Current research interests: new media. Chair of the philosophy department, member of the senate and chairman of the curriculum commission of the Universität Wien. Further information at http://hrachovec.philo.at

Hsin, Lin Hsin is an artist, poet and composer born in Singapore, deeply rooted in mathematics and information technology. She graduated in mathematics from the University of Singapore and received a postgraduate degree in computer science from the University of Newcastle upon Tyne, England. She studied music and art in Singapore, printmaking at the University of Ulster, papermaking in Ogawamachi, Japan, and paper conservation at the University of Melbourne Conservation Services.

Kleiner, Dmytri is a software developer and cultural producer exploring the political economy of network topology. Dmytri is a founder of the Telekommunisten collective and is currently working on the Telekommunist Manifesto, which will be published by the Institute of Network Cultures.

Machulis, Kyle is known as a tinkerer/hacker/pioneer/visionary/deity in the realm of sex technology (or at least, a ton of bloggers seem to think so). Through his Slashdong webpage, he uses the topic of teledildonics (remotely actuated sexual experience) to teach the basic concepts of electrical and mechanical engineering. He also tracks the convergence of sex and technological advances in toys and interaction. An (accidental) expert in the field of sex in video games, he is on the leadership council of the IGDA Sex In Games Special Interest Group, a gathering of game developers, academics, and players interested in discussing the role of sex in interactive entertainment. His MMOrgy Project keeps the community updated on the intimate happenings of the Massively Multiplayer Online Gaming world, where emergent sex (intimate encounters not originally planned as part of the game/world by developers) has become a hot topic and often-seen event.

Mikes, Mela currently lives in Vienna. She dropped out of university after studying philosophy for a while and now works as a software test engineer. She is also a hobby DJ and creator of the melafesto podcasts.

Outhwaite, Sarah is a director, choreographer, and digital muser from New York.

Schneider, Frank Apunkt is an unfree author, unfree artist and unfree lecturer. He lives and works in Bamberg, Germany. In 2007 he published 'Als die Welt noch unterging' (Ventil Verlag), a book dealing with early German punk/new wave culture. Frank Apunkt Schneider is member of monochrom.

Tingley, Jane lives and works in Montreal. Exhibitions: 2010 Solar Branch Prosthetic – Permanent Installation, Marnay-Sur-Seine, Aube, France 2009 Ecology; Water, Air, Sound Artscape Whychwood Barns, Toronto, Ontario. Installation: Plant(iPod)Installation.

Wenhart, Nina is an instructor for the "Prehysteries of New Media" class at the School of the Art Institute of Chicago and an independent artist/researcher. She graduated from Prof. Oliver Grau's Media Art Histories program at the Danube University in Krems with a Master Thesis on Descriptive Metadata for Media Arts. For many years, she worked in the field of archiving media art, most recently at the Ludwig Boltzmann Institute for Media.Art.Research and before as the head of the Ars Electronica Futurelab's videostudio, where she created their archives and primarily worked with the archival material.